The Convergence of Race, Ethnicity, and Gender

Multiple Identities in Counseling

The Convergence of Race, Ethnicity, and Gender

Multiple Identities in Counseling

Second Edition

TRACY L. ROBINSON
Northeastern University, Boston

PEARSON

Merrill
Prentice Hall

Upper Saddle River, New Jersey
Columbus, Ohio

Library of Congress Cataloging-in-Publication Data

Robinson, Tracy L.
  The convergence of race, ethnicity, and gender : multiple identities in counseling
Tracy L. Robinson. -- 2nd ed.
     p. cm.
  Includes bibliographical references and index.
  ISBN 0-13-118610-8
  1. Cross-cultural counseling. I. Title.

  BF637.C6R583 2005
  158′.3--dc22   2004007087

Vice President and Executive Publisher: Jeffery W. Johnston
Publisher: Kevin M. Davis
Editorial Assistant: Amanda King
Production Editor: Mary Harlan
Production Coordinator: The GTS Companies/York, PA Campus
Design Coordinator: Diane C. Lorenzo
Text Design and Illustrations: The GTS Companies/York, PA Campus
Cover Design: Ali Mohrman
Cover Image: Superstock
Production Manager: Laura Messerly
Director of Marketing: Ann Castel Davis
Marketing Manager: Autumn Purdy
Marketing Coordinator: Tyra Poole

This book was set in Korinna by The GTS Companies/York, PA Campus. It was printed and
bound by R. R. Donnelley & Sons Company. The cover was printed by The Lehigh Press, Inc.

Pearson Education Ltd.   Pearson Education Australia Pty. Limited
Pearson Education Singapore Pte. Ltd.   Pearson Education North Asia Ltd.
Pearson Education Canada, Ltd.   Pearson Educación de Mexico, S.A. de C.V.
Pearson Education—Japan   Pearson Education Malaysia Pte. Ltd.

10 9 8 7 6 5 4
ISBN: 0-13-118610-8

Dedicated to students whose
commitment to dialogue, justice, and
healing is an affirmation of life.

PREFACE

> As we learn to bear the intimacy of scrutiny and to flourish within it, as we learn to use the products of that scrutiny for power within our living, those fears which rule our lives and form our silences begin to lose their control over us.
>
> *Audre Lorde, Sister Outsider: Essays and Speeches*

In 1989, as a new Assistant Professor, I started talking about convergence. What I meant by convergence was the intersections of race, ethnicity, gender, and other primary identity constructs within the context of counseling. Each of these constructs is critical to a person's emotional and psychological development and each intersects with other human dimensions. Recently, these intersecting identities have been receiving greater attention in the multicultural counseling literature. Prior to this, much of the literature focused on individual aspects of identity (most often race, culture, or ethnicity) and their subsequent influences on a cross-cultural counseling event in which the client was a person of color and the counselor was not. A consideration of how multiple identities, visible and invisible, converge simultaneously and affect development, behavior, and the counseling event itself was missing.

This new paradigm for imaging differences, both visible and invisible, allows each of us to engage in the unrelenting process of increasing self-awareness as gendered, cultural, racial, ethnic, sexual, and cultural beings influenced by class, ability, and disability. That differences exist is not refuted nor regarded as problematic. The inequity promoted and perpetuated within a society in which immutable human characteristics hold rank is the problem.

Multicultural counseling emphasizes an ecological framework in which person-environment interaction, culture, ethnicity, family, collective society, history, and spirituality are regarded as fundamental to understanding the client in therapy. Multicultural counseling also recognizes the way in which dominant cultural beliefs and values furnish and perpetuate feelings of inadequacy, shame, confusion, and distrust for clients in both the counseling process and the larger society.

The overall goal of this work is to engage in a dialectical, "both/and" discussion about how identity constructs operate conjointly in people's lives to affect personal development and problem presentation in counseling. The response to the first edition from colleagues and students has been inspiring and humbling. This second edition offers an updated format with new chapters, case studies, and storytellings. New and existing theories and research are discussed, and greater attention is devoted to the application of clinical practice. In a spirit of *Umoja* (unity) and *Ujima* (collective work and responsibility), I acknowledge and celebrate the good work that elders, colleagues, and students have done and continue to do in multicultural counseling.

A MESSAGE TO STUDENTS

The material presented in this book can provoke dissonance. Students often feel fatigued, guilty, and put off by their new feelings and the voices of others that they have never truly heard before, both within the book and within the context of the course where this book is used. Once the course is finished and you have your grade, it is easy to retreat to more comfortable pre–cross-cultural class experiences. However, if you are to become a multiculturally competent counselor, your thoughts, actions, behaviors, and beliefs about yourself and others need to "bear the intimacy of scrutiny and to flourish within it." The process of transformation moves you toward strategies and solutions to change the social structure and become an advocate and change agent for the long haul.

I welcome you to this exploration. Please read the storytellings and case studies, and listen to other people's stories, and mine, and your own as well. Although growth cannot happen without disequilibrium, know that you are being prepared to better appreciate the multiple layers and contexts that both you and your clients will bring to the counseling event. Your enhanced sense of self will assist you in knowing your clients from their unique frame of reference. This in turn will help you find the questions to ask and avoid those that should not be asked. As you process your own feelings and endeavor to make sense out of new information, I hope that you will have communities of support who listen, nurture, and challenge. I also hope that you can accept that there may be existing individuals and communities who will be unable to receive or support some of the new insights that you will take from this text.

A MESSAGE TO COLLEAGUES

Teaching multicultural counseling is not easy. As students become aware of unearned skin color privilege, history denied and distorted, and their own internalization of and complicity with racism, sexism, and homophobia, there is disillusionment, sadness, and anger—often directed toward the messenger—you. Faculty of color may be perceived as capable or well suited to teach culturally oriented courses only. Despite being well prepared and ready to teach, White professors may be received suspiciously by both students and faculty across race and ethnicity. White students may fear that faculty of color are going to behave punitively or make them feel guilty for being White. Students of color may feel that they have to carefully weigh their words in class lest they offend their White professors and suffer the consequences with an inferior grade. Untenured professors of any race are concerned about student evaluations, which can have positive and negative implications for promotion and tenure review. Senior faculty and department heads need to understand these dynamics and act wisely. The politics are fierce and often unspoken, yet they represent the landscape of cross-cultural counseling.

With that said, the course is one where teachers are able to bear witness to students being changed at depth. This is a gift but not without a price. It is important that you take care of yourselves and do the best work that you can. This is after all, a calling. Bearing witness to students' newfound ability to truly listen to other people's voices and coexist with different ways of being in the world allows us teachers to contribute to healing and justice. At the same time, some students will receive excellent grades yet will not be significantly altered by their experience. Be prepared to read and hear racist statements from students. However, you must be prepared to hear that which is difficult to receive when you ask students to speak from their own lived experiences. You have to trust that for some of your students, you are nurturing growth and change that you will not see by the semester's end. I encourage new faculty who have taken jobs away from home and other communities of support to have a ready list of people on whom to call and confide after a particularly difficult class that leaves you feeling drained and seriously questioning your decision making that led you to this place you now call home.

OUTLINE OF CHAPTERS

The text is divided into four parts: Imaging Diversity, Valued Cultures, Converging Identities, and Reimaging Counseling. Every chapter has at least one "Storytelling" feature to honor the powerful oral tradition of storytelling that is alive in the world's cultures. To encourage the integration and application of the material, a case study is presented in each chapter.

In the first edition, individual chapters were not devoted to the four primary groups of color in the United States: Native Americans/Alaskan Natives, Latinos, people of Asian descent, and people of African descent. The rationale for not dedicating a chapter to each group of color was to avoid the presentation of the self as so discrete from other people and ecological contexts. However, some of the professors who used the first edition indicated that separate chapters make more pedagogical sense. In this second edition, a separate chapter is devoted to each of these four groups. The reality of bicultural, biracial, and multiracial people as the fastest growing demographic in the United States is recognized as well throughout the book.

PART ONE: IMAGING DIVERSITY Chapter 1, Multiple Identities: Defined, provides an overview of culture, race, ethnicity, gender, sexuality, disability, socioeconomic class, and religion and faith. The importance of counselors' awareness of their attitudes about sources of differences is emphasized. A dominant value structure within the United States that is touted as normal and superior to the exclusion of all others is examined. Dominant cultural values are discussed as a way to orient the reader to core values that are invisible, even to those of us born and reared in the United States.

Chapter 2, Multicultural Competencies and Skills, focuses on the knowledge, attitudes, and skills, both verbal and nonverbal, that are essential for the effective counselor to possess. Competencies are discussed in depth. Information is provided on the integration of competencies in various counseling settings, which includes the ability of the counselor to refer clients when the client's problems exceed the counselor's professional training and skills. Finally, ethical considerations are discussed within a multicultural context.

In Chapter 3, Statused Identities, gender, race, sexual orientation, religion, ability, disability, and class as sources of differences and status characteristics are explored.

Race and gender are presented as primary status traits and an explanation is given for this perspective.

PART TWO: VALUED CULTURES   Chapter 4 focuses on Native Americans and Alaskan Natives. Chapter 5 explores Latinos. Chapter 6 focuses on people of African descent. Chapter 7 is dedicated to people of Asian descent, Native Hawaiians, and Pacific Islanders. A succinct overview of demographic characteristics, historical information, migratory patterns (where applicable), and cultural values are explored. The terms "people of Asian descent" and "people of African descent" are used instead of Asian American and African American for three reasons: to reflect the biracial and multiracial heritages reflected within and across racial categories; to respect the reality that people of African and Asian descent may live in America but hail from other parts of the world, such as the Caribbean or the continents of Asia and Africa; and to honor the reality that many people of African and Asian descent whose people have resided in America for many generations may not choose to self-identify as Asian American or African American but by a particular ethnicity, such as Korean, Jamaican, American, Ghanaian, or another means of identification.

In 1978, the Office of Management and Budget (OMB) adopted the term *Hispanic* to describe people who were perceived to have a similar ethnic background. Instead of Hispanic, *Latino* is used throughout this text because it is a self-defined term. Latinos can be of any race.

PART THREE: CONVERGING IDENTITIES   Chapter 8, Converging Race, explores race from sociopolitical perspectives. Primary stage models of biracial and racial identity development for each of the four groups and relevant research are presented. Via the case study, race, gender, acculturation, and assimilation are explored.

Chapter 9, Converging Gender, discusses gender roles and gender identity, and looks briefly at gender development from a biological perspective. Sex and sex-role typing are explored and distinctions are made among terms. Female and male models of gender identity are discussed. Attention is given to gender socialization, emotion, and potential effects of gender dyads on the counseling event.

Chapter 10, Converging Socioeconomic Class, focuses on class as a status variable both in society and in the counseling event. (Class is inextricably linked to self-worth and income.) The training that counselors receive in traditional counseling programs is discussed within the context of culture. Questions are provided to help students unravel the role of class in their own development and with regard to perceptions of others. The intersections of power, powerlessness, gender, and race are considered.

Chapter 11 is titled Converging Sexual Orientation. Often counselors do not receive adequate training in sexuality, with respect to their own lives and those of their clients. The goal of this chapter is to expose counselors to the heterosexual bias that exists in American culture and to increase sensitivity about the inherent danger to lesbian, gay, bisexual, and transgender clients in a climate of heterosexism. Questions are posed to help students reflect on the meanings they attach to sexual orientation.

Chapter 12, Converging Physical Attractiveness, Ability, and Disability, addresses the need for counselors to be aware of how women and men are conditioned to define beauty. A cultural value of thinness contributes to constant dieting behavior among increasingly large numbers of young girls and women, internalized sense of low self-esteem, anorexia, bulimia, and high dependence on others to validate the self. Attention is also devoted to the silent phenomenon of colorism, self-satisfaction, and physical attractiveness. Steroids and the athletic culture in the lives of men are examined. The able-bodied culture and its impact on perceptions of normalcy, beauty, and well-being are discussed. Counseling people with disabilities is emphasized.

PART FOUR: REIMAGING COUNSELING Chapter 13, Diversity in Relationships, focuses on a variety of interpersonal and intimate relationships, including traditional marriages between women and men, same-gender couples, extended families, and close friendships that function as families although people are not related by blood. Family structure, marital status, and diverse family patterns, such as father-headed households and the extended family, are noted. Strategies for counselors to work effectively with a diversity of relationships are emphasized.

The therapeutic process can foster greater self-understanding toward enhanced functioning, intrapersonally and interpersonally. This is the message of Chapter 14, Mutuality, Empathy, and Empowerment in Therapy. Empowerment is viewed as one of the goals of psychotherapy. Those forces that leave people bereft of power are discussed. Conflict inherent in female and male gender role socialization, empowerment, and the stigma associated with seeking therapeutic assistance is acknowledged. Empathy is defined as critical to effective counseling.

Finally, Chapter 15, Diverse Counseling and Healing Strategies, explores a variety of interventions for enhanced emotional and mental functioning. Empathy, advocacy, and flexibility are identified as essential skills. A resistance model is featured and several case studies are offered as a way of integrating resistance into counseling. Approaches that laypeople can use are highlighted. Alternative counseling approaches are discussed, such as expressive arts, spirituality, and mind/body integration.

An epilogue concludes this work.

ACKNOWLEDGMENTS

Eleven years ago, Mary Howard-Hamilton and I approached a publisher in the exhibition hall at an American Counseling Association Convention. We told her of our desire and our dream: to write a book on multicultural issues in counseling that incorporated race, ethnicity, and culture as well as the muted topics of gender, socioeconomic class, and sexual orientation. We asked the editor if we could buy her a cup of coffee. She graciously accepted. Out of that conversation, her scrutiny of us, our scrutiny of multicultural counseling and of ourselves as women, Black Americans, and academicians, an invitation was extended to us to develop a book prospectus. Linda Sullivan had coffee with Mary and me at the ACA in Maryland and eventually moved us forward to a signed contract for the first edition.

Over a decade later, I offer this second edition. I thank Mary for her invaluable contributions to the first edition of this text. Her support and spirit surround this second edition as well. I am indebted to Mary for her scholarship and creativity. Although I updated the chapter on relationships (it was titled family in the first edition) with current census data, Mary provided much of the framework and theory for this chapter. I also thank Mary for her contributions to the chapters on gender and sexual orientation. Her friendship, sisterhood, and collegiality are the staff of life.

I also want to thank my family, friends, students, graduate assistants, and colleagues for inspiration, encouragement, good distraction, help, prayers, and love. Sharyn Matthews, my NUTA (Northeastern University Teaching Assistant), did an exceptional job of finding and organizing the resources—census data, books, and research articles—for this second edition. She was a breath of fresh air, particularly on those frigid winter days when we complained bitterly about Boston's weather and drank our soothing tea.

Anybody can show up at the celebration party but not everyone can walk with you on the journey when there is no clear end in view. Dad, Robin, Rita, Ro, Ms. Fay, CC, Marilyn, Betsy, Janie, and Brookins have had their walking, dancing, marking-time, and "I've got your back" shoes on for such a long time. How can I say thanks? Carmen and Willie graciously helped me with the Spanish translation of my poem. Karin, Karen, Barbara, Jess, and Rob are newer members to my circle of stones and are precious beyond the expression of words. My angel mother has never left my side. Geoffrey's love has anchored me and lifted me higher than I've ever been lifted before.

I thank Kevin Davis, my editor, for holding this vision with me. His quiet strength has whispered me onward. Autumn Benson has been such a good listener and has consistently provided superb professional assistance. Mary Harlan of Merrill is truly a miracle worker. Wendy Druck of GTS consistently demonstrated professionalism and a gentle spirit throughout the production of this book. I also thank the following reviewers: Greg Granderson, Santa-Rosa Junior College; Brian McNeill, Washington State University; Aneneosa A. Okocha, University of Wisconsin–Whitewater; and Woodrow M. Parker, University of Florida.

Tracy L. Robinson

DISCOVER THE COMPANION WEBSITE ACCOMPANYING THIS BOOK

THE PRENTICE HALL COMPANION WEBSITE: A VIRTUAL LEARNING ENVIRONMENT

Technology is a constantly growing and changing aspect of our field that is creating a need for content and resources. To address this emerging need, Prentice Hall has developed an online learning environment for students and professors alike—Companion Websites—to support our textbooks.

In creating a Companion Website, our goal is to build on and enhance what the textbook already offers. For this reason, the content for each user-friendly website is organized by topic and provides the professor and student with a variety of meaningful resources. Common features of a Companion Website include:

FOR THE PROFESSOR

Every Companion Website integrates **Syllabus Manager**™, an online syllabus creation and management utility.

- **Syllabus Manager**™ provides you, the instructor, with an easy, step-by-step process to create and revise syllabi, with direct links into Companion Website and other online content without having to learn HTML.
- Students may logon to your syllabus during any study session. All they need to know is the web address for the Companion Website and the password you've assigned to your syllabus.
- After you have created a syllabus using **Syllabus Manager**™, students may enter the syllabus for their course section from any point in the Companion Website.
- Clicking on a date, the student is shown the list of activities for the assignment. The activities for each assignment are linked directly to actual content, saving time for students.
- Adding assignments consists of clicking on the desired due date, then filling in the details of the assignment—name of the assignment, instructions, and whether it is a one-time or repeating assignment.
- In addition, links to other activities can be created easily. If the activity is online, a URL can be entered in the space provided, and it will be linked automatically in the final syllabus.
- Your completed syllabus is hosted on our servers, allowing convenient updates from any computer on the Internet. Changes you make to your syllabus are immediately available to your students at their next logon.

FOR THE STUDENT

- **Counseling Topics**—17 core counseling topics represent the diversity and scope of today's counseling field.
- **Annotated Bibliography**—includes seminal foundational works and key current works.

- **Web Destinations**—lists significant and up-to-date practitioner and client sites.
- **Professional Development**—provides helpful information regarding professional organizations and codes of ethics.
- **Electronic Bluebook**—send homework or essays directly to your instructor's email with this paperless form.
- **Message Board**—serves as a virtual bulletin board to post—or respond to—questions or comments to/from a national audience.
- **Chat**—real-time chat with anyone who is using the text anywhere in the country—ideal for discussion and study groups, class projects, etc.

To take advantage of these and other resources, please visit *The Convergence of Race, Ethnicity, and Gender: Multiple Identities in Counseling,* Second Edition, Companion Website at

www.prenhall.com/robinson

RESEARCH NAVIGATOR: RESEARCH MADE SIMPLE!

www.ResearchNavigator.com

Merrill Education is pleased to introduce Research Navigator—a one-stop research solution for students that simplifies and streamlines the entire research process. At www.researchnavigator.com, students will find extensive resources to enhance their understanding of the research process so they can effectively complete research assignments. In addition, Research Navigator has three exclusive databases of credible and reliable source content to help students focus their research efforts and begin the research process.

HOW WILL RESEARCH NAVIGATOR ENHANCE YOUR COURSE?

- Extensive content helps students understand the research process, including writing, internet research, and citing sources.
- Step-by-step tutorial guides students through the entire research process from selecting a topic to revising a rough draft.
- Research Writing in the Disciplines section details the differences in research across disciplines.
- Three exclusive databases—EBSCO's ContentSelect Academic Journal Database, *The New York Times* Search by Subject Archive, and "Best of the Web" Link Library— allow students to easily find journal articles and sources.

WHAT'S THE COST?

A subscription to Research Navigator is $7.50 but is **free** when used in conjunction with this textbook. To obtain free passcodes for your students, simply contact your local Merrill/Prentice Hall sales representative, and your representative will send you the Evaluating Online Resource Guide, which contains the code to access Research Navigator as well as tips on how to use Research Navigator and how to evaluate research. To preview the value of this website to your students, please go to www.educatorlearningcenter.com and use the Login Name "Research" and the password "Demo."

BRIEF CONTENTS

Part One: **Imaging Diversity**

Part Two: **Valued Cultures**

Part Three: **Converging Identities**

Part Four: **Reimaging Counseling**

CONTENTS

Part One
Imaging Diversity

Part Two
Valued Cultures

Chapter 6
People of African Descent
90

Chapter 7
People of Asian Descent, Native Hawaiians, and Pacific Islanders
106

Part Three
Converging Identities

Chapter 8
Converging Race

Chapter 9
Converging Gender

Chapter 10
Converging Socioeconomic Class 168

Chapter 11
Converging Sexual Orientation 186

Chapter 12
Converging Physical Attractiveness, Ability, and Disability 206

Part Four
Reimaging Counseling

Chapter 13
Diversity in Relationships   226

Chapter 14
Mutuality, Empathy, and Empowerment in Therapy   246

Chapter 15
Diverse Counseling and Healing Strategies   258

NOTE: Every effort has been made to provide accurate and current Internet information in this book. However, since the Internet and information posted on it are constantly changing, it is inevitable that some of the Internet addresses listed in this textbook will change .

Part One: **Imaging Diversity**

Chapter 1

Multiple Identities: Defined

Dialogue cannot exist, however, in the absence of a profound love for the world and for men [sic]. The naming of the world, which is an act of creation and re-creation, is not possible if it is not infused with love. Love is at the same time the foundation of dialogue and dialogue itself . . . Because love is an act of courage, not of fear, love is commitment to other men [sic].

Paulo Freire, Pedagogy of the Oppressed

A primary tenet of this text is that effective counselors acknowledge, understand, and appreciate sources of differences among people. The distinction between sources of difference among people and the attitudes people hold about differences is examined throughout this work.

Diversity across age, ethnicity, ability, disability, gender, race, religion, sexual orientation, and socioeconomic class attests to the strengths of a heterogeneous culture. Yet, the United States continues to wrestle with equity for all. Numerous movements and laws, such as the Asian rights movement, the Chicano moratorium, the civil rights movement, the women's movement, the gay rights movement, Section 504 of the 1973 Rehabilitation Act, and the Americans with Disabilities Act (ADA), are evidence of the ongoing struggle for justice, access, and opportunity.

This chapter explores the implications for counselors practicing within a culturally diverse nation that is challenged by the concept of *equality for all*. A case study is provided to allow readers an opportunity to integrate the material discussed throughout this chapter.

The case study is also included to encourage the readers' application of material to real-life examples. Diverse identities within the United States include race, ethnicity, culture, gender, sexual orientation, mental and physical ability, socioeconomic class, age, and religion. All are identity constructs and sources of difference. The interplay of these identity markers influences the process of meaning making throughout life. Identities are multiple, simultaneous, and ever-shifting. Depending on the context, certain identities have more power than do others and can take on different meanings. Within the counseling event, identity affects both a client's problem orientation and the counselor–client relationship.

Admittedly, race and gender are given more attention throughout this text. The rationale for this position is substantiated by two observations. First, gender and race are characteristics into which people are born and are often visible but not always. Second, in this society, race and gender are socially constructed to function as primary status traits (Robinson, 1993). As visible markers, the meanings associated with race and gender status prevail (see the Storytelling "Doctor, Doctor,"). In the storytelling scenario with the doctor, the woman's assumption about black men included low socioeconomic class and criminality. Cose (1993) said that "for most Blacks in America, regardless of status, political persuasion, or accomplishments, the moment never arrives when race can be treated as a total irrelevancy. Instead, too often, it is the only relevant factor defining our existence" (p. 28). This observation is true not only for African Americans but for other non-White people as well.

Within a color-conscious society, people are judged initially by the color of their skin, an immutable characteristic, and often by their gender, more so than by the content of their character. Often, stereotypes associated with race, gender, and other sources of difference have far-reaching implications for one's livelihood, place of residence, employment opportunity, educational quality and access. This process of judging by appearances may be largely unconscious, yet it occurs both outside and within the counseling event.

STORYTELLING: Doctor, Doctor

A prominent African American male heart surgeon was running weekend errands. Dressed casually in jeans and a sweatshirt, he stopped at an ATM to withdraw money. It was apparent that the European American woman in front of him was uncomfortable as she clutched her purse nervously. Noticing the woman's discomfort, the doctor said at the end of her transaction in his inimitable way, "Don't worry. I've got more money than you do." In the context of the hospital with his white coat, stethoscope, and reputation, this doctor is accorded respect and status. In the mall on a weekend afternoon, this same brilliant man is regarded as a potential thief and a societal element to be feared. Class may temporarily mediate the effects of racism, but class neither cancels nor nullifies these effects. If class alone had this type of power, then middle-class people of color, by virtue of their proximity to and possession of traditional markers of middle-class status (titles, degrees, homes, clothing), would not experience racism.

MULTICULTURALISM IN COUNSELING DEFINED

Multiculturalism is not a new force in counseling. Dramatic demographic changes within the United States inform the profession of the need to reconceive basic Western assumptions of counseling that have been shaped and framed by culture and cultural discourses. Embedded deeply in the fabric of daily life, culture is often rendered invisible, largely because of its pervasiveness. These discourses, or uses of language and verbal exchanges of ideas, operate as forms of social practice to communicate and perpetuate particular meanings (Winslade, Monk, & Drewery, 1997).

Racial and cultural **monoculturalism** represents single-system seeing. It assumes that all people come from the same cultural plane and desire the values of the dominant culture, which have been dictated by those with the most racial and ethnic power (McIntosh, 1990). Monoculturalism is inconsistent with multiculturalism.

Multiculturalism is respectful of multiple epistemological and philosophical perspectives. As an ongoing process that includes comfort with, support, and nurturance of people from various cultures (Hoopes, 1979), multiculturalism views differences as indispensable to a healthy society. Multiculturally competent counselors are able to identify similarities and differences among people and coexist with this information without defensiveness or denial. The terms **multiculturalism** and **cultural diversity** tend to be used interchangeably, but they are by no means synonymous. Cultural diversity may more aptly describe the phenomenon of culturally different people coexisting (Robinson, 1992). The nature of this coexistence, whether harmonious or conflictual, is unknown when one is merely observing different people sharing similar space.

Within the context of American socialization, people are culturally socialized to develop an ethnocentric ideology. Equality and justice for all is widely touted and taught by clergy, family, and educators. Yet many students, regardless of race, admit that they are largely ignorant of the contributions that people of color have made to the United States and to the world. As racial and cultural awareness increases, students might appear confused and/or agitated. They may ask, "How is it that I could have earned a bachelor's degree from a reputable institution and have such limited and inaccurate knowledge about myself, and society and the people in it?" Just as school curriculum materials are a reflection of what is valued throughout society, U.S. history, too, is an institutionalized narrative. Most of us memorized "Columbus sailed the ocean blue in fourteen hundred ninety-two." However, school children are often not told of the bloodshed and murder of Indians (Zinn, 2003). Most of us also did not hear "America . . . derived its wealth, its values, its food, much of its medicine, and a large part of its 'dream' from Native America" (Gunn Allen, 1994, p. 193).

DIVERSE IDENTITIES: AN OVERVIEW

An appreciation of diversity is a democratic ideal. Popular sayings in American culture, such as "Different strokes for different folks" and "To each his own," suggest not only an awareness of but an acceptance of difference. However, despite such cultural expressions, a multicultural society remains an ideal and is not yet a reality.

Since its inception in 1776, the United States has been home to an extremely diverse population. Some sources of diversity among people that existed then and continue now are race, ethnicity, gender, sexual orientation, nationality, physical ability, ability, disability, socioeconomic status (SES), and religion (Pinderhughes, 1989).

Of all Americans, about one quarter, or 25%, are persons of color. The designation "people of color" refers to individuals who are African American, Native American Indian/Alaskan Native (Indian/Native), Asian American, Latino, biracial, and multiracial. Nearly 7 million people in the 2000 Census described themselves as being a member of two or more races (U.S. Census Bureau, 2000). The latest census figures indicated that European Americans were 75% of the population; Latinos, who can be any race are 12.5%; and African Americans are 12.3%. According to this latest census, Latinos surpassed African Americans as the largest group of color during the early part of the 21st century. Much of the racial and ethnic diversity in U.S. society has been influenced by persons from Latin America and Asia, the areas from which the majority of current immigrants originate. Asians, 3.6% of the population, are one of the fastest growing groups.

Between 1990 and 2000, the European American population grew 5.8% and the African American population grew 15.7%. During this same period, the growth rate was 26% for Indians/Natives, 41% for Asians and Pacific Islanders, 57.6% for Latinos, and 57% for persons of "other races" (U.S. Census Bureau, 2000). Projections of the total resident population between 2006 and 2010 indicate a 3.3% increase of

9.7 million for a U.S. population of nearly 300 million. The Asian population is projected to see the largest increase of 121% during this time, followed by a 111% increase among Latinos. Less significant increases are projected for Non-Hispanic whites of 10%, 4.7% among American Indians, and 4.6% among Blacks (U.S. Census, 2000).*

During the start of the 21st century, the workplace will undergo many changes. It will be the most highly educated workplace ever, with 38% having a two-year, four year or advanced college degree. Women under 25 now have labor force participation on par with men, and older women in their 30s and 40s are approaching 85% of the male participation rates. The proportion of Black people in management and professional occupations has doubled over the past 30 years. The proportion of Latinos has nearly tripled and the proportion of Asians has increased by over four times (www.epf.org/research/labordayreports/2002/LDRsummary2002.asp).†

In addition to changes in the workplace, U.S. schools will also undergo demographic shifts. Currently, nearly 33% of all children under age 18 are children of color. By 2010, children of color will represent the majority of young people in California, Florida, New York, and Texas—states that will account for a third of the nation's youth (The Children's Partnership, 2000).

Gender and sexual orientation are two other components of the diversity in the United States. Approximately 51% of the population is female and 49% are male—the male-female ratio is dictated, however, by race and age. This topic will be discussed in greater detail in subsequent chapters.

Human sexuality exists on a continuum and includes heterosexuality, bisexuality, and homosexuality (Robinson & Watt, 2001). The incidence of exclusive homosexuality is estimated to range from 5% to 10% for men and 3% to 5% for women (Strong & Devault, 1992). People who identify as transgender do not subscribe to a male/female dichotomy. For instance, a person can be a biological female yet identify as male with respect to dress and identity. The term transgender refers to the full spectrum of persons with nontraditional gender identities including pre- and posttranssexuals, transvestites, and intersex persons. Intersex persons are born with ambiguous genitalia and are assigned a gender by physicians and family members (Carroll & Gilroy, 2002).

Ours is also an aging population, but such demographic trends are impacted by race. According to the 2000 Census, the White population is the oldest, with 7% being 75 years or older. This compares with 2.1% of persons 75 and older among Native Americans and Alaskan Natives and 3.5% among Blacks. The median age for Latinos is approximately 25; it is 26.5 among Native Americans and Alaskan Natives, roughly 29 for Blacks, 32 for Asians, and 38 for Whites.

Across all age, race, and ethnic groups, religion and/or spirituality plays a part in most people's lives. The United States was founded on Christian principles, however there exists much religious and faith diversity within and between religious and spiritual groups. Christianity is clearly the largest religion worldwide and is

*Source: Projections of the total resident population by 5-year age groups, race, and Hispanic origin with special age categories: Middle Series, 2006 to 2010. Population Projections Program, Population Division.

† Source: Internet. Challenges facing the American workplace. The seventh annual workplace report challenges facing the American workplace. The state of the American workplace in 2002.

purported to have 2 billion members or one third of the world's inhabitants. Islam has approximately 1.3 billion members or 15% of the planet's population. Hinduism is third with 900 million. Persons who are secular, nonreligious, agnostic, or atheist number 850 million. Buddhism is considered the fifth largest religion with 360 million people (www.adherents.com, 2002).

Other world religions include Chinese traditionalism, African traditionalism, Sikhism, Judaism, Bahai, and Shinto. Religion, spirituality, and their various expressions are all affected by the identity dimensions of race, ethnicity, gender, sexual orientation, class, and culture.

A, B, AND C DIMENSIONS

As a means of conceptualizing human differences, Arredondo (1992) referred to the characteristics into which people are born as **"A" dimensions** of personal identity. These include age, culture, sex, sexual orientation, language, social class, and physical disability. **"B" dimensions** are characteristics not necessarily visible to others but are influenced by individual achievement; these include educational background, geographic location, income, marital status, religion, work experience, citizenship status, and hobbies. C dimensions are historical events that impact people's present and future lives. For immigrants, historical events can refer to political events that prompted departure from their home countries. The outbreak of diseases (such as polio, SARS, HIV), as well as terrorist events are examples of historical events that intersect with A and B dimensions.

Understanding the convergence of multiple identity constructs (A, B, and C dimensions) in people's lives is crucial to viewing clients holistically. Throughout this text, the convergence of race and gender (A dimensions) is given primary focus yet all dimensions are essential to promoting client development and empowerment in the counseling process.

A dialectical or both/and approach to cross-cultural counseling allows for complexity and strives for balance (Pedersen, 1990). Although culture is directly acknowledged and respected, it is not the sole or even the dominant component of the counseling event. For some people culture is a dominant identity. Others are seemingly oblivious to culture. The counselor needs to be sensitive and respectful of the role that culture and conceptualization of the self plays in people's lives.

CONCEPTUALIZATION OF THE SELF

The primary focus on the individual is not standard in every culture. In many societies throughout the world, the self is conceptualized within the context of the collective or the community, not as a separate entity. Acculturation, migration status, income, education, and racial/ethnic identity development affect internalization of certain values.

Individualism and collectivism have roots in political and economic history, religion, and philosophy (Kagitcibasi, 1997). In **individualism,** the person is regarded as discrete from other beings and is considered the essential cornerstone of society (Kagitcibasi, 1997). Myers (1991) maintained that because Western society is philosophically oriented to individualism, individuals are the primary referent point and are separate from others. Fragmentation between spirit and matter (or *bifurcation of the self*) is thus an outcome of an individualistic frame of reference.

Individualism may also suppress individual expression. For example, external conformity and individualism appear to be in contradiction, yet these are two cultural themes in the United States. Americans are encouraged to be autonomous, to be their own persons, and to do their own thing. They are also told to maintain the status quo and "not rock the boat." There is almost an unwritten edict against extreme levels of individuality because this tends to be indicative of nonconventionality. U.S. society espouses, "Be all you can be," but conflicting messages are also given: "Do not cross the border of what is acceptable thinking and behavior." "Color within the lines and stay within the box!"

By not knowing the self or being able to ask and answer the questions, "Who am I?" "What do I want to be?" and "What and whom do I want?" one is vulnerable to adopting others' answers to these questions. Although excessive forms of individualism can interfere with one's ability to live collectively and ask for help, as well as receive help from others, individuality is critical to forming an identity.

In addition to socialization factors, structural issues mediate individualism. For example, when the United States' economy was agrarian-based and people were less mobile, interdependence was greater than it is in today's technological and highly mobile society in which people are often isolated from extended family and community support. Individualism influences and is associated with other core U.S. cultural values such as empiricism. The scientific tradition in academia emerged from a positivistic-empirical model that emphasizes quantification, statistical measurement, and validation of reality by use of the five senses. In Western ideology, individualism, measurement, and control are cultural values, exerting powerful influence on the policies, programs, and politics of the United States, both past and present. The visible is legitimate and the invisible is suspect because it cannot be proven and counted. Yet Albert Einstein knew that "Not everything that counts can be counted, and not everything that can be counted counts" (Harris, 1995).

IMAGES OF DIVERSE IDENTITIES

CULTURE

Culture is ubiquitous, central to each of our lives, and shapes the way we see the world. It has been defined as the myriad ways of people to preserve society and meet a range of human needs. Belief systems, behaviors, and traditions make up the essence of culture (Pinderhughes, 1989) as do people's relationships with time, nature, other people and mode of activity (Kluckhohn & Strodtbeck, 1961). As pervasive as culture is, people are often oblivious to its impact on their and others' lives because of unstated assumptions and shared values that go unrecognized (Bronstein & Quina, 1988).

Cultural encapsulation, or viewing the world from only one cultural lens (Wrenn, 1962), is regarded as an impediment to effective multicultural counseling. Counselors need to recognize and be willing to address their cultural biases. Dana (1993) identified an **emic perspective** as one that is respectful of, and sensitive to, the native culture's meanings for phenomena and allows for a recognition of persons on their own terms. By contrast, an **etic perspective** emphasizes the observer's culturally driven meanings that are referenced as the standard for interpretation. Within an ethnocentric perspective, there is a belief that one's own culture and belief systems are superior to those who are culturally different from oneself. Such an attitude is in direct contradiction to the goals and aims of multiculturally competent counseling.

Although Berry and Sam indicated that *acculturation* is a neutral term because changes may happen in both groups, acculturation tends to bring about change in one group, which is referred to as the acculturating group. Two questions clarify the outcome of acculturation strategies: (a) "Is it considered to be of value to maintain relationships with the dominant society?" and (b) "Is it considered to be of value to maintain cultural identity characteristics?" (p. 296).

Acculturation appears to be a process of socialization into accepting and adapting to the cultural values of the larger society. Berry and Sam (1997) provided a definition of acculturation from Redfield, Linton, and Herskovits's (1936) definition: "Acculturation comprehends those phenomena which result when groups of individuals having different cultures come into continuous first-hand contact with subsequent changes in the original culture patterns of either or both groups" (pp. 293–294). Acculturation can take place at the expense of one's original cultural values as one internalizes the dominant society's values and traditions. The key difference is that acculturation is not so much identification as it is internalization. Because this process is not always conscious (Sue, 1989), the possibility of cultural alienation from one's traditional culture is high.

Berry and Sam (1997) discussed four acculturation strategies: (a) assimilation, (b) traditionality, (c) integration, and (d) marginality. Although a dimension of acculturation, **assimilation** is different and describes those persons who do not desire to maintain their cultural identities and thus seek sustained interaction with other cultures outside their own. Sue (1989) discussed a similar phenomenon when describing assimilation. He said it refers to a conscious process in which the person desires to identify with the traditional society because its art, language, and culture are perceived to be more valuable than the person's own. Persons who are acculturated are viewed as being low in a knowledge of, and appreciation for, their own cultures while holding the dominant culture in high regard. The original cultures have been lost or relinquished, and persons have given up most cultural traits of their cultures of origin and assumed the traits of the dominant culture (Berry & Kim, 1988).

According to Steinberg (1989), *assimilation* "meant something less than a total obliteration of ethnic difference. Rather the term referred to a 'superficial uniformity' between the minority and dominant groups that could conceal differences in 'opinion, sentiments, and beliefs' " (p. 47).

Traditionality describes persons who choose to hold on to their cultural connections and avoid interaction with others. Here, people have knowledge of, and appreciation for, their own cultures while holding the dominant culture in lower regard. Berry and Sam (1997) pointed out that when the dominant culture engages in these practices, the term is *segregation*.

Integration describes an interest in maintaining one's original culture while simultaneously seeking interactions with the other culture. According to Berry and Kim (1988), these persons are characterized as being *bicultural*. They are high in knowledge of, and appreciation for, their own cultures while esteeming the dominant culture as well. An integration of both an original culture and the dominant culture has transpired. Mental health and acculturation modality are related. Berry and Kim (as cited in Dana, 1993) stated that "mental health problems will be least intense with biculturality and progressively increase in severity with assimilation, traditionality, and marginality outcomes of acculturation" (p. 112).

Little interest in cultural maintenance and limited desire to interact with others from different cultures is defined as **marginality.** According to Dana (1993), "marginality will often occur when the traditional culture is not retained and the dominant society culture is not accepted" (p. 112). Emotional and psychological stress is associated with seeking to become acculturated within a given culture. Gloria and Peregoy (1995) discussed how alcohol and other drug abuse may be by-products of acculturation stress among some Latino populations. This connection between substance abuse and acculturation stress also seems to apply to Native American Indians and other ethnic and racial groups in their attempts to cope amid cultural devastation (Herring, 1992).

RACE

Every human being is a member of the human race, of the species of *Homo sapiens*. Typical conceptions of race often refer to people of color (Christian, 1989), nonetheless, *race* refers to White people as well. Race is an extremely volatile and divisive force in this nation despite the heroic efforts of various movements (e.g., the Asian, Latino, and civil rights movements) that coalesced to create greater racial equity. Race accounts for huge variations in income, occupational distribution, educational levels, quality of and access to health care, and longevity (Anderson, 2003). Some scientists and academics have advanced that ethnicity accounts for marked differences in intelligence (Herrnstein & Murray, 1994).

What is race? According to some biologists, **race** or subspecies "is an inbreeding, geographically isolated population that differs in distinguishable physical traits from members of the species" (Zuckerman, 1990, p. 1297). Healey (1997) said that race was "an isolated inbreeding population with a distinctive genetic heritage. Socially, the term is used loosely and reflects patterns of inequality and power" (p. 309).

The biology of race is heavily debated (Cornell & Hartmann, 1997; Healey, 1997). In fact, most biologists regard race as a social construct only. Even persons who appear very different from one another by virtue of skin color, facial features, and hair texture are very similar genetically. The Human Genome Project discovered that 99.9% of our 30,000 human genes are shared by everyone (Anderson 2003). Yet, properties such as hair texture and the amount of melanin in the skin are typically the dimensions commonly associated with race (Lee, 2001). Melanin is responsible for darker skin color hue and represents "an adaptation to a particular ecology" (Healey, 1997, p. 11). Although race is often based on phenotypic variables, these variables do not accurately reflect one's race but rather represent a basis for assigning people to a particular racial group. This issue is explored in greater depth in Chapter 8. In this work, it is not my intention to locate people into mutually exclusive racial and gender categories in an effort to conceptualize race and other identities in binary terms. Moreover, from the perspective of biracial or mixed-race persons, having to choose a fixed identity negates their other identities that, though perhaps less visible, are substantial parts of their self-definition (Robinson, 1999b).

ETHNICITY

Typical discussions of ethnicity in the United States tend to include the "melting pot." This pot has been brewing and bubbling for generations. Originating in 1910 at the University of Chicago (Steinberg, 1989), the term described the assimilating tendencies of the more than 1 million European immigrants who were entering the United States each year. Sociologists were interested in knowing how the more than 20 nationalities managed conflict. By outward appearances, they seemed to be adapting very rapidly to the dominant culture.

The melting pot theory differed from the theory of "ethnic pluralists," who maintained that ethnicity was an enduring factor throughout American life. Yet, the loss of native tongues, the decline of ethnic cultures, the dispersion of ethnic communities, the increase in ethnic and religious intermarriage, and the transformation of ethnic-sounding names to American-sounding names were and continue to be examples of Americanization (Steinberg, 1989). In addition, the melting pot assailed the preservation of individual differences in that the pot was dominated by a particular ingredient. This image differs from that of a mosaic in which a variety of different and unique colors are depicted together.

The process of assimilation among White ethnic microcultures differs greatly from that among people of color. Race often makes people of color easy targets for discriminatory treatment. Historical differences exist between race and ethnicity as a function of U.S. policy. The 1790 Naturalization Law, which was in effect for 162 years, stated that only free "White" immigrants would be eligible for naturalized citizenship. This meant that general citizenship was denied Asians until 1952, with the Walter-McCarran Act, and even Native American Indians until 1924 (Takaki, 1994).

People often lack an understanding of history, and this misunderstanding is the basis for the maintenance of racist attitudes. For instance Alba (1990) referred to persons from Latin America as "new immigrant groups" (p. 1). His statement is based on the fact that during the late 19th and early 20th centuries Europeans represented the largest group of immigrants to this nation. Yet, in the Treaty of Guadalupe, Hidalgo, Mexico lost half of its national territory, which included Texas, New Mexico, California, Arizona, Nevada, Utah, and half of Colorado (Novas, 1994). It is important to be aware of historical accuracy particularly when refering to people as new immigrants who occupy the homeland of their ancestors.

Race and ethnicity are used interchangeably by some authors and researchers; however, these terms are not synonymous. According to Pinderhughes (1989), **ethnicity** refers to a connectedness based on commonalities (e.g., religion, nationality, regions) in which specific aspects of cultural patterns are shared and transmission over time creates a common history and ancestry. Smith (1991) defined an **ethnic group** as,

> A reference group called upon by people who share a common history and culture, who may be identifiable because they share similar physical features and values and who, through the process of interacting with each other and establishing boundaries with others, identify themselves as being a member of the group. (p. 181)

Both preceding definitions identify commonality in which unique cultural aspects are shared and transmitted. Among some racial groups, ethnicity refers more to nationality and country of origin. For others, religion describes ethnicity or values and lifestyle (Lee, 2001). Despite these different definitions of ethnicity, persons can be of the same ethnicity (e.g., Latino) but represent different racial backgrounds (e.g., White, Black, biracial, Asian). Persons can also be of the same racial group (Asian) but of differing ethnicities (e.g., Chinese, Southeast Asian Indian, Cuban, Filipino). When transmitted intergenerationally within the culture, language, dancing, dressing, singing, storytelling, ways of worship and mourning, quilt making, weaving, and cooking, for example, are ethnic behaviors (Alba, 1990).

GENDER

Traditional notions of gender reference nonmales (Christian, 1989), yet gender refers to males, females, and to transgendered individuals. Gender has socially constructed categories in terms of roles and behaviors based on a biological given of sex (Renzetti & Curran, 1992). **Biological sex** refers to the possession of an XY chromosome pair for a genetically healthy male and an XX chromosome pair for a genetically healthy female, along with the corresponding anatomical, hormonal, and physiological parts (Atkinson & Hackett, 1995). Some people are born with a variety of chomosomal configurations, such as Klinefelter's, in which a male person has an extra X chromosome or XXY. The reader needs to be sensitive to this reality and within the context of counseling, support the client's exploration of the ways in which his life has been affected by their condition. In addition, there are persons who are born with genitalia that are ambiguous; therefore doctors, in conjunction with results from appropriate genetic tests, determine a child's sex to the best of their abilities or affix a sexual assignment. **Gender** refers to the roles, behaviors, and attitudes that come to be expected of persons on the basis of their biological sex. Despite the advent of the women's and men's movements, in U.S. society, "Men are socialized to be emotionally inhibited, assertive, powerful, independent, and to equate sexuality with intimacy, manliness, and self-esteem. Women tend to be socialized to be emotional, nurturing, and to direct their achievement through affiliation with others, particularly men" (Mintz & O'Neil, 1990, p. 382). In truth, men are emotional beings who need to rely on others, do not always feel strong, and desire to express a full range of emotions. Women are leaders, strong, providers, and caretakers of self and others.

Sex and gender are terms that are easily confused. For instance, lactation and penile ejaculation are sex roles that are not biologically interchangeable for men and women, respectively. However, diaper changing and car repair are not sex roles. They are socially constructed gender roles. There are no isolated genes for choosing wallpaper or building a deck, yet the arbitrary divisions of labor that society has constructed based on biological sex are stringent and far too often attributed to biology.

The "uniformity myth," or the assumption that biological sex is synonymous with societal gender roles, has often existed in the literature (Mintz & O'Neil, 1990). Psychological masculinity is not a biological phenomenon, yet it is often equated with characteristics of the U.S. culture, such as rugged self-reliance, competition, and fierce individualism (Robinson & Watt, 2001). The characteristics often attributed to femininity, such as loving children, yielding, and nurturing, are not exclusive to the female sex or to heterosexuals of any gender.

Androcentrism is a traditional systematic construct in which the worldview of men is used as the central premise of development for all individuals, including women (Worell & Remer, 1992). The central image underlying this concept is "males at the center of the universe looking out at reality from behind their own eyes and describing what they see from an egocentric or androcentric point of view" (Bem, 1993, p. 42). The many benefits associated with privilege can limit one's insight into the disadvantages that can accompany privilege, nonetheless, both men and women alike suffer from the constricting consequences of inequities based on biological sex and socially constructed gender roles (see the Storytelling, "Now That I Have My Boy").

STORYTELLING: Now That I Have My Boy

A woman once told me that during her pregnancy she felt incredible pressure from her husband to have a boy. She knew her husband desperately wanted a boy. She also knew that if she had a girl she would have to keep trying until she had a male child. She also told me how relieved she was when her first child was a boy and said that now that she had her boy she did not have to keep on trying to have any more children.

SEXUALITY

Sexuality exists on a continuum and encompasses homosexuality, bisexuality, and heterosexuality. There are different expressions of sexuality within and across the sexuality continuum.

The United States is a heterosexist society. **Heterosexism** is the belief that everyone is heterosexual and that heterosexual relationships are preferred and necessary for the preservation of the family, particularly the nuclear family. Heterosexism is institutionalized through law, religion, education, and the media and leads to homophobia (Pharr, 1988). Related to heterosexism, **homophobia** is the irrational and unreasonable fear of same-sex attractions and "persons whose affectional and erotic orientations are toward the same sex" (King, 1988, p. 168). It also applies to persons perceived to be gay or lesbian and emanates from the perception of homosexuality as an aberration of the correct social order. The term **homosexual** defines attraction to the same sex for physical and emotional nurturance and is one orientation on the sexual orientation continuum. It has become associated with the historical belief that homosexuality is unnatural, a sin, and a sickness. For this reason, the terms *gay* and *lesbian* are preferred and used throughout this work. *Homophobia* comes from the Latin *homo,* meaning "same" (in this case, referring to same-gender attraction), and *phobia,* meaning "fear of."

Heterosexism has implications for a number of relationships, including the client-counselor dyad. Heterosexism could limit the type of advocacy a heterosexual counselor might engage in with a gay, transgendered, or bisexual client. This is particularly true if the counselor is extremely self-conscious about being labeled as gay or lesbian because of affiliation with, or advocacy for, gay men and lesbians.

As a reflection of changing times and sentiments regarding sexuality, some corporations and universities provide same-sex partner benefits for committed couples who are not married and live together. Vermont recognizes same-sex partnerships as legal within civil unions. On March 29, 2004, the Massachusetts legislature voted to ban gay marriage and establish civil unions, approving a proposed constitutional amendment that would reverse the Supreme Judicial Court's historic November 2003 ruling that legalized same-sex marriage (Klein, 2004).

DISABILITY

Section 504 of the Rehabilitation Act of 1973 and the Americans with Disabilities Act of 1990 (ADA) prohibit discrimination against individuals with disabilities. According to these laws, no otherwise qualified individual with a disability shall, solely by reason of his disability, be excluded from the participation in, be denied the benefits of, or be subjected to discrimination under any program or activity of a public entity.

According to the *Americans with Disabilities Act Handbook* (EEOC, 1991), an individual with a disability is a person who has a physical or mental impairment that substantially limits one or more "major life activities," or has a record of such an impairment, or is regarded as having such an impairment. Examples of physical or mental impairments include, but are not limited to, contagious and noncontagious diseases and conditions such as orthopedic, visual, speech, and hearing impairments; cerebral palsy; epilepsy; muscular dystrophy; multiple sclerosis; cancer; heart disease; diabetes; mental retardation; emotional illness; specific learning disabilities; HIV disease (whether symptomatic or asymptomatic); tuberculosis; drug addiction; and alcoholism. According to the U.S. Census Bureau (2002b), there are 49.7 million people (one in five residents) age 5 and over with a disability.

The nature of disabilities among people varies, and the term itself is resistant to precise definition and measurement (Atkinson & Hackett, 1995). Numerous categories exist in describing persons with disabilities, from mild to moderate to severe. People need not be born into a disability, but whether it exists at birth or occurs at some juncture in life, it is a biological reality nonetheless. According to Weeber (1993), persons with disabilities are the only minority with an open membership. Anyone can become a member at virtually any time, and most people will become disabled during their old age. Disability is a reality for millions of Americans, yet persons with physical and mental disabilities continue to face obstacles to access and experience discriminatory attitudes. How many of us have gone to a restaurant with a friend who had a visible disability to find that the waiter or waitress completely ignored this friend and asked the person who did not appear to have a disability what the friend with the disability would like to order? Such attitudes are fueled by a societal perception that persons with disabilities are dependent, helpless, childlike, and incomplete.

Disability intersects with gender and has class implications. Resource allocation for women with physical disabilities is different from that for men with disabilities and women who are able-bodied. According to Fulton and Sabornie (1994), "nearly twice as likely to be employed, men with disabilities earn less than 44% more than women with disabilities" (p. 150). According to the March 2001 supplement to the *Current Population Survey,* the mean earnings in 2000 of year-round, full-time workers ages 16 to 64 with work disabilities was $33,109. By comparison, those without work disabilities earned an average of $43,269 (U.S. Census Bureau, 2002b). In addition, the poverty rate among the population 25 to 64 years of age with no disability was 8% compared with 10% for people with a nonsevere disability and 28% for people with a severe disability (U.S. Census Bureau, 2001b).

Despite the reality that disability is simply one component of a person's overall identity, Fowler, O'Rourke, Wadsworth, and Harper (1992) noted that the term *disabled* "conveys a message of inability which overshadows other identity descriptors of the person and becomes the exclusive role for persons who are disabled" (p. 102). Disability can function as a primary status trait when it is visible and regarded as the most salient component of a person's existence. For instance, a counselor who associates the experience of being able-bodied and middle class with feelings of power may perceive an unemployed client with a disability as helpless and marginal. Actually, the client may feel psychologically empowered and have access to an abundance of emotional and spiritual resources that enable him to feel powerful about his life.

SOCIOECONOMIC CLASS

Socioeconomic class has traditionally referred to a person's or group's relative social position within a hierarchical ranking (Jaynes & Williams, 1989). Factors that affect one's socioeconomic ranking include educational level, employment stability, wages, marital status, income of spouse and/or other persons in the home, size of household, citizenship, and access to medical benefits. Exceptions exist, but increased education tends to be associated with higher incomes (Hacker, 1992).

In the counseling arena, an inordinate emphasis has been placed on career development and assessment with less attention devoted to lower socioeconomic class and people of color (Richardson, 1993).

The intersections of class with gender and race are clear. According to the U.S. Census Bureau, in 2001, the poverty rate for non-Hispanic Whites was 7.8%; 22.7% for Blacks; and 10.2% for Asians and Pacific Islanders. For Latinos, who can be of any race, it was 21.4% (U.S. Census Bureau, 2002).

Socioeconomic class affects other dimensions of one's life, including sense of worth and social status. Schliebner and Peregoy (1994) described its impact on the family:

> The family unit . . . derives its routine and ordering of time, place in a social
> network, status, and economic well-being from the labor force participation
> of its parental members . . . When productivity is halted, profound feelings
> of loss, inadequacy, guilt, and lowered self-esteem can result. (p. 368)

Self-construct and feelings of self-worth are affected by employment and socioeconomic class. Therefore it is not surprising that child-rearing practices would also be affected. Storck (1998) suggested that class has to be expanded to include psychosocial characteristics such as a sense of well-being. In their study of working parents, McLoyd and Wilson (1992) found that parents with fewer economic resources, in comparison to parents who were considered middle class, placed less emphasis on happiness as a goal while they were rearing their children. These parents were less likely to believe that childhood was a protected, carefree, and happy-go-lucky space, or that it was their responsibility as parents to create such a climate for their children. The research presented by McLoyd and Wilson plus Storck's call for an expansion of the concept of social class suggest that class is not independent of other dimensions of one's personhood, such as psychological well-being and attention to happiness. Socioeconomic status is also a major driver of health-behaviors and health related psychological processes, including physical activity, smoking, healthy eating habits, sleep quality, depression, cynical hostility, obesity, and chronic stress (Anderson, 2003).

Wilson (1994) argued that to understand the economic plight of people in society, race needs to be examined in conjunction with structural and infrastructure issues such as technology, unemployment, underemployment, and migrant labor.

> Because fewer Black and White workers are willing to accept an economic
> arrangement that consigns them to dead-end menial and poorly paid jobs,
> low-wage service and manufacturing industries have increasingly used
> immigrant labor, including illegal aliens or undocumented workers to keep
> wages depressed. (p. 250)

Regardless of race, the last few years have not been favorable for Americans. In 2001, there were 6.8 million poor families (9.2%). This figure had increased from 6.4 million (8.7%) in 2000 (U.S. Census Bureau, 2001). The high unemployment rates due to heavy economic losses in the dot.com technology sector and manufacturing declines have been devastating to millions of people. In this example, class converges with race and gender. These intersections have implications for the client's problem presentation and perceived effectiveness of the counseling relationship.

SPIRITUALITY

The United States was founded on Christian principles. The teachings of Jesus as reflected in the New Testament were based on love for everyone in a spirit of justice. The Bible's other teachings include the writings of the apostles and of various church fathers. Other religions throughout the world and within the United States are widely practiced and provide people with a sense of connection with the universe and of harmony, peace, and joy. These religions include Buddhism, Judaism, Islam, Hinduism, Confucianism, Taoism, Shintoism, and tribal beliefs (Wehrly, 1995).

Religion and spirituality are conceptualized differently. **Religion** may be measured by denominational affiliations (e.g., Baptist, Methodist), as well as by empirical, behavioral, or public indicators, such as churchgoing and avoidance of denounced (sinful) behaviors (e.g., alcohol consumption; cigarette smoking; foul language; the revealing of one's face or body; disobedience to one's family, culture, or husband; sexual intercourse outside marriage). **Spirituality** is often private and/or internally defined, transcends the tangible, and serves to connect one to the whole (other living organisms and the universe). Spirituality gives life direction and can help people maintain mental health (McDonald, 1990; Swinton, 2001). It is possible to define oneself as spiritual without being religious and to be religious but not spiritual (Burke & Miranti, 2001). Faith was defined by Fowler and Keen (1978) as being connected to but not the same as religion. It is "a person's or a community's way-of-being-in-relation to other persons and groups, and to the values, causes, and institutions that give form and pattern to life" (pp. 23–24).

Faith helps people cope with stress and make meaning in life (Watt, 1996). Many clients find some degree of comfort in their faith when seeking to answer the questions "Who am I?" or "What will become of me?" or "What am I going to do?" Parker (1985) saw that faith and development were integrated. He said, "The idea that active participation and struggle is necessary, is common not only to discussions of religious development but to discussion of other forms of cognitive growth and change" (p. 45). Undeniably, people find comfort in their faith, particularly during crises or intensely conflictual times in life.

As a crucial cultural attribute, counselors should not overlook faith as key to a client's cultural background (Bishop, 1992). Dissimilarity in religious values between client and counselor may account for a hesitance to explore religion, as well as for a counselor's unwillingness to self-disclose his values. If the counselor lacks knowledge about a client's culture or religion or both, it is crucial that the professional close this knowledge gap. Counselors need to first assess their own cultural and spiritual belief systems to help their clients navigate this oftentimes uneven terrain. Counselors also need to be aware that, for many individual clients, religion represents a definite form of oppression (Robinson & Watt, 2001). In addition, religion has been and continues to be used to justify dominance, racism, and terrorism. During his 1492 exploration of the Americas, Christopher Columbus took Arawak Indians as prisoners and put them aboard one of his ships to Spain. He believed the Arawak to be naive because they were willing to share their possessions. Despite Columbus's enslavement and murder of Indians, he invoked religion and saw it as a form of divine assistance. Columbus said, "Thus the eternal God, our Lord, gives victory to those who follow His way over apparent impossibilities" (Zinn, 2003, p. 4). Counselors need to recognize the historical role of religion as it may impact clients' present-day religious realities.

IMPLICATIONS FOR COUNSELORS

The ultimate aim of multicultural counseling is to recognize and appreciate that differences exist among people. Multiculturalism is an ideal and an ongoing process that takes place over time. Counselors are encouraged to acknowledge where they are in their own cultural and racial development because attitudes about differences can help or hinder the creation of a mutually respectful counseling event. A counselor must understand the strengths of a client's culture and see such strengths as instrumental to healthy development. Counselors also need to learn to communicate effectively with clients about the full range of the clients' values in order to assist the client in their seeing the connection among these values, how they view their problems and think about problem resolution. Counselors should assess their knowledge about differences and supplement this knowledge as necessary. It is all right not to know; what one does with not knowing makes the difference (see the Case Study "Not Wanting to Be Insensitive").

CASE STUDY
Not Wanting to Be Insensitive

Miriam is a 28-year-old, physically healthy Lebanese woman living in a medium-sized city in South Carolina with her husband, Samuel. He is also Lebanese. They have lived in the United States since 1993 and came to the States with their families. They are Arabs, Christians, and heavily involved in their Catholic church. They have been married 6 years and have two small children. Miriam is taking a class at the community college and spends several nights a week studying. Sam and Miriam's lovemaking has become infrequent, and it is clear to Samuel that the relationship is strained. Miriam's time away from the home has increased. She says she is studying with a classmate. Samuel suggests that they speak with their priest. Miriam told Sam that she could not speak to him. When Sam asked why, Miriam told Sam that she was having a sexual relationship with her female classmate—and that she had been having feelings for other women before they were married. She prayed that these feelings would go away but they did not. Miriam would prefer to talk with a Lebanese woman, and although she is close to her family, she believes that she cannot talk with them about this topic. The counseling psychologist at her community college is Judith. Miriam decides to see her.

QUESTIONS
1. What are the dominant discourses regarding Miriam's ethnicity, marital status, gender, and religion?
2. Where does the counselor begin with Miriam?
3. How can the counselor best help Miriam?

DISCUSSION AND INTEGRATION
The Client, Miriam

Miriam's dilemma is real and she requires a safe place to sort out her feelings. As a mother, wife, Catholic, daughter, and Lebanese woman, some of her identities conflict or at least the dominant discourses associated with these identities conflict. For example, good Catholics are heterosexual. Good mothers are not lesbian. Prayer has the power to override same-sex feelings.

Culturally, there are clear expectations for Miriam as a Lebanese woman. Kinship ties are very strong. Lebanese families are "traditionally patrilineal, endogamous, and extended, with wide and complex kin relationships that help to sustain traditional functions of the culture" (Simon, 1996, p. 365). In Lebanon, nearly half of the population are Christians (Abud-abbeh, 1996). In the United States, Miriam and her family maintain traditional attitudes toward a series of issues that are similar to those held by Arab Americans who are Muslim—family, marriage, and children are some of these topics. Miriam also feels ashamed for neglecting some of her family responsibilities such as child care and serving as an appropriate hostess to both her and Samuel's parents during their regular visits. The emphasis on kinship in her culture and the cultural expectations for her to prepare and serve food are strong. Simon (1996) points out, "Identity for the Lebanese does not exist apart from the family. In fact, the proper introduction of a Middle Easterner does not end with the announcement of his name— his family group must also be established" (p. 365).

The Counselor, Judith

As a counselor influenced by a social constructionist perspective Judith realizes Miriam is wrestling with sexual identity issues but also realizes that a person's sexual identity is not determined by sexual behavior and that sexual orientation may be an evolving part of identity. However, the longevity of Miriam's sexual feelings for and attraction to other women, as well as the strength of her conflict, is a strong indication that she may not be just experimenting sexually with her female friend.

Miriam's Catholicism is a crucial part of her life and a source of strength. Nonetheless, her religion also contributes to her guilt. Judith would be wise to help Miriam with the collision of feelings around religion and her sexuality.

In addition to creating a safe place for Miriam to be, Judith may encourage Miriam to do bibliotherapy in which she reads the stories of other women who may be questioning their sexuality. Marriage counseling is also recommended at some point but it should be kept in mind that the focus between a Lebanese couple is often on the children (Simon, 1996).

Often counselors will omit certain information or avoid asking particular questions out of fear of being perceived as ignorant, racist, insensitive, or discriminatory. This fear can paralyze the counseling event and interfere with the client's growth and support in dealing with problems that require the counselor's awareness and leadership to initiate conversation about difficult topics. It is impossible to help clients explore complex issues concerning race, sexual orientation, gender, religion, and culture if counselors have not started this important work for themselves. Cardemil and Battle (2003) offer an axiom that may be helpful: "When in doubt about the importance of race and ethnicity in treatment, err on the side of discussion. Be willing to take risks with clients" (p. 282).

SUMMARY

The various faces of diversity were discussed in this chapter. Included were culture, race, ethnicity, gender, sexuality, disability, socioeconomic class, and spirituality. The multiple identity components in shaping psychosocial development was highlighted. A case study was presented to illustrate the textured lives of clients. Potential biases of the counselor were pinpointed, and recommendations for improvement were offered.

REFERENCES

Abudabbeh, N. (1996). Arab families. In M. McGoldrick, J. K. Pearce, & J. Giordano (Eds.), *Ethnicity and family therapy* (pp. 333–346). New York: Guilford Press.

Adherents.com. (2002). Major religions of the world ranked by number of adherents. Retrieved from http://www.adherents.com/.

Alba, R. D. (1990). *Ethnic identity: The transformation of White America.* New Haven, CT: Yale University Press.

Anderson, N. B. (2003, October). *Unraveling the mystery of racial and ethnic health disparities: Who, what, when, where, how and especially, why?* Boston, MA: Institute on Urban Health Research, Northeastern University.

Arredondo, P. (1992). *Latina/Latino counseling and psychotherapy: Tape 1. Cultural consideration for working more effectively with Latin Americans.* Amherst, MA: Microtraining and Multicultural Development.

Atkinson, D. R., & Hackett, G. (1995). *Counseling diverse populations.* Madison, WI: Brown and Benchmark.

Bem, S. (1993). *The lens of gender: Transforming the debate on sexual inequality.* New Haven, CT: Yale University Press.

Berry, J. W., & Kim, U. (1988). Acculturation and mental health. In P. R. Dasen, J. W. Berry, & N. Sartorius (Eds.), *Health and cross-cultural psychology: Toward applications* (pp. 207–236). Newbury Park, CA: Sage.

Berry, J. W., & Sam, D. L. (1997). Acculturation and adaptation. In J. Berry, M. Segall, & C. Kagitcibasi (Eds.), *Cross-cultural psychology* (Vol. 3, pp. 291–326). Boston: Allyn & Bacon.

Bishop, D. R. (1992). Religious values as cross-cultural issues in counseling. *Counseling and Values, 36,* 179–189.

Bronstein, P., & Quina, K. (1988). *Teaching a psychology of people.* Washington, DC: American Psychological Association.

Burke, M. T., & Miranti, J. (2001). The spiritual and religious dimensions of counseling. In D. Locke,

J. Myers, & E. Herr (Eds.), *Handbook of counseling,* (pp. 601–612). Beverly Hills, CA: Sage.

Cardemil, E. V., & Battle, C. L. (2003). Guess who's coming to therapy? Getting comfortable with conversations about race and ethnicity in psychotherapy. *Professional Psychology: Research and Practice, 34,* 278–286.

Carroll, L., & Gilroy, P. J. (2002). Transgender issues in counselor preparation. *Counselor Education & Supervision, 41,* 233–242.

Christian, B. (1989). But who do you really belong to—Black studies or women's studies? *Women's Studies, 17,* 17–23.

Cornell, S., & Hartmann, D. (1997). *Ethnicity and race: Making identities in a changing world.* Thousand Oaks, CA: Pine Forge Press.

Cose, E. (1993). *The rage of a privileged class.* New York: HarperCollins.

Dana, R. H. (1993). *Multicultural assessment perspectives for professional psychology.* Boston: Allyn & Bacon.

Equal Employment Opportunity Commission (EEOC). (1991). *Americans with Disabilities Act handbook.* Washington, DC: Government Printing Office.

Fowler, C., O'Rourke, B. O., Wadsworth, J., & Harper, D. (1992). Disability and feminism: Models for counselor exploration of personal values and beliefs. *Journal of Applied Rehabilitation Counseling, 23,* 14–19.

Fowler, J., & Keen, S. (1978). *Life maps: Conversations on the journey of faith.* Waco, TX: Word Books.

Freire, P. (1992). *Pedagogy of the oppressed.* New York: Continuum.

Fulton, S. A., & Sabornie, E. J. (1994). Evidence of employment inequality among females with disabilities. *Journal of Special Education, 2,* 149–165.

Gloria, A. M., & Peregoy, J. J. (1996). Counseling Latino alcohol and other substance users/abusers: Cultural considerations for counselors. *Journal of Substance Abuse Treatment, 13,* 119–126.

Gunn Allen, P. (1994). Who is your mother? Red roots of White feminism. In R. Takaki (Ed.), *From different shores: Perspectives on race and ethnicity in America* (2nd ed., pp. 192–198). New York: Oxford University Press.

Hacker, A. (1992). *Two nations: Black and White, separate, hostile, unequal.* New York: Ballantine Books.

Harris, K. (1995). Collected quotes from Albert Einstein. http://rescomp.stanford.edu/~cheshire/EinsteinQuotes.html

Healey, J. F. (1997). *Race, ethnicity, and gender in the United States: Inequality, group conflict, and power.* Thousand Oaks, CA: Pine Forge Press.

Herring, R. D. (1992). Understanding Native American values: Process and content concerns for counselors. *Counseling and Values, 34,* 134–137.

Herrnstein, R. J., & Murray, C. (1994). *The bell curve: Intelligence and class structure in American life.* New York: Free Press.

Hoopes, D. S. (1979). Intercultural communication concepts: Psychology of intercultural experience. In M. D. Psych (Ed.), *Multicultural education: A cross-cultural training approach.* LaGrange Park, IL: Intercultural Network.

Kagitcibasi, C. (1997). Individualism and collectivism. In J. Berry, M. Segall, & C. Kagitcibasi (Eds.), *Cross-cultural psychology: Vol. 3. Social and behavioral applications* (pp. 1–49). Boston: Allyn & Bacon.

King, N. (1988). Teaching about lesbians and gays in the psychology curriculum. In P. Bronstein & K. Quina (Eds.), *Teaching a psychology of people* (pp. 168–174). Washington, DC: American Psychological Association.

Klein, R. (March 30, 2004). Vote ties civil unions to gay-marriage ban. *The Boston Globe,* p. A2

Kluckhohn, F. R., & Strodtbeck, F. L. (1961). *Variations in value orientations.* Evanston, IL: Row, Peterson.

Kromkowski, J. A. (1992). *Race and ethnic relations, 92–93.* Guilford, CT: Dushkin.

Lee, C. (2001). Defining and responding to racial and ethnic diversity. In D. Locke, J. Myers, & E. Herr (Eds.), *Handbook of counseling* (p. 581–588). Thousand Oaks, CA: Sage.

McDonald, A. L. (1990). Living with our deepest differences. *Journal of Law and Religion, 8,* 237–239.

McIntosh, P. (1990). *Interactive phases of curricular and personal revision with regard to race* (Working Paper No. 219). Wellesley, MA: Wellesley College Center for Research on Women.

McLoyd, V. C., & Wilson, L. (1992). Telling them like it is: The role of economic and environmental factors in single mothers' discussions with their children. *American Journal of Community Psychology, 20,* 419–444.

Mintz, L. B., & O'Neil, J. M. (1990). Gender roles, sex, and the process of psychotherapy: Many questions and few answers. *Journal of Counseling and Development, 68,* 381–387.

Myers, L. J. (1991). Expanding the psychology of knowledge optimally: The importance of world view revisited. In R. Jones (Ed.), *Black psychology* (3rd ed., pp. 15–28)., Berkeley, CA: Cobb and Henry.

Novas, H. (1994). *Everything you need to know about Latino history.* New York: Penguin.

Parker, M. S. (1985). Identity and the development of religious thinking. In A. S. Waterman (Ed.), *Identity in adolescence* (pp. 43–60). San Francisco: Jossey-Bass.

Pedersen, P. (1990). The constructs of complexity and balance in multicultural counseling theory and practice. *Journal of Counseling and Development, 15,* 16–24.

Pharr, S. (1988). *Homophobia: A weapon of sexism.* Little Rock, AR: Chardon.

Pinderhughes, E. (1989). *Understanding race, ethnicity, and power: The key to efficacy in clinical practice.* New York: Free Press.

Renzetti, C. M., & Curran, D. J. (1992). *Women, men, and society.* Boston: Allyn & Bacon.

Richardson, M. S. (1993). Work in people's lives: A location for counseling psychologists. *Journal of Counseling Psychology, 40,* 425–433.

Robinson, T. L. (1992). Transforming at-risk educational practices by understanding and appreciating differences. *Elementary School Guidance and Counseling, 27,* 84–95.

Robinson, T. L. (1993). The intersections of gender, class, race, and culture: On seeing clients whole. *Journal of Multicultural Counseling and Development, 21,* 50–58.

Robinson, T. L. (1999a). The intersections of dominant discourses across race, gender, and other identities. *Journal of Counseling and Development, 77,* 73–79.

Robinson, T. L. (1999b). The intersections of identity. In A. Garrod, J. V. Ward, T. L. Robinson, & B. Kilkenney (Eds.), *Souls looking back: Portraits of growing up Black*. New York: Routledge.

Robinson, T. L., & Watt, S. K. (2001). Where no one goes begging: Gender, sexuality, and religious diversity. In D. Locke, J. Myers, & E. Herr (Eds.), *Handbook of counseling* (pp. 589–599). Thousand Oaks, CA: Sage.

Schliebner, C. T., & Peregoy, J. J. (1994). Unemployment effects on the family and the child: Interventions for counselors. *Journal of Counseling and Development, 72*, 368–372.

Simon, J. P. (1996). Lebanese families. In M. McGoldrick, J. K. Pearce, & J. Giordano (Eds.), *Ethnicity and family therapy* (pp. 364–375). New York: Guilford Press.

Smith, E. J. (1991). Ethnic identity development: Toward the development of a theory within the context of majority/minority status. *Journal of Counseling and Development, 70*, 181–188.

Steinberg, S. (1989). *The ethnic myth: Race, ethnicity, and class in America*. Boston: Beacon Press.

Storck, L. E. (1998). Social class divisions in the consulting room: A theory of psychosocial class and depression. *Group Analysis, 31,* 101–115.

Strong, B., & Devault, C. (1992). *Understanding our sexuality*. St. Paul, MN: West.

Sue, D. W. (1989). Cultural identity development [Video]. Anhesto, MA: Microaiming and multicultural development.

Swinton, J. (2001). *Spirituality and mental health care: Rediscovering a "forgotten" dimension*. Jessica Kinglsely Publishers.

Takaki, R. (1994). Reflections on racial patterns in America. In R. Takaki (Ed.), *From different shores: Perspectives on race and ethnicity in America* (2nd ed., pp. 24–35). New York: Oxford University Press.

The Children's Partnership (2000). Tomorrow's youth: A changing demographic. http://www.childrenspartnership.org/pub/children2000/children_of_2000.pdf

U.S. Census Bureau (2000). U.S. Summary: 2000. Washington, DC: U.S. Department of Commerce.

U.S. Census Bureau (2001). Money Income in the United States: 2001. Washington, DC: U.S. Department of Commerce.

U.S. Census Bureau (2001b). Nearly 1 in 5 Americans has some level of Disability, U.S. Census Bureau reports. United States Department of Commerce News. http://www.census.gov/press-release/www/2001/cb01-46.html

U.S. Census Bureau (2002). Poverty in the United States. Washington, DC: U.S. Department of Commerce.

U.S. Census Bureau (2002b). 12th Anniversary of Americans with disabilities (July 26). http://www.census.gov/Press-Release/www/2002/cb02ff11.html

Watt, S. (1996). *Identity and the making of meaning: Psychosocial identity, racial identity, womanist identity, and faith development of African American college women*. Unpublished doctoral dissertation, North Carolina State University at Raleigh.

Weeber, J. (1993). *"We are who you are": The issue of self-definition with disabled women and a reframed feminist response*. Unpublished manuscript, North Carolina State University at Raleigh.

Wehrly, B. (1995). *Pathways to multicultural counseling competence: A developmental journey*. Pacific Grove, CA: Brooks/Cole.

Wilson, W. J. (1994). The Black community: Race and class. In R. Takaki (Ed.), *From different shores: Perspectives on race and ethnicity in America* (2nd ed., pp. 243–250). New York: Oxford University Press.

Winslade, J., Monk, G., & Drewery, W. (1997). Sharpening the critical edge: A social constructionist approach in counselor education. In T. Sexton & B. Griffin (Eds.), *Constructivist thinking in counseling practice, research, and training* (pp. 228–245). New York: Columbia University Teacher's College.

Worell, J., & Remer, P. (1992). *Feminist perspectives in therapy: An empowerment model for women*. New York: John Wiley.

Wrenn, C. G. (1962). The culturally encapsulated counselor. *Harvard Educational Review, 32*, 444–449.

Zinn, H. (2003). *A people's history of the United States. 1492 present*. New York: HarperCollins.

Zuckerman, M. (1990). Some dubious premises in research and theory on racial differences. *American Psychologist, 45*, 1297–1303.

Chapter 2

Multicultural Competencies and Skills

The quiet
companionship of a comforting person is
like balm to the soul. Like Mother Earth,
she absorbs the shock of pain and erases
the wounds and even the scars with time.
These kindred spirits seem to be able to
take our hand and walk with us through
the difficult places they have already
traveled. They keep us from the loneliness
that pervades our experiences, waiting for
a word that we have passed through
safely. And best of all, they never bring it
up again but let the past take care of the
past. Their eyes are on tomorrow, their
hands on the present time so that we
never hear empty echoes and are never
reminded that we were unhappy. And
then, we, in quiet ways, can reach back
and take someone else's hand.

Joyce Sequichie Hifler, A Cherokee Feast of Days

One of my professors at the Harvard Graduate School of Education, Robert Kegan, once said that counseling is similar to the creation of a holding environment for people. In this space, people can heal and gain insight into problems that assail them. Good counseling is not rescuing people, but it does involve journeying the way with people as they struggle.

This chapter explores the development of multicultural competencies in counseling. Strategies for becoming a multiculturally competent counselor and guidelines on monitoring dissonance and measuring cross-cultural effectiveness are reviewed. A case study allows for an integration of the material presented.

The competencies were derived from a 3 × 3 (Characteristics × Domains) matrix in which the characteristics of a "culturally skilled counselor" were cross-classified with the domains of multicultural competence (i.e., awareness, knowledge, and skills) (Holcomb-McCoy, 2000, p. 85).

A little history may be helpful. In 1980, the Division of Counseling Psychology's (Division 17) Education and Training Committee formed a Cross-Cultural Counseling Competencies Committee for the purpose of developing culturally relevant counseling competencies for adoption into graduate counseling and clinical psychology programs (Sue et al., 1982). These competencies were approved in 1982. In that same year, Sue et al. proposed a definition of **cross-cultural counseling** as "any counseling relationship in which two or more of the participants differ in cultural background, values, and lifestyle" (p. 47). Given this definition, any counseling interaction could be regarded as cross-cultural in that human beings vary with respect to their cultural orientations and their lived experiences as cultural beings.

MULTICULTURAL COMPETENCIES: AN OVERVIEW

In 1991, the Association for Multicultural Counseling and Development (AMCD) presented a document to the American Association for Counseling and Development (now the American Counseling Association) toward standardization and establishment of specific guidelines for the profession. The goal was to amend and adopt new standards for practice that would encompass a multicultural worldview (Sue, Arredondo, & McDavis, 1992). In 1992, Sue et al. developed a list of multicultural competencies. In this important document, awareness, knowledge, and skills were described. Four years later in 1996, Arredondo et al. expounded on this list of competencies. Explanatory statements were added to "take the profession further along in the process of institutionalizing counselor training and practices to be multicultural at the core" (p. 56).[*]

* Competencies and explanatory statements on pp. 25–28 of this text are from "Operationalization of the Multicultural Competencies," by P. Arredondo, R. Toporek, S. P. Brown, J. Jones, D. C. Locke, J. Sanchez, and H. Stadler, 1996, Journal of Multicultural Counseling and Development, 24, pp. 42–78. Copyright 1996 by American Counseling Association. Used with permission. No further reproduction authorized without written permission of the American Counseling Association.

A collaborative work on multicultural counseling competencies with 10 authors was published in 1998 (Sue et al.). The focus was on individual and organizational development. In addition to the competencies, a description of multicultural counseling competence was provided and includes: (a) awareness of own assumptions, values, and biases, (b) understanding the worldview of the culturally different client, (c) developing appropriate intervention strategies and techniques, (d) being able to define a multiculturally competent organization, (e) understanding how organizational and institutional forces may either enhance or negate the development of multicultural competence, and (f) being able to define the major characteristics of the culturally competent and inclusive organization (Sue et al., 1998).

In 2003, The AMCD published *Multicultural Counseling Competencies* with editor Gargi Roysircar. It is clear that multicultural competencies have evolved into a framework to be used as a guide for the training and practice of counselors. Much criticism or points of resistance have emerged regarding multicultural competencies. Such resistance, as well as additional research and theory, has resulted in a more conceptually sound and clear set of principles. For example, the competencies have been referred to as too complex and detailed. This criticism was acknowledged and the response provided was that becoming multiculturally competent requires a lifelong commitment and is not an easy endeavor.

Below, the three competencies appear in bold. Each competency is followed by italicized statements about attitudes and beliefs, knowledge, and skills.

COUNSELOR AWARENESS OF OWN CULTURAL VALUES (A) AND BIASES

ATTITUDES AND BELIEFS   The first competency is **counselor awareness of own cultural values and biases**. *Culturally skilled counselors believe that cultural self-awareness and sensitivity to one's own cultural heritage are essential.* They understand the importance of their own cultural heritage and are able to identify their own cultural groups and the associated values and beliefs of these groups. In addition, counselors understand the impact of their cultural groups on them personally.

Second, *culturally skilled counselors are aware of how their own cultural backgrounds and experiences have influenced attitudes, values, and biases about psychological processes.* Explanatory statements include counselors' ability to identify cultural influences on cognitive development, problem solving, and decision making. Counselors are also able to express the beliefs of their particular religions and cultural groups and relate them to dimensions of identity, including disability and sexual orientation.

Third, *culturally skilled counselors are able to recognize the limits of their multicultural competency and expertise.* More specifically, counselors can identify how cultural attitudes, beliefs, and values may interfere with best service delivery to clients.

Fourth, *culturally skilled counselors recognize their sources of discomfort with differences that exist between themselves and clients in terms of race, ethnicity, and culture.* Such differences are acknowledged, ways to handle these differences are understood within the counseling relationship, and the solutions are responsibly implemented.

KNOWLEDGE   Culturally skilled counselors have specific knowledge about their racial and cultural heritage and how it personally and professionally affects their definitions of, and biases about, normality/abnormality and the process of counseling.

Second, *culturally skilled counselors possess knowledge and understanding about how oppression, racism, discrimination, and stereotyping affect them personally and their work.* Counselors are aware of privileges associated with a variety of identities, including race, physical abilities, gender, socioeconomic class, and sexual orientation. They are also knowledgeable of the recent research on racism, ways to combat racism, racial identity development, and the relationship of these themes to counselors' professional development.

Third, *culturally skilled counselors possess knowledge about their social impact on others.* More specifically, counselors are aware of the various dimensions of difference and are clear about how nonverbal communication styles differ within and among cultures.

SKILLS   Regarding skills, first *culturally skilled counselors seek out educational, consultative, and training experiences to improve their understanding and effectiveness in working with culturally different populations.* Essentially, effective counselors know when they need to refer clients to other helpers and maintain an active list of potential referrals (see the Case Study "Across the Pacific, Home" at the end of this chapter).

Second, *culturally skilled counselors are constantly seeking to understand themselves as racial and cultural beings and are actively seeking a nonracist identity.*

COUNSELOR AWARENESS OF CLIENT'S WORLDVIEW (B)

ATTITUDES AND BELIEFS   The second competency is **counselor awareness of client's worldview.** Again, beginning with *attitudes and beliefs* and then moving on to knowledge and eventually skills, first *culturally skilled counselors are aware of their negative and positive emotional reactions toward other racial and ethnic groups that may prove detrimental to the counseling relationship.* Counselors are honest about their biases relevant to certain racial and ethnic groups.

Second, *culturally skilled counselors are aware of their stereotypes and preconceived notions that they may hold toward other racial and ethnic minority groups.*

KNOWLEDGE   Culturally skilled counselors possess specific knowledge and information about the particular group with which they are working. Effective counselors know about their clients' cultural values, history, and differences in verbal and nonverbal behaviors.

Second, *culturally skilled counselors understand how race, culture, and ethnicity may affect personality formation, vocational choices, manifestation of psychological disorders, help-seeking behavior, and the appropriateness or inappropriateness of counseling approaches.* Counselors are clear about how societal oppression affects groups and can interpret traditional systems (e.g., regarding personality development) and interrogate how such a system may or may not relate to particular groups.

Third, *culturally skilled counselors understand and have knowledge about sociopolitical influences that impinge on the lives of racial and ethnic minorities.* Counselors are knowledgeable about institutionalized racism, internalized oppression, poverty, and other themes that affect their clients and the communities in which these clients live. In addition, they are aware of how the media, written and visual, along with certain policies (e.g., affirmative action setbacks), affect the ways people of color and other groups are perceived in society.

SKILLS   Culturally skilled counselors should familiarize themselves with relevant research and the latest findings regarding mental health and mental disorders that affect various racial and ethnic groups. Counselors are mindful of the research in mental health and career issues that affect different cultural groups and are able to identify a variety of multicultural experiences in which they have been involved.

Second, *culturally skilled counselors become actively involved with persons of color and other groups outside the counseling setting.* Counselors seek to engage in activities that both challenge preconceived stereotypes and encourage comfort with people across differences.

CULTURALLY APPROPRIATE INTERVENTION STRATEGIES

ATTITUDES AND BELIEFS   The third competency is **culturally appropriate intervention strategies.** *Culturally skilled counselors respect clients' religious and spiritual beliefs and values.* In doing so, they are able to identify aspects of spirituality relevant to wellness and healing.

Second, *culturally skilled counselors respect indigenous helping practices and respect help-giving networks among communities of color.* Counselors are also able to integrate their efforts with indigenous helps where appropriate.

Third, *culturally skilled counselors value bilingualism and do not view another language as an impediment to counseling.* Monolingualism is recognized as limiting in itself.

KNOWLEDGE   Culturally skilled counselors have a clear and explicit knowledge and understanding of the generic characteristics of counseling and therapy (culture bound, class bound, and monolingual) and how they may clash with the cultural values of various cultural groups. Counselors understand the context in which theories and the current counseling knowledge base have arisen.

Second, *culturally skilled counselors are aware of institutional barriers that prevent people of color, women, persons with disabilities, people from low-income groups, and gay/lesbian clients from using mental health services.* By doing so, counselors can also suggest alternatives to traditional systems of helping and communicate effectively with others about how to intervene appropriately.

Third, *culturally skilled counselors have knowledge of the potential bias in assessment instruments and use procedures and interpret findings in a way that recognizes the cultural and linguistic characteristics of the clients.* Counselors are able to interpret assessment instruments in the context of a client's culture and are also aware of existing bias in traditional systems of diagnosis, including the *DSM–IV-TR* (*Diagnostic and Statistical Manual of Mental Disorders,* 4th ed., Revised).

Fourth, *culturally skilled counselors have knowledge of family structures, hierarchies, values, and beliefs from various cultural perspectives.* Counselors are aware of various resources within the community that can assist their clients with a host of concerns while recognizing that culture can contribute to clients making decisions that are not culturally consistent with that of the counselor.

Fifth, *culturally skilled counselors should be aware of relevant discriminatory practices at the social and community levels that may be affecting the psychological welfare of the population being served.* This would include knowledge of both state and national policies (e.g., repeals of affirmative action in California or Ohio's declaration that marriage is between a man and a woman only).

SKILLS Culturally skilled counselors are able to engage in a variety of verbal and nonverbal helping responses. They are able to send and receive both verbal and nonverbal messages accurately and appropriately. Counselors are aware of why they use particular communication styles at a given time and are able to modify techniques for a variety of contexts.

Second, *culturally skilled counselors are able to exercise institutional intervention skills on behalf of their clients.* Counselors can help equip clients with coping and resistance strategies and effective skills to deal with institutional discrimination.

Third, *culturally skilled counselors are not averse to seeking consultation with traditional healers or religious and spiritual leaders and practitioners in the treatment of culturally different clients when appropriate.* If necessary, counselors are aware of appropriate referrals within indigenous communities.

Fourth, *culturally skilled counselors take responsibility for interacting in the language requested by the client and, if not feasible, make appropriate referrals.* Counselors are able to seek out the services of translators and are familiar with resources that provide appropriate language services to clients.

Fifth, *culturally skilled counselors have training and expertise in the use of traditional assessment and testing instruments.* Counselors understand the cultural context in which traditional assessment tools have developed.

Sixth, *culturally skilled counselors should attend to, as well as work to eliminate, biases, prejudices, and discriminatory contexts in conducting evaluations and providing interventions and should develop sensitivity to the intersections of oppression: sexism, discrimination against people with disabilities, heterosexism, class elitism, and racism.* Counselors are able to address the need for change, regarding discrimination, on an organizational level.

Seventh, *culturally skilled counselors take responsibility for educating their clients to the processes of psychological intervention, such as goals, expectations, legal rights, and the counselor's orientation.* Clients are encouraged by their counselors to advocate for themselves through an educational process.

Arredondo and Arciniega (2001) added grounding principles to these competencies, which place the competencies within an ecological framework. The first principle is of the learning organization. Namely, such an organization is teachable and open to change by questioning and challenging itself. The lone cross-cultural class that characterizes most graduate counseling training programs was criticized as not being representative of a learning organization or responsive to the research available on the significance of multicultural competence.

The second principle is a competency rationale, which provides the profession with guidelines as well as developmental benchmarks for attributes and characteristics that distinguish competent counselors from those who are not. Despite the greater attention given to multicultural counseling competence, the issue still remains regarding how to teach multicultural counseling competencies to graduate students in the most effective way possible (Kim & Lyons, 2003).

DIVERSITY TRAINING IN COUNSELING: AN OVERVIEW

The key to implementing and infusing standards for a multicultural society begins with the code of conduct that governs the assessment, intervention, and evaluation practices of counselors, therapists, and teaching faculty. There is considerable variety in counselor diversity training programs. D'Andrea and Daniels (1991) found that cross-cultural counseling courses are taught very differently. One outcome is certain: Programs that fail to heighten awareness among students about students' own biases and prejudices or that provide only a partial examination of the topic may risk exposing vulnerable clients to mental health professionals who are ill-prepared to provide quality services (see the Storytelling "The Importance of Being Aware").

STORYTELLING: The Importance of Being Aware

After discussing dominant cultural values in the United States, I asked my class if patriarchy was a cultural value. The list that my students and I had created included individualism, self-reliance, protestant work ethic, competitiveness, educational attainment, striving to improve, standard English, rigid time orientation, democracy, freedom, empiricism, meritocracy, control, Christianity, and convenience. The majority of the class, which was 90% female and under 24 years of age, disagreed with me. One student stated that the majority of people in college were women, that women were occupying top positions in government and business never seen before, and that the gap in wages between men and women was closing. So, I asked the students if any of them ever restricted their activities because they would be alone or out at night. I also asked when was the last time they felt fear upon hearing footsteps behind them when out alone, only to be relieved when they saw it was a woman (of any race). I asked them if they kept secrets regarding their sexual histories because they knew that if revealed, such information would be costly in terms of their reputations. All this, I said, is a function of patriarchy, of living within a system where as women they had less advantage, less rank, and often less power and security than do men. I also stated that being young, White, and college educated women affected their ability to see some of the socially constructed disadvantages associated with gender that poor, older, disabled women, and women of color witness daily.

Pinderhughes (1989) provided definitions of *race, ethnicity,* and *culture* because students are often confused about these terms. Although used interchangeably, counseling programs need to offer clear definitions of these and other terms used in cross-cultural counseling. Controversy exists concerning which training models for counselor training are the most appropriate. Dinsmore and England (1996) stated that "no general consensus regarding what set of program characteristics constitutes a standard for multicultural program competence" (p. 59).

In their qualitative review of multicultural training programs, D'Andrea and Daniels (1991) identified four types: (a) culturally entrenched, (b) cross-cultural awakening, (c) cultural integrity, and (d) infusion. Culturally entrenched training does not include multicultural training. Racial and cultural diversity within this type of academic department tends to be limited. The cultural needs of people of color are rarely considered, and emphasis on other worldviews is virtually nonexistent. *Cross-cultural awakening* is characterized by faculty who are likely to recognize that many counseling theories do not speak to the mental health concerns and needs of persons from culturally different backgrounds. Interactions with racially and culturally diverse persons either professionally or personally are rare. However, faculty are more conscientious and behave and think differently from their colleagues in the first stage. At the more advanced third stage, *cultural integrity,* departments understand the importance of cultural, racial, and class issues, which are a core part of the curriculum. At the highest stage, *infusion,* programs integrate the issues of cultural and racial diversity throughout the curriculum in a way that complements existing material. Students are encouraged to think at higher, more conceptually complex levels.

Gender issues in counseling are gaining greater attention, but more emphasis is required with respect to power and equity (Hoffman, 1996). A focus on men, women, and transgender issues is also needed because *gender* and *transgender* encompass a diversity of gender orientations.

A MODEL FOR MULTICULTURAL COUNSELOR TRAINING PROGRAMS

Faculty in counselor education programs have been grappling for some time with how to best teach multiculturalism. Bowman (1996) concluded that "multicultural instruction should not be limited to one course but should be infused in all aspects of the training" (p. 16). One separate multicultural counseling class endorses a bifurcation of multicultural issues from other core curriculum constructs.

There are exercises that can facilitate student introspection and application of multicultural theory. Drawing one's culture with crayons and constructing a genogram outlines family history. Reading McIntosh's (1989) article "White Privilege: Unpacking the Invisible Knapsack" can be very thought provoking. The unearned privileges associated with ability, gender, and sexual orientation can also be investigated.

Journals, personal narratives, participation in cross-cultural activities as a racial minority, and reading about power and oppression are critical aspects of multicultural training. One instructor encourages her students to write a comprehensive racial psychohistory, allowing them to document the role that race has played in shaping their life philosophies, personalities, and coping patterns (Kogan, 2000).

Despite integration, U.S. society is very much segregated along racial lines. It is likely that many graduate students and their faculty do not have intimate friendships outside of their racial, sexual, and class groups. Laboratory experiences, then, are essential. Bowman (1996) stated that "trainees need opportunities to examine the dynamics of establishing relationships with culturally diverse populations and to question how they apply what they know about self and others to successful cross-cultural interactions" (p. 23). As students encounter dissonance, they need safe places where they can ask questions and process newly encountered information. Faculty need to support students in their efforts at risk taking while encouraging all students to be receptive to new, conflicting, and in some cases disturbing ideas from classmates and even professors.

A variety of experiential activities, such as role play, games, and films, are recognized as a means of educating counseling students about the counseling process. According to Kim and Lyons (2003), games, in particular, offer "optimal opportunities to gain multicultural counseling competence across attitudes, beliefs, knowledge, and skills" (p. 402).

ASSESSMENT AND DIVERSITY

To guide counseling departments in their training efforts, Ponterotto, Alexander, and Grieger (1995) developed a multicultural competency checklist. There are six themes, each with several items (a) minority representation, (b) curriculum issues, (c) counseling practice and supervision, (d) research considerations, (e) student and faculty competency evaluation, and (f) physical environment. The first four items on the checklist seek to ascertain *diverse representation*—whether 30% of faculty, students, and program support staff are visibly racially/ethnically diverse. Bilingual skills are also important. The second theme, *curriculum issues* is covered across five items and reflect course work, pedagogy, and student assessment. For example, multicultural issues are integrated into all course work. All program faculty can specify how this is done in their courses. Furthermore, syllabi clearly reflect multicultural inclusion. *Counseling practice and supervision* is the third area and contains three questions. The focus here is on students' practicum, supervision quality, and the "Multicultural Affairs Committee," which is recommended as a way to monitor multicultural activities. *Research considerations* has four questions concerned with a multicultural research presence in the program. Statement 14 of the checklist asks if there is clear faculty research productivity in multicultural issues as is evidenced by journal publications and conference presentations on multicultural topics. The four items in *student and faculty competency evaluation* emphasize proficiency in multicultural issues. Statement 19 asks whether students' "comprehensive exams reflect Multicultural issues." The final two items concern the *physical environment* and whether it reflects diversity in the faculty offices, reception area, and clinic area. The authors of this checklist recognize that very few programs will meet all the competencies in the checklist and suggest that 1-, 3-, and 5-year action plans be developed to address any gaps.

Many traditional psychoeducational measures used for assessment purposes were not validated with diverse populations in their original sample groups and are based on individual performance or self-report or both. Therefore, the appropriateness and validity of many commonly used psychological and psychoeducational assessment instruments, when used with individuals and diverse populations, may be questionable. The validity and reliability of assessment tools have implications for research. Culturally insensitive research accommodates and further perpetuates inadequate training models and subsequent counseling services. According to Ponterotto and Casas (1991), one criticism of current research on people of color is that important intrapersonal and extrapersonal factors, such as client attitudes, client-counselor racial similarity, communication styles, acculturation, and discrimination and poverty, have virtually been ignored. Furthermore, the research has not considered or studied the tremendous heterogeneity in multicultural populations, which has affected, fostered, and perpetuated ethnic stereotypes and global categorizations. Last, easily accessible subject populations (e.g., White psychology college students from large midwestern universities) that tend not to be representative of the larger community have typically been selected as research populations. This overreliance on research using analogue designs "whereby the subject pools have consisted of pseudoclient (e.g., students) and pseudocounselors (e.g., graduate students in counseling) instead of 'real' clients and counselors" (Ponterotto & Casas, 1991, p. 78) limits generalizability to actual client and counselor populations.

Concern has also been raised over the validity and applied pragmatic utility of the many research findings now appearing in the multicultural literature (Ponterotto & Casas, 1991). Simplistic client-counselor process variables have been overemphasized, and significant cultural, as well as psychosocial variables that might affect counseling have been disregarded. In other words, important psychosocial variables (e.g., learning styles, communication patterns, racism, oppression, poverty), which may be more difficult to study but are vital to understanding the role of counseling with people of color, have been overlooked. Concomitantly, a high degree of heterogeneity, such as demographic characteristics, class, and attitudes, exists within multicultural populations, yet these intracultural differences tend not to be noted in the research literature.

To demonstrate competence in multicultural assessment, conceptualization of presenting problems, establishment of appropriate interventions, development of client treatment goals, and the formulation of multiculturally sensitive research, psychological service providers and academicians will need to acquire cultural knowledge, information, and skills.

IMPLICATIONS FOR COUNSELORS

Unlearning oppressive practices that distance counselors from themselves and their clients is lifelong work and an ongoing process. Willingness to be open, to be changed, and to be healed are crucial ingredients in this process of developing not only a nonracist identity but also nonsexist, nonclassist, and nonhomophobic identities. Being honest about the various emotions that are understandably within us as counselors, even during the cross-cultural therapeutic event, is essential. Abernathy (1995) said that "minimal attention has been devoted to addressing the anger that frequently emerges in cross-racial work" (p. 96).

Numerous books, articles, conferences, and associations are in the service of fostering a climate of multiculturalism and equity for all people. The American Counseling Association and American Psychological Association provide excellent resources for students, professionals, and practitioners who want to develop themselves and to connect with others who are like-minded and focused on multicultural competence, which is a challenging endeavor. Hartung (1996) noted the difficulty in developing cultural competencies among both faculty and students:

> The task proves challenging because it calls for examining and confronting one's own perceptions, biases, prejudices, and worldview. The task is multidimensional because it involves heightening personal awareness, expanding cultural knowledge, and honing counseling skills. (p. 7)

Despite these challenges and available resources, having genuine and authentic relationships—not just colleagues, but friends who come to each other's homes and talk honestly about their lives as racial, cultural, and gendered beings is a true gift. This type of sharing and being together allows us to discuss, understand, and ultimately heal from the scourge of race oppression. At the same time, acknowledging the shame experienced by many counselors-in-training is a crucial beginning to their understanding of oppression and inequity (see the Storytelling "Their Stories Make Me Ashamed and Tired"). Such feelings are important and should be worked through as part of the multicultural training process (Parker & Schwartz, 2002).

STORYTELLING: "Their Stories Make Me Tired and Ashamed"

My students had been reading personal narratives in the winter 1999, *Journal of Counseling and Development* special edition on healing racism that I had the privilege of being the special editor. The narratives are compelling as people across race, skin color, age, gender, and ethnicity tell their stories of encountering racism. I walked into class and began the lecture—and engaged in my traditional socratic style. Students were not participating and the energy in the room was low. At first I thought that my students were tired—midterms were in a few weeks and many of them worked and also had families. I asked my students what was going on because it was clear that something was up. Finally, one student spoke and admitted that the stories (personal narratives) made her tired and ashamed. She had grown weary of reading the stories about racism because they left her feeling guilty. She also felt angry that in her 23 years of growing up with liberal parents in the northeast that she had not been aware of the significant role that race and skin color played in people's lives. Other students began to share similar feelings. The students also felt angry with me for introducing this information. I told my students that this was a Toni Morrison moment for me. Ms. Morrison said that if her people could endure tragedy then the least that she could do was write about it. My task was to bring people's lived stories to my students' awareness so that this knowledge would be a form of power even if it initially left my students feeling powerless. After all, powerlessness is what so many clients feel by the time they arrive at the counseling event. Monitoring students' dissonance is a part of effective training in multicultural counseling courses. Checking in with students and asking how they are, acknowledging the hard work they are doing, and honoring the release of emotion, including sadness, shame, and anger, are necessary.

CASE STUDY
Across the Pacific, Home

Moana, age 27, and her family are originally from New Zealand and have lived in Washington for 15 years. Moana's mother is White and her father is Maori (indigenous people of New Zealand who are of Polynesian descent). Although Moana has lived in the United States for the majority of her life, she and her father often speak Maori in their home and visit their homeland every few years. Moana is working on her master's degree in environmental studies and is interested in working for an environmental agency in Brisbane, Australia, so that she can be closer to her place of birth and to the *tangata whenua* (people of the land), to whom she is very committed. Moana's older brother, Timoti, is a dentist and has two children that Moana is very fond of and with whom she spends a considerable amount of time. Moana reports to the counseling center at her university to discuss her career plans, anticipated move, and stress associated with leaving her family and being so far away. Moana has enjoyed living in Washington, but she misses her extended family and being around other Maori people, of which there is a sizeable population in Australia. Reid Simms, who has expertise in the psychological stress associated with career transition, is a European American male counselor who has never heard of the Maori people; has rarely been outside the United States except to Canada, Mexico, and Europe; and has restricted interactions with people of color except for some collegial interactions with his colleagues at work.

QUESTIONS
1. Should Reid, according to the American Counseling Association and the American Psychological Association ethical guidelines, refer Moana to another counselor?
2. What would Reid have to do to become more multiculturally competent?
3. What implications do Reid's current knowledge and skill base have for the quality of counseling services he renders?

DISCUSSION AND INTEGRATION
The Client, Moana

Moana (which means "sea") is Maori (Polynesian) and White. Miscegenation laws did not exist in New Zealand as they did in America, and there is a lot of intermarriage between Maori and Whites in New Zealand (Robinson, 2001). The Maori people tell the story that their ancestors came to Aotearoa/New Zealand (land of the long white cloud) from Hawaiki, somewhere in Polynesia. Another theory maintains that the Maori's ancestors (Tipuna) were Chinese, originally from mainland China, who migrated across the Pacific over the centuries—from Taiwan, through the Philippines and Indonesia to West Polynesia, on into the islands of East Polynesia and then New Zealand (Dunlop, 1998). Moana's ancestors arrived in double-hulled canoes about 800 years prior to Captain Cook's visit in 1769. Soon, more British came and the indigenous people were colonized. Countless Maori died from European diseases and land wars, the Maori's land was stolen from them, and promises were broken. The Treaty of Waitangi, signed on February 6, 1840, stated,

> Her Majesty the Queen of England confirms and guarantees to the Chiefs and Tribes of New Zealand and to the respective families and individuals thereof the full exclusive and undisturbed possession of their Lands and Estates Forests Fisheries and other properties which they may collectively or individually possess so long as it is their wish and desire to retain the same in their possession (Cited in Orange, 1989, p. 31)

Currently, Maori compose approximately 14% of the population in New Zealand. According to Smith (1997), "the term 'Maori' only became meaningful as a category because of colonisation" (p. 35).

Moana has an understanding of the history of her people and is committed to being more involved in the indigenous movement and advocating for *tino rangatiratanga,* which means "self-determination." She is experiencing stress because of the considerable transitions that moving to Australia will hold for her. Yet, she is excited about the change and new opportunities awaiting her. Her cultural longings are admirable, and she needs to be encouraged for listening to herself and responding to a call that obviously comes from deep within. Because Moana is a New Zealand-born citizen, she has easy entry into the world of work in Australia without needing a visa or other documentation.

The Counselor, Reid Simms

Section A.2 (Respecting Diversity) of the American Counseling Association Code of Ethics and Standards of Practice, Subsection b on Respecting Differences reads:

> Counselors will actively attempt to understand the diverse cultural backgrounds of the client with whom they work. This includes, but is not limited to, learning how the counselor's own cultural/ethical/racial identity impacts her/his values and beliefs about the counseling process. (American Counseling Association, 1998)

In light of this ethical guideline, it is important that Reid learn more about Moana's culture. This task may be challenging because Reid is unfamiliar with Moana's history and geography. However, it does not seem appropriate for Reid to refer Moana to another counselor simply because he is unaware of her background. Even though Moana's cultural background is crucial to an understanding of who she is and the way she makes sense of her current dilemma, Reid does know something about the psychological stress associated with her impending move and all that it entails.

What could Reid do given the multicultural competencies? The first competency is **counselor awareness of own cultural values and biases.** Reid would display multicultural sensitivity if he is aware of his attitudes and beliefs, given the cultural and racial diversity between Moana and himself. Reid is of English descent and for this reason has spent considerable time researching his own family tree in England. He understands the importance of his own cultural heritage, is clear about his group's associated values and beliefs, and knows how his parents' Britishness (e.g., formality, individualism) has affected him personally. His history will also tell him that the British, his ancestors, colonized the Maori, Moana's ancestors.

Away from therapy, Reid will need to work through any feelings of guilt or shame he has because of this historical reality. Moreover, if Reid recognizes the limits of his multicultural expertise, this would help him know where his shortcomings are with Moana and how best to overcome them in order not to hamper quality service delivery. Recognizing that his interactions with people from different racial and cultural groups is rather limited and that such lack of exposure may provoke feelings of discomfort within him in this cross-cultural counseling relationship will also help Reid. Acknowledging the differences is important, as is knowing ways to address them within the counseling relationship. It would not be inappropriate for Reid to ask Moana questions about her culture or her traditions. It would be irresponsible, however, for Reid not to do some research on his own or to talk with informed others to reduce his level of inexperience and thus increase his feelings of competence with Moana. Reid, independent of his counseling relationship with Moana, also works to understand himself as a racial being and seeks to eradicate a racist ideology from his life. This would entail confronting any of his stereotypes about Pacific Island people or immigrant groups. Part of Reid's investigation could be to research the effects of colonization on Maori and other indigenous people. For instance, the Treaty of Waitangi is essential knowledge regarding New Zealand and race relations between Maori and Whites (also known as *Pakeha*). Glynn et al. (1997) provided insight into the knowledge of the treaty in which partnership was fractured between Maori and European people (Pakeha) in New Zealand as a result of political oppression by the Pakeha majority. "This history has progressed through armed struggle, biased legislation and successive educational policies and initiatives that have imposed Pakeha language and knowledge codes at the expense of Maori" (p. 102).

The desire for Moana to return to the South Pacific and be involved in the indigenous movement is indicative of her understanding of her country's history and the injustices that describe what has transpired between Maori and Whites. Toward embracing the second competency, **counselor awareness of client's worldview,** Reid needs to know about the land takeovers and the genocide—the oppression of Maori people—to best serve Moana's psychological needs. More specifically, an understanding of Moana's culture and ethnicity and their impact on her personhood and career choice is essential. Maori people value collaborative and collective relationships and are influenced by the sacred connections to their ancestors and to the land.

The third competency is **culturally appropriate intervention strategies.** Moana is largely affected by the traditional spirituality of Maori people and less so by Christian traditions. Reid is a Christian. As a culturally skilled counselor, he would understand aspects of Moana's spirituality that would be relevant for her overall well-being, such as singing traditional songs *(waita)*, honoring the elders, and being on the *Marae* (Maori meeting house). Tate (1998) stated that, among Maori, the making of links is essential and that these links are with *whanau,* or the family. *Whanaungatanga,* or the principles of relationships with family, are eternal. Wehrly (1995) cited other dimensions of Maori culture that are relevant for counseling: *whakamanawa,* which is encouragement and showing compassion; and *mauri,* which is self-esteem and the ability to be in touch with things spiritual. As a culturally skilled counselor, Reid would be able to consult with traditional healers and, if necessary, make referrals within Moana's indigenous community. Although Reid does not speak the Maori language, it would be important for him to value bilingualism and be interested in knowing some Maori terms, such as *kia ora,* which is a greeting and welcome.

If Reid were to administer any type of assessment instrument to Moana to help her clarify career interests and strengths, he would need to understand the potential bias of such instruments, and the cultural context in which they are normed. Despite the fact that Moana has lived in the United States the majority of her life, her cultural context was not part of the norming process.

If Reid does not consider Moana's cultural heritage, then his interactions with her would be problematic and disrespectful of who she is as a cultural being. Moana and her counselor have some gender, racial, ethnic, and religious differences. These visible differences could have strong implications for the counseling event. Lorde (1978), however, reminded her readers that "it is not differences that immobilize but silence. And there are so many silences to be broken" (p. 44).

Reid has neither knowledge of Maori people nor much interaction with people of color outside his work. Yet he might be effective with considerable effort on his part.

SUMMARY

This chapter offered an overview of multicultural competencies and skills. A brief review of counselor education diversity training programs was also provided, as well as strategies for becoming a multiculturally competent counselor. The importance of monitoring dissonance and measuring cross-cultural effectiveness was discussed through the Storytelling. The case study dealt with the question of referring clients to different counselors when a cross-cultural counseling relationship exists.

REFERENCES

Abernathy, A. D. (1995). Managing racial anger: A critical skill in cultural competence. *Journal of Multicultural Counseling and Development, 23,* 96–102. *ACA Ethical Standards Casebook,* American Counseling Association. (1988). Alexandria, VA: American Counseling Association.

Arredondo, P., & Arciniega, G. M. (2001). Strategies and techniques for counselor training based on the multicultural counseling competencies. *Journal of Multicultural Counseling and Development, 29,* 263–273.

Arredondo, P., Toporek, R., Brown, S. P., Jones, J., Locke, D. C., Sanchez, J., & Stadler, H. (1996). Operationalization of the multicultural competencies. *Journal of Multicultural Counseling and Development, 24,* 42–78.

Bowman, V. E. (1996). Counselor self-awareness and ethnic self-knowledge as a critical component of multicultural training. In J. L. DeLucia-Waack (Ed.), *Multicultural counseling competencies: Implications for training and practice* (pp. 7–30). Alexandria, VA: Association for Counselor Education and Supervision.

Cottone, R. R., & Tarvydas, V. M. (1998). *Ethical and professional issues in counseling.* Upper Saddle River, NJ: Merrill/Prentice Hall.

D'Andrea, M., & Daniels, J. (1991). Exploring the different levels of multicultural counseling training in counselor education. *Journal of Counseling and Development, 70,* 78–85.

Dinsmore, J. A., & England, J. T. (1996). A study of multicultural counseling training at CACREP-accredited counselor education programs. *Counseling Education and Supervision, 36,* 1, 58–76.

Dunlop, F. (1998, August 11). World: Asia-Pacific Maoris may have come from China BBC News. Retrieved January 26, 2004, from http://news.bbc.co.uk/1/hi/world/asia-pacific/148892.stm.

Glynn, T., Berryman, M., Atvars, K., Harawira, W., Kaiwai, H., Walker, R., & Tari, R. (1997). Research, training, and indigenous rights to self-determination: Challenges arising from a New Zealand bicultural journey. In *International School Psychology XXth Annual Colloquium, Proceedings*.

Hartung, P. J. (1996). Transforming counseling courses: From monocultural to multicultural. *Counseling Education and Supervision, 36,* 1, 6–13.

Hifler, J. S. (1992). *A Cherokee feast of days: Daily meditations.* Tulsa, OK: Council Oak Books.

Hoffman, R. M. (1996). Gender: Issues of power and equity in counselor education programs. *Counselor Education and Supervision, 36,* 104–112.

Holcomb-McCoy, C. C. (2000). Multicultural counseling competencies: An exploratory factor analysis. *Journal of Multicultural Counseling and Development, 28,* 83–97.

Kim, B. S. K., & Lyons, H. Z. (2003). Experiential activities and multicultural counseling competence training. *Journal of Counseling & Development, 81,* 400–408.

Kogan, M. (2000, July/August). Course exposes hidden racial prejudices: Students confront their hidden biases to better prepare for psychology practice. *Monitor on Psychology, 31*(7). http://www.apa.org/monitor/julaug00/prejudice.html

Lorde, A. (1978). *Sister outside: Essays and speeches.* Freedom, CA: Crossing Press.

McIntosh, P. (1989, July/August). privilege: Unpacking the invisible knapsack. *Peace and Freedom.*

Orange, C. (1989). *The story of a treaty.* Wellington, New Zealand: Bridget Williams Books.

Parker, W. M., & Schwartz, R. C. (2002). On the experience of shame in multicultural counseling: Implications for White counselors-in-training. *British Journal of Guidance and Counseling, 30,* 311–318.

Pinderhughes, E. (1989). *Understanding race, ethnicity, and power: The key to efficacy in clinical practice.* New York: Free Press.

Ponterotto, J. G., Alexander, C. M., & Grieger, I. (1995). A multicultural competency checklist for counseling training programs. *Journal of Multicultural Counseling and Development, 23,* 11–20.

Ponterotto, J. G., & Casas, J. M. (1991). *Handbook of racial/ethnic minority counseling research.* Springfield, IL: Charles C Thomas.

Robinson, T. L. (2001). White mothers of non-White children. *Journal of Humanistic Counseling, Education and Development, 40,* 171–184.

Roysircar, G. (Ed.). (2003). *Multicultural counseling competencies: 2003.* Alexandria, VA: Association of Multicultural Counseling and Development.

Smith, L. T. (1997). Maori women: Discourses, projects, and *mana wahine.* In S. Middleton & A. Jones (Eds.), *Women and education in Aotearoa* (pp. 33–51). Auckland, New Zealand: Auckland University Press.

Sue, D. W., Carter, R. T., Caas, J. M., Fouad, N. A., Ivey, A. E., Jensen, M., LaFromboise, T., Manese, J. E., Ponterott, J. G., & Vazquez-Nuttal, E. (1998). *Multicultural counseling competencies: Individual and organizational development.* Thousand Oaks, CA: Sage.

Sue, D. W., Arredondo, P., & McDavis, R. J. (1992). Multicultural counseling competencies and standards: A call to the profession. *Journal of Counseling and Development, 70,* 477–483.

Sue, D. W., Bernier, J. E., Daran, A., Feinberg, L., Pedersen, P., Smith, C. T., & Vasquez-Nuttale, G. (1982). Cross-cultural counseling competencies. *Counseling Psychologist, 19,* 45–52.

Sue, D. W., Ivey, A. E., & Pedersen, P. B. (1996). *A theory of multicultural counseling and therapy.* Pacific Grove, CA: Brooks/Cole.

Tate, P. H. (1998, March 29). *Whanaungatanga.* Keynote speech at the meeting of the New Zealand Association of Counselors, New Zealand.

Wehrly, B. (1995). *Pathways to multicultural counseling competence: A developmental journey.* Pacific Grove, CA: Brooks/Cole.

Chapter 3

Statused Identities

**You save yourself or
you remain unsaved.**

Alice Sebold, Lucky

The counseling event is affected by the perceptions that clients and counselors have about identity constructs, particularly those that are visible. Attitudes about sources of difference have to be examined, and the impact of these attitudes on the counseling event must be assessed. This chapter explores sources of human differences. The social construction of identities within U.S. society is conveyed via the Contextual and Social Construction of Differences Model. Implications for counselors and their client populations are emphasized throughout.

IDENTITIES AS STATUS: THE CONTEXTUAL AND SOCIAL CONSTRUCTION OF DIFFERENCES MODEL

Nearly 60 years ago, Hughes (1945), a sociologist, addressed dilemmas of occupational and ascribed status. He stated that occupational or vocational status has a complex set of supplementary characteristics that come to be expected of its incumbents. For example, it is anticipated that a kindergarten teacher will be a female. Such expectations are largely unconscious because people do not systematically expect that certain people will occupy given positions. Through a process of cultural socialization from the media, educational systems, clergy, and family, people "carry in their minds" the auxiliary traits associated with many specific positions in society. Persons who newly occupy prestigious positions contend with ongoing suspicions from those who have historically maintained these positions and from those who have observed such people occupying these positions.

At the base of people's thinking is the perception that new incumbents may not be as qualified or worthy as others preceeding them and that their jobs are due primarily to affirmative action or other political processes and are not a result of hard work or merit. As new groups occupy positions that have been held almost exclusively by one racial and/or gender group, stereotypes do not completely disappear. It is possible to internalize negative stereotypes and to embody the belief that luck, injustice, and/or quotas, not merit, equity, and/or skill, are responsible for occupational success.

In the society about which Hughes spoke, race membership was a status-determining trait. This was the case because race tended to overpower any other variable that might run counter to it such as vocational achievement, which is a component of social class. Because racism and sexism are interlocking paradigms of oppression, gender membership, for example, is also a status-determining trait. Hughes's decades-old observations have contemporary relevance.

The **Contextual and Social Construction of Differences Model** (see Figure 3.1) proposes that human characteristics operate as status variables in society. The model advances that, in the United States, identities such as race, gender, and class are socially constructed, are statused, and have particular meanings. Contextual and socially constructed meaning about discourses maintain that in both subtle and blatant ways, persons who hold membership in higher status groups are valued

Visible and Invisible Sources of Difference	Contextual and Socially Constructed Meanings About Difference	Consequences of Socially Constructed Meanings About Difference
Race	Being White is valued. Not being White is less valued	Racism
Skin Color	Being light in skin color is valued. Not being light is less valued	Colorism
Sex	Being male is valued. Not being male is less valued	Sexism
Sexual Orientation	Being heterosexual is valued. Not being heterosexual is less valued	Homo prejudice
Ability	Being physically and mentally able are valued. Not being able is less valued	Able-ism
Class	Being middle-class or wealthy is valued. Not being middle class or wealthy is less valued	Class Elitism
Religion	Being Christian is valued. Not being Christian is less valued	Religious Bigotry

FIGURE 3.1
Contextual and Social Construction of Differences Model

within society differently from persons who hold membership in lower status groups. This stratification of identities is a social construction. Visible and invisible identities (e.g., race, gender, sexual orientation, religion, ability, and disability) are not oppressive. Racism, colorism, sexism, homo prejudice, able-body-ism, class elitism, and religious bigotry however, are oppressive and discriminatory (Robinson, 1999). According to Reynolds and Pope (1991), a customary norm by which people are evaluated in the United States is based on how close they are to being White, male, middle class, Christian, heterosexual, Englishspeaking, young, and mentally, physically, and emotionally able. When an established set of criteria for evaluating people's worth exists, economic exploitation, religious bias, homophobia, able-body-ism, and other sources of discrimination ensue.

"Isms" emanate from a rank-and-file orientation regarding sources of differences among humans (Hughes, 1945; Myers et al., 1991). The basis for all of society's "isms," according to Myers et al. (1991), is "an extrinsic orientation" (p. 56). Within such a conceptual system, most people, independent of race and ethnicity, struggle with maintaining a positive sense of self.

ASSUMPTIONS OF HIERARCHICAL SOCIALIZATION PATTERNS

The Contextual and Social Construction of Differences Model presents sources of differences within the context of socially constructed meanings and the consequences of these meanings about difference. In this section, the underlying assumptions of viewing differences in this manner are considered.

Sources of differences between and among people become primary status-determining traits when they are viewed as possessing rank and having value. Certain characteristics are perceived as normal and, within monoculturalism, are thought to be desired by all. For instance, many students have a difficult time understanding why a person with a disability would not want to be able-bodied because it is thought that life would be so much easier. Characteristics with less rank (such as being old, or short, or fat), are held in lower esteem and tend to be regarded as less desirable. Within this hierarchical framework, the most or least valued aspect of a person may not be an achieved trait, such as an honest character, but an immutable one, such as White skin or a curved spine (see the Storytelling "Identities in Context").

Although human beings are more similar than they are different, a hierarchical framework where differences have rank inflates differences among people. A system where people are worthy because they are "unique expressions of spiritual energy" (Myers et al., 1991, p. 56) honors our humanity.

RACISM

Race is an unchosen characteristic of birth. Racism, however, can be changed because attitudes and actions that are depreciative of racial differences can be unlearned. New cognitions can replace old ones. Racism involves the total social structure in which one group has conferred advantage over another through institutional

STORYTELLING: Identities in Context

I went to New Zealand in 1998 on sabbatical to deconstruct my notions of race, gender, and culture. It soon became clear to me that my accent marked me, as did my braids, which in the words of the teenage girls were "choice." Upon speaking, I was often asked, are you Canadian or American?" Once I told people that I was American, people would launch into a lively discussion of the places in America that they had visited or wanted someday to visit. In New Zealand, my nationality was a dominant identity, not my race. I attribute this to the positive way in which America was viewed at the time and the fact that there are so many other dark-skinned people from Samoa, Tonga, Fiji Islands, and the Solomon Islands in New Zealand. Although an uncomfortable reality, it felt easier to be an American in New Zealand. In America, my nationality as an American is muted and dictated by the negative ways in which my race as a Black person are socially constructed.

policies. **Racism** is a social construction based on sociopolitical attitudes that demean specific racial characteristics, as Pinderhughes (1989) makes clear:

> Racism raises to the level of social structure the tendency to use superiority
> as a solution to discomfort about difference. Belief in the superiority of
> Whites and the inferiority of people-of-color based on racial difference is
> legitimized by societal arrangements that exclude the latter from resources
> and power and then blame them for their failures, which are due to lack of
> access. (p. 89)

Discussing racism is unsettling and provokes dissonance. People are often reluctant to engage in dialogue about racism, yet racism is a major part of this country's origins. Other terms may be used instead of racism, such as manifest destiny or progress or ambition. However, part of being committed to the process of transformation and social change is to bear witness to the truth. Ambition and racial exploitation should not be confused.

It has been said that America was built by taking land from a people and people from a land. Racially discriminatory practices were underway when Africans built the infrastructure for major cities in the South and were not remunerated. Americans behaved arrogantly and perceived themselves as superior to Native American Indians when, during the 20th century, they stole the American Indians' land and devastated their way of life. Americans behaved in a racist manner when scores of first and second-generation Japanese Americans were interred in U.S. concentration camps during World War II. Small numbers of German and Italian Americans were interred also, but not to the same extent as were the Japanese. A racist ideology existed when the Southwest, which was once Mexico, was ceded to the United States by the Treaty of Guadalupe Hidalgo in 1848. People became "foreigners in their native land" that they had inhabited for centuries. A racist ideology existed when laws, such as the 1882 Exclusion Act, restricted Chinese from this country while white-skinned European immigrants flooded in. Racism was practiced when the 1790 Naturalization Law was in effect for 162 years; this policy reserved naturalized citizenship for Whites only (Avakian, 2002). At various junctures in U.S. history, laws forbade women across racial groups and men of color from voting, becoming literate, marrying White people, becoming educated at all-White institutions, owning property, working, and drinking water from public facilities. Such policies attested to the institutionalization of racism and sexism as blatant devaluations of race and sex diversity.

Racist attitudes portrayed in sentiments against racial intermixing were not simply between races but within ethnic groups as well. In the Nazi publication *Neues Volk,* it was written, "Every German and every German woman has the duty to avoid association with other races, especially Slavs. Each intimacy with a people of inferior race means sinning against the future of our own people" (cited in Rogers, 1967, p. 19).

Scientific notions about intelligence were developed against a sociopolitical backdrop of racism. Herrnstein and Murray (1994), in their controversial work *The Bell*

Curve, examined ethnic differences on intelligence tests. They concluded that "for every known test of cognitive ability that meets basic psychometric standards of reliability and validity, Blacks and Whites score differently" (p. 276). These authors indicated that the differences are reduced once the testing is done outside the South, after age 6, and after 1940. Herrnstein and Murray argued that even once socioeconomic differences are controlled for, the differences do not disappear, but class may reduce the overall differences in intelligence testing by about one third.

Grubb (1992) investigated the claim that Blacks are genetically inferior to Whites on intelligence testing. As a clinical psychologist specializing in the treatment of childhood and adolescent disorders, he examined 6,742 persons with developmental disabilities from three western states. If this argument that Blacks were genetically inferior to Whites was true, then one could expect to see a higher proportion of Blacks identified as having mental retardation, in comparison with Whites. Grubb found that, of the total population included in this project, 0.03% had developmental disabilities. This figure was consistent across racial groups. He concluded that the assumptions regarding heredity among the Black race were not upheld in this study, leading one to reject this line of reasoning.

Nisbett (1995) also challenged Herrnstein and Murray (1994). Nisbett argued that comparing Blacks at high socioeconomic status (SES) with high-SES Whites is inherently flawed, given the higher income levels of these Whites in comparison with Blacks. In addition, Nisbett stated that socialization and social factors affect ability levels. Claims by Jensen and other authors stating that "g-loaded" tests differed between the races, with Whites having faster reaction times on complex maneuvers, was subjectively interpreted. According to Nisbett, "For skills such as spatial reasoning and form perception, the g-loading was relatively low and B/W gap relatively low" (p. 44).

Did you know that during slavery, two forms of psychopathology were common among slaves? The first, "drapetomania," consisted of a single symptom of slaves running away. The second, "dysathesia aethiopica," consisted of numerous conditions such as destroying plantation property, showing defiance, and attacking the slave masters. This second condition was also known as "rascality," and both were nerve disorders coined by reputable physicians (Bronstein & Quina, 1988). Liberty and the pursuit of happiness are explicit in this nation's charter, yet the desire for these entitlements among Blacks during this time in history was appraised as pathological. Black people took care of White people, yet they were perceived of and depicted as childlike, incapable of providing for themselves, and dependent on their benevolent White masters. Clinicians of the day interpreted 1840 Census data that reported higher rates of psychopathology among Blacks to support the belief that "the care, supervision, and control provided by slavery were essential to the mental health of Blacks" (Bronstein & Quina, 1988, p. 39). This paradigm supported a false belief that Blacks were not only different but inferior. It was not possible to be diagnosed accurately when the psychological community perceived people to be inherently flawed and chattel. The distrust of the mental health community that exists today in many communities of color cannot be adequately appreciated without an understanding of this history.

CONSEQUENCES OF RACISM FOR EUROPEAN AMERICANS   Just as there are consequences of racism for people of color (e.g., stress, disparities in health care), there are also consequences for Whites (Pinderhughes, 1989). How can there not be consequences, given the pernicious nature of racism that impacts all people? Whites may lack understanding about the effects and consequences of race and racism on their own lives: however, this is largely because race often refers to non-White people and is partly due to misperceptions among many Whites about racial inequities and discrimination. More specifically, there are large numbers of White Americans who believe that there is equity for Blacks and Whites in this country and that Blacks are as well off in terms of jobs, incomes, health care, and schooling (Institute of Medicine, 2003).

One way to facilitate the discussion of racism is through an examination of unearned White skin color privilege. McIntosh (1989) maintained that privilege is an invisible knapsack of assets an entitled group can refer to on a regular basis to negotiate their daily lives more effectively. It is unearned and yet is a fugitive subject, partly because many European Americans are oblivious to it and partly because non-Whites do not share in the privileges Whites take for granted. Unpacking privilege produces dissonance among many Whites because it assails fundamental Western beliefs of meritocracy and creates confusion about the meaning of being White.

One consequence of racism for European Americans is that it limits emotional and intellectual development (Pinderhughes, 1989). Inattention to race as a factor in identity formation can contribute to a void in self-conception due to the construction of the self apart from a conscious and often accurate understanding of the dynamic of race. Ethnocentrism limits awareness of other legitimate worldviews besides one's own. Ethnocentrism also supports ignorance about oppression, which contributes to domination and exploitation.

Among many Whites, the consequences of racism in their lives are invisible, as are the skin color privileges. Two conditions seem to intensify obliviousness to unearned privilege. The first is unawareness of the circumstances surrounding group membership, which entitles an individual to privileges. The second is the inability to see how others who do not share group membership also do not share privileges. Among counselors, this nonseeing could translate into reduced empathy. As the quintessential tool in counseling, counselors are severely limited in their effectiveness when they are unable to empathize. There are certain groups in which people have unchosen membership and unearned privilege; however, one can choose how to respond to earned and unearned privileges and decide whether to relinquish some of that privilege. Privilege in its various forms can also be used to empower or equalize systems of injustice.

McIntosh (1989) identified several benefits that enabled her to negotiate her daily existence more effectively. She could choose not to teach her children about race or racism if teaching it would cause them some discomfort. (The growing numbers of White women who are mothering non-White children are finding that this privilege is not afforded to them [Robinson, 2001].) She could move to most any neighborhood, confident that she would be treated well and welcomed. She also knew that her children would be given school curricular materials that testified to the existence of their race.

Not having skin color privilege does not leave one bereft of invaluable resources. Having unearned skin color privilege does not supply moral fiber or self-knowledge. This point is illuminated in the docudrama *Rabbit-Proof Fence*. The primary characters are three "half-caste" Aboriginal girls who were legally abducted from their family by the Australian government. The abduction was part of an effort to stamp out the last vestige of Aboriginal culture and prepare these children for White society. (This law remained on the books until the 1970s.) The oldest child, a teenage girl, walked more than 800 miles back home using ingenious ways to avoid being recaptured. This child's sense of home, self, and belonging to her family was far superior to those who used their power over her. Her power to love, persevere, and stand in her own convictions were obvious and a reflection of her sense of identity. This act of resistance—of confronting messages that seek to demean and replacing them with knowledge that empowers and informs—may enable marginalized groups to thrive in the face of racism.

PATRIARCHY

Patriarchy is a sex/gender system that involves the total social structure (Renzetti & Curran, 1992). Within this system, men have advantage conferred on them because of their prescribed rank or societal status or both. For example, during the more than 2 decades of the women's movement there have been increases in the college attainment rates of women and dramatic increases among women in the workforce. In fact, women under 25 are on par with men in labor participation. Amidst these and other advances, gender inequity continues. In the United States, women earn $.86 to men's $1.00. Compared to men, women pay more for dry cleaning and automobiles.

Once the layers of class and race are imposed, the extent and effects of gender inequity intensify, but so does the possibility of resistance and personal empowerment (Robinson & Kennington, 2002). Because patriarchy is intertwined with power and privilege, the ascribed status of sex becomes elevated as a primary-status trait over achieved status. This system is inherently unjust because biological sex is not chosen; nonetheless, it is an extremely powerful determinant of how people are treated. Both women and men are necessary to society's maintenance, yet through an elaborate gender socialization process, expectations and behaviors are disseminated and internalized. These socialization practices, both blatant and subtle, maintain a system not only in the United States but also in other countries throughout the world, where women are not as advantaged because of their less prominent status as females. Haider (1995) discussed this phenomenon from both global and historical perspectives:

> In many cultures, the notion of male dominance—of man as woman's
> "god," protector and provider—and the notion of women as passive, sub-
> missive, and chaste have been the predominant images for centuries. In
> many cases, customary practices have been based on a pecking order that

has not always been conducive to the well-being and personal development of those lower down the status line, (p. 53).

One consequence of patriarchy for men is that it creates a skewed emotional existence. Many men are unable to experience comfortably and thus express a full range of emotions, such as fear, dependency, and uncertainty, because of the narrow parameters of patriarchy. By its very nature, patriarchy is a system of wide-scale inequity to which many people, including women, are oblivious.

Given the potential disadvantages of patriarchy for men, are there possible benefits of patriarchy for women? Patriarchy has its genesis in injustice. If any presumable benefits of patriarchy result for women, they are temporary and elusive, primarily because the benefits would be dictated by women's adherence to the parameters of patriarchy and their compliance with subscribed gender roles. Does equality for women apply primarily to those women who subscribe to at least some but not too many of the characteristics associated with masculinity (e.g., self-sufficiency, assertiveness, competition)? According to Bem (1993), any such benefits accorded to women are most likely a by-product of androcentrism, or male-centeredness, in which the male standard prevails. Counselors need to understand this dynamic, for example, as they educate female clients about engaging in self-care, which tends not to be supported by conventional norms of gender behavior. Some clients will encounter opposition, from women and men alike, as they attend to self. Counselors can help clients identify what they want while helping them cope with significant others who may not be supportive.

SEXISM

The women's movement challenged many traditional stereotypes about women, their work, and their place in society. That women wanted equal pay for equal work, respect in a society that too often reduced them to sexual objects, and denied them choice about their bodies and minds was the message echoed across numerous platforms. Another part of these platforms encouraged women to consider seriously the socialization experiences that contributed to their reliance on others for their emotional and financial well-being. **Sexism**, an institutionalized system of inequity based on biological sex, was brought to the nation's attention.

Bem (1993), author of the Bem Sex Role Inventory, maintained that androcentrism responds to men as human and to women as other. Given this perspective, it is easy to understand that men enjoy certain privileges that women do not. For the most part, ours is a society in which men benefit over women. Yet male privileges do not bestow power on all men and ultimately deny all women. In fact, one benefit of the men's movement is that it has called attention to the myth that women's powerlessness translates into men's power. Individual men may feel powerful but not all men do. Swanson (1993) recognized this as the "new sexism" and noted "Some men, rather than feeling like patriarchs, often feel like workhorses, harnessed with the burden of being family provider, trying to pull the family wagon up a muddy hill of financial debt" (p. 12).

Despite the assets and benefits associated with unearned privilege, it does not dictate real power. Many White men, men of color, or poor, disabled, and/or gay men do not share the same privileges that some economically privileged, able-bodied, and/or heterosexual men do. Thus, many men may not perceive a sense of personal power because they do not possess crucial markers that society deems normative. The presence of these critical markers, however, does not ensure that individual men will automatically feel powerful. Because of the underlying assumption that persons who share gender are monolithic, use of the phrase *men in general* is problematic (Carrigan, Connell, & Lee, 1987). Making inappropriate attributions regarding clients' identity constructs is called a *miss*—for example, assuming a person without a visible disability is not disabled or in pain.

Another identity construct that can mitigate the privileges that men have is sexual orientation. Some of the privilege associated with maleness has a qualifier of hetero-sexuality. Gay men who are "out" experience attacks from a homophobic society in the form of ostracism, discrimination, and in some instances violence. Despite these clear disadvantages, being gay does not cancel all privileges associated with being male. Within a society where skin color is associated with unearned privilege, gay White men mediate the effects of homophobia with White skin privilege. Gay men of color receive male privilege yet contend with both racism and homophobia (Loicano, 1989).

The irony of socialization is that although, most men are conditioned to be providers, protectors, and ready for combat, they often experience pressure from women to be nurturing, soft, and intimate (Skovholt, 1993). These messages are confusing. Part of being a protector is not asking for help or appearing to be vulner-able, which is what intimacy and nurturance entail.

CONSEQUENCES OF SEXISM FOR MEN   Racism contributes to a dehumanizing stance and limits human development (Pinderhughes, 1989) for people regardless of their race and ethnicity. Sexism adversely affects all people, men included. The male gender role often results in men being restricted in their emotional expressive-ness and promotes a limited range of behaviors available to them. "Restrictive emo-tionality involves the reluctance and/or difficulty men have in expressing their feel-ings to other people and may be related to their hesitancy to seek help from others" (Good, Dell, & Mintz, 1989, p. 295). Men have gender and are influenced by rigid and sexist discourses whereby they are oriented toward success, competi-tion, and the need to be in control (Robinson, 1999). The danger in the male role is that it has been connected to "Type A" behavior patterns and to depression (Good & Mintz, 1990).

HOMOPHOBIA

Homophobia is "the unreasonable fear of same-sex attractions, attentions, rela-tionships, and persons whose affectional and erotic orientations are toward the same sex" (King, 1988, p. 168). This fear emanates from the perception of homo-sexuality as an aberration of the correct social order.

Undoubtedly, similar stereotypes may be associated with a man's gay identity, such as being promiscuous or untrustworthy around young children.

CONSEQUENCES OF HOMOPHOBIA FOR HETEROSEXUALS Many men are often concerned that engaging in any behaviors deemed "feminine" will be misconstrued as the absence of masculinity and thus an indicator of homosexuality. Men are often taught that anything associated with femininity is anathema. Within this restrictive context, heterosexual men may feel real fear in expressing physical affection with another man because of connotations of homosexuality. This concern may explain why many men, on greeting one another, engage in roughhousing, evidenced by vigorous slaps on the back. Such behavior, however, is culturally dictated. In Ghana, West Africa, or in Cairo, Egypt, for example, it is quite natural to see men holding hands while walking together. Within these cultural contexts, affection and endearment support this behavior. In the United States, similar behavior is interpreted as a blatant expression of homosexuality.

Homophobia also interferes with the formation of cross-sexual orientation friendships out of fear that such interaction and proximity would be misinterpreted by others. In this context, heterosexual counselors can be inhibited in their ability to be allies to lesbian, gay, bisexual, and/or transgender (GLBT) clients.

ABLE-BODY-ISM

People with disabilities have a long history of being discriminated against. An understanding of this type of discrimination is enhanced by an assessment of the "mastery-over-fate" orientation descriptive of American society. The U.S. culture places inordinate emphasis on youth and fitness and preoccupation with the body beautiful. A disability is seen as an imperfection, which is contrary to the culturally sanctioned values of control and domination (see the Storytelling "Try Harder").

A clear bias for the able-bodied exists. Because most buildings have been constructed for able-bodied persons, persons without disabilities are often oblivious to their unearned privileges. How much thought do most able-bodied people give to the accessibility of a house or other building? Having disabled people in our lives or being

STORYTELLING: Try Harder

A few years ago, a European American, able-bodied female graduate student expressed her anger and embarrassment over her feelings toward a disabled graduate student. The disabled student, also a White female, found it difficult to walk given her disability and started using a scooter. In the nondisabled student's mind, the disabled student was succumbing to her disability as opposed to attempting to overcome it by at least trying to walk. Part of the able-bodied student's anger was fueled by the fact that the disabled student, as a White person, was not overcoming the disability, which was inconsistent with appropriate behavior for a White American. This story illustrates the dynamics of identity, in its multiple forms, and the expectations that one status places on others.

temporarily disabled (e.g., after foot surgery) increases our awareness. Architectural space and design are outgrowths of cultural attitudes and assumptions that are biased against persons, and in particular, women with disabilities. As Weisman (1992) pointed out:

> Placement in barrier-free housing and rehabilitation services favors
> men. . . . Disabled women are not usually thought of as wives and mothers
> who often manage households with children and husbands. The wheelchair-
> accessible two- and three-bedroom unit is a rarity. (p. 118)

The myth that people with disabilities are childlike, dependent, and depressed contributes to maltreatment, ignorance from the larger society, and denial about the fact that, at any time, able-bodied people can and most likely will become disabled if they live long enough. Multiculturally competent counselors have the ability to regard clients with disabilities as whole human beings wherein the disability is under-stood as a component of identity and not the entire focus of the counseling event or an exhaustive account of the client's essence (Fowler, O'Rourke, Wadsworth, & Harper, 1992). The counselor's facility at beholding the client's multiple spiritual, occupational, sexual, and social identities is commentary about the counselor's moral and ego development.

CONSEQUENCES OF ABLE-BODY-ISM AMONG THE ABLE-BODIED   Society was cre-ated for persons who are able-bodied. Our society of concrete sidewalks and curbs is uninviting to persons with temporary and permanent disabilities.

Stereotypes abound regarding people with disabilities. One of the most perni-cious is that persons with disabilities desire to be able-bodied. This mistaken belief is similar to the belief that people of color desire to be White or that women desire to be men. Equating the experience of having a disability with living a lesser life is prob-lematic for two reasons. First, such an attitude is not characteristic of a multicultur-ally competent counselor who possesses accurate beliefs and attitudes of diverse client populations. Second, this attitude is arrogant and psychologically restrictive for able-bodied persons, who at any time can become disabled. Having a disability can deflate a sense of self and depress self-esteem (Livneh & Sherwood, 1991), yet this is not the experience of all persons with disabilities. For this reason, disability identity development models are greatly needed.

CLASS ELITISM

Much of the formal training counselors receive in traditional counselor education programs emanates from a middle-class bias. This bias is characterized by empha-sis on meritocracy, the Protestant work ethic, Standard English, and adherence to 50-minute sessions (Sue & Sue, 1990). The difficulty with this type of partiality is that it can alienate counselors from poor clients. Persons who have limited access to material wealth in a materialistic culture are not perceived as being as viable as those with greater resources. A dangerously close relationship exists between self-worth and income in our capitalistic culture. Thus, the poor, regardless of their work ethic, tend to be perceived as being lazy and even immoral (Gans, 1992). Conversely, the rich are esteemed and admired, often independent of their moral or immoral conduct.

The relationship between class and power is dubious (Pinderhughes, 1989). Low-income status (despite being hard working) is not valued in a consumeristic society, and having membership in this devalued group can provoke feelings of powerlessness and depression (Pinderhughes, 1989).

CONSEQUENCES OF CLASS ELITISM Because socioeconomic class converges with gender, race, ability, and personal power, as well as other identity constructs, it is simplistic to conclude that being able-bodied or male or having a high income is automatically associated with feelings of safety, security, less tendency to depression, and less pain. Counselors in particular are mistaken in assuming that not having high status is related to feelings of less power, thus ascribing low status to non-White persons, ethnic group members, and persons who have low income (Gibbs, Huang, & Associates, 1989).

AGEISM

Ageism refers to discrimination against people because of their age. This discrimination is often aimed at the middle-aged or the elderly (Nuessel, 1982). Ageist terms vary and include primarily negative expressions. Examples are *crotchety, fuddy-duddy, fart, senility, golden-ager, graybeard,* and *Lawrence Welk generation* (Nuessel, 1982).

Atkinson and Hackett (1995) stated that "delineating the elderly as being 65 and over is a purely arbitrary separation" (p. 192). Its genesis is in the decades-old Social Security system, which was instituted when people did not live as long as they do now.

Ageism is compounded with other layers of discrimination. For instance, until very recently, limited attention had been devoted to the study of breast cancer. On the surface, this lack of focus can easily be attributed to sexism; however, is ageism also at fault? Does the fact that the majority of women survivors of breast cancer are not in their 20s or 30s, but rather in their 50s, contribute to the limited (but thankfully growing) research on this disease? Is it less important for an aging woman to lose the commodity of beauty that esteems her with worth and power given its association with sexuality? This is an unsettling question, yet counselors need to know how adversely affected they are by the intersecting layers of discrimination.

Elders ought not be treated as monoliths. Doing so greatly impedes the delivery of effective services. Differences exist between a 65-year-old healthy person and a 90-year-old elder whose health has begun to decline. Atkinson and Hackett (1995) described the "young-old" and the "old-old" (p. 14). The young-old is in fairly good health with stable financial supports. The old-old is experiencing deficits in several psychological, physical, social, and financial resources.

Counselors need to be mindful of the social supports available to the elderly client. Sturdy social supports with both friends and family results in less dependency on formal psychological help (Phillips & Murrell, 1994). Part of a counselor's assessment, then, should be an examination of an elder's level of involvement in meaningful and purposeful social activity. The elder's sense of personal autonomy or control over life is also an important component of overall wellness. Some illnesses, such as Alzheimer's disease, will require that the counselor work in sync with other caregivers to maximize the quality of living during a stressful, disquieting, and potentially chaotic time. Age biases contribute to some counselors seeing little merit in providing psychotherapy to aging persons. For example, one weakness of psychoanalytic theory is that it is not generally regarded as viable for persons age 50 or older or for poor people. Identifying a client's strengths, regardless of the presenting problem, is a crucial step in facilitating growth or bolstering coping abilities.

CONSEQUENCES OF AGEISM FOR THE NON-ELDERLY   Unlike most traditional cultures in which the elderly tend to be respected and valued, in the U.S. culture, inordinate emphasis is placed on youthfulness. The societal significance attached to doing, productivity, and maintaining mastery over nature may explain this cultural preoccupation with youth and the herculean effort to defy and, in some instances, deny aging. Aging appears to be viewed as a loss of control and of diminishing power. Discrimination against a segment of the population that is composing a higher percentage of the total and of which all will be members, if they are fortunate, culminates in fear-based stereotypes about the experience of being an elder. It is heartening to see how a culture of menopausal women is redefining hot flashes as power surges and recognizing the "change" in life as a time of ascendancy and coming into one's own.

IMPLICATIONS FOR COUNSELORS

Not acknowledging the meaning of race in one's life can restrict the development of a racial self. This lack of clarity about a core identity construct adversely affects counselors' empathy toward their clients. American society socializes people into attitudes that are often not honoring of difference. Counselors need to recognize these and other biases within themselves and not allow shame to fan denial. The ongoing process of unlearning these attitudes is tumultuous, but the good news is that it is possible. Counselors need to ascertain whether they are able to work effectively with a variety of clients.

Counselors have a professional and ethical obligation to refer clients to other professionals when they are unable to provide necessary assistance (see the Case Study "Multiple and Textured Identities"). However, the counselor who is highly judgmental of a White woman involved in an interracial relationship needs to be concerned if intolerance in one area of her life also extends to persons who, for example, do not practice her same religious affiliation.

CASE STUDY
Multiple and Textured Identities

Tasha Long is a 38-year-old Black American female. She works as a career counselor with a mental health agency and has held this job for 6 years. Tasha has been divorced from her husband Jeff for 8 months. They were married for 12 years and have an 11-year-old son, Jason. Jason lives with Tasha. Tasha divorced Jeff because of his cocaine and alcohol problems. Jeff is HIV positive, and 2 years ago, Tasha discovered that she had contracted the disease from Jeff. Tasha has not revealed her HIV-positive status to any friends or family members. Her medical doctor knows and Tasha plans to consult a psychologist in a neighboring state with this information. Tasha received her test results anonymously from a call-in testing center after conducting a home test. Mike is Tasha's fiancé, and they are planning to be married in a few months. Mike has children from a previous marriage, and Tasha does not want any more children. Tasha feels that if she tells Mike of her condition, he will not want to marry her. Mike is a good man that Tasha has come to love and respect. He is a good role model for Jason, and Tasha wants this for her son, given the instability that Jeff brought into their lives. Tasha's job performance has been excellent and is not impacted by her medical condition, divorce, and other life changes. Tasha decides to drive to a neighboring state to seek out a professional counselor regarding the many stressors in her life which fill her with guilt, anger, and sadness.

QUESTIONS

1. How does the issue of identities as status affect Tasha's life?
2. Which of the consequences of socially constructed meanings about difference manifest in Tasha's life? How are they manifested?
3. Among the stressors in Tasha's life, which contribute most significantly to her emotional state?
4. What are the multiple identities in Tasha's life?
5. On which identity constructs might an inexperienced counselor focus?

DISCUSSION AND INTEGRATION
The Client, Tasha

Tasha is silent about her HIV-positive status, but she is not alone. According to the Centers for Disease Control, there are an estimated 42 million people living with HIV/AIDS. Of these, 38.6 million are adults and 19.2 million are women. In 2001, 63% of women and adolescent girls or 7 million people reported with AIDS were Black (Centers for Disease Control, 2003). Blacks are only 12% of the U.S. population and Black women are roughly 6% of the U.S. population. It is clear that Black women are disproportionately overrepresented among persons impacted with this illness.

Tasha contracted HIV through heterosexual contact. Most of the AIDS cases diagnosed in 2001 among females older than 13 years of age were also attributed to heterosexual contact. There are different modes of transmission between the sexes. The majority of men who are exposed to HIV is through having sex with other men. Jeff was exposed in the second most common way: through intravenous (IV) drug use.

Tasha's dilemma is very real as she struggles with multiple identities. When she was married, Tasha did not perceive herself to be at risk although it was clear that Jeff was using drugs. Nonetheless, theirs was a monogamous relationship that Tasha saw as long term and committed. Such a perception often contributes to women not perceiving themselves to be at risk (St. Lawrence et al., 1998).

As an engaged woman, daughter, and mother, Tasha hides a terrible secret that threatens her relationships and her quality of life. "HIV infection can lead to mental impairment, from minor cognitive disorder to full-blown dementia, as well as precipitate the onset of mood disorders or psychosis" (U.S. Department of Health and Human Services, 2001, p. 57).

The revelation of her condition and the fact that she withheld information from Mike for as long as she did may impact Mike's willingness to remain in the relationship. Tasha was not taking drugs but was having sex with her husband. His use of IV drugs exposed him to the virus, which subsequently infected Tasha. Tasha feels enraged at this unjust situation. She is also angry with herself for putting up with Jeff's drugging behavior for years, which escalated from marijuana use to more serious addictions. Part of Tasha's silence exists within the context of the Black community's cultural response in which there tends to be an avoidance of open discussion of sexual behavior and drug use (Worth, 1990). Such silence has implications for prevention and AIDS education.

Tasha is also a professional woman. In this regard, she differs from low-income Black women who are HIV positive. Clearly, both groups are at risk of contracting the disease from heterosexual contact; however, in poor communities, the risks of intravenous drug use are higher (Weeks, Schensul, Williams, Singer, & Grier 1995).

Tasha's guilt and shame over not being honest with Mike reminds her of Jeff's betrayal and dishonesty with her. Within the African American community, condoms can be viewed negatively. Their use is often associated with infidelity, casual relationships, disease, and beliefs that detract from trust (St. Lawrence et al., 1998). Tasha is very careful with condom use, but she knowingly exposes Jeff to the virus every time she is sexually intimate with him. This is a unilateral decision based on secrecy that is damning to a relationship.

The Counselor, Ruth

Instead of focusing on weaknesses and powerlessness, Ruth can assist Tasha by helping her to realize that despite her vulnerability she is still able to make choices. This knowledge can ultimately be empowering.

Ruth can also help Tasha explore the options of either "coming out" to Mike, Jason, and her parents or remaining closeted. Waiting to decide which course of action to take is also an option, but procrastinating could be a form of denial as well as a form of control over a situation in which Tasha feels powerless. That her medical doctor and now her therapist know of her HIV-positive status may decrease some of her feelings of secrecy and inauthenticity.

It is important that Ruth unravel any feelings of discomfort that she may have in working with a client who is HIV-positive. Ruth may need to supplement her knowledge about this disease and its multiple effects on women's lives. Ruth can also help Tasha with a variety of legal (power of attorney, a will) and other services, such as a support group, once Tasha is ready to acknowledge her condition to others. There are plenty of people who are HIV-positive who live fulfilled lives with partners who love and care for them. A support group would help Tasha develop some new skills for living with her changed life, with or without Mike. Her responsibility for Jason, given Jeff's substance-dependent state, is not negated by her medical condition. It is clear that Tasha needs assistance with how to make sense out of this overwhelming and potentially debilitating stressor in her life.

Ruth looks at Tasha's situation from a perspective of power. Ruth understands that personal power does not come from denying injustice or oppressive acts, but rather comes from recognizing them and realizing one's vulnerabilities (Pinderhughes, 1989). Ruth sees that Tasha is in a state of crisis and is not operating from an empowered position but from a place of fear, shame, dishonesty, and desperation.

Tasha may think that her silence protects her, but it does not. Through cognitive restructuring, Ruth can help Tasha see that being silent does not make her HIV-positive condition go away. Her silence denies her the right to live her life with integrity and honesty. Her silence also denies Mike the right to decide what he wants to do with the information of Tasha's HIV-positive status. Both of these scenarios represent lesser lives. As Alice Sebold said at the beginning of this chapter, "You save yourself or you remain unsaved." Tasha can save herself but not through her silence and dishonesty. She needs to realize that she was victimized by Jeff's behavior but in time, she need not feel or behave like a victim or an oppressor to Mike.

Tasha's sense of responsibility for Jeff's behavior may also fuel her sense of guilt. Gender and race dictate that Black women are responsible for their health, the health of their children, and that of their husbands or sexual partners. Being accustomed to providing care for others when they are ill, who will care for Tasha? This is a role with which she is very unfamiliar (Richie, 1994).

Ruth may also struggle with ethical considerations regarding Tasha's behavior. Ruth knows that Tasha is HIV-positive and is having sex with someone who is unaware of her condition. Ruth may not be legally or ethically bound to tell Jeff about Tasha's condition—although in some states, such as in North Carolina, the public health department is required to inform a spouse of their spouse's HIV-positive status. At the same time, Ruth has to balance Tasha's confidentiality with legal responsibilities such as duty to warn or duty to protect (Norsworthy & Fajardo, 1996). If Ruth were to tell Mike of Tasha's HIV-positive status, she would be justified in doing so. According to Section B.1.d of the Ethical Standards of the American Counseling Association,

A counselor who receives information confirming that a client has a disease commonly known to be both communicable and fatal is justified in disclosing information to an identifiable third party, who by his or her relationship with the client is at a high risk of contracting the disease. Prior to making a disclosure the counselor should ascertain that the client has not already informed the third party about his or her disease and that the client is not intending to inform the third party in the immediate future." ACA, 2000, p. 5.

There are situations in which ethical codes do not provide the counselor with specific information to follow. In some states, there are criminal charges that may accompany an act of sexual intercourse when someone is HIV-positive, conceals this information, and knowingly has unprotected sex with another person. Tasha needs to know that although she is having protected sex, she may be making herself increasingly liable by not telling Mike about her HIV-positive status. If he contracts the disease from her, the extent of her liability is more clearly seen. It would help Ruth to be aware of the state laws associated with HIV where she resides so that she can provide Tasha with sound counsel.

Tasha is a professional counselor, yet her personal decisions are not impacting her professional life as of yet. Ruth, then, is not in a position to report her to the Ethics Board.

There are formal assessments that Ruth might use to ascertain Tasha's depression and anxiety levels. These include the Beck Depression Inventory and the Hamilton Anxiety Inventory. Overall, Ruth can help Tasha confront a number of pressing issues such as the social stigma associated with her condition; existential concerns, such as death, freedom, and living; health and medical concerns; sexuality, such as safer sexual practices; and loss and grief (Norsworthy & Fajardo, 1996).

SUMMARY

In this chapter, the presentation of human differences as status variables was explored through an examination of the Contextual and Social Construction of Differences Model. Hughes's (1945) work on the dilemmas and contradictions of status was also useful. The consequences of hierarchical socialization were presented, and the advantages of a model based on cultural pluralism were envisioned. The importance of counselors recognizing systems of inequity was articulated, and a case study allowed readers to synthesize the ideas presented.

REFERENCES

American Counseling Association. (2002). ACA Code of Ethics and Standards of Practice, eff. 1995. Alexandria, VA: Author. http://aca.convio.net/site/PageServer?pagename=resources_ethics#ce

Atkinson, D. R., & Hackett, G. (1995). *Counseling diverse populations.* Madison, WI: Brown and Benchmark.

Avakian, M. (2002). *Atlas of Asian-American history.* New York: Checkmark Books.

Bem, S. L. (1993). *The lenses of gender: Transforming the debate on sexuality inequality.* New Haven, CT: Yale University Press.

Bronstein, P., & Quina, K. (1988). *Teaching a psychology of people.* Washington, DC: American Psychological Association.

Carrigan, T., Connell, B., & Lee, J. (1987). Toward a new sociology of masculinity. In H. Brod (Ed.), *The making of masculinities: The new men's studies* (pp. 63–100). Boston: Allen and Unwin.

Centers for Disease Control and Prevention. (2003). Divisions of HIV/AIDS Prevention Web site: http://www.cdc.gov/hiv/dhap.htm.

Fowler, C., O'Rourke, B. O., Wadsworth, J., & Harper, D. (1992). Disability and feminism: Models for counselor exploration of personal values and beliefs. *Journal of Applied Rehabilitation Counseling, 23,* 14–19.

Gans, H. J. (1992, January 8). Fighting the biases embedded in social concepts of the poor. *Chronicle of Higher Education,* p. A56.

Gibbs, J. T., Huang, L. N., & Associates. (1989). *Children of color: Psychological interventions with minority youth.* San Francisco: Jossey-Bass.

Gladding, S.T. (1997). *Community and agency counseling.* Upper Saddle River, NJ: Merrill/Prentice Hall.

Good, G. E., Dell, D. M., & Mintz, L. B. (1989). Male role and gender role conflict: Relations to help seeking in men. *Journal of Counseling Psychology, 36,* 295–300.

Good, G. E., & Mintz, L. B. (1990). Gender role conflict and depression in college men: Evidence for compounded risk. *Journal of Counseling and Development, 69,* 1, 17–21.

Grubb, H. J. (1992). Intelligence at the low end of the curve: Where are the racial differences? In A. Burlew, W. Banks, H. McAdoo, & D. Azibo (Eds.), *African American psychology: Theory, research, and practice* (pp. 219–228). Newbury Park, CA: Sage.

Haider, R. (1995). *Gender and development.* Cairo, Egypt: American University in Cairo Press.

Herrnstein, R. J., & Murray, C. (1994). *The bell curve: Intelligence and class structure in American life.* New York: Free Press.

Hughes, E. C. (1945). Dilemmas and contradictions of status. *American Journal of Sociology, 50,* 353–357.

Institute of Medicine. (2003). *Unequal treatment: Confronting racial and ethnic disparities in healthcare.* Washington, DC: National Academies Press.

King, N. (1988). Teaching about lesbians and gays in the psychology curriculum. In P. A. Bronstein & K. Quina (Eds.), *Teaching a psychology of people: Resources for gender and sociocultural awareness* (pp. 168–174). Washington, DC: American Psychological Association.

Livneh, H., & Sherwood, A. (1991). Application of personality theories and counseling strategies to clients with physical disabilities. *Journal of Counseling and Development, 69,* 525–538.

Loiacano, D. K. (1989). Gay identity issues among Black Americans: Racism, homophobia, and the need for validation. *Journal of Counseling and Development, 68,* 21–25.

McBride, M. C. (1990). Autonomy and the struggle for female identity: Implications for counseling women. *Journal of Counseling and Development, 69,* 22–26.

McIntosh, P. (1989, July/August). White privilege: Unpacking the invisible knapsack. *Peace and Freedom,* pp. 10–12.

Myers, L. J., Speight, S. L., Highlen, P. S., Cox, C. I., Reynolds, A. L., Adams, E. M., & Hanley, P. (1991). Identity development and worldview:

Toward an optimal conceptualization. *Journal of Counseling and Development, 70,* 54–63.

Nisbett, R. (1995). Race, IQ, and scientism. In S. Fraser (Ed.), *The bell curve wars: Race, intelligence, and the future of America.* New York: Basic Books.

Norsworthy, K. L., & Fajardo, E. (1996). Counseling the HIV-infected client. In P. Pedersen and D. Locke (Eds.), *Cultural and diversity issues in counseling* (pp. 87–89). Greensboro, NC: Eric Counseling and Student Services Clearinghouse.

Nuessel, F. H. (1982). The language of ageism. *Gerontologist, 22,* 273–276.

Phillips, M. A., & Murrell, S. A. (1994). Impact of psychological and physical health, stressful events, and social support on subsequent mental health help seeking among older adults. *Journal of Consulting and Clinical Psychology, 62,* 270–275.

Pinderhughes, E. (1989). *Understanding race, ethnicity, and power: The key to efficacy in clinical practice.* New York: Free Press.

Renzetti, C. M., & Curran, D. J. (1992). *Women, men, and society.* Boston: Allyn & Bacon.

Reynolds, A. L., & Pope, R. L. (1991). The complexities of diversity: Exploring multiple oppressions. *Journal of Counseling and Development, 70,* 174–180.

Richie, B. (1994). AIDS: In living color. In E. C. White (Ed.), *The Black women's health book: Speaking for ourselves* (pp. 182–186). Seattle, WA: Seal Press.

Robinson, T. L. (1999). The intersections of dominant discourses across race, gender, and other identities. *Journal of Counseling and Development, 77,* 73–79.

Robinson, T. L. (2001). White mothers of non-White children. *Journal of Humanistic Counseling, Education and Development, 40,* 171–184.

Robinson, T. L., & Kennington, P. A. D. (2002). Holding up half the sky: Women and psychological resistance. *Journal of Humanistic Counseling, Education and Development, 41,* 164–177.

Rogers, J. A. (1967). *Sex and race.* St. Petersburg, FL: Helga Rogers.

Sebold, A. (2002). *Lucky.* New York; Little, Brown, & Company.

Skovholt, T. M. (1993). Counseling and psychotherapy interventions with men. *Counseling and Human Development, 25,* 1–6.

St. Lawrence, J. S., Eldridge, G. D., Reitman, D., Little, C. E., Shelby, M. C., & Brasfield, T. L. (1998). Factors influencing condom use among African American women: Implications for risk reduction interventions. *American Journal of Community Psychology, 26,*(1), 7–28.

Swanson, J. L. (1993). Sexism strikes men. *American Counselor, 1,* 10–13, 39.

U.S. Department of Health and Human Services. (2001). Mental health: Culture, race, and ethnicity—A supplement to Mental health: A report of the Surgeon General. Rockville, MD: U.S. Department of Health and Human Services, Public Health Services, Office of the Surgeon General.

Weeks, M. R., Schensul, J. J., Williams, S. S., Singer, M., & Grier, M. (1995). AIDS prevention for African-American and Latina women: Building culturally and gender-appropriate intervention. *AIDS Education and Prevention, 7,* 251–263.

Weisman, L. K. (1992). *Discrimination by design: A feminist critique of the man-made environment.* Urbana: University of Illinois Press.

Worth, D. (1990). Minority women and AIDS: Culture, race, and gender. In D. Feldman (Ed.), *Culture and AIDS* (pp. 111–135). New York: Praeger.

Part Two: **Valued Cultures**

Chapter 4

Native Americans and Alaskan Natives

The man who sat on the ground in his tipi meditating on life and its meaning, accepting the kinship of all creatures and acknowledging unity with the universe of things, was infusing into his being the true essence of civilization.

Chief Luther Standing Bear. From Joyce Sequichie Hifler, A Cherokee Feast of Days

American Indian and *Alaskan Native* refer to people having origins in any of the original peoples of North and South America (including Central America) and who maintain tribal affiliation or community attachment (U.S. Census Bureau, 2000).

The origins of Native American/Alaskan Native people have been greatly debated. One of the most insightful theories regarding the people who occupied the New World was proposed by José de Acosta, a Jesuit missionary. He theorized that North America, which was a continent clearly separate from Asia, had been settled before the birth of Christ by a group of hunters and their families who, in following animal herds, passed overland from Asia to the Americas (cited in Hoxie, 1996). Many anthropologists agree with de Acosta's theory. The debate wages over timing issues, whether the first people arrived in America more than or less than 15,000 years ago. DNA studies comparing Native Americans to other population groups found three distinct genetic mutations in Mongolia and Siberia, which suggests a separation as early as 30,000 years ago. It is widely accepted that the first Americans arrived in North America by way of the Bering Strait Land Bridge, or Beringia. Temporary ice melts for several thousand years most likely created natural passageways for large game and their human spear-wielding predator (Waldman, 2000).

Native American Creation stories tell of being brought into existence by the Great Spirit or having come from the womb of Mother Earth. In writing of these origins, Gunn Allen (1994) honored Woman:

> There is a spirit that pervades everything, that is capable of powerful song and radiant movement, and that moves in and out of the mind. The colors of this spirit are multitudinous, a glowing, pulsing rainbow. Old Spider Woman is one name for this quintessential spirit, and Earth Woman is another, and what they together have made is called Creation, Earth, creatures, plants, and light. (p. 13)

HISTORY

It is estimated that in 1492 when Christopher Columbus arrived in the New World, that there were approximately 1 million inhabitants within the continental United States (Russell, 1994). Because Columbus mistakenly thought he had landed in India, he referred to the Native people as Indios. The different European dialects represented pronounced the word as Indien or Indianer (Brown, 1981).

The treatment of Native Americans and Alaskan Natives in the United States has been disgraceful. Within 400 years after the Europeans' arrival, the Native population was decimated by wars, starvation, slavery genocide, and disease, with typhus, small-pox, and measles being the greatest killers (Vernon, 2002). In 1790, the enactment of federal policies began with the goal of displacing Indian people. The Bureau of Indian Affairs (BIA), which today is responsible for the United States' relationship with the 562 federally recognized tribes and Alaskan communities, was created in 1824. The job of

Thomas McKenney, the first director of the BIA, was to manage Indian schools, administer Indian trade, and handle the various negotiations associated with Indian trade. For many tribes, the BIA represented betrayal and broken promises. One Native person remarked; "They made us many promises, more than I can remember, but they never kept but one; they promised to take our land, and they took it" (Brown, 1981).

The Indian Removal Act of 1830, under the leadership of President Andrew Jackson, who was known as "Sharp Knife" among some of the Native people, was intended to relocate Indians to Indian country west of the Mississippi, not to include Missouri, Louisiana, or the territory of Arkansas (Hoxie, 1996; Russell, 1994). America's defeat of the British during the War of 1812 prompted little concern for European alliances. The annexation of Spanish Florida contributed to America's perception of Indians as hindrances to the interests of expansionism from the millions of White Europeans who were coming to America. The cultural and psychological violence are evident in Jackson's Second Annual Message to Congress, given shortly after he became the president of the United States:

> It gives me pleasure to announce to Congress that the benevolent policy of the government, steadily pursued for nearly thirty years, in relation to the removal of the Indians beyond the white settlements is approaching to a happy consummation. . . . It will relieve the whole state of Mississippi and the western part of Alabama of Indian occupancy, and enable those states to advance rapidly in population, wealth, and power. It will separate the Indians from the power of the States; enable them to pursue happiness in their own way and under their own rude institutions; will retard the progress of decay, which is lessening their numbers, and perhaps cause them gradually under the protection of the Government and through the influence of good counsels, to cast off their savage habits and become an interesting, civilized, and Christian community. (1908)

Jackson considered this act of removal to be benevolent because the government was funding the relocation. To the Native people, it was their "trail of tears" or the westward herding of the "Five Civilized Tribes" (Cherokees, Chickasaws, Choctaws, Creeks, and Seminoles) to Oklahoma. During the cold and brutal winter, people traveled by foot, horseback, wagon, and steamboat. They were hungry, cold, and sick, and hundreds died from starvation, exhaustion, disease, exposure, and accidents (Brown, 1981; Hoxie, 1996). Native resistance to removal was fierce but their oppressors were opportunistic and destructive. For example, the Georgia militia in Echota destroyed the printing press of the Cherokee Phoenix, a newspaper written in Cherokee syllabary created by Sequoyah (Waldman, 2000).

In 1934, the Indian Reorganization Act was passed, with a goal of ending restrictions against Native religions. Albeit shortlived, during this time there was greater understanding and acceptance of Indian culture. World War II ushered in a period of greater restriction and attempts by the government to integrate Native people into American society. But as was characteristic of the past, more sacred lands were lost during this time and cultures were destroyed. During the 1970s, many traditional

Indians found themselves arrested for possessing sacred objects such as eagle feather or for the use of peyote. Protests against this interference contributed to the 1978 passage of the American Indian Religious Freedom Act. Congress concluded that Native ways of worship were an essential part of Native life, and this law sought to protect and preserve such religious liberties (Hoxie, 1996).

Today, Native American and Alaskan Natives are a heterogeneous group, with 252 tribal languages and 562 federally recognized Indian tribes in the 32 contiguous United States and in Alaska (U.S. Department of the Interior, 2002). Among these tribes is tremendous diversity across custom, language, and family structure (Hoxie, 1996). Apache, Arapahoe, Arikara, Blackfoot, Catawba, Cherokee, Cheyenne, Chickasaw, Chippewa, Choctaw, Comanche, Coushatta, Cree, Creek, Crow, Erie, Eskimo, Haida, Hopi, Hupa, Iroquois, Lumbee, Osage, Mi'kmaq, Mohave, Narragansett, Navajo, Ottawa, Paiute, Pima, Potawatomi, Seminole, Seneca, Shawnee, Shoshone, Sioux, Tlingit, Tununak, Ute, Winnebago, Yaqui, and the Zuni represent only a fraction of Native American and Alaska Native tribal groups. The 10 largest Native American tribes in the United States are Cherokee, Navajo, Latin American Indian, Choctaw, Sioux, Chippewa, Apache, Blackfeet, Iroquois, and Pueblo.

DEMOGRAPHY

The increase in numbers among Native people is a reflection of better census methods and people's acknowledgement of mixed ancestry. According to the 2000 Census, there are 281 million people living in the United States. Of these, 2.4% reported two or more races. Native Americans and Alaskan Natives represent 2.47 million or 0.9% of the total U.S. population (U.S. Census Bureau, 2000). An additional 1.6 million people reported Native American and Alaskan Native ancestry, along with another race. More specifically, 1 million people reported that they were both Native and White, and nearly 183,000 people indicated that they were both Native and Black or African American (U.S. Census Bureau, 2000). Clearly, the majority of American Indian and Alaska Natives have mixed backgrounds as biracial and multiracial people. Consequently, a variety of phenotypic characteristics are found among Native American Indians.

Forty-eight percent of Native Americans and Alaskan Natives live in the West, 2% reside in the South, 16% make the Midwest their home, and nearly 7% live in the Northeast. Alaska has approximately 16% American Indian and Native people, followed by New Mexico with 9.5%, South Dakota with 8.3%, Oklahoma, 7.9%, Montana, 6.2%, and Arizona with 5%.

Native Americans and Alaskan Natives are a young group. Fifteen percent of the total population are younger than age 5, whereas only 2.1% are 75 years or older. The median age is 27.9 years.

About one quarter of Native American and Alaskan Native elderly live on Native American Indian reservations or in Alaskan Native villages. In addition to earlier federal laws that played a role in the populating of urban areas with Native people, high unemployment on the reservations has contributed to the move of Native people to urban areas. Horse (2001) maintains that Native people are geographically dislocated from their homeland within a culture bombarded by the Internet, the U.S. school system, peer pressure, and the mass media. Despite the reality of cultural discontinuity for some Native people, which refers to the gulf between mainstream expectations and Native people's cultural values, most Native people have learned to survive by becoming bicultural (Garret & Pichette, 2000).

Approximately 280,000 Native American and Alaskan Natives speak a language other than English at home, and more than half of Alaskan Natives who are Eskimos speak either Inuit or Yup'ik (U.S. Department of Health and Human Services, 2001). More than half of the total Native American Indian population resides in urban areas.

Among persons 18 to 24 years of age in the 25 largest American Indian tribes, 63% were high school graduates, compared with the U.S. high school graduation rate of 76.5% (U.S. Census Bureau, 1995). Nearly 31 different tribal groups have established their own tribal colleges (Horse, 2001).

CULTURAL PHILOSOPHIES AND ORIENTATION

Tribe is a source of belonging and security for Native American and Alaskan Native people. Personal accomplishments are honored and supported if they serve to benefit the entire tribe or collective. Competition, the hallmark of the educational school system and a dominant cultural value, can be considered at extreme odds with a spirit of cooperation and sharing of resources that belong to everyone (see the Storytelling "Right Relationship with One Another").

Although values vary from tribe to tribe, American Indian and Alaskan Native people believe in a Supreme Creator that is considered both male and female and is in command of all the elements of existence. Paula Gunn Allen (1994) said, "There are many female gods recognized and honored by the Nations. Females were highly valued, both respected and feared and all social institutions reflected this attitude" (p. 193). Indians/Alaskans also believe that all things in the universe are connected, have

STORYTELLING: Right Relationship with One Another

After giving a talk to a group of people assembled at a church on a Sunday morning, the Native American scholar was asked by the event coordinator to offer a blessing from her people to the group assembled. A bit taken aback, the scholar indicated that she was not expecting to do so. At that point, the coordinator said, "You don't have to if you don't want to." The woman replied, "Yes, I do, you asked me." In the Native woman's response, I saw the values of reciprocity, the extended self, and being in harmonious relationship with one another.

purpose, and exemplify personhood (Garrett & Garrett, 1994, 1996), "including plants (e.g., 'tree people'), animals ('our four-legged brothers and sisters'), rocks and minerals ('rock people'), the land ('Mother Earth'), the winds ('the Four Powers'), 'Father Sky,' 'Grandfather Sun,' 'Grandmother Moon,' 'The Red Thunder Boys'" (p. 138).

Honoring the Creator is sacred to Native American and Alaskan Native people and is central to Indians'/Alaskans' harmonious relationships with nature and all things. Garrett (1998) said that "the wellness of the mind, body, spirit, and natural environment is an extension of the proper balance in the relationship of all things" (p. 78). In these cultures, sharing is valued over materialism because all things belong to Earth.

Elders are valued among Native American and Alaskan Natives "because of the lifetime's worth of wisdom they have acquired" (Garrett & Garrett, 1994, p. 137). Elders are accorded respect, and as they age, there is an increase in sacred responsibility for the tribe and family. They understand that their purpose is to care for and guide young people, yet a spirit of curiosity and openness to life's lessons prevails (Garrett & Herring, 2001).

Native American cultural values emanate from a spiritual center that emphasizes coexisting in harmony with nature. This entails a respect for Earth as natural medicine (Peregoy, 1993). Native people have always depended on the land, for it was life and medicine. The Paiute boiled sagebrush to relieve headaches and rheumatism. Even dandruff was cured by rubbing boiled willow leaves into the hair and scalp (Ballentine & Ballentine, 1993).

Implicit in this value system is reverence for and acceptance of the gifts from the earth. In their reverence for the earth, a variety of plants, wild and cultivated, were used for both religious and practical purposes as well as for pleasure. Clearly some Indian people, particularly where agriculture was highly developed, used alcohol prior to contact with Europeans, but for the most part, drinking alcohol was a postcontact reality (Waldman, 2000). Native American people believe that to be human is a part of the Sacred, thus there is an acknowledgment that human beings make mistakes (Trujillo, 2000). Nature, in its natural, undisturbed state, is respected, and coexisting (not interfering) with nature is paramount because all things have spiritual energy. The universe, or Mother Earth, belongs to all people. For the Indian, the concept of land ownership was foreign and made as much sense as did carving up the sky (which is what currently exists in terms of defined air-space boundaries).

Honoring traditional ways suggests a respect for the past and the contributions of the ancestral spirits. According to Peregoy (1993), "The traditional Indian/Native's system of life is intertwined with the tribe and extends further into a metaphysical belief system" (p. 172).

Native American and Alaskan Natives see the extended family and the tribe as taking precedence over the self (Garrett & Garrett, 1994; Gunn Allen, 1994; Peregoy, 1993). Among many Native American and Alaskan Native people, the concept of self tends to be fluid and includes the individual as well as the tribe, the extended family, and even plants and animal spirits (Dana, 2000). A belief or knowledge in unseen powers and reference to deities and mystery is core to many tribal values, as is the importance of balance (Trujillo, 2000).

Respect for and coexistence with helpful animal spirits are enduring values found in nearly all Native American and Alaskan Eskimo societies. It was believed that the animals made themselves available to humans only for as long as there was respect from the hunters for the animal spirits. This involved ritual treatment of the animals so that the animals would, upon their death, return to the spirit world with a good report, which would ensure the success of future hunters. If a hunter was unsuccessful, it could be stated that the animal spirits had not been treated properly; therefore, proper rituals were needed to restore harmony and to correct the imbalance (Hoxie, 1996).

ACCULTURATION

According to Herring (1992), Indian/Alaskan people are "more unalterably resistant to assimilation and integration into mainstream society than are other minority groups" (p. 135); some, however, are acculturated.

Acculturation and assimilation influence value structures and are important to an understanding of cultural adaptation. Garrett and Pichette (2000) identify five levels of acculturation among Native people: (a) Traditional, (b) Marginal, (c) Bicultural, (d) Assimilated, and (e) Pantraditional. These levels exists on a continuum and are a function of a person's life experiences. The Traditional Native person may or may not speak English and will hold traditionally Native values, including tribal customs. The Marginal person identifies with neither mainstream values nor traditional values. Bicultural describes the person who knows and practices both mainstream and traditional values. Assimilated persons hold the mainstream American values in high esteem to the exclusion of those Native. Finally, Pantraditional describes the assimilated person who consciously seeks to return to the "old ways." These people seek to embrace lost traditional values and beliefs and are often bilingual.

Garrett and Pichette (2000) offered a clear definition of acculturation in their discussion of Native American acculturation. It was stated that acculturation is "the cultural change that occurs when two or more cultures are in persistent contact . . . A particular kind of acculturation is assimilation, in which one culture changes significantly more than the other culture and as a result comes to resemble it. This process is often established deliberately through force to maintain control over conquered people, but it can occur voluntarily as well" (p. 6).

Acculturation may take place at the expense of one's original cultural values as one internalizes values and traditions. This process is not always conscious (Sue, 1989), and there is the likelihood of cultural alienation from one's traditional culture because the dominent culture is esteemed over one's own.

One dimension of acculturation is assimilation. Assimilation is different in that it describes those persons who consciously do not desire to maintain their cultural identities and thus seek sustained interaction with other cultures outside their own. The original cultures have been lost or relinquished, and persons have given up most cultural traits of their cultures of origin and assumed the traits, behaviors, and attitude of the dominant culture (Berry & Kim, 1988).

Christianization was one way assimilation was accomplished among many Native Americans. Some Native Americans do not regard the two to be incompatible. In the

Native American Church (NAC), Christian and Native beliefs coexist (U.S. Department of Health and Human Services, 2001). In addition to Spanish and French, European colonizers brought English to America. Language is a medium of culture and English functioned as a way to deny the existence and relevance of Native languages. Such a policy existed in the U.S. government-sponsored Indian boarding schools designed to mainstream American Indian youth. The first school was established in 1879 in Carlisle, Pennsylvania, under the influence of General Henry Pratt. His motto was "kill the Indian and save the man" (Hoxie, 1996; Lesiak & Jones, 1991). In these colonizing contexts, children's hair was cut, traditional clothing was taken away, American Christian names replaced Native names, and only English was allowed. The virtues of White American Christian traditions were espoused and the Native ways were regarded as uncivilized (Cameron & turtle-song, 2003).

Native Americans and Alaskan Natives who possess a strong sense of heritage and honor tradition may be more likely to feel at peace on the reservation where cooperation with others and respect for tribal values based on ritual are commonplace (Gunn Allen, 1994).

SOCIAL, PSYCHOLOGICAL, AND PHYSICAL HEALTH ISSUES

Between the years 1999–2001, the poverty rate for American Indians and Alaskan Natives was 24.5% with 0.8 million poor. This rate was higher than the poverty rates for non-Hispanic Whites, Asians, and Pacific Islanders but equal to the rate for Blacks (U.S. Census Bureau, 2000). Nationally, one third (32.8%) of American Indians and Alaskan Natives do not have a usual source of health care where they are regularly seen by a doctor or a clinic that can provide preventive care (U.S. Department of Health and Human Services, 2001; IOM, 2003). The lack of health insurance among the general population is 17.5%. As a result of treaty obligations, Native Americans receive their health services largely through the federal government and the Indian Health Service. Since 1955, a part of the U.S. Public Health Service was to provide health care to all Native Americans/Alaskan Natives who belonged to federally recognized tribes and lived on or near the reservations throughout 12 service areas (Byrd & Clayton, 2003). Only 38% of Native Americans reside on federal trust lands, and although the federal government has played a key role in health care delivery for Natives, unlike other groups of color, the quality of and access to such care has been adversely impacted by the way in which Native people are scattered throughout the country (Joe, 2003). In light of these and other data that reveal the poor quality of life for unacceptably high numbers of American Indian and Alaskan Native people, many American Indians and Alaskan Natives feel a distrust for the dominant culture (Heinrich, Corbine, & Thomas, 1990).

Partly as a result of this legacy and continuing cultural conflict, alcoholism presents social problems for many Native Americans, affecting their family life, the health of new-borns, and the sustainability of employment. Comorbidity is likely given the relationship between substance addictions and mental health problems. Alcohol abuse is a substantial problem, with the estimated rate of alcohol-related deaths for Indian men to be 27% and for Indian women, 13% (U.S. Department of Health and Human Services, 2001). In addition to the adverse health effects of alcohol abuse on the body, alcoholism is linked to high-risk behaviors such as unprotected sex because it decreases inhibition. The introduction of black tar heroin on many reservations has contributed to an increase in substance dependency. Currently, the number of reported Native American AIDS cases as of December 1999 was 2,132. Although this number seems low, AIDS is the eighth leading cause of mortality among Native Americans between ages 15 and 34 living on or near reservations (Vernon, 2002). Related to poor diet, diabetes ranges from 5% to 50% among tribes and Native communities and colon and rectal cancers are the highest among any racial or ethnic group in the country (Institute of Medicine, 2003). As major causes of morbidity and premature death, these and other poor health outcomes contribute to nearly one in three Native people's death before the age of 45 (Vernon, 2002).

Despite chronic and contemporary challenges, commitment to peoplehood, a spirit of resilience, and a strong sense of identity are evident. American Indian people have been overlooked for their inestimable contributions to the Western world.

> In various parts of the Americas, Indians invented items as varied as the hammock, snowshoes, the bulb syringe, kayaks, and the process of using acid to etch designs onto shell. Indians invented the blowgun, developed animal and bird decoys for use in hunting, wove cloth from feathers, made rubber boots, and invented various musical instruments. (Hoxie, 1996, p. 270)

Gunn Allen (1994) reminds us of the irrefutable influence of American Indian and Alaskan Native people. Elaborate systems of thought and governments based on egalitarianism, service, pacifism, and freedom characterized many tribal societies prior to the presence of patriarchy. Portman and Herring (2001) stated:

> Native American Indian women were integral to the economic and social survival of their nations and tribes. They also held positions of political importance. Native American Indians provided guidance and influenced governance decisions and served as leaders and advisers in many Native American Indian tribes and nations. (p. 187)

Among Native American Indians, a leader's influence was based on personal qualities. Authority within a group was derived from the ability to make useful suggestions and a knowledge of traditional ways and tribal love (Waldman, 2000).

CASE STUDY
A Wounded Spirit

Jerry is a married 55-year-old Hopi American Indian Vietnam veteran. He has two adult children and lives on a large reservation in Arizona with his wife, his mother, and his 7-year-old granddaughter. Jerry has a history of alcohol abuse and is currently in recovery. His drinking started soon after his patrols in Vietnam began. During that time as a squad leader involved in heavy combat, Jerry experienced physical injury and witnessed the death and injury of men in his squadron. For a few years, Jerry has been participating in a Veterans Affairs (VA) counseling program following his post-traumatic stress disorder (PTSD) diagnosis. His symptoms are classic and include nightmares, irritability, difficulty concentrating, exaggerated startle response, restricted range of affect, and feelings of detachment or estrangement from others. Jerry also has been diagnosed with Type II diabetes. On the reservation, Jerry is considered a leader and has been identified as a warrior. Tribal leaders refer to his PTSD as a "wounded spirit" and "heartbreak syndrome." They recognize that Jerry's combat experiences were disruptive to his spiritual, physical, emotional, and social balance. The assistance from the VA that Jerry received in the recovery group with other American Indian men contributed to his sobriety. As a Hopi Indian, Jerry's tribe is very important to him. Horse (2001) maintains that "one's tribal affiliation is usually the first criterion of Indian identity" (pp. 92–93). Most Native adults whose ancestry is both Native and non-Native retain their traditional values but also seek to live in the dominant culture (Garrett & Herring, 2001). Jerry is involved with the Native American Church (NAC). The church has helped Jerry to cultivate peace and prayer in his life. With the support of his family and tribal members, Jerry is ready to participate in the Hopi tribe's major ceremony intended to purify warriors. Donald, Jerry's counselor, is a second-year counseling psychology intern at the VA center.

QUESTIONS

1. What are Donald's value orientations?
2. What are Jerry's value orientations?
3. How do Donald's therapeutic intentions complement Jerry's culture?

DISCUSSION AND INTEGRATION
The Client, Jerry

Jerry's symptoms are characteristic of someone with PTSD. In fact, research conducted by the American Indian Vietnam Veterans Project (AIVVP) suggests that Northern Plains and Southwestern Vietnam veterans had higher PTSD and alcohol abuse rates than did their White, Black, and Japanese counterparts (U.S. Department of Health and Human Services, 2001). Jerry's family situation also has to be considered. In American Indian families, the dependency index is higher. This particular index compares the proportion of people in a home between ages 16 and 64 to those under 16 combined with those 65 and older. It is understood that the 16–64 group will contribute economically to a household in ways that dependent children and elders will not (U.S. Department of Health and Human Services, 2001).

Although there are many alcoholism treatment programs that have special programs for Native Americans, Thomason (2000) maintains that there are no empirical, research-based findings on the efficacy of various treatments for alcohol problems in Native Americans. The term *nativized treatments* refers to standard treatments that have been adapted to be more culturally appropriate for Native populations. These nativized treatments would include, for example, Native American cultural values and traditional healing techniques and ceremonies.

Implications for Counselors

Donald, Jerry's counselor, has been assisting his supervisor, a licensced psychologist, with support groups for Vietnam vets. Donald is 27, single, and biracial. His mother is Filipino and his father is Black. Although old enough to be Donald's "old man," Jerry feels comfortable talking with Donald. He appreciates Donald's pacing—his tendency to not interrupt Jerry's long silences and his understanding of tribal traditions. The last intern tended to talk too much, interrupted often, and seemed uncomfortable with Jerry's pauses and silences.

According to Garrett and Pichette (2000), there are verbal and nonverbal communication style differences between contemporary mainstream American cultural values and those of traditional Native people. More specifically, immediate responses, frequent interruption, and emphasis placed on verbal skills are characteristic of dominant U.S. cultural styles, whereas delayed responses, less frequent interjection, and emphasis placed on nonverbal skills characterize Native cultural traditions. Donald's effectiveness is also related to his respect for the tribal elders' wisdom in treating Jerry's PTSD in addition to some of the traditional Western modes of healing, such as psychopharmacology and medication, that are used to treat Jerry's diabetes. Donald understands that many Native Americans view wellness not only in terms of the body but also the spirit and the mind. According to Dana (1993), "This harmony entails a holistic sensing of the state of continuous fusion among the elements of self with all life, including the creator" (p. 84). In addition, Donald sees Jerry at the Vet center but also comes to his home, and in many cases, their sessions are not limited to the 50-minute hour. Donald's ability to use humor appropriately is in line with Jerry's culture of not taking himself too seriously (Garrett & Herring, 2001).

As part of his assessment and treatment of Jerry, Donald needs to consider Jerry's level of acculturation, his life on the reservation, and the fact that Jerry honors both tribal (the presence of the medicine man and traditional ceremonies) and some mainstream customs (the Native American Church, which has been influenced by Christianity). A comprehensive program may be the best approach to treating Native clients with alcohol abuse issues. Such a program is descriptive of Donald's approach because it includes medical care, self-help groups, and purification ceremonies (Thomason, 2000). What helps Donald is his awareness that he is an outsider, and as such he seeks to develop trust with Jerry and work in conjunction with local and tribal resources (Dana, 2000). Finally, Donald needs to be prepared to deal with the extent of Jerry's pain and sadness around generations of loss, transgression, and trauma (Olson, 2003).

SUMMARY

This chapter provided a history of Native American and Alaskan Native people. Representation in the United States, demographic information, history, and common cultural values among American Indian/Alaskan Natives were provided. A summary of these values can be found in Figure 4.1. A case study was provided for purposes of application of material and relevance to counseling.

FIGURE 4.1
Common Cultural Values Among Native Americans and Alaskan Native People

Spirituality (Great Spirit)

Nature (Mother Earth)

The Sacred

Ritual

Tradition

Balance

Explanation of natural phenomena according to the spiritual realm

Noninterference

Cooperation

Sharing

Extended and present time orientation

Hozhq (An expression of happiness, harmonious relationships, the beauty of the land)

Tiospaye (Shared responsibility, extended family, reciprocity)

Oral Traditions

The Extended Family (The Tribe)

Selflessness

Deference to and respect for elders

Storytelling
Speak softly at a slower rate

Time is always with us

REFERENCES

Ballentine, B., & Ballentine, I. (1993). *The Native Americans: An illustrated history*. Atlanta, GA: Turner.

Berry, J. W., & Kim, U. (1988). Acculturation and mental health. In P. R. Dasen, J. W. Berry, & N. Sartorius (Eds.), *Health and cross-cultural psychology: Toward applications* (pp. 207–236). Newbury Park, CA: Sage.

Berry, J. W., & Sam, D. L. (1997). Acculturation and adaptation. In J. Berry, M. Segall, & C. Kagitcibasi (Eds.), *Cross-cultural psychology* (Vol. 3, pp. 291–326). Boston: Allyn & Bacon.

Brown, D. (1981). *Bury my heart at Wounded Knee*. New York: Henry Holt & Company.

Byrd, W. M., Clayton, L. A. (2003). Racial and ethnic disparities in healthcare: A background and history. In Institute of Medicine (Ed.), *Unequal Treatment: Confronting Racial and Ethnic Disparities in Health Care*. Washington, DC: The National Academies Press.

Cameron, S. C., & turtle-song, i. (2003). Native American mental health: An examination of resilience in the face of overwhelming odds. In F. Harper and J. McFadden (Eds.), *Culture and Counseling: New Approaches*. Boston: Allyn & Bacon.

Dana, R. H. (1993). *Multicultural assessment perspectives for professional psychology*. Boston: Allyn & Bacon.

Dana, R. H. (2000). The cultural self as locus for assessment and intervention with American Indians/Alaska Natives. *Journal of Multicultural Counseling and Development, 28,* 66–81.

Garrett, J. T., & Garrett, M. W. (1994). The path of good medicine: Understanding and counseling Native American Indians. *Journal of Multicultural Counseling and Development, 22,* 134–144.

Garrett, J. T., & Garrett, M. W. (1996). *Medicine of the Cherokee: The way of right relationship.* Sante Fe, NM: Bear.

Garrett, M. (1998). *Walking on the wind: Cherokee teachings for harmony and balance.* Santa Fe, NM: Bear.

Garrett, J. T., & Pichette, E. C. (2000). Red as an apple: Native American acculturation and counseling with or without reservation. *Journal of Counseling and Development, 78,* 3–13.

Garrett, J. T., & Herring, R. D. (2001). Honoring the power of relation: Counseling Native adults. *Journal of Humanistic Counseling, Education, and Development, 40,* 139–160.

Gunn Allen, P. (1994). Who is your mother? Red roots of White feminism. In R. Takaki (Ed.), *From different shores: Perspectives on race and ethnicity in America* (2nd ed., pp. 192–198). New York: Oxford University Press.

Heinrich, R. K., Corbine, J. L., & Thomas, K. R. (1990). Counseling Native Americans. *Journal of Counseling and Development, 69,* 128–133.

Herring, R. D. (1992). Understanding Native American values: Process and content concerns for counselors. *Counseling and Values, 34,* 134–137.

Hifler, J. S. (1992). *A Cherokee feast of days: Daily meditations.* Tulsa, OK: Council Oak Books.

Horse, P. G. (2001). Reflections on American Indian identity. In C. Wijeyesinghe and B. Jackson III (Eds.), *New perspectives on racial identity development: A theoretical and practical anthology* (pp. 91–197). New York University Press.

Hoxie, F. E. (Ed.). (1996). *Encyclopedia of North American Indians: Native American history, culture, and life from paleo-Indians to the present.* Boston: Houghton Mifflin.

Institute of Medicine (Ed.) (2003). *Unequal Treatment: Confronting Racial and Ethnic Disparities in Health Care.* Washington, DC: The National Academies Press.

Jackson, A. (1908). Second annual message. In J. D. Richardson (Ed.), *A compilation of the messages and papers of the presidents 1789–1902,* Volume II. Retrieved January 10, 2003 from http://www.pbs.org/wgbh/aia/part4/4h3437t.html

Joe, J. R. (2003). The rationing of healthcare and health disparity for the American Indians/Alaskan Natives. In Institute of Medicine (Ed.), *Unequal Treatment: Confronting Racial and Ethnic Disparities in Health Care.* Washington, DC: The National Academies Press.

Lesiak, C., & Jones, M. (1991). In the White man's image (The American Experience Series), Public Broadcasting Source.

Olson, M. J. (2003). Counselor understanding of Native American spiritual loss. *Counseling and Values, 47,* 109–117.

Peregoy, J. J. (1993). Transcultural counseling with American Indians and Alaskan Natives: Contemporary issues for consideration. In J. McFadden (Ed.), *Transcultural counseling: Bilateral and international perspectives* (pp. 163–191). Alexandria, VA: American Counseling Association.

Portman, T. A. A., & Herring, R. D. (2001). Debunking the Pocahontas paradox: The need for a humanistic perspective. *Journal of Humanistic Counseling, Education, and Development, 40,* 185–199.

Russell, G. (1994). *A map of American Indian history.* Phoenix, AZ: Thunderbird Enterprises.

Sue, D. (Presenter). (1989). *Cultural identity development* [Video]. Amherst, MA: Microtraining and Multicultural Development.

Thomason, T. C. (2000). Issues in the treatment of Native Americans with alcohol problems. *Journal of Multicultural Counseling and Development, 28,* 243–252.

Trujillo, A. (2000). Psychotherapy with Native Americans: A view into the role of religion and spirituality. In P. S. Richards & A. E. Bergin (Eds.), *Handbook of psychotherapy and religious diversity.* Washington, DC: American Psychological Association.

U.S. Census Bureau (1995). Selected social and economic characteristics for the 25 largest American Indian tribes. Washington, DC: Racial Statistics Branch Population Division.

U.S. Census Bureau (2000). *U.S. Summary 2000.* Washington, DC: U.S. Department of Commerce Economics and Statistics Administration.

U.S. Department of Health and Human Services. (2001). *Mental health: Culture, race, and ethnicity—A supplement to mental health: A report to the Surgeon General.* Rockville, MD: U.S. Department of Health and Human Services, Public Health Service, Office of the Surgeon General.

U.S. Department of the Interior (2002). *Federal Register.* Washington, DC: Bureau of Indian Affairs.

Vernon, I. (2002). *Killing us quietly: Native Americans and HIV/AIDS.* Lincoln, NE: Bison Books.

Waldman, C. (2000). Atlas of the North American Indian. New York: Checkmark Books.

Chapter 5

Latinos

Ahora Mismo La Mañana

Yo soy la historia y la familia.

Yo soy tambien los muertos y los ninos no
nacidos.

Me gusta tambien el mañana porque hoy
quiero bailar y soy feliz amando.

Right Now Tomorrow

I am history and I am family.

I am also the dead and the unborn
children.

I am pleased with tomorrow because
right now I want to dance and I am
happy to love.

Tracy Robinson, 2004

This chapter profiles Latinos and includes a brief look at history, cultural values, and demographic trends. A case study is provided for the integration of material in a therapeutic context.

THE SPANISH, INDIANS, ASIANS, AND AFRICANS

According to Novas (1994), the racial diversity among Latinos is very old and connected to political movements and to war. *Hispanic* comes from España, Spain, the country from which the conquistadors hail. The Spanish encountered various Native people throughout millenia and across the various lands: the Arawak, Mayas, Aztecs, and Incas. African people who were brought involuntarily to the Caribbean and to North and South America as slaves intermarried and intermixed with the Spanish. In the Phillipines, the Spanish encountered Asian people and made their claim to the land in 1522; thus Filipinos are categorized as Asian but have Spanish ancestry. Also in 1522, the Spanish infiltrated Central America, including Nicaragua, Honduras, El Salvador, and Guatemala. These countries were conquered 2 decades later. During the colonial period when Spain ruled these countries, a Spanish elite ruled. Others were considered of a lower class. Class divisions were connected to skin color. Unions between the Spanish and the indigenous Indian people resulted in mestizos. Mestizos were not regarded as equals to the Spaniards but emerged as a higher class than pure Indians. Once African slaves arrived, new class and color configurations emerged. Today, non-White Latinos still experience discrimination that is politically, socially, and racially motivated (Hernandez, 1996). In addition to European, Indian, and African ancestries, some Latinos claim an Asian heritage (Santiago-Rivera, Arredondo, & Gallardo-Cooper, 2002). Latinos can be of any race and represent a range of phenotypical characteristics.

DEMOGRAPHY

Novas (1994) clarified that for many Latinos, " 'Hispanic' is merely a bureaucratic government census term." The term Latino or Latina, depending on gender, is widely used and refers to persons with Spanish ancestry. Many Latinos prefer to be called by their country of orgin.

Representing 12.5% of the U.S. population or 32.8 million people as of the 2000 Census (U.S. Census Bureau, 2001b), Latinos have exceeded the number of African Americans and now represent the largest group of color. High rates of immigration and high fertility rates account for this increase. For instance, among the 31.1 million people from the 2000 Census reporting to be foreign born, 51.7% are from Latin America (U.S. Census Bureau, 2000). One in five births in the United States was to Latinas, and the fertility rate for Latinas in 2000 was 47% higher than the overall average. In comparison to native-born Latinas, foreign-born Latinas have a higher fertility rate (U.S. Census Bureau, 2001b).

Whereas the average age of non-Latinos in the United States is 38.6, the average age among Latinos is roughly 25 years (U.S. Census Bureau, 2001a). The largest 5-year age group among Latinos is children under the age of 5. Among non-Latinos, the largest 5-year age group is 40–44 year olds. Latinos have had the lowest proportion of elderly in each census. High fertility rates and immigration have given rise to the low proportion of elderly Latinos.

The Western world's Latinos are *la raza,* which means, "the race" or "the people." Places of origin among Latinos are diverse and varied: Puerto Ricans (*Puertorriquenos*), Cubans (*Cubanos*), Central Americans and South Americans, Latin Americans (which include Dominicans [*Dominicanos*]), and Mexican Americans (*Mejicanos*).

Central America includes Belize, Costa Rica, El Salvador, Guatemala, Honduras, Nicaragua, and Panama. The countries of South America include Argentina, Bolivia, Brazil, Chile, Paraguay, Peru, and Uruguay. Columbia and Venezuela represent the northern part of South America. Brazil is another country in South America; however, Brazilians speak Portuguese and are of Portuguese, not Spanish, descent. Millions of Latinos from countries such as Argentina and Costa Rica are not of Spanish or Indian descent, but rather descend from European or Antillean nations (Beals & Beals, 1993). Some British left England during the 18th century and other Europeans went to Latin America to escape Nazi oppression (Santiago-Rivera, et al., 2002).

Latinos in the United States are united by the Spanish mother tongue, yet there are language differences. Beals and Beals (1993) stated that the majority of Spain's citizens speak Castellano, whereas the majority of Chicanos (Mexicans) speak Pocho. According to Carballo-Dieguez (1989), many Latinos are fluent in both Spanish and English, others know very little English, others have limited knowledge of Spanish, and others speak "Spanglish," a mixture of both languages.

Another unifying force or common theme for the country's Latinos is that the 20th century witnessed the mass migration of Latinos to the United States. Clearly, their points and periods of entry have differed from legal to illegal, from post-Castro for Cubans, to citizenship status issues for Puerto Ricans, to the illegal and extralegal status of Mexicans who die daily en route to America. Clearly, this country has been enhanced, enriched, and truly transformed as a function of the presence of Latino people (Sanchez, 2002).

The diversity among Latinos is tremendous. Despite this diversity, Latinos are descendents of the oppressed and the oppressor with a history marked by social oppression, conquest, liberation, and struggle (Garcia-Preto, 1996). Among the diverse group of Latinos, differences exist across geography, country of origin, race, class, traditions, acculturation, and the time and sociopolitical circumstances in which persons entered the United States (Beals & Beals, 1993; Nicolau & Santiestevan, 1990). Stavans (1995) said, "We Latinos have an abundance of histories, linked to a common root but with decisively different traditions. At each and every moment, these ancestral histories determine who we are and what we think" (p. 20).

Mexican Americans comprise 66% of Latinos. Mexico has been and continues to represent a country with one of the highest immigration rates to the United States. Central and South Americans represent 14.5% of Latinos; Puertorriquenos represent

9%; Cubans, 4%; and other countries, 6.4% (U.S. Census Bureau, 2001a). Mexicans are more likely to live in the West at 57% and in the South at 33%. Puerto Ricans are highly concentrated in the Northeast (64%), and Cubans are most likely to live in the South (80%). Central and South Americans are concentrated in the Northeast (32%), the South, (35%), and the West (28%) (U.S. Census Bureau, 2001a).

Although Latinos are spread throughout the entire United States, California is home to nearly 11 million Latinos. Texas is next with 6.7 million. New York is third with 2.8 million Latinos. Florida ranks fourth with 2.6 million Latinos, and Illinois is fifth with 1.5 million. Although there are less than 800,000 Latinos living in New Mexico, they comprise 42% of the state's population (U.S. Department of Health and Human Services, 2001).

SOCIAL, PSYCHOLOGICAL, AND PHYSICAL HEALTH ISSUES

As for educational attainment among Latinos, there are variations among ethnic groups across the educational pipeline. More than one quarter or 27% of Latinos have less than a ninth grade education compared to 4% of non-Hispanic Whites. The high school graduation rate is 57% compared to 88.4% among non-Hispanic Whites. Cubans and other Latinos are most likely to have graduated from high school, at 73% and 72%, respectively. Among Mexicans, 51% have graduated from high school, and 64% of Puerto Ricans and Central and South Americans have graduated from high school. The college attainment rate among Latinos is 10.6% compared to 28% of non-Hispanic Whites. Cubans have the highest college attainment rate at 23% compared to 7% for Mexicans (U.S. Census Bureau, 2001a).

In addition to geographic diversity, income varies as well. Latinos are more likely to be unemployed at 6.8%, compared to 3.4% of non-Hispanic Whites. Puerto Ricans have the highest unemployment rate at 8.1% and 5.1% among Central and South Americans, respectively. When employed, Latinos are more likely to work in service occupations at a rate of 19.4% or in operator or labor positions at 22%. Compared to non-Hispanic Whites, their rates in these positions are 11.8% and 11.6%, respectively. Non-Hispanic Whites are more than twice as likely to work in managerial positions at a rate of 33.2%. In 2000, only 14% of Latinos worked in managerial or professional positions, with Mexicans being the least likely of Latinos to work in such positions, at a rate of 11.9% (U.S. Census Bureau, 2001).

Among Latinos, nearly one quarter (23.8%) live in poverty, yet they represent only 12.5% of the total population. Puerto Ricans have the highest poverty rate at 25.8%, and Central and South Americans have the lowest at 16.7%. What these data tell us is that the poverty rate among Latinos is nearly triple that of the non-Hispanic White population, which is 7.7%. High poverty rates contribute to Latinos having the highest (35%) probability of being medically uninsured (Institute of Medicine, 2003). Compared to the White population, Latinos have disproportionately higher rates of diabetes and obesity (Institute of Medicine, 2003). However, despite the high poverty rates among

Latinos, substantial income gains have been made. As of 2000, 23.3% of Latinos have incomes $35,000 or above. Mexicans have the lowest proportion (20.6%), earning $35,000 or more (U.S. Census Bureau, 2001).

MIGRATORY PATTERNS FROM MEXICO

Mexico is currently one of the largest sources of new immigrants to the United States. Mexicans in America represent the largest group of Latinos and number nearly 21 million. Nearly 90% of Mexicans live in Texas, California, New Mexico, Arizona, and Colorado. North Carolina had the largest percentage of growth of Latinos between the 1990 Census and the 2000 Census. A number of push and pull factors influenced the migratory patterns of Mexico's people to the United States. During the early 1900s, there was a need for cheap labor to work in U.S. agriculture. The harsh economic conditions in Mexico, high unemployment along with Mexico's proximity to the United States set the stage for large-scale migration (U.S. Department of Health and Human Services, 2001).

There was a time when the land that the majority of Americans now occupy was once Mexico. In 1821, Mexico won its independence from Spain, but this freedom was truncated. In 1848, the Treaty of Guadalupe Hidalgo was the result of Mexico's defeat in a series of wars a decade earlier. Through this formal agreement between Mexico and the United States, Mexico lost 50% of its territory. The cultural and geographic decimation was enormous. Mexicans who had lived on their own land, where their almas (souls) resided, now became migrant farm workers. Mexicans who had been landowners found themselves working for White men. Once Texas, New Mexico, California, Arizona, Nevada, and half of Colorado officially became United States territory, the Spanish language was ousted, with English becoming the primary and official mode of school instruction.

CULTURAL ORIENTATION AND VALUES

Cultural heritage commonalities are strong. For instance, among most Latinos, cooperation rather than competition is stressed. The extended family and friendship networks are held in high esteem and are the basis of Latino culture (Gloria & Peregoy, 1995) (*see Figure 5.1*). Family members feel a sense of obligation to provide for, and to receive support from, one another both emotionally and materially (Vasquez, 1994). In many Mexican American families, the extended family is strong and includes *compradazgo,* or godparents, and among Puerto Ricans, *compadres,* or special friends, who often act as coparents and receive a high place of honor, affection, and respect in the family (Santiago-Rivera et al., 2002). Gloria and Peregoy (1995) stated that more status is given to a person who honors family than to someone with material possessions.

FIGURE 5.1
Common Cultural
Values Among Latinos

> Personalismo (Intimacy)
>
> Dignidad (Personal honor)
>
> Familism (Faith in friends and family)
>
> Respeto (Respect)
>
> Confianza (The development of trust)
>
> Simpatia (Being a nice, gentle person)
>
> Carino (A demonstration of endearment in verbal and nonverbal communication)
>
> Orgullo (Pride)
>
> Loyalty to Family
>
> Collectivism
>
> Service to others
>
> Education as a means of development

Family structure and personal honor are highly valued. *Dignidad* is linked to both *personalismo* and *respeto*. Personalism is an orientation in which the person is more important than the task. *Respeto* refers to "sensitivity to a person's position and creates a boundary within which conversations should be contained to avoid conflict" (Santiago-Rivera et al., 2002, p. 113). *Dignidad* encourages actions that cultivate pride for people independent of their position and refers to a strong sense of self-worth and personal dignity. A focus is also placed on being in the moment, with emphasis on the present.

Family structures are often formal and hierarchical, in that deference to elders and males is practiced. Although often misunderstood as related to men's sexual prowess and women's objectification, *machismo* is a part of Latino culture that describes stoicism, the need for *dignidad,* or dignity, *respeto,* or respect, and in some instances, dominance within the family (Vasquez, 1994) (see the Storytelling, "Once a Teacher"). Adherence to family roles, such as males outside the home and

STORYTELLING: Once a Teacher

When travelling in Cuba a few years ago, I met a maid at the hotel. I wanted to practice my Spanish. She wanted to practice her English. We spoke in English given that her English was better than my Spanish. She told me that prior to being a maid, she had worked as a teacher in a secondary school. She did this for several years and had received the appropriate training at the university. I asked her what events had transpired in her life for her to work now as a maid. She indicated that as a maid, with access to European and American tourists who use the American dollar, her tips were better than the salary that she received as a teacher. The work was harder, but the tips gave her money for her family. In speaking with other Cubanos during my trip, I heard similar stories in which taxi drivers, wait staff at restaurants, and maids were earning higher salaries than people who had gone to the university. This was sobering to hear but it was real.

females inside, represents another value orientation practiced by some Latino fami-lies (Arredondo, 1992).

In Latino culture, a premium is placed on personal relationships. *Personalismo,* or a desire to be close, to know one another intimately, and to communicate personally rather than impersonally, represents a value orientation common to many Latinos (Arredondo, 1992; Gloria & Peregoy, 1995). *Simpatia* refers to the value of smooth and harmonious interpersonal interactions (Gloria & Peregoy, 1995). Latino familes are more likely to live within family units and, similar to Asian Americans and Pacific Islanders, are least likely to live alone. Children also tend to remain with the family (espe-cially girls) until they marry (U.S. Department of Health and Human Services, 2001).

Demonstrated through loyalty for one's family, cultural pride is significant (Rendon & Robinson, 1994). According to Comas-Diaz (1993), the concept of *respeto* "governs all positive reciprocal interpersonal relationships, dictating the appropriate deferential behavior toward others on the basis of age, socioeconomic position, sex, and authority status" (p. 250).

For most Latinos, the bond to Catholicism is strong. In fact, the concept of *Marianismo* "is based on the Catholic cult of the Virgin Mary, which dictates that when women become mothers they attain the status of Madonnas and, accordingly, are expected to deny themselves in favor of their children and husbands" (Vasquez, 1994, p. 202). Clearly, conflicts can emerge within this cultural value system, particularly for Latinas who may be more acculturated. Overall, the church and faith play a crucial role and shape core beliefs, such as (a) the importance of sacrifice, (b) charitability and service to others, and (c) long suffering, even in the face of adversity (Sue & Sue, 1990). As is consistent with other groups who are more oriented toward collectivism than individualism, there is a holistic connection between the mind and body. *Curanderos,* or spiritual and herbal "folk" healers, who are primarily women, practice an ancient Native American art (Novas, 1994). They hold special status in many Mexican and Mexican American communities and often work in consultation on psychiatric cases with priests and other religious authorities (Arredondo, 1992). Given the rich his-tory of the Aztecs as herbalists, healers, botanists, and medical doctors (Padilla, 1984), it is not surprising that their descendants would have the gift of healing.

Communication styles represent a significant part of the way meanings are expressed and interpreted. Many Latinos tend to speak softly, avoid eye contact when listening to or speaking with persons perceived as having high status, and interject less. Often, the manner of expression is low-key and indirect (Sue & Sue, 1990). For many Latino youths and adults, being a linguistic minority represents a real barrier to education and employment.

Colorism refers to differential and often inequitable treatment because of skin color hue (Robinson & Ward, 1995). As with African American communities, col-orism affects Latino communities. Sue and Sue (1990) indicated that "the more a person resembles an Indian, the more prejudice and discrimination he or she will encounter" (p. 298). A variety of hues—white, black, brown, and red—compose the Latino population. This attests to roots from Africa, Asia, Spain, and other parts of Europe, and a Native American heritage.

CASE STUDY
La Mujer y La Familia

Cecelia Hernandez, a 37-year-old college-educated Dominican client, presents to counseling through the Employee Assistance program at her job with what she calls "career difficulties." Cecelia is a floor manager at a wireless communications company that has recently merged with another conglomerate. She is a single parent and has been divorced from her child's father for 3 years. Cecelia's ex-husband is White and their child is 13. They divorced because of constant conflicts that she admits she should have seen before she ever walked down the aisle. She was hopeful that in marrying someone White she might have a greater chance at a more egalitarian relationship. Cecelia states that her employer is asking her to relocate to Montana from Massachusetts or to take a severance package because her work site is being downsized. Cecelia does not know anyone in Montana—all her family, including her mother, two sisters, and uncle are in Massachusetts. She has lived there since she and her family came to the states when she was a child; her child, Cooper, does not want to move. Cooper repeated the sixth grade this past year because of learning difficulties. He was diagnosed with a reading disorder and also has ADHD (Attention Deficit/Hyperactivity Disorder). Cecelia does not know what else she can do with her skills and training except work for a similar company, and based on her inquiries so far, there is little available in this tight job market. The severance package will only last a few months, and already Cecelia has considerable debt.

Cecelia's counselor, Ben, is 25 years of age. When Ben enters the room he warmly introduces himself by his first name and addresses Cecelia similarly. Cecelia is embarrassed by Ben's actions but does not correct him, although she prefers to be addressed as Ms. Hernandez. Ben's first thought is that he does not have much experience working with African American clients but feels comfortable doing so. As Ben listens to Cecelia discuss her career and financial concerns, he expresses confusion as to why Cecelia does not simply take the job in Montana. The benefits

and salary are tremendous. He tells her, "I know that you will miss your family, but planes fly and trains ride. The real challenge may be not having other Black people to interact with." Cecelia is taken aback by Ben's statement and indicates to him that she is a Latina from the Dominican Republic "and not a Black." Ben apologizes and asks Cecelia to continue. Cecelia explains to Ben that she is very close with her family, has never lived apart from them, and that she is the oldest daughter with family responsibilities. Ben begins to suspect that Cecelia is too close to her family and is reminded of a statement that she had told him as to the explanation her husband gave for leaving their marriage—"You are unable to go to the bathroom without your family's input!" Ben proceeds to encourage Cecelia to consider the consequences of staying in Massachusetts without employment. He also suggests that she take a variety of interest and values inventories that would give her a sense of her strengths. Prior to the end of the session, Cecelia tears up and says, "This is too hard and I feel alone all the time." In addition to her work and family stresses, Cecelia says that she has a constant headache and feels chest pain nearly every day. Her doctor cannot find anything wrong with her. Cecelia worries about Cooper. She does not want him to drop out of school like her younger brother did.

QUESTIONS
1. What are Cecelia's cultural dimensions that may impact her problem presentation?
2. What are Ben's cultural dimensions that may impact his conceptualization of Cecelia's issues?

DISCUSSION AND INTEGRATION
The Client, Cecelia

Cecelia's psychosocial identity and orientation to her problems have been shaped by a constellation of factors. These include her ethnicity, gender, culture, family, geographic region, education, religion, and personality, as well as other dimensions, such as her acculturation level. To see Cecelia holistically, it is imperative that Ben not define Cecelia by only one visible identity construct, such as being Latina. There are other dimensions in Cecelia's life that profoundly shape her and her presenting issues, such as being in transition as a single parent with a male son who is experiencing difficulty in school. The affective dimension of Cecelia's life also needs to be addressed. She is experiencing a great deal of stress and her sadness exists, albeit underneath the surface. Cecelia has the highest level of educational attainment and English language proficiency in her family. Her family relies on her for a variety of issues, including translation, interacting with school personnel for her nieces and nephews, and organizing her mother's finances.

According to Santiago-Rivera et al. (2002), acculturation is a psychosocial stressor. Thus, for first-generation immigrants who are attempting to adjust to a new environment, acquire a new language, and deal with a host of internal and external demands, the stress may be much greater than previously thought, with chronic acculturation stress having enormous psychological implications. According to the U.S. Department of Health and Human Services (2001), "Recent immigrants of all backgrounds, who are adapting to the United States, are likely to experience a different set of stressors than long-term Hispanic residents" (p. 133). Acculturation, according to some epidemeological studies, may even lead to an increase in mental disorders. Thus, the length of time that Cecelia has resided in the United States need not preclude the presence of culture-bound syndromes that could be associated with the stress of acculturation (Gonzalez et al., 1997).

Cecelia's headaches and chest pains could be a function of somatization in which she is expressing her emotional and psychological discomfort through physical sensations within her body. Ben could ascertain from his client what she thinks her physical symptoms mean and how they may be related to some of her concerns about her family and career situation (U.S. Department of Health and Human Services, 2001).

As a woman and a Latina, Cecelia has been socialized to see herself within the context of her relationships with others. Her multiple identities as a woman of color, oldest daughter, single mother, and professional manager can and do conflict. Although it is clear that some women of color receive support from their families and loved ones, balancing multiple roles and conflicting demands produces stress for women (Comas–Diaz & Greene, 1994).

As a mother, Cecelia is worried about her child and she has reason to be. Latino youth are at higher risk for poor mental health outcomes, and they are more likely to drop out of school and to report feelings of depression and anxiety. In addition, Latino youth represent 18% of juvenile offenders in residential placement (U.S. Department of Health and Human Services, 2001). Research suggests biracial children also have a high incidence of academic and behavioral problems, which are often connected to identity conflicts and related challenges (Gibbs, 1989). Cooper is biracial, and Cecelia is concerned that he is becoming too Western in his orientation. Cecelia complains about the way Cooper speaks to her. She often tells him that if she spoke to her mother that way, even now as an adult, she would get slapped. Santiago-Rivera et al. (2002) encourage parents of bicultural children not to impose their culture on the child, particularly adolescents. It is suggested that children will internalize a variety of experiences and beliefs into their own value system that encompasses multiple identities and worldviews.

Implications for Counselors

There are several misses and mistakes that the counselor Ben made during the first counseling session. As a result, the counseling event is unnecessarily hampered by Ben's initial insensitivity to a woman of color and to an older client. There is such informality in Western culture—everyone is on a first-name basis—but some clients of color as well as some White people are put off by a casual air that feels disrespectful. Ben should have asked how the client wanted to be addressed. This is a basic concept when working with clients who are older.

The concept of *falta de respeto* (lack of respect) is considered to be a major cause for breakdown in communication across a number of relationship dyads (Santiago-Rivera et al., 2002). Ben needs to recognize that Cecelia's unilateral decision to pick up and move could be considered harmful to family stability. Cecelia's family is not composed of just herself and her child but of her entire extended family. Cecelia remembers the sacrifices that both her mother and deceased father made to send her to college. Her family, like many Latina families, valued education as a means of development for family and community (Comas-Diaz & Greene, 1994).

The Western view of the nuclear family is limiting for many Latinos and is connected to the cultural tendency to bifurcate and separate the self into discrete categories. Like other Latinos, Dominicans have a variety of phenotypes. There were African slaves in the Dominican and many Dominicans, due to their African roots, have dark skin and other Negroid features. Upon first looking at Cecelia, Ben assumed that she was a Black American woman. After listening to her, he did not hear an accent and made a faulty assumption to which Cecelia took offense. A key ingredient to effective counseling is to wait and listen for valuable information that the client and the counseling process can and will reveal. In time, ask appropriate questions. Despite Ben's miss, Cecelia's very strong reaction to being mistaken for a Black American is good clinical information. According to Garcia-Preto (1996), "A source of conflict for many Dominicans has been that even though about 80% of the population is mulatto, a mixture of Black and White races, the government has held an unofficial policy against negritude or descendants of African slaves and an official policy in favor of the island's Spanish roots" (p. 149).

It would also help Ben to know where the Dominican Republic is. It occupies two thirds of the island of Hispaniola. Haiti occupies the other one third on the Western side and was the first colony to be settled by the Spaniards in 1492.

Ben needs to attend to Cecelia's ethnicity and culture while transcending it as well. Ben used dominant cultural orientations in perceiving Cecelia. There is extreme individualism in the West that has unfortunate consequences for Westerners— hedonism and the tendency to see the environment

and relationships as disposable. Many Latino families value close and intimate communication styles in which there is greater emphasis on the group and less on the individual acting as a lone agent. If the clinician is not careful, there can be a misinterpretation of such closeness as enmeshment or dysfunctionality because the self seems so fused or not reflective of mature and independent decision making. Although it is true that in many Latino families the husband is the primary and only breadwinner, with gender roles well prescribed, this is by no means the case in all Latino families (again class, acculturation, and individual differences need to be considered). This traditional scenario is not the case for Cecelia in that she is a single parent and is college educated.

Cecelia's family came to the United States with the same dreams as other immigrants—to have access to economic opportunity and to raise their families in peace. Political instability, unemployment, and devastation of a country's infrastructure compel people in search of a better life to leave their homes. Although their homelands are rich in beauty, culture, and natural resources, they are poor in terms of economic and social development (Suarez-Orozco & Paez, 2002).

In working with Latinos, it is important to consider the client within the broader context of the family. Ben would do well to ask about Cecelia's role in the family and how this role is manifested in her life during the evenings and on the weekends. In other words, after working a full day, Cecelia helps Cooper with his homework and drives down the street to check in on her mother—read her mail, go to the grocery store, and visit with her. Cecelia's aging mother is overweight and has diabetes. Cecelia oversees her mother's insulin intake and talks often with her mother's doctors. According to Santiago-Rivera et al. (2002), a multidimensional ecological comparative model may help Ben to devise a relevant and respectful treatment approach. There are four domains to the model: (a) the impact of migration and cultural change, (b) family organization, (c) the current ecological environment and the family, and (d) the family life cycle or transitions.

How Cecelia has traditionally dealt with stress would also be helpful for Ben to assess.

People across a variety of ethnic groups use alternative forms and sources of health care. Cecelia's family's traditions, proverbs or *dichos*, and reliance on prayers or religion can all be extremely helpful to Ben in helping Cecelia formulate a plan for dealing with her very real stressors.

Diagnosing Cecelia's health condition might be difficult. Oftentimes, the symptoms associated with a particular disorder or level of distress may fall short of meeting all of the diagnostic criteria. This could result in a failure to adequately diagnose a condition, particularly when cultural patterns may impact the manifestation of a disorder (U.S. Department of Health and Human Services, 2001). The areas for clinical focus (V codes) include Acculturation Problem, which although coded on the first Axis and possibly more benign and more accurate, may not allow Ben to be reimubursed by his insurance company.

Ben could help Cecelia deal with her stress through a variety of stress reduction activities, such as relaxation training and deep-breathing exercises. He could also help Cecelia, within a culturally respectful framework, identify what is most important to her and help her learn to delegate responsibility. For example, Cecelia could enlist the support of her siblings with the care of her mother. She could also require Cooper to do laundry and clean the house. If Cecelia does not use stress reduction techniques, she could become immobilized by the stress (Comas-Diaz & Greene, 1994).

SUMMARY

This chapter focused on Latinos. A demographical snapshot was provided and included information about representation in the population by ethnic group, the most populated states where Latinos reside, and educational attainment. Immigration was discussed, as were push and pull factors contributing to immigration. A detailed case study was included and cultural elements were discussed. Conflict among cultural values, gender expectations, and acculturation influences were highlighted.

REFERENCES

Arredondo, P. (1992). *Latina/Latino value orientations: Tape 1. Cultural considerations for working more effectively with Latin Americans.* Amherst, MA: Microtraining and Multicultural Development.

Beals, M. J., & Beals, K. L. (1993). Transcultural counseling and the Hispanic community. In J. McFadden (Ed.), *Transcultural counseling: Bilateral and international perspectives* (pp. 213–238). Alexandria, VA: American Counseling Association.

Carballo-Dieguez, A. (1989). Hispanic culture, gay male culture, and AIDS: Counseling implications. *Journal of Counseling and Development, 68,* 26–30.

Comas-Diaz, L. (1993). Hispanic Latino communities: Psychological implications. In D. Atkinson, G. Morten, & D. W. Sue (Eds.), *Counseling American minorities: A cross-cultural perspective* (pp. 245–263). Madison, WI: Brown and Benchmark.

Comas-Diaz, L., & Greene, B. (1994). Women of color with professional status. In L. Comas-Diaz & B. Greene (Eds.), *Women of color: Integrating ethnic and gender identities in psychotherapy* (pp. 347–388). New York: Guilford Press.

Garcia-Preto, N. (1996). Latino families: An overview. In M. McGoldrick, J. Giordano, & J. Pearce (Eds.), *Ethnicity and family therapy* (pp. 141–154). New York: Guilford Press.

Gibbs, J. T. (1989). Biracial adolescents. In J. T. Gibbs & L. N. Huang and Associates (Eds.), *Children of color: Psychological interventions with minority youth* (pp. 322–350). San Francisco: Jossey-Bass.

Gloria, A. M., & Peregoy, J. J. (1995). Counseling Latino alcohol and other substance users/abusers: Cultural considerations for counselors. *Journal of Substance Abuse Treatment, 13,* 1–8.

Gonzalez, M., Castill-Canez, I., Tarke, H., Soriano, F., Garcia, O., & Velasquez, R. J. (1997). Promoting the culturally sensitive diagnosis of Mexican Americans: Some personal insights. *Journal of Multicultural Counseling and Development, 25,* 156–161.

Hernandez, M. (1996). Central American families. In M. McGoldrick, J. Giordano, & J. Pearce (Eds.), *Ethnicity and family therapy* (pp. 214–224). New York: Guilford Press.

Nicolau, S., & Santiestevan, S. (1990). *The Hispanic almanac.* New York: Hispanic Policy Development Project.

Novas, H. (1994). *Everything you need to know about Latino history.* New York: Penguin.

Padilla, A. M. (1984). Synopsis of the history of Chicano psychology. In J. Martinez & R. Mendoza (Eds.), *Chicano psychology* (pp. 1–19). Orlando, FL: Academic Press.

Rendon, L. I., & Robinson, T. L. (1994). A diverse America: Implications for minority seniors. In W. Hartel, S. Schwartz, S. Blue, & J. Gardner (Eds.), *Ready for the real world: Senior year experience series* (pp. 170–188). Belmont, CA: Wadsworth.

Robinson, T. L., & Ward, J. W. (1995). African American adolescents and skin color. *Journal of Black Psychology, 21,* 256–274.

Santiago-Rivera, A. L., Arredondo, P., & Gallardo-Cooper, M. (2002). *Counseling Latinos and la familia: A practical guide.* Thousand Oaks CA: Sage.

Sanchez, G. J. (2002). "Y tu, que?" (YzK): Latino history in the new millennium. In M. Suarez-Orozco & M. M. Paez (Eds.), *Latinos: Remaking America* (pp. 45–58). Berkeley: University of California Press.

Stavans, I. (1995). *The Hispanic condition: Reflections on culture and identity in America.* New York: Harper Perennial.

Suarez-Orozco, M., & Paez, M. M. (2002). *Latinos: Remaking America.* Berkeley: University of California Press.

Sue, D. W., & Sue, D. (1990). *Counseling the culturally different: Theory and practice.* New York: John Wiley.

U.S. Census Bureau (2000). U.S. Summary: 2000. Census 2000 Profile. Washington, DC: U.S. Department of Commerce.

U.S. Census Bureau (2001a). The Hispanic population in the United States. March 2000. Washington, DC: U.S. Department of Commerce Economics and Statistical Administration.

U.S. Census Bureau (2001b). Labor force participation for mothers with infants declines for first time, Census Bureau reports. U.S. Department of Commerce Economics and Statistical Administration Retrieved from http://www.census.gov/Press-Release/www/2001/cb01-170.html

U.S. Department of Health and Human Services. (2001). *Mental health: Culture, race, and ethnicity—A supplement to mental health: A report to the Surgeon General.* Rockville, MD: U.S. Department of Health and Human Services, Public Health Service, Office of the Surgeon General.

Vasquez, M. J. T. (1994). Latinas. In L. Comas-Dias & B. Greene (Eds.), *Women of color* (pp. 114–138). New York: Guilford Press.

Chapter 6

People of African Descent

Balm in Gilead
Is there no balm in Gilead
to set your people free?
What would you have for us to do
with what we know and see?
How can we sojourn through this world
with these questions on our souls?
Is there no balm in Gilead
to heal and to make whole?

Tracy Robinson, 1991

This chapter is about people of African descent. The majority of Black people in this country are descendents of African slaves. The term *people of African descent* is used to honor and recognize this majority as well as the other Black people throughout the Diaspora who reside in America.

DEMOGRAPHY AND THE DIASPORA

As the second largest group of color in the United States, the 34.6 million people of African descent come from diverse cultures, including Africa, the Caribbean, central Europe, and South America. African Americans are 12.3% of the population (U.S. Census Bureau, 2000b). Nearly 800,000 people in the 2000 Census identified themselves as having two races (U.S. Census Bureau, 2001). Of all African Americans, 6% are foreign born. Most have come from the Caribbean, Dominican Republic, Haiti, and Jamaica. Since 1983, over 100,000 refugees have come to the United States from African nations (U.S. Department of Health and Human Services, 2001).

HISTORY, 500–1500 A.D.

According to social historian Bennett (1982),

> Civilization started in the great river valleys of Africa and Asia, in the Fertile
> Crescent in the Near East and along the narrow ribbon of the Nile in Africa
> . . . Blacks, or people who would be considered Blacks today, were among
> the first people to use tools, paint pictures, plant seeds, and worship gods.
> (p. 5)

The skeletal remains of the earth's earliest human come from East Africa, representing all of our ancestors—we are family in the truest sense of the word!

Between 500 and 1600 A.D., Africa had empires, governments, and systems of trade in regions throughout the continent. The exalted West African empires of Ghana, Mali, and Songhai emerged in the western Sudan and were in existence during that time (Christian, 1995). Each of these three states had a powerful king and was very wealthy, with an abundance of gold, thriving agriculture, manufacturing, and successful international trading efforts. Ghana dominated the Sudan for 3 centuries and reached its peak in the early part of the 11th century. Mali rose in the 13th century, and Songhai was a formidable power in the 15th and 16th centuries. During this time, Timbuktu represented one of the world's greatest cities, with a reputation as the intellectual center of the Songhai empire.

THE SLAVE TRADE

The majority of Blacks in America trace their ancestry to the slave trade. The slave trade operated for 4 centuries. In 1501, for instance, the Spanish government authorized the use of African slaves in the Americas. Portugal was actually the first country to land a cargo of slaves in the Western Hemisphere (Christian, 1995) and remained the dominant slave trader well until the end of the 16th century (Stewart, 1996). In addition to the Portuguese, the Spanish, Dutch, British, and the colonies provided fierce competition for this lucrative industry in which human beings were traded for gold, salt, sugar, wine, and tobacco. Nations that controlled most of the American waters controlled most of the trade. Slaves were shipped to Cuba, Spain, the West Indies, and to the colonies. The first American slave ship bound for Africa was called the Rainbow and sailed from Boston.

During the slave trade throughout Europe, the Americas, and the Carribbean, nearly 12 million people were taken out of Africa, mainly from West and Central Africa. Slave ships brought kidnapped Africans to the Western Hemisphere, which included the colonies, Brazil, and the Caribbean. According to Bennett (1982), most slaves came from an area bordering a 3,000 mile stretch on the West Coast of Africa. They hailed from different tribes, including the Hausas, the Mandingos, the Yorubas, the Efiks, the Krus, the Ashantis, the Dahomeans, the Senegalese, and the Fantins.

It is estimated that as many as 2 million people perished at port, at sea, or upon arrival during the slave trade. The *middle passage* typically refers to the journey from Africa to the Americas, Europe, or the Caribbean. From roughly 1450 to 1600, about 367,000 Africans were removed from Africa, with this number increasing dramatically to over 6 million during the 18th century. A history of resistance and revolt characterize the experience of slaves. In 1526, in the San Miguel settlement which is now known as present day South Carolina, slaves set fire to the settlement and fled to live among the Native Americans. Those slaves who managed to make it safely to the Gracia Real de Santa Teresa de Mose settlement, founded by escaped slaves, were granted their freedom by the King of Spain.

Africans played a role in capturing other Africans for sale to White slave traders. Slavery existed in the African states prior to European enslavement of Africans. This historical reality was used to justify the use of African slaves among Europeans. Although enslavement of any human being is morally reprehensible, there were two important differences between the slavery of Africans by other Africans and the slavery of Africans by Europeans. African slavery was not plantation or mining slavery. It did not strip African people of family linkage nor was it based on racial hatred that reduced people's humanity. African slaves owned by other Africans would sometimes marry, own property, and become a member of the family (Zinn, 2003). The extent of Africans' participation in the selling of other Africans to Europeans depends on which version of history one reads. According to Bennett (1982), there has been an attempt to overemphasize the degree of African involvement. Bennett said, "It is true that some

Africans, corrupted by Europe's insatiable desire for human flesh, sold their country-men. But many Africans, like King Almammy and Captain Tobba, loathed the whole business and forbade their subjects to take part in it" (p. 47). According to Stewart (1996b), "Most of the Africans who became slaves were sold into slavery by other Africans . . . A lucrative trade for European goods, especially weapons, facilitated the selling of slaves to the Europeans" (p. 10). Africans captured by other Africans and sold to White slave traders who sold them to the highest bidder in Virginia became part of the social structure of the colony (Christian 1995).

The year 1619 is designated as the date when the first African settlers reached North America on a Dutch man-of-war ship in Jamestown, Virginia. This group of African indentured servants were not regarded as slaves. In exchange for their passage over, people sold their labor for a period of time. Thousands of Whites used this method as a means of coming to the colonies, and life for them was often similar to that of Black indentured servants. They worked alongside each other doing farming, clearing forests, and cutting tobacco. For these first 40 years, Black settlers moved about with relative ease and had voting rights, and even after surviving indentured servitude, purchased other Blacks. This system began to erode with the arrival of greater numbers of Africans, which made the profits from the slave trade escalate for both the slave trader and slave owner.

These servants were not, however, the first Africans to arrive in North America. Estevanico was the most important African explorer of America and the first for-eigner to discover New Mexico. He was born in Morocco around 1500 and left Spain in 1527 as the slave of Andres Dorantes. These two were members of the expedition of Pánfilo de Narváez, the Spanish governor of Florida. Estevanico became the first foreign explorer of the southwestern United States and explored the area that became Arizona and New Mexico (Christian, 1995; Stewart, 1996). In 1539, Estevanico was murdered by Zuni Indians who were protecting their land.

During the latter part of the 1700s, southeast Native American tribes, such as the Choctaws, Seminoles, and Creeks, were slave owners, with the Cherokees having the largest number of slaves. Prior to Native people's removal to Indian Territory, Native Americans used Black slaves on their plantations in both Georgia and Tennessee.

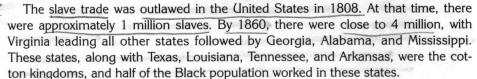

The slave trade was outlawed in the United States in 1808. At that time, there were approximately 1 million slaves. By 1860, there were close to 4 million, with Virginia leading all other states followed by Georgia, Alabama, and Mississippi. These states, along with Texas, Louisiana, Tennessee, and Arkansas, were the cotton kingdoms, and half of the Black population worked in these states.

RESISTANCE TO SLAVERY

The resistance to slavery was multifaceted; it was political, literary, and appeared on the podium as preachers spoke against this abomination to humankind. Many slaves ran away often seeking to be reunited with loved ones risking life and limb to escape their enslavement. Frances E. W. Harper, a Black poet, was born to free Blacks in Maryland. Some thought her to be a man or a White person with a black painted face given how intelligent and articulate she was (talk about discourses!); however, she protested the unequal treatment of people on the basis of gender and race. Her poem "The Slave Auction" appeared in her 1854 *Poems of Miscellaneous Subjects:*

> The sale began—young girls were there,
> Defenseless in their wretchedness,
> Whole stifled sobs of deep despair
> Revealed their anguish and distress.
>
> And mothers stood with streaming eyes,
> And saw their dearest children sold;
> Unheeded rose their bitter cries,
> While tyrants bartered them for gold.

Slavery was a barbaric institution supported by the government and often sanctioned by the church. The impact on and implications for Black people's mental health, self-image, psyches, and earning potential can never be truly assessed.

The ways in which Black people coped or resisted took on a number of different forms, with religion and spirituality being critical. "In the slave quarters, African Americans organized their own 'invisible institution.' Through signals, passwords, and messages not discernible to Whites, they called believers to 'hush harbors' where they freely mixed African rhythms, singing, and beliefs with evangelical Christianity" (Maffly-Kipp, 2000, p. 2). Negro spirituals had double meanings of salvation and liberation. It was in this context that spirituals were created and remain to this day.

Although the slave trade had been outlawed, slavery itself continued in the South until Lincoln, out of military necessity, signed the Emancipation Proclamation in 1863. The purpose of this document was to deplete the South of its slave labor power. Lincoln had no authority to free slaves in the loyal states, only in the states of rebellion. In 1865, on June 19th, a day better known as "Juneteenth," slavery was outlawed in Texas. Later that year, on December 18, slavery became illegal with the passage of the 13th Amendment to the U.S. Constitution.

The only way for many Blacks to gain access to opportunity was to leave the South. Baltimore was considered a border city and represented a popular place for newly freed slaves to start a new life, after looking from town to town for displaced loved ones. In the same year that the 13th Amendment was ratified, the Ku Klux Klan was organized in Pulaski, Tennessee. Its purpose was to undermine racial equality through acts of terrorism, which often went unpunished, and in some municipalities, were sanctioned by political officers who were themselves Klan members.

The 14th Amendment in 1868 extended citizenship to African Americans, whereas the 15th Amendment was put in place to assure the right to vote, but poll taxes, grandfather clauses, and literacy tests kept Blacks from voting. *De jure* (by law) *segregation* replaced slavery—also known as Jim Crow. This inferior status of Blacks was sanctioned by law and required that Blacks ride at the back of the bus, sit in different sections of movie theaters and sports stadiums, drink at separate water faucets, live in separate neighborhoods, and eat at separate restaurants.

Many Blacks sharecropped after passage of the 13th Amendment. Sharecroppers worked the landowner's land for a share of the profit once the crop went to market. Landowners kept the accounts. Keeping landowners honest was very difficult for sharecroppers who had little power or literacy.

To this day, the majority of Blacks in the United States continue to reside in the South. This percentage declined during the 20th century. World War I created a huge demand for unskilled labor in the urban North; recruiters went to the South to bring Black workers to northern cities such as Pittsburgh, Chicago, Detroit, and Indianapolis. Between 1916 and 1919, 500,000 African Americans migrated north (Stewart, 1996). After World War II, nearly 5 million Blacks went north between 1940 and 1960.

DEMOGRAPHIC TRENDS

Nearly 55% of Blacks live in the South, with 19% residing in the Midwest, 17.6% living in the Northeast, and only 9% living in the West (U.S. Census Bureau, 2000b) Washington, DC, has the highest percentage of Blacks, followed by Mississippi, Louisiana, South Carolina, Georgia, Maryland, Alabama, North Carolina, Virginia, and Delaware.

The median age of African Americans is 29.8 years. Persons between the ages of 35 and 44 represent the largest single age category at 16%. Children under the age of 5 compose 8.5% of the population, and persons 75 to 84 years of age are 2.4% of the population (U.S. Census Bureau, 2000b).

Between the race and Hispanic-origin groups, Blacks have the lowest sex ratio, with Black females outnumbering Black males throughout every decade. There have been increases in the high school graduation level, now at 78.5%. This compares to 84.1% for the general population (U.S. Census Bureau, 2000b). Just under 12% (11.4) have completed a bachelor's degree (U.S. Census Bureau, 2000b). Compared to the population at large, Blacks have higher rates of marital divorce, separation, and never-married rates. In 2000, 43.5% of Blacks ages 15 and older had never been married, compared with 28.1% of the general population. Less than one third (32.5%) of Blacks are married with their spouses present compared to 53% for the U.S. population. Rates of separation are double those in the general population: 5.1% among Blacks compared to 2.1% for the total (U.S. Census Bureau, 2000b).

SOCIAL, PSYCHOLOGICAL, AND PHYSICAL HEALTH ISSUES

To understand demographic data and the experience of Blacks living in America, sociopolitical factors need to be considered. For instance, in 2001 the poverty rate for African Americans was 22.9% (U.S. Census Bureau, 2002), compared with 11.6% for the nation at large. Black people are more likely to live in severe poverty in comparison to Whites. Blacks tend to have less money saved, lower rates of home ownership, and few investments (U.S. Department of Health and Human Services, 2001). Black children are more likely to live in female-headed households, which are disproportionately among the poor. There is, however, another side to Black economic conditions. Over 30% of Blacks in America have incomes between $35,000 and $75,000, and nearly 32% live in the suburbs (U.S. Department of Health and Human Services, 2001). Although there is a discernible middle class among African Americans, regardless of income, Black people in America tend to have fewer resources (e.g., public services, access to health care), tend to be segregated in neighborhoods and have higher levels of health risks (IOM, 2003).

Compared to the general population, Black people are more likely to be exposed to violence, which of course has implications for mental illness symptoms such as depression and post-traumatic stress disorder (PTSD). Nearly 25% of Blacks do not have health insurance despite the fact that over 8 in 10 African Americans are in working families (IOM, 2003). Access to mental health care is limited. Among Blacks who have health insurance, treatment-seeking behavior for mental health services does not automatically increase. Some of this behavior is related to the stigmatizing attitudes that exist regarding mental health care. One study found that the number of Blacks who feared mental health treatment was 2.5 times greater than the proportion of Whites (U.S. Department of Health and Human Services, 2001). Other research found that Blacks were less likely than Whites to be properly diagnosed when suffering from affective disorders, such as depression. The tendency of clinicians, both Black and White, was to diagnose Blacks with schizophrenia (Good et al., 2003).

African American adult men are less than 6% of the U.S. population, yet in jails and state or federal prisons they represent 48% of the incarcerated population (U.S. Census Bureau, 2000a). According to the Washington-based research and advocacy group Justice Policy Institute (JPI), African American men are more likely to go to jail than go to college. From 1980 to 2000, the number of African American men in jail or prison grew three times as fast as the number in colleges and universities. The JPI report compared 2 decades of data from the Bureau of Justice Statistics and the National Center for Education Statistics and found that although states had plenty to spend on prisons, they had much less to devote to education (Schulte, 2002). It should be noted that in 2000, 32% of Black men were not in the civilian labor force compared to 25.8% of men in the general population (U.S. Census Bureau, 2000b).

Health outcomes are related to lifestyle choices, such as smoking and nutrition. Nonetheless, Blacks have a myriad of health problems that should not be looked at separate from the experiences of poverty, substandard housing, underemployment, unemployment, and chronic racial discrimination. Blacks have diabetes at a rate more than three times that of Whites; heart disease is 40% higher than that of Whites; prostate cancer is more than double that of Whites; HIV/AIDS is more than seven times that of Whites; and infant mortality is twice that of Whites (U.S. Department of Health and Human Services, 2001).

CULTURAL ORIENTATION AND VALUES

Despite struggle and hardship, strengths of persistence, forgiveness, resistance, and resilience are evident (Exum & Moore, 1993). According to Nobles (1972), African Americans' sense of self and cultural traditions have been derived from several cultural and philosophical premises shared with West African tribes. Myers (1991) states:

> Afrocentricity refers to a worldview that believes reality is both spiritual and material at once . . . with highest value on positive interpersonal relationships between men/women; self knowledge is assumed to be the basis of all knowledge, and one knows through symbolic imagery and rhythm. (p. 19)

Within Africentric thought, the self is extended in unity with others and emphasis is on the collective. An African proverb, "I am because we are and since we are, therefore I am," summarizes the saliency of the collective. Among some African Americans, *consubstantiation,* or the sense that everything within the universe is connected as a part of a whole, is a way of seeing the world (Parham, 1992). Myers (1991) stated that, in the Africentric paradigm, spirit and matter are one and is a representation of one spirit manifesting good.

Common values that many Blacks in America share include the extended family and outside blood relatives. Collateral relations are valued over highly individualistic styles (Sue & Sue, 1990). Education as a means of self-help and a strong work ethic are often taught to children from a very early age. Communication patterns are not limited to verbal dialogue or standard English—the dialect has survived rather well as has a sense of humor in order to deal with injustice and things ludicrous (see the Storytelling "Everybody's Raconteur!"). Most Black people depend on nonverbal modes of communication patterns—how something is said rather than what is actually verbally spoken. Body movement, postures, gestures, and facial expressions represent dominant patterns of communication within the African American community. These tend not to be strictly linear as in Western society (Exum & Moore, 1993). Another value often manifested in the Black community is giving people status as a function of age and position. A present time orientation is seen at church, parties, and other events. This, of course varies by individual differences and acculturation levels. Value is also placed on the use of proverbs (e.g., "Every goodbye ain't gone") and spiritual wisdom ("God don't make no mistakes") to not only cope but to resist well and to thrive (see *Figure 6.1*).

STORYTELLING: Everybody's Raconteur!

The following story was told by Gloria Melton in Drylongso (Gwaltney, 1980).

These three astronauts were in this ship which was overloaded. There was a black one, a Jew, and an Italian. So, the command told them that they would have to throw out as much as they could. Well, they did that and it still wasn't enough, so the command told them they had to answer a question and the one who couldn't get his question was going to have to be put out to lighten the load enough. So the command asked the Italian, "Who discovered America and when?" So the Italian said, "Christopher Columbus in 1492." The command said, "Good, you can stay." Then they asked the Jew, "What was the name of a famous ship that got in a little trouble?" So he said, "That would be the Titanic, sir. They had 18 thousand people aboard. Sixteen thousand people were saved and 2 thousand people drowned." So they said, "Good, you can stay too!" Then they looked at the colored fellow and said, "Give me the first and last names of the 2 thousand people who were drowned."

This story speaks to the sociopolitical awareness that most Black people have about racial inequity. A keen ability to tell a story while using humor is evident.

There is great diversity among people of African descent in country of origin, language, ethnicity, class, education, acculturation level, point of entry into America, and religious orientation. Black people seem to be united by strong and rich spiritual traditions that infuse educational systems, cultural values, kinship networks, and political revolutions. Cultivating one's spirit and maintaining a strong connection with the church represent a foundation for the experience of most Blacks in America. Black

FIGURE 6.1
Common Cultural Values Among
People of African Descent

Oral traditions
Reliance on proverbial wisdom
Spirituality
Firm child rearing practices
Education as a means of self-help
Collateral interpersonal relations
Formal communication styles with elders and authority figures
Nonverbal modes of communication
Extended family based on blood and strong ties
Unity
Self-determination
Collective work and responsibility
Cooperative economics
Purpose
Creativity and faith
Fluid time orientation

STORYTELLING: "I understand"

I was talking with my grandmother one night while I was in graduate school in Massachusetts. I was bemoaning the cold weather, the cold people, the lack of money, and my desire to finish my masters but begin my doctorate at another graduate school. My grandmother listened attentively. She then asked me, "Is Harvard giving you any money?" I said "yes, ma'm." She asked me if the school where I wanted to attend was giving me any money. I said, "no." She said, "then you stay at Harvard." I responded, "but Grandma, you don't understand, I don't want to stay here." She said, "oh yes I do understand. Sometimes you have to do what you don't want to do until you can do better. Dry your eyes and return to your books." And that I did. My grandmother had a fourth-grade education. She had to drop out of school to pick cotton in Woodbury, Georgia. My grandmother was one of the most intelligent people I have ever known; I am so grateful to be her granddaughter.

people may not go to church or even have a church home, but they may still "pray to the Lord" (Boyd-Franklin, 2003, p. 270) when confronted with difficult times, such as illness, death, loss, and bereavement. (See the Storytelling "I understand"). Historically, the Black church has been a focal point in the African American community and a place where advocacy and social and political change have taken hold. The Black church played a prominent role in the civil rights movement, voter registration, fundraising for college students, health promotion, and personal and spiritual development. Many musicians and other celebrities had their talents recognized and nurtured by participating in the choir, youth programs, and leadership forums. A variety of religions and spiritual expressions exist among African Americans, with growing numbers counted as Muslims, Buddhists and agnostic; however, the majority of Blacks in American regard themselves as Christians.

Worldview refers to the way people make meaning. Adapted from Hilliard's work, Exum and Moore (1993) summarized elements of African American worldview. These include emphasis on the whole as opposed to the parts; preference for approximations over accuracy; focus on people rather than things; and acceptance and integration with the environment. In addition to these values is a respect for nature and emphasis on groupness.

The *Nguzo Saba,* or classical African values, also provide insight into African American values (Karenga, 1980) and are discussed in greater detail in Chapter 15. The first and third principles are *Umoja* and *Ujima* and refer to unity and collective work and responsibility. These principles endorse solidarity, harmony, cooperation, and connection with others toward a common destiny. The second principle, *Kujichagalia,* means self-determination and naming for the self who the self will be, despite others' definitions. *Ujaama,* the fourth principle, refers to cooperative economics, in which resources are shared for the good of all. Within an Africentric framework, the *I* is not separate from the *We. Nia,* the fifth principle, is purpose that benefits not only the self but also the collective, for which one has responsibility. The sixth principle is *Kuumba,* or creativity. Creativity is inextricably linked to imagination, ingenuity, and leaving the world a better place than it was when you first arrived. *Imani,* or faith, is the last principle and encompasses the past, present, and future.

Several publications reflect a theory of resistance based on the Nguzo Saba principles (Brookins & Robinson, 1995; Robinson & Ward, 1991). The goal of resistance theory is to empower marginalized groups with optimal tools to name, confront, repudiate, and replace dominant and demeaning messages with knowledge of self and community. This topic is discussed further in subsequent chapters.

Resistance theory is regarded as an important response to the chronic stress of racism, particularly given the limited research related to the use of specific modes of coping with perceived racism (Clark, Anderson, Clark, & Williams, 2002).

African tradition includes a strong tie between the living and the world of the dead in defining the scope of community. J. A. Opoku (personal communication, April 3, 1994) said about Ghanaian culture, "The dead are still with us."

CASE STUDY
Chronic Post-Traumatic Stress Disorder

Ken is a 20-year-old African American male in his third year of college who was born and raised in St. Louis, Missouri. He was taken into state custody as a 15-month-old infant after his mother had been murdered. He had been found in the apartment next to her dead body. When Ken was 7, he was adopted by his foster parents. From this time on, he grew up in a stable working-class family in which weekly church attendance was standard. His father is a postal carrier and his mother is a vocational nurse. During a 4-week in-service residential advisor (RA) training, a speaker spoke about the prevalence of sexual abuse among college males and females during their early childhoods. To his surprise, Ken found himself deeply disturbed by this information and began to sweat and feel nauseous. Prior to coming to live with his parents, Ken was sexually abused repeatedly in a foster home by one of his older brothers. He never told anyone about the abuse. Ken feels enormous shame and anger about his experience. Because he wanted to be adopted and desired a home, he sought to be the perfect kid and never gave his parents any trouble. Ken has found that he has started having nightmares of being chased, caught, and subdued. He also finds it difficult to concentrate, and has missed the last two in-service sessions on sexual abuse. Estevan is Ken's residential director (RD). He has noticed Ken's absence at the trainings, observed his reaction at the

first session, and has noticed his intolerance of others and difficulty with concentration at subsequent meetings. Estevan suggests that Ken speak to one of the on-campus psychologists. Ken reacts angrily and is reluctant to do so. Ken is concerned that asking for help would be interpreted as a sign of weakness and an indication that his problems are too large for him to continue working effectively as an RA. Ken is dependent on the RA position to provide his room and board. Ken assures Estevan that he is fine and refuses any help seeking. Ken has very limited experience with dating women. Although he would like to, he has been unable to reciprocate with strong feelings. He is concerned that his sexual experiences as a child may mean that he is gay, but he does not talk with anyone about this or similar concerns. Ken has no interest in dating other guys. Ken's RD stated that he will need to make up the missed sessions from the in-service as part of his RA requirements. Ken has a 3.8 grade point average, is a member of the concert band, and also sings in the choir.

QUESTIONS
1. What are Ken's value orientations?
2. Is Ken's avoidance of help seeking a function of his race, gender, or both?
3. What is the best way to approach Ken therapeutically?

DISCUSSION AND INTEGRATION
The Client, Ken

It is clear that Ken is distressed and appears to be triggered by the ongoing trauma of being sexually abused when he was a young boy. Sexual abuse can be both contact and noncontact. Exposing children to pornography or masturbating in their presence is noncontact abuse. Contact abuse involves penetration or attempted penetration or some type of stimulation of the child's body (Gartner, 1999). Ken's abuse was both contact and noncontact in that he was forced to listen to his older foster brothers talk about their sexual exploits. Ken was also sodomized.

Prior to the trauma of the sexual abuse, he was traumatized as a child by being in the home with his murdered mother, lying in wait with her body before being found by the authorities. Although he was an infant at the time and preverbal, the extent of this trauma should not be underestimated. There is tremendous stress associated with growing up in violence, and Black children are more likely to be exposed to it. Boyd-Franklin (2003) stated "many are acquainted from an early age with violence in their homes in the form of child abuse, sexual abuse, drug overdose, and AIDS" (p. 266).

Ken has some of the classic symptoms of PTSD, namely avoidance of the stimuli associated with the trauma, nightmares, difficulty concentrating, and physiological reactivity on exposure to internal or external cues. Washington (1987) stated that, when counseling a Black man,

> The ante is greatly raised. . . . There are more walls, blocks, and barriers evident. He struggles not only with the cultural scripts that define manhood but with a true double-edged sword of gender-role constraints plus racism. The latter, racism, being more formidable than the first. (p. 192)

Ken is not unusual as a male in underutilizing the help that is available to him. At the same time, his cultural experiences, as amplified by Washington, play a major role as well.

If anyone is entitled to ask for or need help, it is Ken. His multiple identities as a college student, student leader, adopted son, incest survivor, and 20-year-old all collide to make for some very confusing feelings. The in-service training triggered an experience that Ken had, throughout most of his life, blocked out. However, the trainer indicated that sexual abuse in children is unfortunately rather common. What this information may do is help to normalize Ken's experience in that he sees that other people, including men, have been abused. According to Addis and Mahalik (2003), "Depending on the context in which a problem occurs, individual men may or may not perceive the problem as normative" (p. 10). Descriptive norms also operate and communicate to men how other men are responding or are not responding. Ken, most likely, had male role models in his life who did not ask for help, openly express their vulnerability, or share experiences of being overpowered by persons bigger and stronger.

Ken's symptoms reflect the literature regarding sexually abused boys and men. Gartner (1999) summarized research on the sexual abuse of boys and men by stating that sexually abused men are more likely than are sexually abused women to have dysfunctional and physiological reactions to stress, as well as chest pains, nightmares, and shortness of breath. These men also have difficulty relating intimately to women and men. Men who are sexually abused often question their sexual orientation and gender identity.

Another issue for Ken is the fact that he is adopted. Rampage, Eovaldi, Ma, and Weigel-Foy (2003) indicated that children adopted after infancy (Ken was adopted as a school-age child) may lose relationships with birth family and extended family members. Ken should be commended for his academic excellence and extensive involvement in a variety of activities. His insistence on remaining busy at all times may be unconsciously related to the hypervigilance that characterizes many children exposed to traumatic circumstances. Many times these children will evidence difficulty with emotional and behavioral regulation (Rampage et al., 2003). Ken's extensive involvement in activities could also be indicative of a mood disturbance. Parham (1992) noted that among some African Americans, depression manifests not as psychomotor retardation but as increased activity in order to "keep on keeping on" (Parham, 1992). So much of the Black experience in America is coping, surviving, and putting up with injustice and annoying aspects of racism, yet people still have to function—go to work and school, feed the kids, and pay the bills. In a doing-oriented culture, a counselor needs to avoid mistaking Ken's behavior for adaptive functioning when it is more descriptive of chronic post-traumatic stress disorder.

Ken can still be considered a teenager, which means that he is trying to negotiate a variety of identities that feel conflicting at times. Parental, faculty, residential director, church, peer, and self-imposed expectations operate simultaneously and can feel overwhelming. According to Ward (2000), "Black teenagers face the daunting task of developing strong personal and racial identities and of combining the two while resisting a barrage of identities that others, even well-meaning family members, would impose on them" (p. 129).

Implications for Counselors

The residential director, Estevan, is in a precarious situation. He is not certain of Ken's issues but suspects they are related to the in-service training done on child sexual abuse. At the same time, he has noticed changes in Ken's behavior that could have an impact on Ken's effectiveness as a leader of other students. Although he cannot make Ken seek counseling, his insistence that Ken finish the training does require Ken to confront an issue that he has been avoiding. Doing so may land him in the counselor's chair sooner rather than later. Estevan may seek additional information about this issue or issues in general and offer his support to Ken to decrease Ken's feelings of isolation. Researchers realize that the rate of abuse among boys is higher than what had been previously thought (Blume, 1990). Gartner (1999) reports a 1984 study done on men in which it was found that 33% of Canadian men were sexually victimized at some point in their lives. This rate is as high as

that reported by Russell (1986) in her study of 900 random women.

There are many barriers that interfere with men seeking psychological assistance. This is particularly the case if men perceive other men to be disparaging of the process. Fortunately, Estevan is encouraging of help seeking. Ken's internal dictates against asking for help prevent his ability to access help at this time.

Once in counseling, cognitive restructuring may help Ken hear and reflect on the conscious and unconscious messages he learned from an early age, such as "Real men do not ask for help" or "Men cannot be sexually abused." These early tapes received from society, the educational system, and the media at large should be reviewed. Yet Washington (1987) pointed out that although the assumptions about men as powerful and masters of their fate describe many White male Americans, this is not necessarily the case for certain Black men, who may be benefactors of male privilege but contend, nonetheless, with an oppressive and racist society.

Estevan, as a multiculturally competent counselor, would be aware of his own culture, his biases, and his client's worldview. In addition, he would be clear about interventions that might help Ken. Estevan continues the ongoing work of (a) engaging in self-examination, (b) increasing self-knowledge, (c) learning the truth about racism and sexism (that it is limiting to emotional and psychological development), and (d) being conscious of change agents and initiating institutional changes (Washington, 1987).

Gary (1987) reported that among a group of African American men who brought their interpersonal conflicts to the attention of mental health providers, the major presenting problem was depression. The resarch indicates that Black people with mental health needs are unlikely to receive treatment. If Ken receives help, it is likely to come from primary care providers. African Americans receiving speciality care are more likely to leave treatment prematurely (U.S. Department of Health and Human Services, 2001).

Ken was raised in the church. His spirituality could be a coping tool and/or a way to blame himself for the sin that befell him. There is most likely not a congregation in this nation that does not have a member who has not been sexually abused (Pellauer, 1987). Because Ken is reluctant to seek out help from a psychologist, especially one on his campus, he may be able to talk with his or another minister. Unfortunately, many churches are silent about the abuse and other forms of violence that their members have been and continue to be exposed to. Their silence does not protect those who are suffering and places the congregation and the community at large in an even more vulnerable position due to a lack of responsible and responsive spiritual leadership. Some ministers and churches are not silent but are change agents for justice, educating and healing, and praying for and with their members. For the counselor to acknowledge that a terrible wrong was done, that the counselor is so sorry, and that she walks with the client now through the path of healing is a balm to the soul. Ken needs this balm.

SUMMARY

This chapter provided history, demographic trends, and cultural values for people of African descent. A lengthy case study was presented for students to gain practice with integrating multiple issues: adoption, childhood sexual trauma, cultural influences on coping with mood disturbances, and the influence of race and gender on help seeking. Implications for counseling with people of African descent are discussed in the case study.

REFERENCES

Addis, M., & Mahalik, J. R. (2003). Men, masculinity, and the contexts of help seeking. *American Psychologist, 58*(1), 5–14.

Blume, E. S. (1990). *Secret survivors: Uncovering incest and its aftereffects in women*. New York: John Wiley & Sons.

Boyd-Franklin, N. (2003). Race, class, and poverty. In F. Walsh (Ed.), *Normal family process* (pp. 260–279). New York: Guilford Press.

Brookins, C. B., & Robinson, T. L. (1995). Rites of passage as resistance to oppression. *Western Journal of Black Studies, 19*(3), 172–185.

Christian, C. M. (1995). *Black saga: The African American experience (a chronology)*. Boston: Houghton Mifflin.

Clark, R., Anderson, N. B., Clark, V. R., & Williams, D. R. (2002) Racism as a stressor for African Americans: A biopsychosocial model. In T. LaVeist (Ed.), *Race, ethnicity and health* (pp. 319–339). San Francisco, CA: Jossey-Bass.

Exum, H. A., & Moore, Q. L. (1993). Transcultural counseling from African-American perspectives. In J. McFadden (Ed.), *Transcultural counseling: Bilateral and international perspectives* (pp. 193–212). Alexandria, VA: American Counseling Association.

Gartner, R. B. (1999). *Betrayed as boys: Psychodynamic treatment of sexually abused men*. New York: Guilford Press.

Gary, L. E. (1987). Predicting interpersonal conflict between men and women: The case of Black men. In M. Kimmel (Ed.), *Changing men: New directions in research on men and masculinity*. Newbury Park, CA: Sage.

Good, M. J. D., James, C., Good, B. J., & Becker, A. E. (2003). The culture of medicine and racial, ethnic, and class disparities in health care. In *Institute of Medicine* (pp. 594–625). Washington, DC: The National Academies Press.

Gwaltney, J. L. (1980). *Drylongso: A self-portrait of Black America.* New York: Random House.

Karenga, M. (1980). *Kawaida theory.* Los Angeles: Kawaida.

Maffly-Kipp, L. (2000). African-American religion in the nineteenth century. University of North Carolina at Chapel Hill. http://www.nhc.rtp.nc.us/tserve/nineteen/nkeyinfo/nafrican.htm

Myers, L. J. (1991). Expanding the psychology of knowledge optimally: The importance of world view revisited. In R. Jones (Ed.), *Black psychology* (2nd ed., pp. 15–28). Berkeley, CA: Cobb & Henry.

Nobles, W. (1972). African philosophy: Foundations for Black psychology. In R. H Jones (Ed.), *Black psychology.* New York: Harper & Row.

Parham, T. (Presenter), (1992). *Counseling African Americans* [Video]. Amherst, MA: Microtraining and Multicultural Development.

Pellauer, M. D. (1987). Violence against women: The theological dimension. In M. Pellauer, B. Chester, & J. Boyajian (Eds.), *Sexual assault and abuse* (p. 51–61). CA: Harper San Francisco.

Rampage, C., Eovaldi, M., Ma, C., & Weigel-Foy, C. (2003). Adoptive families. In F. Walsh (Ed.), *Normal family processes: Growing diversity and complexity* (pp. 210–232). New York: Guilford Press.

Robinson, T. L., & Ward, J. V. (1991). A belief in self far greater than anyone's disbelief: Cultivating resistance among African American adolescents. *Women & Therapy, 11,* 87–103.

Russell, D. (1986). *The secret trauma: Incest in the lives of girls and women.* New York: Basic Books.

Schulte, E. (2002). More black men in jail than college. http://www.socialistworker.org/2002.

Stewart, J. C. (1996). *1001 things everyone should know about African American history.* New York: Doubleday.

Sue, D. W., & Sue, D. (1990). *Counseling the culturally different: Theory and practice.* New York: John Wiley.

U.S. Census Bureau. (2000a). Correctional populations in the United States, 1997. Washington, DC:

U.S. Census Bureau. (2000b). Population by age, sex, and race and Hispanic origin. Current population survey. Racial Statistics Branch, Population Division. Washington, DC:

U.S. Census Bureau. (2001). Overview of race and Hispanic origin: Census 2000 brief. Washington, DC: U.S. Department of Commerce.

U.S. Census Bureau (2002). Poverty in the United States. Washington, DC: U.S. Department of Commerce.

U.S. Department of Health and Human Services. (2001). *Mental health: Culture, race, and ethnicity—A supplement to mental health: A report to the Surgeon General.* Rockville, MD: U.S. Department of Health and Human Services, Public Health Service, Office of the Surgeon General.

Ward, J. V. (2000). *The skin we're in: Teaching our children to be emotionally strong, socially smart, and spiritually connected.* New York: Free Press.

Washington, C. S. (1987). Counseling Black men. In M. Scher, M. Stevens, G. Good, & G. A. Eichenfield (Eds.), *Handbook of counseling and psychotherapy* (pp. 192–202). Newbury Park, CA: Sage.

Zinn, H. (2003). *A people's history of the United States: 1492–present.* New York: Harper Collins.

Chapter 7

People of Asian Descent, Native Hawaiians, and Pacific Islanders

He who stands on tiptoe is not steady.

He who strides cannot maintain the pace.

He who makes a show is not enlightened.

He who is self-righteous is not respected.

He who boasts achieves nothing.

He who brags will not endure.

According to followers of the Tao,

"These are extra food and unnecessary
luggage."

They do not bring happiness.

Therefore followers of the Tao avoid them.

Lao Tsu, Tao Te Ching

This chapter is a focus on people of Asian descent. The diverse ethnic groups among Asians are highlighted. Demographical information, history, and cultural values are also presented.

DEMOGRAPHY

There are 10.2 million Asians living in the United States (U.S. Census Bureau, 2000b). Although Asians comprise 3.6% of the U.S. population, they represent one of the fastest growing groups in the nation. Between 1990 and 2000, the Asian population in the U.S. grew 48%.

Almost 399,000 people reported being Native Hawaiian or other Pacific Islander, which includes Guamanian, Chamorro, Samoan, or of another Pacific Island. Pacific Islanders also encompass dispersed areas, including Australia, New Zealand (the Maori), Tasmania, Polynesia, Fiji Islands, the islets of Micronesia and Melanesia, and extending through New Guinea (U.S. Census Bureau, 2000b).

In the 2000 Census, another 1.65 million people identified themselves as both Asian and one or more other races (U.S. Census, 2000b), the most common being White, with 868,395 people. Fifty-two percent of the population reporting Asian with another race were Asian and White. The high rates of intermarriage between Asians and Whites, particularly among Asian women and White men, explain respondents' reporting of their biracial heritage. According to Wu (2002), "Among Asian Americans under the age of thirty-five who are married, half have found a spouse of a non-Asian background" (p. 263).

Among these biracial respondents, 138,802 reported that they were Asian, Native Hawaiian, and other Pacific Islander; 106,782 were Asian, Black, or African American. Native Hawaiians and other Pacific Islanders alone or in combination with one or more other races were less than 1 million at 874,414, or 0.3% of the entire U.S. population.

Highly concentrated in the West, nearly 54% of the Asian population resides in this part of the country. Hawaii alone has 51% of the Asian and Pacific Islander population. The West also has the highest percentage, at 21%, of people who reported as more than one race in 2000. Nine of the 10 cities in the United States with over 100,000 Asian residents are in California. California has 11% of the U.S. Asian population. Washington State has nearly 6% and Nevada has 4.9%. The Northeast has nearly 18% of the Asian population. Less than 6% (5.7% and 5.6%, respectively) of the Asian population reside in New Jersey, New York State, and the South.

The Chinese are the largest group of Asians, representing 2.4 million or 24% of the Asian population. The second largest group are the nearly 2 million Filipinos. Among Filipinos, 5 million report Filipino in combination with one or more other races or Asian groups (U.S. Census Bureau, 2000b). The third largest ethnic group among Asians are Asian Indians at nearly 1.7 million. There are higher numbers of

Vietnamese and Koreans in the population than there are Japanese, according to the 2000 Census, 1.12 million, nearly 1.1 million, and just under 800,000, respectively (U.S. Census Bureau, 2000b).

Southeast Asia represents the Asian subcontinent south of China and east of India. Persons from Vietnam, Laos, and Cambodia are neighbors. Indonesia, Malaysia, Thailand, Burma, Bhutan, and Bangladesh are also included. According to Sandhu (1997), more than 40 cultural groups compose Asian and Pacific Islander Americans. Many of these groups are less researched and perhaps less well known than other groups who have lived in the United States for several generations. Asian newcomers speak hundreds of languages and dialects and practice a broad array of religions. Many ethnic Asian newcomers are more likely to identify with specific national or regional ties (e.g., Vietnamese, Korean, Hmong, Punjabi Sikh, Cantonese, Taiwanese).

In the 2000 Census, nearly 1.3 million people referred to themselves as "other Asian," which can also mean two or more Asian categories (U.S. Census Bureau, 2000b). The median age among Asians of 32.6 years has decreased from what was seen at the turn of the 20th century when the median age was approaching 40 years. This was a function of the predominantly adult male migration to the United States, primarily from mainland China. More will be discussed later in this chapter about this phenomenon.

Tremendous diversity is found within the Asian community. As Uba (1994) pointed out, "The term 'Asian culture' is technically a misnomer. The tenets of these belief systems are shared by many cultures—there are also significant differences among Asian cultures" (p.12). Over 100 languages and dialects are spoken, and in some communities such as the Hmong and Cambodians, high rates of linguistic isolation exist, which describes the phenomenon of persons over the age of 14 not speaking English "very well" (U.S. Department of Health and Human Services, 2001).

Ethnicity, nationality, migration or generational status, assimilation, acculturation, facility with the English language, political climate in country of origin, religion, socioeconomic status, occupation, transferability of skills, foreign credentials to the United States, and educational level depict some of the many sources of differences within the group (Sue & Sue, 1990; Tsai & Uemura, 1988).

MIGRATORY PATTERNS

The Chinese are the Asian ethnic group with the longest history in the United States and were the first Asian ethnic group to be recruited to the West Coast during the 1840s. At that time, there was a need for cheap labor to work on the transcontinental railroads (Tsai & Uemura, 1988). U.S. policymaker Aaron H. Palmer predicted that with a connection to the East Coast, San Francisco would become the "great emporium of our commerce on the Pacific" (Takaki, 1993, p. 192). Chinese were perceived to be more suited for "cleaning wild lands and raising every species of agricultural product" (Takaki, 1993, p. 192).

In 1863, Congress authorized construction of the U.S. transcontinental railroad. The eastward track was laid from Sacramento, California through the Sierra Nevada, and eventually into Utah. During the winter months, working conditions were often brutal and snowdrifts would bury entire work crews. Come spring, their frozen bodies would be discovered. The westward track was built mainly by Irish immigrants and started in Omaha, Nebraska. Both the Irish and Chinese received a monthly wage of $31. Unlike the Irish, the Chinese worked longer days and slept in tents near the side of the road. The Irish worked 8-hour days and resided in boarding rooms.

Despite the harsh realities of work on the railroad, many Chinese were motivated to come to America. In China, floods were making it difficult to harvest their crops. Political instability, such as taxation and ethnic conflict were also factors. Between 1865–1869, the total number of Chinese railroad workers increased from 50 to almost 12,000 (Avakian, 2002). Finding gold in California was also a dream of many Chinese (Cao & Novas, 1996).

Life was not only difficult for Chinese men, Chinese women were suffering as well. In 1860, over 80% of Chinese women were prostitutes and many were teenage girls of 15 and 16 years of age. As a result of slavery, kidnapping, and deception, Chinese girls found themselves on the auction block where they worked as concubines or prostitutes, sexually serving both White and Chinese men (Avakian, 2002).

Shortly after the arrival of the Chinese in 1840, 141 Japanese men, women, and children arrived in Hawaii in 1868. The Japanese, along with Koreans, Filipinos, and Puerto Ricans who came later near the turn of the 20th century, were recruited to Hawaii to work in the sugar cane plantations.

Known as the Meiji Restoration (after Emperor Meiji), the Japanese migrated to the United States during Japan's period of rapid modernization. Because of tax increases levied to pay for sweeping reforms, Japan's peasant farmers suffered greatly from economic hardships and lost their land. Persons from the districts of Yamaguchi, Hiroshima, and Kumamoto were hit hardest by poverty and composed the majority of immigrants hailing from Japan (Avakian, 2002).

Between 1885 and 1925, 200,000 Japanese left for Hawaii, and another 180,000 went to mainland United States. By the turn of the 20th century, 70% of Hawaii's sugar plantation labor was from Japan. In 1900, with the passing of the Organic Act, the U.S. Congress voted for the creation of the Territory of Hawaii. Despite the fact that Chinese and Japanese Hawaiians represented more than half of the population, they were not allowed to vote, and Whites, the minority, represented the elite and ruling class. Fortunately, the Organic Act allowed for laborers to have greater power in organizing themselves more effectively. Such resistance, led by the Japanese, encouraged planters to look for new labor sources, primarily from Korea and the Philippines.

Prior to the arrival of other Asians into the United States, Congress passed the Chinese Exclusion Act of 1882, which barred the "immigration of all Chinese laborers, lunatics, and idiots into the United States for a 10-year period" (p. 51). This act was the first and only law in U.S. immigration that ordered an entire group of people of a specific nationality to be banned from the United States (Avakian, 2002).

On December 7, 1941, a major base of the U.S. Navy, the Oahu port at Pearl Harbor, was attacked by the Japanese. Bases in the Philippines, Guam, the Midway Islands, and other ports in the Pacific were also attacked. Nearly 3,000 soldiers, sailors, and civilians were killed. This surprise attack fueled existing anti-Japanese sentiments. With the passing of Executive Order 9066, wartime curfew and internment measures were enacted primarily against the Japanese—most of whom were *the Nisei,* or second-generation, American-born Japanese. In addition, small numbers of Germans, Italians, and Eastern Europeans were also relocated to camps to safeguard the security of the United States. Although the order was a constitutional violation as well as a legal violation of due process, more than 110,000 Japanese Americans were forced to leave their homes and move to cramped internment camps. The construction plans used were for unmarried army recruits, thus up to six families resided in long army barracks with very little privacy. The traditional diet of many Japanese people, such as fresh vegetables and fruits, was not available, and waiting in lines for meals and bathroom facilities were commonplace (Avakian, 2002).

Compared to the Chinese, Japanese, Koreans, Filipinos, and Asian Indians, the Vietnamese are the most recent immigrant group to arrive in the United States. Between April and December 1975, 100,000 refugees from Vietnam and Cambodia were admitted to the United States as parolees, as announced by the U.S. attorney general (Avakian, 2002).

ACCULTURATION AND EXPERIENCES IN AMERICA

There are differences in the values expressed in Asian cultures and in the United States. Much of this difference, in addition to personality, is related to acculturation. Over 26% of people of Asian descent were born in Asia (U.S. Census Bureau, 2000b). Length of time in the United States, access to resources, facility with the English language, educational level, and employment status are factors that affect adjustment. Other moderator variables include generational status, age, ethnic density of neighborhood, country of birth, kinship structures, and purposes of immigration. According to Berry and Sam (1997), cultural maintenance and contact and participation are important issues that groups and individuals consider in their interpersonal interactions. Two different immigrant streams are associated with huge diversity within the Asian and Pacific Island population. The first stream represents people from countries that have large populations in the United States and tend to have better health. Included are Chinese, Filipinos, Koreans, and Asian Indians. The second stream consists of lower socioeconomic groups. Many refugees are included in this number (Frisbie, Cho, & Hummer, 2002).

Cultural maintenance refers to cultural identity characteristics that are considered important and for which people strive. Contact and participation refers to the extent to which groups deem it important to become involved with other cultural groups or remain primarily among themselves. The assimilation strategy is defined when persons do not wish to maintain their cultural identity and seek interactions with other cultures. Separation is referred to when the nondominant group places a value on holding onto their original culture and wishes to avoid interactions with persons from other cultures. Segregation is the term used to describe the dominant group's stance with respect to the nondominant group. Integration refers to the maintenance of cultural integrity while seeking to participate in the larger social network of a multicultural society. Marginalization defines little possibility or interest in cultural maintenance and little interest in having relations with others.

Research conducted by Sodowski, Wai, and Plake (1991) with 524 Latino and Asian American students, faculty, and staff at a large midwestern university revealed that Vietnamese were less acculturated into the majority society than were Japanese and Korean Americans. No significant acculturation differences were found among Chinese and Japanese Americans, and Asians from the Indian subcontinent.

Prior to arrival in the United States, most Asian immigrants and refugees have primary exposure to their own culture. Upon arrival, cultural adaptation is required, and a relinquishing of native aspects of their culture to function in school and work contexts is part of this process. In addition to the factors cited earlier that affect adaptation, age of migration (before or after the age of 12), reason for migration (economic development or political refuge), and mode of migration (with or without parents or family members) are critical issues (Tsai & Chensova-Dutton, 2002).

Asian Americans are the most highly educated ethnic group. Nearly 28% of Asian people have bachelor's degrees, compared to 19.7% of Whites. One in five Asian adults has an advanced degree compared to 11% of Whites (U.S. Census Bureau, 2000b). Asian Indians, more than any other Asian group, occupy higher percentages of managerial and professional positions. In 1980, 47% of Asian Indians held professional managerial jobs in the United States, compared to 30% of Chinese, 28% of Japanese, and 22% of Koreans. Based on 1997 data, 58% of Americans who descended from the Indian subcontinent (Bangladesh, India, Pakistan, and Sri Lanka) had undergraduate, graduate, or professional degrees (U.S. Department of Health and Human Services, 2001). Among many, arranged marriages are still practiced (see the Storytelling "Arranged Marriage").

STORYTELLING: Arranged Marriage

I met a young Asian Indian woman once while conducting a diversity training workshop. She confided in me that she had an American boyfriend but that back home in India, her parents were already planning her arranged marriage. The ad that her parents had placed in the paper referred to her as "wheat" in color. She told me that her parents believed that such a description sounded much better than dark brown, the color of her skin.

The successes and creativity of many newly migrated groups from Asia have been attributed largely to the informal network system of valuing the group, being a member of the group, and attending to the needs of others through sharing financial and human resources, from employment information to housing, for the betterment of all (Chang, 1996; Sue & Sue, 1990). Among some Asian groups, even among newly arrived immigrants, a substantial number have higher education and extensive career experience. Much of the success in business noted among many Korean Americans can be explained by a system called *kae,* which is similar to the Chinese concept of *woi* and the Japanese system known as *tanomoshi*. This system enables successful people to help newcomers through a lending and borrowing system. In addition, many of the Korean banks are under the authority of Korean banks. In this way, newcomers face less discrimination than would be seen at an American bank (Avakian, 2002).

SOCIAL, PSYCHOLOGICAL AND HEALTH ISSUES

Sue and Sue (1990) cautioned against acceptance of well-known myths and stereotypes concerning Asians in America as "model minorities" who do not face difficulties that other groups of color experience (see the Storytelling "Activism and Struggle"). The "model minority" myth also denies the tremendous diversity that exists among individual Asian Americans. According to Takaki (1994),

> Asian-American "success" has emerged as the new stereotype for this ethnic minority. While this image has led many teachers and employers to view Asians as intelligent and hardworking and has opened some opportunities, it has also been harmful. (p. 57)

The model minority myth often interferes with economically disadvantaged Asian American communities receiving the necessary emotional and financial resources and creates division among groups of color as one group is pitted against another. Some suffer because of unemployment, and some newly immigrated groups, such

STORYTELLING: Activism and Struggle

Fueled by the victories won during the African American civil rights movement, the late 1960s and early 1970s were a time when many young Asian Americans protested and spoke out on a variety of issues related to their rights as Asian Americans. Many Asians felt a sense of solidarity with the Vietnamese during the antiwar movement. In addition, many young Asian Americans were inspired to develop a sense of ethnic pride and self-esteem when leaders in the Black Power movement encouraged African Americans to find empowerment (Avakian, 2002).

as Southeast Vietnamese, have very high poverty rates and difficulties with social adjustment due to the trauma they experienced prior to immigration. In fact, Vietnamese Americans have an average family income that is about half that of AAPI populations as a whole (Byrd & Clayton 2003). Pacific Islanders tend to have higher rates of poverty than other Asian groups, with Tongans and Samoans having some of the highest rates (U.S. Department of Health and Human Services, 2001). Many Pacific Islanders reside across more than 22 islands including Micronesia (Guam, Belau, and the Carolines Marianas, Marshalls, and Gilberts) and Melanesia (Fiji). Because of autonomous governments with a variety of political relationships with the United States, varying levels of health and health care exist. For instance, Guam has a relatively high level of health care, with the Republic of Belau and the Federated States of Micronesia having older hospitals that provide a "generally poorer level of care" (Byrd & Clayton, 2003, p. 480).

Among refugees, such as Cambodians, Laotians, and the Vietnamese, post-traumatic stress disorder (PTSD) and depression are not uncommon given war and poverty. Prime Minister Pol Pot is known for Cambodia's "killing fields," which references an inhumane period of genocide led by the communist guerilla organization the Khmer Rouge. Between 1975 and 1979, one third of Cambodia's population, or between 1.5 and 2 million Cambodians, were slaughtered. Anti-communists, students, intellectuals, the wealthy, and doctors were considered to be enemies of the state and tragically lost their lives (Avakian, 2002). One study found that Cambodian high school students had symptoms of PTSD as well as depressive symptoms. Among Cambodian adults who had been resettled in Massachusetts, 43% reported the death of between one and six children (U.S. Department of Health and Human Services, 2001). This distress was captured as intense sadness that is invisible to other people.

Asians also suffer discrimination on the job, and career choices are skewed because of racial inequities. Educationally, some Asians have problems with the English language on standardized tests, and conflicts exist between American and Asian values. The stereotype of the model minority permeates the culture. Asian students who internalize this myth may find it extremely hard to ask for needed assistance or feel increasingly isolated in their attempts to achieve academic success (Gloria & Ho, 2003).

For some youths, the pressure to succeed academically can cause enormous stress. Chang's (1996) research on coping styles of Asian students is a welcome contribution to the literature, given the stress experienced by many Asian youths. He found in his study of 111 Asian college students and 111 White college students that the Asian students used more problem avoidance and social withdrawal than the White students. Also, the Asian students, though more pessimistic in their orientations than the White students, were not less optimistic. Amid the expectation of negative events, the Asian students employed active coping styles.

In addition to concerns about traditional coping strategies, there are other reasons that explain the reluctance among many Asian Americans to discuss their problems. According to Uba (1994), it is not uncommon for many Asian Americans to perceive talking about themselves or disclosing private personal information to a stranger as reflective of low maturity and lack of discipline.

CULTURAL ORIENTATION AND VALUES

Confucianism, Taoism, and Buddhism underlie many Asian cultural values. Founded in the 5th and 6th centuries B.C. by followers of Siddharta Gautama, later known as Buddha (Avakian, 2002), the basic teachings of Buddhism maintain that there is suffering, the first Noble Truth. Understanding the roots of suffering, the cessation of suffering, and being on the path to refrain from that which causes suffering are also emphasized (Nhat Hanh, 1998). Older than Buddhism is Hinduism, which dates back to 1500 B.C. Hindu beliefs are presented in two sacred books, the *Vedas* and the *Upanishads*. People are ranked into caste systems from the Brahmans or priests to the sundras or peasants and laborers. Confucius, born in about 551 B.C., was China's most influential philosopher. Family loyalty, hard work, and respect for one's parents and elders were emphasized. In addition to being a philosophy, Taoism was also a religion. It emphasized harmony in nature and contemplation (Avakian, 2002). Such a philosophy is seen in the eighth chapter of the *Tao Te Ching:* "In dwelling, be close to the land. In meditation, go deep in the heart. In dealing with others, be gentle and kind. In speech, be true. In ruling, be just. In business, be competent. In action, watch the timing. No fight: No blame" (Lao Tsu, trans. 1972). *We wei,* which literally means "doing nothing" or inaction, was emphasized, but it could also refer to modesty, simplicity, and absence of ambition for power (Hong & Domokos-Cheng Ham, 2001).

Values common to many Asian ethnic groups include emphasis on harmony in relationships, emotional restraint (emotional expression may be interpreted as a sign of immaturity), precedence of group interests over individual interests, extended family, deference to authority, obedience to and respect for parents, emphasis on hard work, fulfilling obligations, and high value associated with education (Sandhu, 1997; Uba, 1994) (*see Figure 7.1*) According to Ying (2002), "The primary objective of socialization is *tsuo jen* (which literally means to make/become human), that is, to teach a child proper social rules of conduct and submission of personal desires to that of others in order to avoid interpersonal conflict and social disapproval" (pp. 174–175).

Among the Chinese, selflessness, obedience to authority, or deference to the collective unit is a primary value and is manifested in relations with elders or those in authority. Body parts are used to describe intimate relationships. For instance, biological children are referred to as bone and flesh and siblings are referred to as hand and foot (Ying, 2002). The concept of *jen,* or personhood, is emphasized. Jen is a Confucian virtue and is written with two strokes. Each represents one person and refers to responsibility for kin as expressed through respect, loyalty, and love (Dana, 1993).

Among the Chinese, the self is conceptualized in a social way (Ying, 2002). In the West, the self is primary and exerts influence on expectations concerning psychological well-being. For instance, personal happiness is considered an inalienable right and an essential goal, an entitlement if you will. In many Asian cultures, including Chinese but also Southeast Asians, achievement of personal happiness may be a less salient

Enryo (Reserve, Constraint)

Jen (Benevolence, Personhood, Humanity)

Yuan (The influence of past relationships on present social relationships)

Face (Concern for maintaining face)

Thrift

Interpersonal Harmony in Relationships

Ren Qing (Social favors exchanged in the form of money, goods, information—according to an implicit set of social rules)

Precedence of group interests over individual interests

Obediance to authority

Emotional self-control

FIGURE 7.1
Common Cultural Values Among People of Asian Descent

goal and might well be constructed within a collectivistic framework because appraisal of the self is based on external social standards (Tsai & Chensova-Dutton, 2002).

Despite diversity among Asians, certain ethnic groups share some similarities, such as the Chinese and the Japanese. According to Sue and Sue (1995), in both cultures, the families are patriarchal and communication styles tend to be formal, well defined, and flow from top downward. Relationships among family members are highly interdependent, with one's actions reflecting on the entire family unit. Control of the children is maintained by fostering feelings of shame and guilt. Although parenting children in this manner may characterize many Asian families, it also applies to other cultures as well. Hsu (1953) observed that the most important thing to Americans is what parents should do for the children: to Chinese, what children should do for their parents is of greatest importance.

Family is given respect and honor. Among the Vietnamese, it is not uncommon for multiple generations to reside collectively in one home. Elders are honored, respected, and cared for because of the importance of family. Compared with other groups, Asian Americans are more likely to live in households composed of family members only. They are less likely to live on their own and are characterized by low percentages of female-headed households. Pacific Islanders are also more likely to have larger families than most Asian Americans and Americans (Byrd & Clayton, 2003; U.S. Department of Health and Human Services, 2001). According to McFadden (1993), Asians tend to believe that marriage is the most important event that can occur in a person's life and is perceived to be long-lasting, until the end of one's life, with divorce being considered the greatest possible tragedy that could occur.

Restraint of emotions represents a value for many Asian Americans. This is not to be confused with the absence of a sense of humor; however, *enryo,* or reserve and constraint, is an important value and represents a primary mode of communication. Uba (1994) said, "This syndrome may be manifested in a number of ways, as in a hesitancy to speak up in class or to openly contradict a person in a position of authority . . . Another part of the *enryo* syndrome is a modest devaluation of oneself and one's possessions" (p. 18).

Humility is regarded as a cultural value, as is the notion of loss of face. Self-effacement and modesty are highly valued and reflect wisdom and function to increase social harmony (Ying, 2002). Leong, Wagner, and Kim (1995) stated that communication styles among Asians allow participants to maintain face. Therefore, direct communication styles, reflective of a Western style and involving confrontation and challenges, tend to be less desirable.

CASE STUDY
Dual Diagnosis

Kara McGuire is a 32-year-old university librarian. She lives in San Jose, California, where she was born and raised. Kara's mother is Japanese and her father is Irish. Kara is the oldest child in a family with three children. She has a younger sister and in her words, a "baby brother." Kara has always wondered from where in the family she inherited her looks. Kara's sister is tall, thin, and "looks white." Kara has always struggled with her weight, has dark and very Asian eyes, and dark skin. Recently Kara and her colleagues were talking about the wife of a coworker. One of her White colleagues said, *"she may have married White and rich, but she will always be a slanty-eyed Chinc."* Embarrassed, her colleague said, *"don't take offense Kara, I don't see you as Asian."* Kara felt awkward but smiled and said, "don't worry about it." Kara has been married 6 years but is currently separated from her husband, Tyler, who moved out 2 months ago. He has been involved with various women throughout their marriage. For nearly 2 years, Kara had been feeling suspicious about Tyler. Often, he was out late or away from his job as a chiropractor for business or professional development. Kara also found some receipts for gift purchases that were for a woman. When she asked Tyler if anything was wrong, he told her there wasn't. Kara has been under a lot of stress at work given the budget shortfalls that have left her understaffed. She has a hard time getting out of bed in the morning, has gained 35 pounds in 3 months, cries a lot, is socially withdrawn from her friends and family, finds it difficult to concentrate at work where she has been making many mistakes, and has been drinking more alcohol to the point of becoming intoxicated most evenings. At a recent physical examination, Kara's physician noticed that in addition to her significant weight gain, that her blood pressure was elevated. Kara had also been complaining of frequent headaches. Kara tearfully confided in her doctor about the challenges both at work and at home. Dr. Clemson diagnosed Kara's clinical depression and gave her a prescription for Wellbutrin. She also wrote down the name of a counseling psychologist and strongly recommended that Kara call her. Kara feels ashamed about her need for professional help, but she presents for counseling on the recommendation of her doctor. Her therapist is Ms. Carson, an African American woman with an M.S. in Counseling Psychology.

QUESTIONS
1. How do Kara's cultural values impact her approach to seeking psychological help?
2. How might the "model minority myth" interfere with Ms. Carson's empathy for Kara's psychological distress?
3. Given Kara's dual diagnosis along with marital status transitions and gender and body image issues, what is the best approach for Ms. Carson to pursue in helping Kara?

DISCUSSION AND INTEGRATION
The Client, Kara

Kara is not very verbal about feelings of depression related to the dissolution of her marriage. This could be a result of personality and cultural dimensions. Although raised in the United States, Kara, who resided in the same household as her Japanese-born grandmother, was very influenced by many traditional Asian values. To this day, she spends quality time with her great maternal aunt and finds talking with her to be a source of strength and reassurance. Bradshaw (1994) discussed the cultural inconsistency of anger among Asian women, given the values of deference and meekness. Uba (1994) also discussed the hesistancy to discuss feelings openly.

Many Asian Americans are hesitant to discuss their feelings and problems openly and may feel rather skeptical about how effective counseling may be (Hong & Domokos-Cheng Ham, 2001). Some of the same attitudes that discourage Asian Americans from seeking mental health services discourage them, once in therapy, from discussing their problems. Nonetheless, because of the way in which many Asian communities deal with challenges to mental health by deferring to nonprofessionals, elders, and older relatives within the community (Yeh & Wang, 2000), Kara needs to be applauded for the help-seeking avenues that she has already explored.

Chow (1994) identified four cultural dilemmas facing Asian American women: (a) obedience versus independence, (b) collective (or familial) versus individual interest, (c) fatalism versus change, and (d) self-control versus self-expression or spontaneity (p. 186). Some of these forces were operating in Kara's life, particularly self-control and the construction of the self from a collectivistic orientation.

In a counseling situation, high adherence to Asian values can be an asset. Kim, Li, and Liang (2002) investigated the effects of client adherence to Asian cultural values, counseling session goal, and counselor emphasis of client expression on client perceptions of the career counseling process with 78 Asian American college students at a large mid-Atlantic university. Asian American clients who had high adherence to Asian cultural values, as measured by the Asian Values Scale, perceived greater client-counselor working alliance and counselor empathic understanding than did clients who had low adherence to Asian cultural values. Such values representing related aspects of Asian cultural values included collectivism, conformity to norms, emotional self-control, family recognition through achievement, filial piety, and humility. The authors concluded, "Asian Americans who adhere to Asian cultural values try to be understanding, accommodating, conciliatory, and not directly confrontational, and they expect the same from others" (pp. 351–352).

This type of research with a scale developed for and normed on Asians is very important to collecting reliable data. According to Uba (1994), "Just as there are few normative data on the behaviors of Asian Americans, there often are not data on normative responses of Asian Americans to various tests" (p. 165).

Kara's facility with the English language is one of the factors, from a study of Chinese Americans in the Bay Area of California, found to be associated with a more positive attitude regarding help seeking for a nervous or emotional problem (Ying & Miller, 1992). In a study by Lin (1994) of 145 adult Chinese Americans, when qualified ethnic and language-matched therapists were provided, the Chinese Americans were found to stay in therapy as long as the general American public. Kara's therapist is not Eurasian, yet she can be extremely helpful to Kara.

There are multiple issues in Kara's life. She most likely feels enormous shame regarding her weight gain, failed marriage, and alcohol consumption. These feelings are fueled by a sense of having neglected her community and/or family responsibilities. She is also depressed and has reason to be—she has lost a significant relationship that she values. The antidepressant medication prescribed by her physician may provide symptomatic relief and equip her with greater ability to cope with her feelings of sadness. The medication may, in time, allow Kara to function more effectively in the workplace. Kara's headaches may be stress related and a somatization of her inner state. According to Dana (2002), "Somatization constitutes an attempt to communicate an experience of bodily symptoms and distress in response to psychosocial stressors often associated with depression and anxiety disorders, or worry and preoccupation with well-being" (p. 37). Some research suggests that some groups of Asians may have higher rates of somatoform issues compared to the general population. Headaches are one way in which somatization is manifested.

It is likely that Kara has a sense of rejection from her husband's dishonoring of the marriage relationship. Such feelings of rejection and betrayal may well trigger feelings of personal inadequacy that are most likely associated with body image. In a culture obsessed with external standards of beauty such as ours, Kara is not alone in feeling the burden of this inordinate emphasis placed on being thin and pretty.

Much of the literature that is available would suggest that Asian Americans, in comparison to the general population, consume less alcohol and drugs (Mercado, 2000). The myth of the model minority fuels this dearth of information. The truth of the matter is that Asians like other groups contend with substance addictions as well. There is research to suggest that substance abuse among Asians is on the rise (Zane & Huh-Kim, 1998).

According to Chang (2000), "Most Asian cultures are historically patrilineal and patrilocal and favor male offspring over female. Consequently, women often grow up feeling devalued and suffer emotional and psychological consequences from these sexist customs throughout their lives" (p. 201). The stringent beauty standards that impact Kara's life is a function of patriarchy.

Implications for Counselors

There is great diversity within racially similar groups of people. Ms. Carson, Kara's counselor, understands this diversity while also having a sense of Kara's history and cultural values. Kara is very uncomfortable with asking for help. According to Hong & Domokos-Cheng Ham (2001), the concept of talk therapy is foreign to many Asian American clients. While seeking professional help may be a strange concept among many Asians, it is also foreign to other groups of color and to some White people as well. There is research to suggest that in spite of this lack of familiarity with psychotherapy, many Asian Americans might expect quick relief from their symptoms.

The multiple issues in Kara's life were alluded to earlier and include depression, job stress, racial identity/family issues, alcohol intoxication, and body-image challenges. Given her depression and the intersecting nature of Kara's issues, several months of regular counseling may benefit Kara; however, Ms. Carson might want to avoid telling Kara that part of her treatment plan involves months of therapy (Hong & Domokos-Cheng Ham, 2001). This information could be both overwhelming and discouraging.

Kara is biracial. It is not uncommon for biracial persons to struggle with converging their various identities. According to Mass (1992), Japanese people in Los Angeles had higher rates of outmarriages compared to other Asian groups. In a study conducted among interracial Japanese Americans, Mass (1992) sampled 53 college-age White Japanese respondents and 52 monoracial Japanese American college students. She measured ethnic identity, acculturation, self-concept, and the Japanese American ethnic experience, and administered a personality inventory. No differences in the psychological adjustment and self-esteem of the two groups were found. However, it was discovered that interacial Japanese Americans showed less identification with being Japanese than monoracial Japanese Americans. Japanese Americans who were raised in parts of the country (Hawaii and certain California communities) where there were larger numbers of Japanese Americans tended to have few or no problems with race. Kara grew up in a state with a large Asian population, yet her racial identity struggles are real and not unusual.

Kich (1992) developed a three-stage biracial model for Japanese and White Americans from semistructured interviews with 15 biracial adults. Such a developmental model may be helpful for Ms. Carson to bear in mind when counseling Kara. The first stage is awareness of differentness and dissonance between self-perceptions and the perceptions from other people. In this stage, biracial people are seen as different. Dissonance or discomfort about this difference can occur when the comparison process is regarded as devaluation. The second stage, Struggle for acceptance from others, can extend into adulthood and often occurs in the context of school or community settings. In cases where a biracial person is the only one in a particular context, the question, "What are you?" may be asked, especially in light of differences in one's name or phenotype. The final stage is self acceptance and assertion of an interracial identity. Kich (1992) says, "The biracial person's ability to create congruent self-definitions rather than be determined by others' definitions and stereotypes may be said to be the major achievement of a biracial and bicultural identity" (p. 314).

The nature of Kara's internal dissonance suggests that she is aware of differentness, has experienced dissonance around this recognition, and struggles with an acceptance of her multiple identities.

Kich (1992) discussed the ways in which biracial Japanese Americans achieved a sense of identity development. Some traveled to Japan and learned the language. Others met and spoke with extended family members who may have been less emotionally available in the past. Others who had endorsed the European American community exclusively may have explored their Japanese heritage anew or for the first time.

To best treat substance abuse issues, Mercado (2000) suggests a family counseling/therapy intervention. In addition, respecting cultural values and understanding the extent of acculturation are paramount to treating the client, even if the client is being seen alone (Chang, 2000). A genogram is suggested that might go back to three generations within the family. Cultural mapping could also be used, as well as an examination of the role that Kara has historically played within her family. Finally, gender roles need to be considered.

A combination of psychopharmacology and individual therapy may be extremely beneficial for Kara. She will need to be monitored by a medical doctor if taking antidepressants in light of her increased alcohol use. In addition, Ms. Carson may suggest journaling, walking to relieve stress and maintain physical health and strength, and deep breathing to relax. Given the influence of Kara's grandmother's wisdom on her life, Kara could be encouraged to reflect on this cultural strength. Ms. Carson would be wise to assess the role of spirituality in Kara's life and ascertain if it can be integrated into the treatment plan as a means of coping and resilience and resistance from discrimination and various forms of stress, including work and matters of the heart.

SUMMARY

This chapter focused on people of Asian descent. An extensive case study provided insight for counseling in working with a woman of mixed ethnic and racial heritage. Dual diagnosis (mood and substance disorders) were presented. The client's multiple identities: gender, ethnic, and cultural were discussed and considered as dimensions of problem presentation and resolution.

REFERENCES

Avakian, M. (2002). *Atlas of Asian-American history*. New York: Checkmark Books.

Berry, J. W., & Sam, D. L. (1997). Acculturation and adaptation. In J. W. Berry, M. H. Segall, & C. Kagiticibasi (Eds.), *Handbook of cross-cultural psychology: Volume 3—Social and behavioral applications* (pp. 291–326). Boston: Allyn & Bacon.

Bradshaw, C. (1994). Asian and Asian American women: Historical and political considerations in psychotherapy. In L. Comas-Diaz & B. Greene (Eds.), *Women of color: Integrating ethnic and gender identities* (pp. 72–113). New York: Guilford Press.

Byrd, W. M., & Clayton, L. A. (2003). *Racial and ethnic disparities in healthcare: A background and history*. In Unequal treatment: Confronting racial and ethnic disparities in healthcare (pp. 455–527). Institute of Medicine. The National Academies Press.

Cao, L., & Novas, H. (1996). *Everything you need to know about Asian-American history*. New York: Penguin.

Chang, E. C. (1996). Cultural differences in optimism, pessimism, and coping: Predictors of subsequent adjustment in Asian American and Caucasian American college students. *Journal of Counseling Psychology, 43*, 113–123.

Chang, P. (2000). Treating Asian/Pacific American addicts and their families. In J. Krestan (Ed.), *Bridges to Recovery: Addiction, family therapy, and multicultural treatment* (pp. 192–218). New York: Free Press.

Chow, E. N-L. (1994). The feminist movement: Where are all the Asian American women? In R. Takaki (Ed.), *From different shores: Perspectives on race and ethnicity in America*. New York: Oxford University Press.

Dana, R. H. (2002). Examining the usefulness of DSM–IV. In K. Kurasaki, S. Okasaki, & S. Sue (Eds.), Asian *American mental health: Assessment theories and methods* (pp. 29–46). New York: Kluwer.

Dana, R. H. (1993). *Multicultural assessment perspectives for professional psychology*. Boston: Allyn & Bacon.

Frisbie, W. P., Cho, Y., & Hummer, R. A. (2002). Immigration and the health of Asian and Pacific Islander adults in the United States. In T. A. LaVeist (Ed.), *Race, ethnicity, health: A public health reader* (pp. 231–251). San Francisco: Jossey–Bass.

Gloria, A. M., & Ho, T. A. (2003). Environmental, social, and psychological experiences of Asian American undergraduates: Examining issues of academic persistance. *Journal of Counseling and Development, 81*, 93–105.

Hong, G. L., & Domokos-Cheng Ham, M. (2001). *Psychotherapy and counseling with Asian American clients: A practical guide*. Thousand Oaks, CA: Sage.

Hsu, F. L. K. (1953). *American and Chinese: Two ways of life*. New York: Abeland-Schuman.

Kich, G. K. (1992). The developmental process of asserting a biracial, bicultural identity. In M. P. P. Root (Ed.), *Racially mixed people in America* (pp. 304–317). Newbury Park, CA: Sage.

Kim, B. S. K., Li, L. C., & Liang, C. T. H. (2002). Effects of Asian American client adherence to Asian cultural values, session goal, and counselor emphasis of client expression on career counseling process. *Journal of Counseling Psychology, 49*, 342–354.

Lao Tsu. (1972). *Tao Te Ching* (G. F. Feng & J. English, Trans.). New York: Vintage.

Leong, F. T. L., Wagner, N. S., & Kim, H. H. (1995). Group counseling expectations among Asian American students: The role of culture-specific factors. *Journal of Counseling Psychology, 42*, 217–222.

Lin, J. C. H. (1994). How long do Chinese Americans stay in psychotherapy? *Journal of Counseling Psychology, 41*, 288–291.

Mass, A. I. (1992). Interracial Japanese Americans: The best of both worlds or the end of the Japanese American community. In M. P. P. Root

(Ed.), *Racially mixed people in America* (pp. 265–279). Newbury Park, CA: Sage.

McFadden, J. (1993). *Transcultural counseling: Bilateral and international perspectives.* Alexandria, VA: American Counseling Association.

Mercado, M. M. (2000). The invisible family: Counseling Asian American substance abusers and their families. *The Family Journal: Counseling and Therapy for Couples and Families, 8,* 267–272.

Nhat Hanh, T. (1998). *The heart of the Buddha's teaching.* Berkeley, CA: Parallax Press.

Sandhu, D. S. (1997). Psychocultural profiles of Asian and Pacific Islander Americans: Implications for counseling and psychotherapy. *Journal of Multicultural Counseling and Development, 25,* 7–22.

Sodowski, G. R., Lai, E. W. M., & Plake, B. (1991). Moderating effects of sociocultural variables on acculturation attitudes of Hispanics and Asian Americans. *Journal of Counseling and Development, 70,* 194–204.

Sue, D. W., & Sue, D. (1990). *Counseling the culturally different: Theory and practice.* New York: Wiley.

Sue, D. W., & Sue, D. (1995). Asian Americans. In N. Vaac, S. B. Devaney, & J. Witmer (Eds.), *Experiences and counseling multicultural and diverse populations* (3rd ed., pp. 63–90). Bristol, PA: Accelerated Development.

Takaki, R. (1993). *A different mirror: A history of multicultural America.* Boston: Back Bay Books.

Takaki, R. (1994). The myth of the "model minority." In R. C. Monk (Ed.), *Taking sides: Clashing views on controversial issues in race and ethnicity* (pp. 55–61). Guilford, CT: Dushkin.

Tsai, J. L., & Chensova-Dutton, Y. (2002). Models of cultural orientation: Differences between American-born and overseas-born Asians. In K. Kurasaki, S. Okasaki, & S. Sue (Eds.), *Asian American mental health: Assessment theories and methods* (pp. 95–106). New York: Kluwer Academic.

Tsai, M., & Uemura, A. (1988). Asian Americans: The struggles, the conflicts, and the successes. In P. Bronstein & K. Quina (Eds.), *Teaching a psychology of people* (pp. 125–133). Washington, DC: American Psychological Association.

Uba, L. (1994). *Asian Americans: Personality patterns, identity, and mental health.* New York: Guilford Press.

U.S. Census Bureau. (2000a). Current population survey. Washington, DC: Racial Statistics Branch, Population Division.

U.S. Census Bureau. (2000b). The Asian population: 2000. Washington, DC: U.S. Department of Commerce.

U.S. Census Bureau. (2000c). Profile of selected social characteristics: Current Population Survey. Washington, DC: Racial Statistics Branch. Population Division.

U.S. Census Bureau. (2001). Overview of race and Hispanic origin: Census 2000 brief. Washington, DC: U.S. Department of Commerce.

U.S. Department of Health and Human Services. (2001). *Mental health: Culture, race, and ethnicity—A supplement to mental health: A report to the Surgeon General.* Rockville, MD: U.S. Department of Health and Human Services, Public Health Service, Office of the Surgeon General.

Wu, F. (2002). *Yellow: Race in America beyond Black and White.* New York: Basic Books.

Yeh, C., & Wang, Y. (2000). Asian American coping attitudes, sources, and practices: Implications for indigenous counseling strategies. *Journal of College Student Development, 41,* 94–103.

Ying, Y. (2002). The conception of depression in Chinese Americans. In K. Kurasaki, S. Okasaki, & S. Sue (Eds.), *Asian American mental health: Assessment theories and methods* (pp. 173–184). New York: Kluwer Academic.

Ying, Y., & Miller, L. S. (1992). Help-seeking behavior and attitude of Chinese Americans regarding psychological problems. *American Journal of Community Psychology, 20,* 549–556.

Zane, N. W. S., & Huh-Kim, J. (1998). Addictive behaviors. In L. S. Lee and N. Zane (Eds). *Handbook of Asian American Psychology* (pp. 527–554). Thousand Oaks, CA: Sage.

Part Three: **Converging Identities**

Chapter 8

Converging Race

It isn't easy to call people on their unconscious errors. If I point out that they said "American" when they meant "White," they will brush it off with, "Well, you know what I mean," or "Why are you bringing up race?" Yet it is worth pondering exactly what they do mean. What they have done through negligence, with barely any awareness, is equate race and citizenship. They may even become embarrassed once the effect is noticed.

Frank Wu, Yellow: Race in America Beyond Black and White

The multiculturally competent counselor recognizes that race converges with other identity constructs and for the client may be less of an important identity in the client's life. Throughout this chapter, racial identity theory is discussed. The discussion expands race beyond the limiting contexts of phenotype, oppression, and privilege.

RACE AND SCIENCE

The recently completed Human Genome Sequencing Project has confirmed what scientists have known for a very long time—that humans do not fit into the biological criteria that define race. The widely held belief in the biological differences between racial groups is simply incorrect (LaVeist, 2002). "Any way you measure, the amount of divergence between people is essentially zero," according to Joseph L. Graves, an evolutionary biologist. He went on to say that "the scientific case for the nonexistence of human race is overwhelming" ("Genetic Research," 2003).

Despite this scientific reality, a substantial portion of the dialogue about race includes conceptual frameworks that argued the inferiority of African and Semitic people attributable to inherent biological deficiencies (see Pedersen, 1994). Charles Darwin's (1859) work *The Origin of Species by Means of Natural Selection* was used to support the genetic intellectual superiority of Whites and the genetic inferiority of non-Whites, who were referred to as the "lower races." There are claims regarding racial purity and racial superiority but these are bogus and represent a false hope (Cooper, 2002). Everyone comes from the same source (Zuckerman, 1990). Still, outdated racial categories such as Negroid, Mongoloid, and Caucasoid remain. Human beings are products of migratory patterns and world conquests throughout the centuries; the argument of a pure race does not exist (Dobbins & Skillings, 1991).

As early as 1870, the U.S. Bureau of the Census divided the U.S. population into five races: White, Colored (Black), Colored (mulatto), Chinese, and Indian (Root, 1992). Since this time and in the present day, controversy among biologists, anthropologists, and other scholars has surrounded the topic of number of races.

For instance, Gossett (1963) recognized the diversity of opinion and observed the following:

> Linnaeus had found four human races; Blumenbach had five; Curvier had three; John Hunter had seven; Burke had sixty-three; Pickering had eleven; Virey had two "species," each containing three races; Haeckel had thirty-six; Hurley had four; Topinard had nineteen under three headings; Desmoulins had sixteen "species"; Deniker had seventeen races and thirty types. (p. 82)

Zuckerman (1990) sought to clarify misconceptions surrounding racial similarity and difference. He reported that, in his analysis of 18 genetic systems (blood groups, proteins, and enzymes) in 40 populations within 16 subgroups around the world, "the major component of genetic diversity is between individuals in the same tribe or nation; it accounts for 84% of the variance. Of the remaining variance, 10% is accounted for by racial groupings and 6% by geographic regions" (p. 1300). The existence of definable groups or races is not self-evident although human variation indeed is (Cooper, 2002).

Alan Goodman, dean of natural science at Hampshire College, said that, depending on which trait is used to distinguish races, "you won't get anything that remotely tracks conventional race categories" (cited in Begley, 1995, p. 67). Spickard (1992), a scholar on biracial identity, argued, "The so-called races are not biological categories at all. Rather, they are primarily social divisions that rely only partly on physical markers as skin color to identify group membership" (p. 17). Scientists studying the human genome announced recently that "the DNA of human beings is 99.9 percent alike, meaning that no matter what the color of our skin, when you look at humans on the genetic level, we are indistinguishable from one another" ("Race and the Human Genome," (2004).

ORIGINS OF RACIAL GROUPS

Considerable uncertainty surrounds racial origins. Rogers (1967), a historian, wrote that "for us of the present day, the earliest history of all peoples and nations is lost in a fog" (p. 21). Agreement among reputable historians and archaeologists is that the color of primitive humans was Black. Zuckerman (1990) concurred and wrote, "Although there is considerable speculation on the origin of races, little can be proved other than that a species, *Homo sapiens,* gradually evolved from its predecessor *Homo erectus* about 200,000 years ago in East Africa and spread through Africa and Eurasia" (p. 1297). On the basis of an examination of skeletons and art on the continents, early humans might have lived anywhere from 600,000 to 8,000 B.C. Rogers (1967) said that these people were of "small stature, probably from four and a half to five feet tall. Their nearest living descendants are believed to be the Bushmen of South Africa; the Mincopies of the Andaman Islands off the coast of India; the hill-folk of Southern India; the Tapiro of New Guinea; and the Negritos of the Philippines" (pp. 28–29).

If the origins of the human race are Black, from where did Whites originate? Rogers (1967) cited several scholars who believe that the White race is a function of lack of pigmentation, lost over time because it was not needed in cold environments. Sergi, of the University of Rome, stated that European man was African man, *Eur-African,* transformed by European environmental effects. There are three categories of *Eur-African*: "(a) the African with red, brown, and black pigmentation, (b) the Mediterranean or brunette complexion, inhabiting the great basin, including part of Northern Africa . . . and finally, (c) a Nordic variety of blond skin and hair, blue or gray eyes, most universally represented as Scandinavia, North Germany, and England" (Rogers, 1967, pp. 29–30).

RACE AS A SOCIAL CONSTRUCTION

Race often refers to phenotypic appearances, such as skin color, hair type (straight or curly), skin hue, eye color, stature, body size, nose, eyes, and head shape. Clearly, these characteristics alone do not accurately assign one to a particular racial classification or negate the larger biological similarity all human beings are destined to share (see the Storytelling "United by Blood"). Race represents one of the most salient identity constructs and is used as a marker by police, bankers, judges, teachers, employers, potential suitors, and others throughout society to assign people who share certain phenotypic characteristics to racial group membership. Assumptions about these assignments ensue and often dictate the ways in which people experience daily life. The social construction of race is sociopolitical and looms large. It contributes to race labeling, which depends on phenotype to assign people to categories that are caste-like in nature.

At the time in U.S. society when the Census listed five races, to be *colored* (Black or mulatto) was not just a source of difference. Race functioned as a status variable. More specifically, the experience of being "colored" meant no voting rights, no educational access to predominantly White institutions, inexistent or woefully inadequate health care, extreme vulnerability to being lynched, and no legal protection under the law. Yet, the mere classification of races was not solely responsible for differential treatment. Attitudes about race were pivotal to the creation of a social structure in which institutional policy bestowed privilege and conferred disadvantage on persons because of race (Cornell & Hartmann, 1997; McIntosh, 1988; Pinderhughes, 1989). The 2000 Census, for the first time, enabled people to select more than one race as a way of describing themselves. Of the 282 million Americans who responded to the Census, 2.4% indicated that they belonged to more than one race—that's nearly 7 million people.

STORYTELLING: United by Blood

I was donating blood at the Red Cross. After completing all the paperwork, which asks the most personal and intimate questions known to humankind, I was waiting to be taken to the bloodletting station. Before they called me, a nurse gave me several small plastic bags. This was different from the single large plastic bag to which I was accustomed. I asked what these little bags were. The nurse told me that I was special—that I was giving enough blood to help three babies. The thought of giving three innocent babies my blood was magical. Those babies and I were united, not by race, ethnicity, genetics, age, class, or gender. We were united by our humanity—that as a universal donor, I was able to help sustain life and they were able to receive it. We are more similar than we are different. The social construction of race cannot change this irrefutable fact.

In an effort to address racial and gender inequity, affirmative action was created through the provision of opportunity for groups that had been targets of historical discrimination. Takaki (1994), a scholar on race and ethnicity stated that:

> Affirmative action is actually designed to address the legacy of past racial discrimination and existing inequality by training and identifying qualified individuals of excluded racial minorities and allowing them greater access to equality and opportunity in education and employment. (p. 7)

Many believe that affirmative action seeks to impose quotas, which results in unqualified people (meaning people of color and women) taking jobs away from those who are qualified (often regarded as White males). The goal of affirmative action, however, was to encourage employers to create opportunity for people of color, given their exclusion throughout history and in current-day America. Eventually, this provision extended beyond racial classification to include gender, sexual orientation, physical disability, and religion.

RACIAL IDENTITY DEVELOPMENT

More differences exist within groups than between them. As such, differences in racial identity and value orientations are to be expected among racially similar but individually unique people. Racial identity development theory underscores the reality of psychological differences within racial and ethnic groups and discourages a monolithic perspective when seeking to understand people who are racially or ethnically similar. Racial identity theory also assumes that individuals at early levels of development have the potential to change over time as they encounter dissonance to existing cognitive schema (Robinson, 1999). By integrating racial identity into a discussion of race, race is then conceptualized as one component of psychosocial identity. The goal is to move race beyond the framework of unearned privilege and oppression. Toward this end, several racial identity development models are discussed in the following sections.

CROSS'S NIGRESENCE MODEL

Cross's (1991) theory of racial identity development, called the **Negro-to-Black conversion experience,** or **Nigresence,** is the most widely used racial theory about African Americans. It presumes a sociopolitical perspective and refers to the process of developing healthy racial collective identities, as a function of discrepancies in sociopolitical power across racial groups. In Cross's work, a distinction is made between *personal identity (PI)* and *reference group orientation (RGO)*. The former refers to self-esteem and interpersonal competence; the latter refers to racial identity and racial self-esteem. Cross's work on Black racial identity has been extremely influential in the development of models related to other aspects of identity, including racial and cultural identity models for other groups of color and the womanist identity model (see Ossana, Helms, & Leonard, 1992).

Within Cross's (1991) theory, identity development is a maturation process whereby external negative images of the self are replaced with positive internal conceptions. Cross's five-stage nigresence model—(a) preencounter, (b) encounter, (c) immersion and emersion, (d) internalization, and (e) internalization and commitment—refers to "a resocializing experience" that "seeks to transform a preexisting identity (a non-Africentric identity) into one that is Africentric" (p. 190). Robinson and Howard-Hamilton (1994) discussed **Africentricity** as a conscious ideology with a strong connection to one's spirituality and kinship via African culture, culminating in the shared belief "I am because we are and since we are, therefore I am." An optimal Africentric worldview can be measured by an instrument called the Belief Systems Analysis Scale (BSAS), developed by Fine and James-Myers (1990). *Africentrism* involves an awareness of Black identity, knowledge of cultural customs and traditions, liberating psychological resistance strategies, and an understanding of oppression and strategies to resist it (Dana, 1993; Robinson & Howard-Hamilton, 1994).

At *preencounter*, the acculturated African American views the world through the lens of the White dominant culture. Essentially, race has low salience. When people are asked to describe themselves, identifiers other than race, such as work, church, profession, and club affiliation, surface as key descriptors. Cross (1991) maintained that many preencounter African Americans are psychologically healthy and that anti-Black attitudes among African Americans in this stage are rare, although they do exist. Despite indices of psychological health among African Americans at this base stage of racial identity, Cross stated, "Preencounter Blacks cannot help but experience varying degrees of miseducation about the significance of the Black experience" (p. 192). African Americans in this first stage are more likely to operate from a Euro-centric cultural perspective in evaluating beauty and art forms.

At the *encounter* stage, one's new view of the world, as a result of a shocking personal experience, is inconsistent with the old. According to Cross (1991), the two aspects of this stage are (a) experiencing an encounter and (b) personalizing it. In every year of a person's life, myriad encounter experiences could encourage movement from preencounter to encounter. If the experiences are not internalized and personalized, however, movement up to this next stage cannot occur. Other identity constructs, such as religion, class, and education, can delay racial identity formation, particularly when similarity with the referent group (e.g., being Christian, middle class, academically gifted) is encouraged, and differences (e.g., race) that may be perceived as threatening or divisive are ignored (Robinson, 1999).

In the *immersion and emersion* stage, the focus is on being Black to the exclusion of others, particularly Whites. Cross (1991) indicated that this is a transitional stage with respect to identity transformation: "The person's main focus in life becomes a feeling of 'togetherness and oneness with people' " (p. 207).

The fourth stage of Cross's model, *internalization*, is characterized by more peace and calm. At this juncture, dissonance regarding an emerging identity has been resolved, evidenced by high salience attached to Blackness.

Internalization and commitment persons seek to eradicate racism for all oppressed people. According to Cross, this stage is similar to the internalization stage but is reflective of sustained long-term interest and commitment, as opposed to a brief period in one's life. At the higher stages of Cross's model, the African American is more able than at the lower stages to reconceptualize the self outside the narrow confines of oppression. At initial stages, the African American has little awareness of racial oppression because race has minimal importance. Cross has developed the Cross Racial Identity Scale (Vandiver, 2001) to measure the revised dimensions of his Nigresence model.

NATIVE AMERICAN IDENTITY

According to Horse (2001), ethics, or the principles or moral values which guide people's actions, provide Horse with a clear way of conceptualizing Indian identity. Part of this ethic is within the context of a collective consciousness that is influenced by (a) the degree to which one is grounded in the native language, tribe, family, and culture; (b) the worldview which one embraces; (c) recognition as a member of an Indian tribe by the government of the tribe; and (d) the validity of one's genealogical heritage as an Indian, which Horse (2001) asserts is more connected to one's consciousness as an Indian person and not on human-made laws. Concern over blood quantum is an identity issue among Native Indians in urban and rural environments (Wilson, 1992).

Consciousness requires memory, which Gunn Allen (1994) said is not encouraged within a Western tradition. She stated, "The American idea that the best and the brightest should willingly reject and repudiate their origins leads to an allied idea—that history, like everything in the past, is of little value and should be forgotten as quickly as possible" (p. 192).

MULTIRACIAL IDENTITY DEVELOPMENT

Wijeyesinghe (2001) presented a factor model of multiracial identity (FMMI) developed from a qualitative study of African American/European American multiracial adults. The beauty of this model is that it is nonlinear and represents factors or dimensions of identity. These dimensions include (a) racial ancestry or family tree; (b) early experiences and socialization, which include exposure to culture, such as food, music, holiday, dialect, and language; (c) cultural attachment that may influence racial designation; (d) physical appearance, which includes skin hue, body shape, and hair texture; (e) social and historical context, such as the presence of other multiracial people or the 2000 Census allowing people to choose more than one box to designate themselves racially/ethnically; (f) political awareness and orientation, which is connected to the awareness of race and racism within a larger sociopolitical context; (g) other social identities, such as sexual orientation and social class; and (h) spirituality or being guided by spirit, which fosters connection to others and allows people to transcend the divisions of race and ethnicity.

The U.S. Census data documents the reality of increasing numbers of persons who are biracial. Because many existing models assume racial homogeneity among persons, a biracial model is greatly needed.

Poston (1990) proposed a model of biracial identity development with five linear stages: (a) personal identity, (b) choice of group categorization, (c) emeshment/denial, (d) appreciation, and (e) integration. Kich's (1992) model on biracial and bicultural development is discussed in Chapter 7.

LATINO IDENTITY DEVELOPMENT

That Latinos can be and are of any race is confusing and difficult for counseling students to grasp. When students are told that Latinos are not a racial group but an ethnic group with different ethnic and racial subgroups, the confusion magnifies. When I make the point to students that sharing race does not mean sharing ethnicity, and sharing ethnicity does not mean sharing race, I often draw a venn diagram or say something like: "A White-skinned woman with blond hair and blue eyes might identify herself ethnically as Cubana but racially she considers herself to be White. Is she a Latina?" Yes. At the same time, a sister Cubana may have African roots, dark skin, and very curly hair. Ethnically, she is also Cubana but considers herself Black. The difficulty surrounding the understanding of Latinos racially and ethnically is connected to the bifurcation of racial categories. A dichotomized way of perceiving people has had implications for a model of racial or ethnic identity development for Latinos. A dialectic embraces a "both/and" way of being in the world and is needed to appreciate multiple identities within people and across groups of people. In addition, the existing models of racial identity cannot be applied to Latinos. Latinos are not a racial group.

According to Ferdman and Gallegos (2001), there are key dimensions involved in defining a nonlinear Latino orientation. The first dimension is the *lens* toward identity, how a person prefers to identify herself, how Latinos as a group are seen, how Whites are seen, and how *race* fits into the equation.

LATINO INTEGRATED   Persons who are Latino integrated are able to embrace the fullness of their Latino identity and integrate this into other identities, such as class, profession, and gender. A dialectic, as mentioned earlier, is characteristic of the Latino integrated. This person is comfortable with all types of Latinos as there is a broad lens used to see themselves, White people, and others.

LATINO IDENTIFIED   This group has more of a pan-Latino identity, with a view of race, *la raza*, as uniquely Latin. There is a deep and abiding understanding of a history of political struggle and a desire to be united with other Latinos in racial unity. Despite the awareness of and vigilant stand against institutional racism, Latino-identified persons may see Whites, Blacks, and other groups in rigid ways.

SUBGROUP IDENTIFIED   Persons of this group see themselves as distinct from White people but do not necessarily identify with other Latinos or with people of color. The broad pan-Latino orientation discussed in the previous orientations is not reflected here. Other Latino subgroups may be viewed in an inferior way. People's allegiance to a particular subgroup is nearly exclusive. Race is not a central or clear organizing concept, but nationality, ethnicity, and culture are primary.

LATINO AS "OTHER"   Persons with this orientation see themselves as people of color. This may be a function of biracial or multiracial status, ambiguous phenotype, or dominant constructions of race. In certain contexts, the person sees herself as a minority person and not White. There is no identification with Latino cultural norms or with White culture, and an understanding of Latino history and culture is missing.

UNDIFFERENTIATED   Persons with this orientation regard themselves as simply "people" with a color-blind eye. The emphasis on racial classification is not a part of their framework. The desire to associate with other Latinos is not prominent because contact with others is distinct from a person's race or ethnic identity. Life is lived apart from attention to and thoughts of difference.

WHITE IDENTIFIED   White-identified persons perceive themselves as White and thus superior to people of color (*non-White skinned people*—emphasis mine). Assimilation into White culture is a possibility as is connection primarily to only one other group (e.g., light-skinned Cubans) while denying connection to other subgroups. There is an acceptance of the status quo and a valuing of Whiteness to the extent that marrying White is preferred over marrying dark. Latinos with this orientation are *mejorar la raza* (i.e., improve the race).

The strength of this model is that it helps counselors and clients ascertain identity development for Latinos who differ greatly across acculturation level, skin color, national origin, and political ideology. This is also not a linear model; nonetheless, it is clear that there are orientations more conducive to unity with others across race and skin color wherein people are valued because they are human and not because of what they look like.

ASIAN AMERICAN IDENTITY DEVELOPMENT

There are many problems facing Asian people in their experience in America. One of the most pervasive is related to the psychological conflict around racial identity. This conflict is connected to the experience of institutional racism, which is often subtle but damaging nonetheless to people who are targeted as inferior due to being different from a standard of White acceptability (Kim, 2001). According to Kim, "At some point in their lives, many Asian Americans have either consciously or unconsciously expressed the desire to become White, and tried to reject their identity as Asians" (p. 70.).

Underlying assumptions for an Asian American identity development model include (a) the predominance of White racism and its impact on Asian American identity development must be acknowledged, (b) internalized racism has to be unlearned unconsciously, and (c) a healthy identity requires the transformation of a negative racial identity into a positive and healthy one. The proposed stage model is sequential but not linear or automatic.

STAGE ONE: ETHNIC AWARENESS   This first stage represents the period prior to children's entry into the school system. The social environment and reference group consists largely of family. The extent of one's participation in Asian-oriented activities can bolster a sense of positive ethnic awareness.

STAGE TWO: WHITE IDENTIFICATION   This stage is marked by children's painful awareness that they are different from White people and that this difference is not regarded as a good thing. Feeling a sense of shame for being Asian can result in desperate attempts by Asian children to fit into White society. To compensate for feelings of inferiority, many Asian children will seek leadership in organizations and excel academically. Active White identification refers to the Asian student not con-sciously perceiving herself as different from Whites, thus there is a desire to alienate herself from and not be regarded as Asian. Passive White identification Asians enter this stage during their later years and are buffered by early exposure to predomi-nantly Asian communities that nurtured self-esteem. The distancing from Asians and seeking to pass for White is not evident here, but fantasizing, (e.g., "I wish") about being White does occur.

STAGE THREE: AWAKENING TO SOCIAL POLITICAL CONSCIOUSNESS   A shift from personal to social responsibility for racism allows Asian Americans to understand racism and transform their negative sense of self into a positive one. At this stage, White people are no longer the reference group and Asians do not regard them-selves as inferior. The person essentially asks the question, "Why should I be ashamed of who I am?" There is a connection to other people of color.

STAGE FOUR: REDIRECTION TO AN ASIAN AMERICAN CONSCIOUSNESS   In this stage, the sense of oneself as a minority is crystallized into one being Asian. There is often an immersion into the Asian experience and the ego is centered on things/people Asian. Racial pride is experienced as is a positive self-concept. In addi-tion to pride, people feel angry at the way in which the dominant White culture per-petuates racism and cultural violence.

STAGE FIVE: INCORPORATION   One's racial identity is blended into other social identities. The self is seen as whole, with race representing only one aspect of social identity. The immersion of the previous stage is relaxed. A clear Asian American identity has been achieved, yet people in general are the person's reference group.

This model is clearly influenced by other racial identity development theories, yet takes into consideration the unique experiences of Asian Americans.

WHITE RACIAL IDENTITY DEVELOPMENT

Traditional conceptions of race refer to people of color, but European Americans are also racial beings and experience racial identity development. As racial beings, White people are shaped by the construct of race in their and other people's lives, impacted by both skin color privilege and the adverse consequences of racism (Robinson, 1999).

It is an infrequent experience or encounter that would encourage a White person to assess her attitudes about being a racial being (Pope-Davis & Ottavi, 1994). In a society where unearned skin color advantages are conferred, European American counselors need to develop a positive racial identity that does not emanate from oppression and domination. This transformation may be difficult for two reasons. First, it is possible for White people to live in U.S. society without having to acknowledge or give much consideration to the meaning of being White. Second, denial about one's own race impedes self-awareness, a crucial factor in racial identity development.

Helms (1995; Helms & Parham, 1984) has been the predominant voice in the development of White racial identity theory. Hardiman (1982, 2001) developed the White identity development model (WID), which was the first model on White racial identity development.

Helms's (1984, 1995) White racial identity development model (WRID) has six statuses. The term status is preferred over stage in that the latter is more reflective of a fixed state. Helms believed that people could be characterized by more than one status at a given time. These statuses are (a) contact, (b) disintegration, (c) reintegration, (d) pseudoindependence, (e) immersion-emersion, and (f) autonomy. Helms's revised model includes information processing strategies for each of the six statuses.

A person enters the _contact_ status from encountering the idea or actuality of Black people. Family background and environment affect whether the attitude toward Black people is one of trepidation or naive curiosity. In contact, the European American automatically benefits from institutional and cultural racism without the conscious awareness of doing so. The identity ego status and information processing strategy for contact is obliviousness. White people are satisfied with the status quo and are fairly oblivious to the role of racism and their involvement in it.

White people in the contact status tend to have positive self-esteem. They are idealistic about the equal treatment of African Americans; however, in actually interacting with them, they may experience some anxiety or arousal. Through interaction with African Americans, the European American realizes that, independent of economic conditions, clear distinctions exist in the treatment of people across race.

Continuing to have socialization experiences will move the person into Helms's second status, _disintegration_. Entry into disintegration is characterized by conscious conflict that has its origins in dissonance. Here, the White person realizes that people are treated differently as a function of race. The identity ego status and information processing strategy for disintegration are suppression and ambivalence. White people in this status are truly confused by anxiety-provoking racial moral dilemmas that require them to choose between own-group loyalty and humane behavior.

The third status is *reintegration*, which is entered as the White person realizes that, within the dominant culture, the covert and overt belief of White superiority and Black inferiority exists. The desire to be accepted by her White racial group is very strong. It is important in reintegration that a racial identity be acknowledged. Here, White privilege is protected even though it is unearned. People of color are not entitled to privilege because they are morally, socially, and intellectually inferior. Because honest dialogue about race between racially different people does not often take place, it is fairly easy for a person to fixate here. A jarring event can trigger movement into the fourth status, *pseudoindependence*. The identity ego status and information processing strategy for reintegration are selective perception and negative out-group distortion. White people are idealized and others are not tolerated well at all.

According to Helms (1990), "Pseudoindependence is the first stage of redefining a positive White identity" (p. 61). This status is primarily one of intellectualization wherein the person acknowledges responsibility for White racism. The negativity of the earlier stages does not exist; nonetheless, White norms continue to be used to interpret cultural or racial differences. Socially, the person is met with suspicion by both Whites and Blacks. Discomfort with their ambiguous racial identity may move the person into the fifth status. The identity ego status and information processing strategy for psuedoindependence are reshaping reality and selective perception. The commitment to racism is largely intellectual. The goal is to reach out and assist other racial groups.

This fifth status, *immersion-emersion*, is characterized by the replacement of old myths and stereotypes with accurate information. It is a period of unlearning. Here, the person may participate heavily in White-consciousness groups in which the goal is to help the person abandon a racist identity. The focus is not on changing Black people but rather on seeking to change White people. The successful resolution of this status requires that the individual recycle or reexperience earlier emotion that was distorted or repressed. The identity ego status and information processing strategy for immersion-emersion are hypervigilance and reshaping. There is a diligent search for the personal meaning of racism and the ways in which one benefits from racism.

Autonomy, the sixth and last status of Helms's (1984, 1995) model is an ongoing process. In this status, a primary goal is internalizing and experiencing new ways of being racial that were learned from previous stages. Race, one's own and other people's, is not a threat. The identity ego status and information processing strategy for autonomy are flexibility and complexity. Internal standards are for defining the self, and there is a capacity to relinquish the privileges of racism. Helms (1990) stated that the second phase, development of a nonracist White identity, begins with the pseudoindependent stage and ends with the autonomy stage.

ADDITIONAL MEASURES OF IDENTITY

Other measures of identity for various ethnic groups are available. For example, the Ethnic Identity Questionnaire measures preferences of Japanese kinship ties, sex roles, interracial attitudes, and personality characteristics (Dana, 1993). The Acculturation

Rating Scale for Mexican Americans has been used to "represent Hispanic cultural origins" (Dana, 1993, p. 122). This 20-item scale looks at ethnicity of friends, language preference, and contact with Mexico. A similar scale, the Hispanic Acculturation Scale, has 12 items and examines three factors: (a) language use and ethnic loyalty, (b) electronic media preferences, and (c) ethnic social relations.

The Indian Assimilation Scale was developed in 1937–38 and is considered the best example of a pan-Indian measure. It includes attitudes toward native customs, marriage preferences, participation in organizations, and desire to become assimilated (Dana, 1993).

The Cultural Adaptation Pain Scale (CAPS), developed by Sandhu, Portes, and McPhee (1996), assesses the cultural adaptation and psychological pain associated with becoming acculturated. Fifteen major themes of psychological pain are explored. The four factors identified were (a) pain, (b), learned helplessness, (c), positive adaptation, and (d) bigoted. It was not developed for any particular racial or ethnic group.

OPTIMAL THEORY APPLIED TO IDENTITY DEVELOPMENT

Myers et al. (1991) developed a theory of optimal identity that is neither linear nor categorical. In criticizing some psychosocial identity models, she observed that they have limited the role of the individual in the identity process, did not consider people with multiple identities, and were based on a Eurocentric worldview. Myers maintained that the dichotomy of the spirit world and matter within American society makes it difficult to attain a positive self-identity in the United States, regardless of race, because self-worth is based primarily on external validation. Persons who turn outside themselves for meaning, peace, and value have adopted a suboptimal worldview. According to Myers, within an optimal perspective, self-worth is intrinsic in being. Thus, the purpose of life is becoming clearer about how the self is connected with all of life. Spiritual development is an integral part of identity development.

In Phase 0, known as *absence of conscious awareness,* the person lacks awareness of being. This is regarded as an infancy stage. Phase 1 is *individuation.* Here, the world is the way it is in that people simply lack awareness of any view of self other than the one to which they were initially introduced. They rarely assign meaning or value to the various aspects of their identity. Phase 2 is *dissonance;* persons begin the exploration of their true self and effectively explore dimensions of the self that may be demeaned by others. In Phase 3, *immersion,* one's energy is focused on those who are regarded as similar. Phase 4, *internalization,* occurs as people feel good about who they are and have successfully incorporated feelings of self-worth. Phase 5, *integration,* happens as people's deeper understanding of themselves allows them to change their assumptions about the world. The self is more secure internally, and peaceful relationships are a manifestation of this. The final stage, Phase 6, is *transformation.* The self is redefined toward a sense of personhood that includes ancestors, the unborn, nature, and community. The universe is understood as benevolent, orderly, and personal.

A BIRD'S-EYE VIEW OF THE RESEARCH

An abundance of research on racial identity has been done with a predominantly college- and graduate-student population. The purpose here is to examine some of the research to identify common themes related to identity development.

Vandiver (2001) reviewed the Cross Racial Identity Scale (CRIS), a 40-item, 7-point Likert-type inventory to measure Cross's revised theory of Nigresence. Reference group orientation and race salience are also assessed. There are six scales: Preencounter Assimilated (PA), Preencounter Miseducation (PM), Preencounter Self Hatred (PSH), Immersion/Emersion Anti-White (IEAW), Internalization Afrocentriocity Black Nationalist (IA), and Internalization Multiculturalist Inclusive (IMCI). The psychometric properties of the CRIS report acceptable Cronbach alphas: PA = .85, PM = .89, PSH: = .85, IEAW = .85, IBN = .79, IMCI = .76. Newsome (2003) reported comparable reliability coefficients in her research using the CRIS with Black college students at a historically Black college in the Southeast.

Increasing numbers of researchers are conducting empirical research on the multicultural counseling competencies (Holcomb-McCoy, 2000). In one study, the Multicultural Counseling Inventory (MCI) was used to explore whether the ethnicity of rehabilitation counselors would affect the results of the MCI among rehabilitation counselors (n = 303). Of the participants, 86% were European American, 11% were African American, and 3% were members of other races. The researchers found that the Black counselors identified themselves as being more multiculturally competent than did the White counselors. There were no differences between the racial groups on skills or knowledge. There was a tendency, however, for Black counselors to answer in what is considered to be a socially desirable direction (Holcomb-McCoy, 2000).

Holcomb-McCoy (2000) reviewed the literature on multicultural counseling competence. She developed a survey of 61 items that was then sent to professional counselors selected from the ACA membership. Out of 500 surveys mailed, the total number returned was 151. Five factors were identified: (a) knowledge, (b) awareness, (c) definition of terms, (d) racial identity development, and (e) skills. According to the author, in addition to awareness, knowledge, and skills, racial identity development and multicultural terminology are critical factors of multicultural competence. This finding is consistent with the multicultural literature regarding the importance of counselors-in-training being aware of not only their own racial identity levels but also those of their clients. Avoiding confusion in terms, such as race and ethnicity or gender and sex, distinguishes the trained counselor from the layperson.

Fortunately, more researchers are examining the constructs of race and gender among college students. For example, Cokley (2001) conducted research on academic self-concept, racial centrality, and academic motivation of 257 African American college students. Ninety-two were male and 165 were female. Packets were given to students during summer school at two historically Black colleges. The purpose of the study was to examine gender as an important variable in understanding the psychosocial development of African American students. The researchers found that women scored significantly higher on one of the extrinsic motivation scales (the Extrinsic Motivation Identified Regulation scale). Men had significantly higher scores on the Atrinsic Motivation scale, which represents neither intrinsic nor extrinsic motivation. The researchers concluded that Black female students were more motivated about being in college than were Black male students. Black male students evidenced a lack of motivation. It is possible to conclude that the college and overall school experience for many Black males is perceived as alienating. The number of Black males enrolling in and graduating from college has fallen off sharply over the years (Cokley, 2001). Thus, the majority of the research done in this area is on middle school and high school students. The lack of difference in race centrality scores between males and females may suggest that for both genders, race is a central and dominant construct.

Watt, Robinson, and Lupton-Smith (2002) conducted a study of ego identity and Black and White racial identity among 38 graduate students (30 White, 6 Black, and 2 Middle Eastern) at the beginning, middle, and end of their counseling training in a program that included student counseling, community agency, and school counseling tracks. The researchers used the Washington Sentence Completion Test to measure ego identity and used Black and White versions of the Racial Identity Attitude Scale. It was hypothesized that the ego developments of students enrolled in Prepracticum (a second-year class) would be higher than the ego development of students enrolled in Theories and Cross-Cultural (both first-year classes). It was found that students in Theories had lower ego development than students in Cross-Cultural and Prepracticum; however, there were no differences in ego development between students in Cross-Cultural and students in Prepracticum. It was also found that students enrolled in Theories had a lower mean score at the Psuedo-Independence status than did the Prepracticum students. In addition, the racial identity status of students enrolled in Cross-Cultural was higher than the racial identity status of students enrolled in Theories. These data are important in understanding ego and racial identity development for students at different developmental stages in their programs. The study needs to be replicated with a much larger and racially and culturally diverse sample.

Ancis, Sedlacek, and Mohr (2000) studied 578 African American, Asian American, Latino, and White college student responses to a questionnaire assessing perceptions and experiences of the campus cultural climate (CACQ). This scale has 100 statements regarding campus climate. The 11 factors include racial tension, fair treatment, cross-cultural comfort, racial pressures, comfort with own culture, and lack of support. The researchers found racial differences among respondents. African American students reported more negative experiences in comparison to Asian American, Latino, and White students. More specifically, Black students experienced "greater racial-ethnic hostility, greater pressure to conform to stereotypes, less equitable treatment by faculty, staff, and teaching assistants, and more faculty racism than did the other groups" (p. 183). The Asian American and Latino students reported experiences of stereotyping and prejudice. They indicated limited respect and unfair treatment by faculty, teaching assistants, and students, and pressure to conform to stereotypes. Compared to other racial groups, Latinos experienced the least racism and a campus climate relatively free of racial conflict. White students reported less racial tension, few expectations to conform to stereotypic behavior, an experience of being treated fairly, a respectful and diverse campus climate, and the most overall satisfaction.

IMPLICATIONS FOR COUNSELORS

In a recent survey conducted by the Kaiser Family Foundation (U.S. Department of Health and Human Services, 2001), it was found that 12% of African Americans and 15% of Latinos, compared to 1% of Whites, felt that a doctor or health care provider would judge them unfairly or treat them with disrespect because of their race or ethnic background. There is a climate of mistrust around race. Poor Black families are often stigmatized as disorganized, lazy, and deprived (Boyd-Franklin, 2003). Part of multicultural competence is knowledge of these sociopolitical dynamics.

The counseling relationship is influenced by a client's racial identity development because it can directly affect the client's preference for a counselor. For example, clients of color in preencounter (Black), White identified (Latino), or White identification (Asian) are more likely to prefer a White counselor over a counselor of color. The belief exists that "Whites are more competent and capable than members of one's own race" (Sue & Sue, 1990, p. 108). In this scenario, if the counselor is White, the client will typically be overeager to identify with the counselor. If the counselor is non-White, then the counselor will experience feelings of hostility from the client even if the client and the counselor are of the same race. Independent of the counselor's race, the counselor has a responsibility to help reeducate the client as they work together through the client's conflicts. Regardless of race, counselors who choose not to face their biases with courageous introspection are not appropriate candidates for the mental health profession.

During the encounter and dissonance stages, clients are preoccupied with questions concerning the self and identity. They may still prefer a White counselor; however, counselors can take advantage of clients' focus on self-exploration toward resolution of identity conflicts. During the immersion/emersion, resistance and immersion stage of racial/ethnic identity, clients of color tend to view their psychological problems as an outgrowth of oppression and racism. In this stage, clients of color are prone to prefer counselors of their own race. In fact, people of color may tend to perceive White counselors as enemies. Thus, it is important for White counselors to not personalize any attacks from clients of color. Many statements regarding the unjust sociopolitical nature within the United States have legitimacy. It is also wise for counselors to anticipate that resistance/immersion clients will test them, because this stage is one of great volatility. Finally, counselors are apt to be more effective with a client when they use action-oriented methods aimed at external change.

Clients of color at the more integrated phases of racial identity experience an inner sense of security regarding their self-identities. They are able to choose counselors, not on the basis of race, but on the basis of the professional's ability to be empathic and understanding of the issues clients bring to counseling. Sue and Sue (1990) stated that "attitudinal similarity between counselor and client is a more important dimension than membership-group similarity" (p. 112). Nonetheless, clients at higher stages of racial identity may accept a counselor of a different race while preferring one of their own racial or even ethnic or gender group. This preference need not be an indication of discriminatory attitudes but may instead reflect a desire or need for a connection that may or may not occur.

All counselors need to acknowledge their biases and assess their personal readiness prior to engaging in counseling across sources of diversity (see the case study "Not Wanting to Be Racist" at the end of this chapter). To not do so is to place the client in jeopardy. Richardson and Molinaro (1996) found that the reintegration counselor may be impatient toward clients of different races and less likely to establish rapport with these clients. Cook (1994) suggested that White counselors may also engage in ethnocentric behavior if they operate at Helms's reintegration stage and recognize their own race as standard for "normal" behavior of the client. Not until the immersion/emersion stage do White counselors acknowledge clients' race, respect cultural influences, and examine the sociopolitical implications. At the pseudoindependence stage, the White counselor will discuss racial issues but only when interacting with persons of color (Cook, 1994). Generalized assumptions still frame people's thinking.

The importance of a supervisor assisting with a supervisee's racial identity has been researched by Ladany, Brittan-Powell, and Pannu (1997). They found in their research of 105 racially diverse counselors that when supervisee and supervisor were at parallel levels of high racial identity stages, agreement about the supervision process was higher. In addition, when supervisor and supervisee had high levels of racial identity or when the supervisor had a higher level of racial identity than the supervisee, the supervisee's perception of the supervisor's multicultural development influence on her was greater.

Ultimately, our beliefs and attitudes will inform the quality of our listening and our talking. Delpit (1997) eloquently said, "We do not really see through our eyes . . . but through our beliefs. To put our beliefs on hold is to cease to exist as ourselves for a moment—and that is not easy . . . but it is the only way to learn what it might feel like to be someone else and the only way to start the dialogue" (p. 101).

CASE STUDY
Not Wanting to Be Racist

Tiffany has just completed her master's degree in counseling psychology in Conneticut. She is 24 years old and European American. Tiffany is a resident director (RD) in the residence halls at a small private school. She supervises the resident counselors who live in the residences with the students. One of the counselors, Nia, who is Black, tells Tiffany about Fatima, a 21-year-old senior from Iran.

Fatima appears depressed, and has dealt with ostracism from other students since the 9/11 terrorists attacks, despite the university president's appeal for a welcoming and tolerant campus. Nia is aware that Fatima has expressed an interest in returning home despite the fact that she is less than 3 months away from graduating. Nia has seen Fatima looking distraught as she has walked around campus. She has also found Fatima taking her meals from the dining hall to avoid having to sit with the other students. Fatima has been living on campus for 3 years since she started college. She has an aunt and uncle who live in Virginia. She often visits them during school holidays. Tiffany is concerned about Fatima, who is one of the few students from the Middle East attending the college. Fatima is a Muslim and wears the traditional headdress, the hijab, associated with her religion. Tiffany grew up in upstate New York and has never interacted with Muslims and did not cover this particular ethnic group during her sole graduate-level cross-cultural psychology class. Tiffany is at a loss because she does not know what to do. She is afraid of offending Fatima because of her lack of information about Muslim culture. The last thing that she would want to do is be insensitive or have Fatima think that she is racist. So she does not bring up race-related topics. Nia also does not know what to do, and there are no other people from the Middle East on campus with whom to confer. Tiffany is not connected to the Muslim community and is unaware of any resources that may be available to Fatima, herself, or to Nia.

QUESTIONS

1. What can Tiffany do about her fears in working with Fatima?
2. Are Tiffany's fears shared by other counseling students in training or even among new counselors?
3. How can new counselors get the help they need while being in a leadership role themselves?
4. What are the sources of difference between Tiffany and Fatima, and which ones are causing Tiffany the greatest discomfort? Why?

DISCUSSION AND INTEGRATION
The Client, Fatima

Fatima is extremely uncomfortable on her college campus, feels the anger and ostracism from the culture at large and from the campus in particular, and longs to be in an environment where she is welcomed and respected. Fatima is fluent in English, French,

and Farsi. She is extremely intelligent and is proud of her accomplishments. She expects to do well and has functioned fairly independently on campus. However, the ostracism, name-calling, and ignorance have not only saddened her but made her very angry and determined not to put up with such "idiotic attitudes."

Fatima's aunt and uncle came to the United States during the second wave of Iranian immigration between 1970 and 1978. Like many Iranian immigrants, her aunt and uncle are professionals. He is a physician and she is a master seamstress and an extraordinary hostess, treating guests like royalty when visiting their home. According to Fatima, her aunt can make anything without a pattern by looking at a picture only once. Her uncle is clearly the head of the household and has been culturally socialized to expect such authority, deference, and obedience within the family that he provides for materially and socially. Fatima's aunt is not without her own power within the family; it is simply a different form than her husband's. Many families that have been influenced by Western culture may experience a shift from the traditional and prescribed gender roles to those that are more egalitarian (Jalali, 1996). This has not been the case for Fatima's aunt and uncle.

Iranians have survived a variety of invasions from foreign powers as well as contended with turmoil from within their country's government. Despite the instability, Iranians have held tenaciously to a sense of identity. For instance, the majority of the Muslim world are Sunnis, whereas Iranians practice Shiism. Iranians have been characterized as prideful, individualistic, fatalistic, and slow to trust others not connected to the family.

According to Jalali (1996), "Iranians' social code prescribes correct behavioral patterns toward those in each position in the hierarchy. People of a lower rank respond to those of higher rank with deference, politeness, and respect, even though they may feel resentment and hostility toward them" (p. 350).

The Counselor Trainee, Nia

Tiffany and Nia have limited exposure to and understanding of Middle Eastern culture. A good first step for becoming familiar with Iran is for them to be able to locate Iran on the world map. Often counselors will omit certain information or avoid asking particular questions out of fear of being perceived as ignorant, insensitive, or racist. This fear can paralyze the counseling event and interfere with the client's growth. Counselors are required, at times, to initiate conversation about difficult and sensitive topics.

Clearly, "Counselors need to enhance themselves personally and professionally by reading and exposing themselves to various artistic art forms" (Lee, 2001). Reading newspaper articles and attending films and other culture-specific activities can inform a counselor's sense of another person's culture. In addition, there are mosques that may have a community outreach program that functions to educate people within the community about Muslims or people from the Middle East. The international student affairs office may be of assistance and if it is not, Tiffany might want to contact a similar office on a larger campus that serves a more diverse and international student body. The key point to remember is that there are resources available, but the counselor may have to work rather diligently to find this information. The true source of resistance may be an internal reluctance to talk about race even after taking a graduate-level cross-cultural psychology course. Most students have been taught that society is fair and just, and White people tend to not con-

front the role of racism in their own lives (Tatum, 1992). The Internet provides a wealth of information. A good search engine can yield more information than one truly needs, but specific and relevant resources can be found.

The specifics of Fatima's culture are missing for Tiffany and Nia; however, Fatima is a college student who feels frightened and alienated. Nia and Tiffany may identify with Fatima's social class background or her status as a college student because these characteristics are most similar to their own backgrounds. What they may not understand is the cultural and self-imposed expectation that Fatima will request her father's permission to marry and that premarital sex is not something she has done or intends to do until she is married. Through marriage, Fatima will gain status, which "increases further when she has a child, especially a boy" (Jalali, 1996, p. 353).

Culture-free service delivery does not exist; therefore, it is impossible to help clients examine cultural identity and self-esteem issues if counselors have not done this important work for themselves (Pinderhughes, 1989). To increase Nia's cultural awareness, Tiffany, while helping to expand her own awareness, could expose Nia to relevant materials regarding sources of differences in society and multicultural counseling competencies. Both Nia and Tiffany would also benefit from assessing their own levels of racial and cultural development.

SUMMARY

This chapter examined race as a social construction and a status variable. Other constructs were considered in relationship to race in an effort to provide an understanding of the saliency of race as an identity construct that intersects with other multiple identities. Also discussed in this chapter were primary stage models on racial identity development and attending attitudes among various ethnic and racial groups. Implications for efficacy in multicultural counseling were considered. A multicultural and inclusive framework has as its most fundamental premise a celebration and acknowledgment of differences and is reflective of the more advanced stages of development. In contrast, the lower levels of stage models characterize ethnocentric and suboptimal ideologies in that self-awareness is relatively untapped and people are judged by immutable characteristics, such as skin color. Counselors and teachers are not exempt from harboring attitudes that foster discriminatory practices.

REFERENCES

Ancis, J. R., Sedlacek, W. E., & Mohr, J. J. (2000). Student perceptions of campus cultural climate by race. *Journal of Counseling and Development, 78,* 180–185.

Begley, S. (1995, February 13). Three is not enough. *Newsweek,* 67–69.

Boyd-Franklin, N. (2003). Race, class, and poverty. In F. Walsh (Ed.), *Normal Family Process* (pp. 260–279). New York: Guilford Press.

Cokley, K. O. (2001). Gender differences among African American students in the impact of racial identity on academic psychosocial development. *Journal of College Student Development, 42,* 480–487.

Cook, D. A. (1994). Racial identity in supervision. *Counselor Education and Supervision, 34,* 132–241.

Cooper, R. (2002). A note on the biological concept of race and its application in epidemiological research. In T. A. LaVeist (Ed.), *Race, ethnicity, health: A public health reader* (pp. 99–114). San Francisco: Jossey-Bass.

Cornell, S., & Hartmann, D. (1997). *Ethnicity and race: Making identities in a changing world.* Thousand Oaks, CA: Pine Forge Press.

Cross, W. E. (1991). *Shades of Black: Diversity in African American identity.* Philadelphia: Temple University Press.

Dana, R. H. (1993). *Multicultural assessment perspectives for professional psychology.* Boston: Allyn & Bacon.

Darwin, C. (1859). *The origin of species by means of natural selection.* New York: Modern Library.

Delpit, L. D. (1997). The silenced dialogue: Power and pedagogy in educating other people's children. In A. Halsey, H. Lauder, P. Brown, & A. Wells (Eds.), *Education: Culture, economy, society* (pp. 582–594). Oxford, UK: Oxford University Press.

Dobbins, J. E., & Skillings, J. H. (1991). The utility of race labeling in understanding cultural identity: A conceptual tool for the social science practitioner. *Journal of Counseling & Development, 70,* 37–44.

Ferdman, B. M., & Gallegos, P. I. (2001). Racial identity development and Latinos in the United States. In C. Wijeyesinghe & B. Jackson III (Eds.), *New perspectives on racial identity development: A theoretical and practical anthology* (pp. 32–66). New York University Press.

Fine, M. A., & James-Myers, L. (1990). The development and validation of an instrument to assess an optimal Afrocentric worldview. *Journal of Black Psychology, 17*(1), 37–54.

Genetic research confirms: There's only 1 human race (2003, July 15). St. Louis Post-Dispatch.

Gossett, T. (1963). *Race: The history of an idea in America.* New York: Schocken.

Gunn Allen, P. (1994). Who is your mother? Red roots of White feminism. In R. Takaki (Ed.), *From different shores: Perspectives on race and ethnicity in America* (2nd ed., pp. 192–198). New York: Oxford University Press.

Hardiman, R. (1982). *White identity development: A process-oriented model for describing the racial consciousness of White Americans.* Unpublished doctoral dissertation, University of Massachusetts, Amherst.

Hardiman, R. (2001). Reflections on White identity development theory. In C. Wijeyesinghe and B. Jackson III, (Eds.), *New perspectives on racial identity development: A theoretical and practical anthology* (pp. 108–128). New York University Press.

Helms, J. E. (1984). Toward a theoretical explanation of the effects of race on counseling: A Black and White model. *Counseling Psychologist, 12*(3), 153–165.

Helms, J. E. (1990). *Black and White racial identity: Theory, research, and practice.* New York: Greenwood Press.

Helms, J. E. (1995). An update of white and people of color racial identity model. In J. G. Ponterotto, J. M. Casa, L. A. Suzuki, & C. M. Alexander (Eds.), *Handbook of multicultural counseling* (pp. 181–198). Thousand Oaks, CA: Sage.

Helms, J. E., & Parham, T. A. (1984). *Racial Identity Attitude Scale.* Unpublished manuscript.

Herring, R. (1990). Understanding Native American values: Process and content concerns for counselors. *Counseling and Values, 34,* 134–137.

Holcomb-McCoy, C. C. (2000). Multicultural counseling competencies: An exploratory factor analysis. *Journal of Multicultural Counseling and Development, 28,* 83–97.

Horse, P. G. (2001). Reflections on American Indian identity. In C. Wijeyesinghe & B. Jackson III (Eds.), *New perspectives on racial identity development: A theoretical and practical anthology* (pp. 91–197). New York University Press.

Jalali, B. (1996). Iranian families. In M. McGoldrick, J. Giordano, & J. K. Pierce (Eds.), *Ethnicity and family therapy* (pp. 347–363). New York: Guilford Press.

Kich, G. K. (1992). The developmental process of asserting a biracial, bicultural identity. In M. P. P. Root (Ed.), *Racially mixed people in America* (pp. 304–317). Newbury Park, CA: Sage.

Kim, J. (2001). Asian American identity development theory. In C. Wijeyesinghe & B. Jackson III (Eds.), *New perspectives on racial identity development: A theoretical and practical anthology* (pp. 67–90). New York Press.

Ladany, N., Brittan-Powell, C. S., & Pannu, R. K. (1997). The influence of supervisory racial identity interaction and racial matching on the Supervisory Working Alliance and Supervisee Multicultural Competence. *Counselor Education and Supervision, 36,* 284–304.

LaVeist, T. A. (2002). Why we should study race, ethnicity, and health. In T. A. LaVeist (Ed.), *Race, ethnicity, health: A public health reader* (pp. 1–7). San Francisco: Jossey-Bass

Lee, C. (2001). Defining and responding to racial and ethnic diversity. In D. Locke, J. Myers, & E. Herr (Eds.), *Handbook of counseling* (pp. 581–588). Thousand Oaks, CA: Sage.

McIntosh, P. (1988). *White privilege and male privilege: A personal account of coming to see correspondences through work in women's studies* (Working Paper, No. 189). Wellesley, MA: Wellesley College Center for Research on Women.

Myers, L. J., Speight, S. L., Highlen, P. S., Cox, C. I., Reynolds, A. L., Adams, E. M., & Hanley, P. (1991). Identity development and worldview: Toward an optimal conceptualization. *Journal of Counseling and Development, 70,* 54–63.

Newsome, G. (2003). Racial identity, coping, and stress among African American college students. Unfinished dissertation. North Carolina State University.

Ossana, S. M., Helms, J. E., & Leonard, M. M. (1992). Do "womanist" attitudes influence college women's self-esteem and perceptions of environmental bias? *Journal of Counseling and Development, 70,* 402–408.

Pedersen, P. (1994). *A handbook for developing multicultural awareness.* Alexandria, VA: American Counseling Association.

Pinderhughes, E. (1989). *Understanding race, ethnicity, and power: The key to efficacy in clinical practice.* New York: Free Press.

Pope-Davis, D. B., & Ottavi, T. M. (1994). The relationship between racism and racial identity among White Americans: A replication and extension. *Journal of Counseling and Development, 72,* 293–297.

Poston, W. S. C. (1990). The biracial identity development model: A needed addition. *Journal of Counseling and Development, 69,* 152–155.

Race and the human genome: Researchers definitely trump the notion of race with DNA research. (2004). Retrieved January 30, 2004 from http://racerelations.about.com/library/weekly/aa021501a.htm.

Richardson, T. Q., & Molinaro, K. L. (1996). White counselor self-awareness: A prerequisite for developing multicultural competence. *Journal of Counseling and Development, 71,* 238–242.

Robinson, T. L. (1999). The intersections of identity. In A. Garrod, J. V. Ward, T. L. Robinson, & B. Kilkenney (Eds.), *Souls looking back: Stories of growing up Black.* New York: Routledge.

Robinson, T. L., & Howard-Hamilton, M. (1994). An Afrocentric paradigm: Foundation for a healthy self-image and healthy interpersonal relationships. *Journal of Mental Health Counseling, 16,* 327–339.

Rogers, J. A. (1967). *Sex and race.* St. Petersburg, FL: Helga Rogers.

Root, M. P. P. (1992). Within, between, and beyond race. In M. P. P. Root (Ed.), *Racially mixed people in America* (pp. 3–11). Newbury Park, CA: Sage.

Sandhu, D. S., Portes, P. R., & McPhee, S. A. (1996). Assessing cultural adaptation: Psychometric properties of the cultural adaptation pain scale. *Journal of Multicultural Counseling and Development, 24,* 15–25.

Spickard, P. R. (1992). The illogic of American racial categories. In M. P. P. Root (Ed.), *Racially mixed people in America* (pp. 12–23). Newbury Park, CA: Sage.

Sue, D. W., & Sue, D. (1990). *Counseling the culturally different: Theory and practice.* New York: John Wiley.

Takaki, R. (1994). *From different shores: Perspectives on race and ethnicity in America.* New York: Oxford University Press.

Tatum, B. D. (1992). Talking about race, learning about racism: The application of racial identity theory in the classroom. *Harvard Educational Review, 61*(1), 1–24.

U.S. Department of Health and Human Services. (2001). *Mental health: culture, race and ethnicity—A supplement to mental health: A report to the surgeon general.* Rockville, MD: U.S. Department of Health and Human Services, Public Health Service, Office of the Surgeon General.

Vandiver, B. J. (2001). Psychological nigrescence revisited: Introduction and overview. *Journal of Multicultural Counseling and Development, 29,* 165–173.

Watt, S. K., Robinson, T. L., & Lupton-Smith, H. (2002). Building ego and racial identity: Preliminary perspectives on counselors-in-training. *Journal of Counseling and Development, 80,* 94–100.

Wijeyesinghe, C. (2001). Racial identity in multiracial people: An alternative paradigm. In C. Wijeyesinghe & B. Jackson III, (Eds.), *New perspectives on racial identity development: A theoretical and practical anthology* (pp. 129–152). New York University Press.

Wilson, T. P. (1992). Blood quantum: Native American mixed bloods. In M. P. P. Root (Ed.), *Racially mixed people in America* (pp. 108–126). Newbury Park, CA: Sage.

Wu, F. H. (2002). *Yellow: Race in America beyond Black and White.* New York: Basic Books.

Zuckerman, M. (1990). Some dubious premises in research and theory on racial differences. *American Psychologist, 45,* 1297–1303.

Chapter 9

Converging Gender in Counseling

What if a woman allowed herself to leave a mode of doing that does not nourish her, that actively makes her unhappy? What if it were not so difficult? If her upbringing had not sought to teach her to be dutiful, moral, caring, giving, helpful, productive and loving . . . at all times . . . to all others.

Judith Duerk, Circle of Stones

Gender shapes each of our lives in primary ways. It influences core information regarding what we and others come to believe about ourselves. Across race, class, culture, and sexual orientation, some common gender themes seem to exist for men and women. Among people of color, gender is often obscured by race, in that race appears to vie for more attention as the salient identity construct.

In this chapter, gender is emphasized as both a social construct and a status characteristic. It is acknowledged that gender differences exist between men and women and within groups of women and men. This truth is neither refuted nor regarded as problematic. However, the way gender inequity is perpetuated as a primary status characteristic within society is examined. Selected literature is presented that examines relationships with the self and others as a function of gender, gender roles, and sex role typology. The subsequent impact on gender identity is also investigated, as is gender from a biological perspective. Myths about biological differences between males and females are exposed.

GENDER DEFINITIONS

Sex roles and *gender roles* differ. Typically, **sex roles** are behavioral patterns culturally approved as more appropriate for either males or females (Worell & Remer, 1992); however, in this work, *sex roles* refer to roles related to the function of one's biology, such as erection, ejaculation, menstruation, ovulation, pregnancy, and lactation. **Gender roles** are a consequence of society's views regarding appropriate behavior based on one's biological sex, such as diaper changing, garbage takeout, spider killing, dinner making, and primary breadwinning. The meaning of **gender** varies among different cultures and changes throughout time; nonetheless, the most common definition is the culturally determined attitudes, cognitions, and belief systems about females and males. Haider (1995) said, "The focus of gender is on social roles and interactions of women and men rather than their biological characteristics which is sex. . . . gender is a matter of cultural definition as to what is considered to be masculine or feminine" (p. 35). Conflicted and rigid behavior is categorized as **gender role conflict,** which "describes the detrimental consequences of gender roles either for the person holding them or for those associated with this person" (Mintz & O'Neil, 1990, p. 381).

Masculinity refers to traditional societal roles, behaviors, and attitudes prescribed for men, whereas **femininity** references traditional societal roles, behaviors, and attitudes prescribed for women (Mintz & O'Neil, 1990). **Androcentrism** refers to males at the center of the universe, looking out at reality from behind their own eyes and describing what they see from an egocentric—or androcentric—point of view (Bem, 1993).

GENDER AND BIOLOGY

Confusion arises when the sex category to which one should be assigned is ambiguous. With the application of rigorous criteria that are socially derived, people are placed within indigenous categories as male or female, man or woman (West & Zimmerman, 1991). West and Zimmerman said, "Not only do we want to know the sex category of those around us (to see it at a glance, perhaps), but we presume that others are displaying it for us in as decisive a fashion as they can" (p. 21).

In each human body cell, chromosomes are the genetic material carried. Except for the reproductive cells (sperm and ova) and mature red blood cells, each cell has 46 chromosomes arranged into 23 pairs. Twenty-two pairs of chromosomes, called **autosomes,** are matching sets in both males and females. The 23rd pair, called **sex chromosomes,** differs between the two sexes. Among genetically normal males, the sex chromosomes are XY; among genetically normal females, they are XX (Moir & Jessel, 1991).

From conception to about the 6th week in utero, all human embryos are anatomically identical. During the 6th week, sexual differentiation begins. The genetic information in the Y chromosome stimulates the production of a protein called *H-Y antigen.* This protein promotes the change of the undifferentiated gonads into fetal testes. The fetal testes synthesize myriad hormones known as **androgens.** Two important androgens are *Mullerian inhibiting substance (MIS)* and *testosterone.* MIS is involved in the degeneration of the female duct system (Renzetti & Curran, 1992). Testosterone promotes further growth of the male Wolffian duct, the duct system that leaves the testes; it is often referred to as the aggression, dominance, and sex hormone (Moir & Jessel, 1991).

In the 8th week, the hormone dihydrotestosterone encourages the formation of external genitals. It is suggested that, for the female, the lack of testosterone may prompt the undifferentiated gonads of an XX embryo to transform into ovaries around the 12th week of gestation (Renzetti & Curran, 1992).

THE SOCIAL CONSTRUCTION OF GENDER

Gender is a status characteristic that manifests in multiple ways throughout society. Males tend to enter into the world as the preferred sex. It is not uncommon for couples with just girl children to keep having children until a male child is born. The devaluation of women and the esteem given to men is culturally rooted. The process of preparing boys to be masculine men and girls to be feminine women is largely an unconscious one within the culture. Socializing influences include parents,

STORYTELLING: He Knows

Danny, age 6, of Kentucky, wrote the following letter to Santa:

Dear Santa:

I want a transformer, an army doll and a teddy bear. But could you please put the teddy bear in a G. I. Joe box so that no one will make fun of me?

grandparents, the extended family, teachers, the media, and other children. The family influences children in their most important identity formation, the gender role.

An individual's personality develops through the interplay of both biological inheritance and social experience. At birth, males and females are ascribed certain roles, characteristics, and behaviors associated with explicit values and expectations according to a constructed gender role that is socially generated (Haider, 1995). Society places men's work on a higher level for remuneration and recognition. Even in female activities, male involvement gives men expertise.

Once upon a time, before cable, video games, and PlayStations, children would go outdoors and play. Then and now, parents ensure that children are exposed to games, activities, and household chores compatible with the children's gender—and children are rewarded for acting appropriately and punished when there is deviation from a standard. Rewards may be in the form of toys, accolades, encouragement, playing with the children, or actually offering advice and instructions. Punishments may be in the form of ridicule, denial of privilege, or removal of an offensive object (e.g., a Barbie doll for a little boy) (see the Storytelling "He Knows").

Pressure is put on girls to be obedient, good mothers, selfless, dependent, and trustworthy (McBride, 1990). There has to be a relationship between these types of gender socialization experiences and girls' tendency to attribute their success to luck as opposed to skill (Sadker, Sadker, & Long, 1993). Dealing with novelty or the unexpected can be a challenge for girls because they tend to be protected and sheltered. Boys are taught to be outgoing, independent, and assertive. Good and Mintz (1990) found that boys' games, though rule governed, rewarded creativity, improvisation, and initiative and involved teams composed of a larger number of peers and encouraged both cooperation and competition. Boys are also prepared to engage in the world and explore it and to play by themselves. In doing so, they develop improvisational and problem-solving skills and are given important practice in the art of negotiation. Achievement and success are emphasized for boys, which may explain why boys enter an activity with a premise that they should master, create, and make a difference.

SEX ROLE TYPOLOGY

Until gender roles ascribed by society change and the inherent sexism is transformed, men and women alike will be constricted and suffer from the consequences of inequities based on biological sex and accompanying socially constructed roles

(Gertner, 1994). Despite the fact that there are serious consequences associated with rigid sex based gender roles that can limit the range of behaviors available to people, why are they adopted and perpetuated? This question was asked by psychologist Sandra Bem, who developed the concept of androgyny. She also designed the Bem Sex Role Inventory (BSRI), which has been used in hundreds of research studies to help in understanding the concept of *gender role socialization* and androgyny. *Androgyny* is from the Greek *andro,* meaning "male," and *gyne,* meaning "female" (Bem, 1993). Androgyny has been conceptualized as synonymous with a world in which people as gendered beings can fully develop without restricting and confining sex roles.

Psychological differences between the sexes are not biological destiny but rather are learned after birth through the sex role socialization process (Cook, 1987). Although this is the case, a uniformity myth tends to make sex synonymous with gender roles. Often, men are connected with masculine characteristics that are instrumental, agentic, and goal oriented in nature. Emphasis is placed on self-development and separation from others. Masculine characteristics are associated with goal directedness, achievement, and recognition by others for one's efforts.

Highly valued traits within the culture of the United States are deemed masculine—competitiveness, assertiveness, high achievement, and individualism (Burnett, Anderson, & Heppner, 1995). Not only are males valued over females in this culture, but masculinity also has greater "social utility" than does femininity. This, according to Burnett et al. (1995), is known as the masculine supremacy effect. "This position suggests a cultural bias toward masculinity such that individuals who are masculine receive more positive social reinforcement and hence develop higher self-esteem" (p. 323). Masculinity was viewed as more valuable not only for men but also for women. Women who were low in individual masculinity were at greater risk for decreased self-esteem. But there is a flip side. Women who demonstrate too much masculinity are regarded as aggressive and bitchy, whereas boys and men who exhibit an excess of feminine qualities are ridiculed and called derogatory names, such as fag and sissy (Haddock, Zimmerman, & Lyness, 2003).

Femininity may influence how others respond to a person, but it is not surprising that masculinity is strongly related to various indexes of psychological health (Burnett et al., 1995), with masculinity having a more positive impact on how one sees oneself. Women are associated with the feminine characteristics of expressiveness and communality, with a focus on emotionality, selflessness, sensitivity, and interpersonal relationships.

A fascinating history of the measurement of masculinity and femininity was done by Hoffman (2001). Hoffman observed:

> There are numerous instruments that are widely used today by a range
> of individuals from researchers in counseling, psychology, and education
> to human resource personnel. Unfortunately, what is being assessed is
> often given only cursory consideration by researchers and consumers
> alike. (p. 472)

Despite the murky waters of masculinity and femininity, these terms are popular within the culture. Sex role typology, which references a psychological dimension, is not predicated on sex. Masculinity or femininity should refer to behaviors, not physical makeup, but this is not the case. Men can be psychologically feminine and women can be psychologically masculine. Sex-typed persons (e.g., men ascribing to a strictly masculine role, women to a feminine role) have internalized society's sex-appropriate standards for desirable behavior to the relative exclusion of the other sex's typical characteristics. The traditional masculine role, which has been found to be unhealthy on many indices of functioning, is related to status, toughness, and antifemininity. Sex-role rigidity contributes to narrow and restricted behaviors. An example of this was seen in research conducted by Stevens, Pfost, and Potts (1990). They found that "masculine-typed men and feminine-typed women reported the most avoidance of existential issues, with sex-typed persons indicating the least openness to such concerns . . . the findings also complement evidence of behavioral rigidity among sex-typed individuals" (p. 48).

Androgynous refers to persons who are high in both feminine and masculine psychological and behavioral traits, not to persons' biological, male or female, physical characteristics. According to Bem (1993), an individual can be both masculine and feminine; expressive, instrumental, and communal; and compassionate and assertive, depending on the situation. Limiting oneself to one domain could be costly to human potential in that individuals may be required to mitigate agency with communion, and strength with yielding. Bem stated that balance is necessary because extreme femininity untempered by a sufficient concern for one's own needs as an individual may produce dependency and self-denial, just as extreme masculinity untempered by a sufficient ability to ask for help from others may produce arrogance and exploitation. An individual with both masculine and feminine characteristics would arguably be more flexible and function more productively than a sex-typed individual. Androgynous persons demonstrate a lack of statistically significant differences between masculinity and femininity scores, thus showing a blend of both dimensions.

Spence and Helmreich (1978) developed the Personal Attributes Questionnaire (PAQ). Like the BSRI, the PAQ identified four groups: feminine, masculine, androgynous, and undifferentiated. This model recognized that masculinity and femininity coexist to some degree in every individual, male or female. The androgynous person, less bound to the restrictive sex-appropriate standards for behavior, is theoretically able to develop psychologically to the fullest and respond receptively to a wide range of situations, perhaps in ways that the less integrated person is unable to do.

Western philosophy dictates that masculinity and femininity be mutually exclusive or dichotomous. Common language used when referring to the two genders is "the opposite sex," or reference is made to one's partner as "the other half." Masculinity in the Western worldview is associated with an instrumental orientation, a cognitive focus on getting the job done, or problem solving. Femininity, in contrast, is associated with a concern for others and harmony with the group.

Cross-culturally, the concepts of *masculinity* and *femininity* have been represented as complementary domains, traits, and behaviors for thousands of years. For example, the yin-yang theory of the harmony and balance of forces in nature is based in Confucian thought and Chinese cosmology. Uba (1994) said that the yin is representative of feminine, negative, inferior, and weak, whereas the yang is symbolic of masculine, positive, superior, and strong. "If this supposedly natural balance is upset (e.g., if a wife domineers over her husband), the equilibrium within the family would be disrupted" (p. 29).

SEX AND GENDER ROLES

Several models help in understanding women's development (Enns, 1991). These models seek to highlight the relational strengths that women embody and, according to Enns, attempt "to correct the inadequacies of mainstream theories and conceptualize women's experiences in their own terms" (p. 209). Women's psychosocial development is different from men's. For instance, Gilligan (1982) criticized major identity development theorists who depict women as inferior to men because of important gender differences. According to Gilligan, women's development "relies more on connections with others, on relatedness rather than separateness" (p. 271). Erikson (1968) has been observed as focusing the majority of his attention on the masculine version of human existence. The primacy of men in the human life event reflects the sexism of the time (Horst, 1995). Recently, other psychologists have written about the unique experience of women and the implications of this on their development. Jordan (1997a) and Nelson (1996) commented that relational skills are highly functional and involve a complex array of competencies essential to preserving family and culture.

Compared to men, women may emphasize relationships, and the importance of autonomy for women cannot be underestimated. McBride (1990) argued that **autonomy** refers to being able to define oneself, rather than being defined by others. This definition is not seen as an isolated and extremely individualistic self. Rather, autonomy refers to interdependence, mutual cooperation, and individuation. McBride stated that **instrumental autonomy** refers to the ability to act on the world, carry on activities, cope with problems, and take action to meet one's needs. **Emotional autonomy** is the freedom from pressing needs for approval and reassurance. Women are often unaware of how much energy they invest in doing things for others versus developing healthy interdependence. The capacity to commit to concrete affiliations and partnerships and to develop the ethical strength to abide by such commitments even though they may call for significant sacrifices and compromises is a source of strength. Yet it is questionable as to whether such commitments and mutuality can be achieved when there is a considerable power differential (Haddock et al., 2003).

GENDER AND EMOTION

The history of gender relationships in this country is steeped in patriarchy and inequality. Elizabeth Cady Stanton, one of the cofounders of the first Women's Rights Convention held in 1840, observed the burden of caring for everyone other than oneself on the faces of women. She said,

> The general discontent I felt with women's position as wife, mother, housekeeper, physician, and spiritual guide, the chaotic condition into which everything fell without her constant supervision, and the wearied, anxious look of the majority of women, impressed me with the strong feeling that some active measures should be taken to remedy the wrongs of society in general and of women in particular (cited in Zinn, 2002, p. 123).

This socialization process of being selfless can contribute to women equating self-care with being a destructive and selfish person. Women who sacrifice their own development to meet the needs of others often inhibit the development of self-expression, self-knowledge, and self-esteem (McBride, 1990). Yet the culture encourages women to sacrifice their development and needs for the benefit of others' needs, usually men's. Depression is associated with the behavior of women constantly putting others' needs first and discounting their own needs. It is important however not to pathologize women for behaving in this manner. Women who are selfless and sacrificial have had cultural, institutional, and relational help becoming that way (Lemkau & Landau, 1986). Choosing to care for the self might be perceived as an unacceptable proposition, since it is likened to the denial of others (McBride, 1990). When women feel that they have failed to be in nurturing and sustaining relationships, there is a sense of shame. Gender socialization is riddled with shame for women and men. There is not enough room in this book to speak about the shame heaped upon transgender people through the gender socialization process. Researchers found that shame proneness among women was the dominant affective response related to living up to female gender role norms (Efthim, Kenny, & Mahalik, 2001). For shame to be experienced, a person appraises the self as having violated group norms or as having failed to live up to the standards of the social group. Five factors of the Female Gender Role Stress Scale (FGRS) examined women's gender role stress: (a) emotional detachment (e.g., having others believe that you are emotionally cold); (b) physical unattractiveness (e.g., being perceived by others as overweight); (c) victimization (e.g., having your car break down on the road); (d) unassertiveness (e.g., bargaining with a salesperson when buying a car), and (e) failed nurturance (e.g., having someone else raise your children).

Gender socialization takes place for both males and females, but for boys there is an explicit message that boyness is very different from girlness. "Learning rigid masculinity—the skill that prepares one to fight and defend—is a major task of childhood and adolescent male socialization" (Skovholt, 1993, p. 3).

In the Efthim et al. study, five factors of the Male Gender Role Stress Scale (MGRS) examined men's gender role stress and reinforced the dimensions of masculinity: (a) physical inadequacy (e.g., losing in a sports competition); (b) emotional inexpressiveness (e.g., admitting that you are afraid of something); (c) subordination to women (e.g., being outperformed by a woman); (d) intellectual inferiority (e.g., having to ask for directions when lost); and (e) performance failure (e.g., being able to become sexually aroused when you want to).

One consequence of a socialization pattern that emphasizes strength, self-reliance, and independence is retrictive emotionality. Its correlation with depression and negative attitudes toward seeking professional psychological help has been noted in the research (Good & Mintz, 1990).

Another way of understanding restrictive emotionality on men's lives is by comparing an underused muscle to the difficulty many men have in receiving assistance during emotional stress or accepting responsibility when necessary. In this same study with 207 college students (17% non-White), men were found to experience shame proneness, guilt, and externalization. Externalization is the act of shifting blame outward for negative events and is a defensive manuever in dealing with shame and guilt (Skovholt, 1993). Men's tendency to avoid expressing affection toward other men is associated with increased likelihood of depression.

Many men leave intimacy to women. The requirement then for intimacy in adult relationships, to join in mutuality and to surrender to another, may be a tremendous source of conflict and anxiety for men (Jordan, 1997b). Many men need to be educated on the benefits of emotional expression. As human beings, men have basic needs to love and to be loved, to care and to be cared for, to know and to be known, but socially prescribed gender roles tend to require men to be inexpressive and competitive with one another. Evaluating life success in terms of external achievements rather than interdependence is emphasized.

The instrument commonly used to measure masculine role conflict is the Gender Role Conflict Scale (GRCS). It is based on the notion that the traditional gender socialization of boys asks more than what is possible to give. To be regarded as masculine, men are expected to have power, compete with one another, demonstrate control over themselves and their environment, and show power over women. Vulnerability is frowned upon as is weakness and irrationality. The inability to shoulder all of these expectations ushers in distress.

In the Good, Robertson, Fitzgerald, Stevens, and Bartels (1996) study, masculine role conflict was associated with psychological distress, such as paranoia, psychoticism, obsessive-compulsivity, depression, and interpersonal sensitivity. According to Good et al., four behavioral patterns emerge when men experience gender role conflict. The first behavioral pattern is *restrictive emotionality*, which refers to men's reluctance or difficulty in expressing their emotions. The second behavioral pattern is *restrictive affectionate behavior between men*. Men may also be afraid of sharing a full range of emotions for fear of being seen as gay (Good, Dell, & Mintz, 1989). Gertner (1994) said that men may also be limited in how they express their sexuality and affection to others. *Obsession with achievement and success* is the third behavioral pattern, which references a disturbing and persistent preoccupation with work, accomplishment, and eminence as a means of demonstrating value. Seeking help may be experienced as antithetical to being in control and having power. This may help explain why men remain less likely than women to seek therapeutic assistance (Gertner, 1994). It is not that women are more psychologically distressed than men, it is that men's socialization patterns do not encourage them to seek needed psychological help. Further, feeling sad or depressed may be seen as unmanly (Good et al., 1989). *Balancing work and family relations* is the fourth behavioral pattern. Because men are socialized to focus on achievement, other areas of life, such as home and leisure, can easily be ignored or sacrificed or both. These four behavioral patterns have been related to depression (Good & Mintz, 1990). Gertner (1994) added homophobia and health care problems to this as well.

Despite the findings between depression and masculine role conflict, healthy male development can be accomplished with the expansion of gender roles (Skovholt, 1993). Skovholt (1993) said that "this narrow funnel of acceptable masculinity may give males a solid sense of gender identity, but it can, in time, also become a prison that constricts personal growth and development" (p. 13). Men are fearful of being perceived as or labeled feminine, which is part of the narrow funnel through which they must conduct their lives. From a psychosocial perspective, this fear stems from the arduous task men must complete: separate from their mothers toward developing their male identities (Skovholt, 1993). This particular socialization process dictates that men should never engage in opposite-sex behaviors and attitudes.

Men travel through their developmental paths unduly conflicted yet trying to maintain power over women and other men (Pleck, 1984). A key task of the men's movement was to articulate the male experience of power and powerlessness, which assumed that female powerlessness translates into male power (Swanson, 1993). It is clear that the wounds of patriarchal power and control are damaging to men and women (Brown, 1994). The roles for men need to be transformed so that men become "acutely aware of their power to influence self and to break the bonds to patriarchy, emotional handcuffs in the form of assumptions and interpretations that favor patriarchal values above the worth of human beings and the meaning of their experiences" (Brown, 1994, p. 118).

GENDER-BASED IDENTITY MODELS

THE WOMANIST MODEL

Ossana, Helms, and Leonard's (1992) womanist identity model, adapted from Cross's four-stage Nigrescence model, is helpful in illuminating the process of self-awareness. The first stage in the womanist identity model is *preencounter,* which maintains that women at this stage accept traditional or stereotypical notions of womanhood. Such notions are often steeped in women's reliance on others for approval and legitimation. Naturally, the locus of control for women in this stage would be external. The second stage, *encounter,* occurs when a woman has an experience wherein she begins to question notions of womanhood and becomes aware of the prevalence of sexism in society. A woman's discovery that her male colleague with less education and experience is paid significantly more than she is, could be described as an encounter. In the third stage, *immersion/emersion,* the woman surrounds herself with other women and literature about and by women. She is critical of the patriarchal context of society and may experience turbulent emotions, such as guilt and anger, toward herself for having been selfless for so long and at society for its history of promoting gender inequity. During the fourth and last stage, *internalization,* the woman defines womanhood on her own terms and is not bound by external definitions or dictates about what it means to be a woman. Research conducted by Carter and Parks (1996) using the womanist scale on Black and White women found a relationship between womanist identity attitudes and mental health. No relationships were found among African American women, but they were found among European American women. More specifically, White women ($n = 147$) who were not at the highest or internalization stage of womanist identity were more likely to feel depressed, anxious, and scrutinized or under attack. These findings suggest that white women pay a psychological tax for pushing back against the dictates of hegemony. They also pay for their dependence upon hegemony.

WHITE MALE IDENTITY DEVELOPMENT MODEL

Scott and Robinson (2001) presented a circular White male racial identity model. According to the model, movement occurs in multiple directions; however, one type, a term preferred over stage, is most descriptive. It is a theoretically driven model and influenced by Helms (1995), Myers et al. (1991), and Sue and Sue (1990). This model addresses "the convergence of race and gender attitudes that White men exhibit as a result of socially constructed attitudes regarding appropriate displays of manhood" (p. 418). It could be used when counseling White men to help them gain insight into how race and gender intersect and contribute to problem presentation.

Type I, Noncontact, describes men who represent the status quo, deny racism, and seek power and privilege. Type II, The Claustrophobic, characterizes the man who feels that other races are closing in on him. Men whose lives are characterized by this type are disillusioned by the American dream. There is a feeling that power and privilege are going to other races. Type III, Conscious Identity, describes the man who is in dissonance and feels this dissonance between existing belief systems and realities. The Type IV Empirical man questions his role in racism and oppression. Finally, Type V, Optimal, describes the man who understands how his struggle for power and privilege has contributed to racism and oppression.

IMPLICATIONS FOR COUNSELORS

One reverberating point throughout this text is that U.S. society is highly gendered and has rather rigid notions about appropriate modes of being for men and women (Kaplan, 1987). Thus, the power of the therapeutic event is found in the interpersonal relationship between client and therapist. The importance of clinical skills and training is not being minimized; however, the relational bond based on mutuality and trust is primary.

Counselors need to realize that, over time, women and men maintain and modify their sex role-related perceptions, attitudes, and behaviors. Counselors also need to remember that sex role typology is complicated. Individual differences in determining sex roles must be allowed so as not to stereotype people, yet it is important to incorporate gender role socialization in working with clients. For instance, practitioners need to know that men usually feel comfortable with side-by-side intimacy and that face-to-face intimacy, to many men, feels like an invasive and aggressive, highly confrontational experience (Swanson, 1993).

Gender dyad makes a difference in the counseling event. Often, the male and client roles are rather discontinuous. For instance, the personal characteristics of the male role often focus on physical strength and accomplishment, whereas the client role emphasizes acknowledgment of weakness. In the male role, men are often punished for seeking help, whereas in the client role, help seeking is reinforced (Skovholt, 1993).

Gender can add another dimension to the therapeutic process. Good and Mintz (1990) found that, between two men, a male counselor and a male client, restricted emotionality and homophobia present themselves as issues. As unfortunate as it is, homophobia may prevent male counselors from showing concern and care for male clients. A male client may feel tremendous angst and fear if he experiences warmth toward a male counselor. It is also likely that a male counselor could be embarrassed at his feelings toward another man's emotional expressions. The client could also be ashamed to disclose. When the counselor is male and the client is female, a different dynamic can surface. One form of bias is for male counselors to respond to female clients as sex objects. Moreover, because of socialization, a male counselor may adopt a one-up type of position with the client. The client may also have difficulty expressing to the counselor emotion that she may subconsciously feel is intolerable. Kaplan (1987) found that women with male therapists saw themselves as less self-possessed, less open, and more self-critical than did the women with female therapists.

Certain reactions to women in therapy are the product of socialization. Bernardez (1987) found three specific reactions to women in therapy: (a) the discouragement and disapproval of behavior that did not conform with traditional role prescriptions, such as mother; (b) the disparagement and inhibition of expression of anger and other "negative" affects, such as hatred and bitterness; and (c) the absence of confrontation, interpretation, and exploration of passive-submissive and compliant behavior in the client. Despite these reactions from therapists, Bernardez reported that female therapists showed greater empathy and ability to facilitate self-disclosure than males. There are exceptions; male therapists may be more inclined to reproduce the dominant-subordinate position by unconscious encouragement of the female's compliance, submissiveness, and passivity.

A problem for both sexes is the strong gender role prohibition against female anger, criticism, rebellion, or domination. Anger is often equated with hatred, destructiveness, or bitterness. Helping clients realize that they have the right to take care of themselves even if those in their environment tell them they are hurting others is an important step on the road to self-mastery. Some clients "may exclude information that they assume the counselor will not understand or include details designed to counteract the counselor's presumed prejudices" (Hays, 1996, p. 36). The very exploration of bitterness and resentment can lead to the identification of sources of dissatisfaction.

The female counselor–male client dyad represents the typical care-giving pattern in society. Most men would feel very challenged entering therapy and abdicating power to a woman. If a woman is uncomfortable with her power, given some of her socialization tapes that sing the power-of-men-over-women song, she may acquiesce her power.

Female counselor–female client is probably one of the most emotionally intense dyads. This dyad was found to allow for a fuller exploration of childhood experiences. Female clients, because of socialization, may challenge the female counselor and question her competence. Because of gender role socialization, therapists of both genders have difficulties with a whole array of aggressive behaviors in their women clients (Kaplan, 1987). When both the client and counselor are lesbians, the therapeutic relationship is shaped by the intersections of gender and sexuality in that both parties attempt to honor the mutuality inherent in empathic counseling (Slater, 1997). The very process of the counselor "coming out" to her client is an act of mutuality, and yet lesbian therapists should not be the only therapists engaging in this type of self-disclosure. It is also the task of the heterosexual counselor to disclose. Robinson and Watt (2001) summarized this point and stated, "The socially endorsed experience of heterosexuality and the unconscious and unearned privilege afforded heterosexuals often deems them unaware of the importance to transition through sexual identity formation. It is presumed that sexual identity formation pertains to gay people only" (p. 594).

Regardless of the gender of the counselor and the client, empathy is the key ingredient in the counseling event (Pinderhughes, 1989). **Empathy** is the ability of the therapist to surrender him- or herself to the affect of another while cognitively structuring that experience so as to comprehend its meaning in terms of other aspects of the client's psyche (p. 13). It requires that the counselor be comfortable and familiar with the world of affect and the nature of connections between people (Kaplan, 1987). Empathy allows for a merger of people's experiences and understanding—not toward enmeshment but attunement. "In true empathic exchange, each is both object and subject, mutually engaged in affecting and being affected, knowing and being known" (Jordan, 1997a, p. 15). There are power differentials within counseling that are part of the professional relationship, yet empathy and mutuality are impeded by unacknowledged hierarchies within the counseling event when they reinforce hegemonic power dynamics (Mencher, 1997).

Therapists may disapprove of women who show power and controlling, competitive, and autonomous behavior while disliking behavior typically regarded as feminine (e.g., self-depreciation, submissiveness). Some male therapists may subconsciously dread women dominating them and fear their own vulnerability to female aggression. Female therapists may also fear the eruption of their own anger toward men, which can have an adverse impact on the therapeutic relationship. It is also possible that some therapists are afraid to experience the powerlessness that comes with examining social injustice, racism, and oppression (Bernardez, 1987).

Depression among college men and the low likelihood of their seeking out psychological services suggests that college counseling centers are in a prime position to do outreach (residence halls, orientations, classrooms, student development). Helping people to reclaim the parts of themselves they have forfeited to conform to society's role expectations, both at home and at work, is a form of healing. In addition, men can be encouraged to reframe their notions of counseling. Good and Wood (1995) said that "changing men's view of counseling might consist of efforts to emphasize that participating in counseling is an activity involving personal courage and strength that is displayed through facing and sharing one's concerns" (p. 73).

Independent of race, ethnicity, and sexual orientation, male and female children and adolescents receive similar gender-appropriate messages. Poor White men and upper-class men of color are socialized to function and be in positions of control (whether they actually are is a different matter). For this reason, seeking help is incompatible with the masculine role. Middle-class White women and poor women of color are socialized to emphasize the needs and wants of others, usually before their own. Despite the similarities, more research is needed on the specific effects of class and other sources of differences as mediating traditional gender role messages.

The value of both masculine and feminine characteristics for men and women is tremendous. Practitioners need to recognize that some behaviors evidenced by clients may not be indicative of deviation or even of sex atypicality. Individual differences must be accounted for. A primary theme articulated throughout this work is that more differences are found within groups than between them.

CASE STUDY
I Wish

Morgan is a 41-year-old Black school psychologist in private practice. One of her clients, Tory, is a biracial 15-year-old. Tory's mother is White and her father is Black. Tory presented for counseling at the insistence of her mother because of Tory's declining grades, chronic irritability, swearing, smoking, fighting with other girls, disrespect of her mother and other adults, and skipping school. Tory has been engaging in this behavior for about 3 months. Her mother does not know what to do. Tory rarely sees her father and, according to her mother, "looks just like him." Tory has been raised in predominantly White neighborhoods, attended White-majority schools, and has little interaction with her African American heritage. Morgan, after the brief intake with Tory's mother, suspects that Tory is angry and having an identity crisis due to normal adolescence, being biracial, and experiencing isolation from the Black community. During their first session, Morgan asked Tory how she felt about being in counseling. Tory shrugged her shoulders and said it was okay. Morgan told Tory she was glad that Tory was there and she could talk about what she wanted. Morgan asked Tory what kind of music she liked. Tory said she liked R. Kelly. Morgan replied that she loved his song, "I Wish." Tory's eyes lit up and she said that was her favorite song. Morgan asked her why and Tory responded that she wished that she could see her father again. Morgan told Tory she could bring music in to the session and they could talk about what the words meant to her. As Tory was leaving, she asked Morgan, "Where do you get your hair done and is it true that if you get a boy excited then he can't control himself?"

QUESTIONS

1. What appear to be the critical issues facing Tory?
2. What DSM–IV diagnosis might be missed for Tory?
3. What are some of the gender dynamics operating in Tory's life?
4. What might help Tory's mother in parenting her child?

DISCUSSION AND INTEGRATION
The Client, Tory, and Her Counselor, Morgan

A major gender script that both males and females receive is that men are entitled to their sexuality in ways that women are not. Part of this entitlement absolves men of responsibility given the enormity and legitimacy of their desire. A huge bur-

den is heaped on the woman to control the man's sexuality (Jordan, 1997a). Prior to Tory leaving the office, Morgan needs to ascertain the meaning of Tory's question about boys' arousal. Was she in a situation where she was with a boy who was sexually aroused and he was unable to stop? If so, what happened? Was Tory sexually assaulted?

Racism and sexism subject Tory to discrimination that she may not be mindful of. Many Black mothers raise their daughters with the responsibility of educating them about racism and sexism (Turner, 1997). Wilkinson (1997) said, "In the racially structured and multicultural evolution of this country, sex and gender alone have not been the principal determinants of the experiences or self-definitions of Native Americans or Americans, Mexican Americans, Japanese, and certainly not of African Americans" (p. 267). And while this is true, the question becomes, How would the African American community and other communities of color be transformed if gender were more central to the analysis or if the intersections of race and gender were seen as relevant to the improvement of both men and women's lives (Cole & Guy-Sheftall, 2003)?

Although White women contend with sexism, race and racism are constructs that many do not think about (Robinson, 2001). Among White women, race is often not the most organizing construct in their lives. The majority of White mothers are unaware of or may not have personal histories with race to give their non-White daughters socialization messages about race and racism. This is a challenge for the large numbers of biracial and multiracial children with White mothers. For girls and women of color, race, culture, social class, and urbanization interact with gender and create female responses and positions that are diverse and fluctuating (Abrams, 2002). How can Tory develop healthily as a young biracial adolescent with no exposure to or knowledge of her Black identity?

Tory is angry. Often adolescents who are depressed exhibit irritable behavior that is mistaken for behavioral misconduct (e.g., oppositional defiant disorder) but is deep sadness. In some instances, there is a combination of conduct disturbance and a mood disorder; however, the context and, of course, the length of time that the child has had the symptoms needs to be known. Tory could be angry and depressed for many valid reasons: she rarely sees her father, she is a young woman of color in a discriminatory world, she lacks a circle of women with whom to confide about her multiple identities, she's 15, she has concerns about being objectified sexually, and she does not know what to do with her hair or where to go to have something done to it. It is highly possible that Morgan, as a Black therapist who is old enough to be Tory's mother, is able to hold Tory's anger.

Tory's mother loves her child but there are narratives which Tory has to share that may be hard for her mother to hear. Garcia-Coll (1997) identified that White women have a difficult time holding Black women's anger and will go to great lengths to suppress, deny, and repress expressions of this anger. White women's historical role in the oppression of Black women and their enjoyment of present-day privileges earned as a function of that history discourage Black and White women from coming together and bearing witness to one another's anger, shame, and guilt. Good and effective therapy is not possible with all of this unspoken angst, and the client should neither have to pay nor wait for the counselor to work through her unresolved issues.

Women tend to be socialized not to express anger; sadness and fear are more readily tolerated.

Tory needs to learn that anger is acceptable and there are positive and nondestructive ways to release it. Brown (2003) is critical of the culture and its suppression of girls' strong feelings. To mediate their frustrations, fears, marginalization, and anger, girls will fight with other girls. Tory's feelings of rejection and betrayal from a father she rarely sees and does not know contribute to her anger. These feelings should not be discounted when seeking to better understand her aggressive behavior with other girls. Tory can be taught and encouraged to talk to her therapist, cry, write, shout, run, work, study, pray, curse (but not at her mother or teachers), eat well, take care of herself, read, dance, resist, and trust that things do get better in time. Tory's mother, her therapist, and other wise women can offer Tory, a circle of stones, a place to go and to be as healing occurs. May Tory experience what Duerk (1989) envisions.

> How might your life have been different if, through the years, there had been a place where you could go? A place of women . . . who understood your tiredness and need for rest? A place of women who could help you to accept your fatigue and trust your limitations and to know in the dark of winter, that your energy would return, as surely as the spring, women who could help you to learn to light a candle and wait (p. 60).

SUMMARY

In this chapter, the construct of gender in women's and men's lives was considered. The socialization process, as well as biological dimensions, was explored. Counselors need to be aware of the consequences of gender socialization on their personal lives and on those of their clients. Not to do so is to ignore the powerful role of gender in life. A case study examined multiple themes in the life of an adolescent biracial teen. Issues in clinical diagnoses were discussed.

REFERENCES

Abrams, L. S. (2002). Rethinking girls "at-risk": Gender, race, and class intersections and adolescent development. *Journal of Human Behavior in the Social Environment, 6,* 47–64.

Bem, S. L. (1993). *The lenses of gender: Transforming the debate on sexuality inequality.* New Haven, CT: Yale University Press.

Bernardez, T. (1987). Gender-based countertransference of female therapists in the psychotherapy of women. In M. Braude (Ed.), *Women and therapy* (pp. 25–39). New York: Haworth Press.

Brown, L. (1994). *Subversive dialogues: Theory in feminist therapy.* New York: Basic Books.

Brown, L. M. (2003). *Girlfighting: Betrayal and rejection among girls.* New York University Press.

Burnett, J. W., Anderson, W. P., & Heppner, P. P. (1995). Gender roles and self-esteem: A consideration of environmental factors. *Journal of Counseling and Development, 73,* 323–326.

Carter, R. T., & Parks, E. E. (1996). Womanist identity and mental health. *Journal of Counseling and Development, 74,* 484–489.

Cole, J. B., & Guy-Sheftall, B. (2003). *Gender talk: The struggle for women's equality in African-American Communities.* New York: Random House.

Cook, E. P. (1987). Psychological androgyny: A review of the research. *Counseling Psychologist, 15,* 471–513.

Duerk, J. (1994). *Circle of stones: Woman's journey to herself.* San Diego, CA: Lura Media.

Efthim, P. W., Kenny, M. E., & Mahalik, J. R. (2001). Gender role stress in relation to shame, guilt, and externalization. *Journal of Counseling and Development, 79,* 430–438.

Enns, C. Z. (1991). The "new" relationship models of women's identity: A review and critique for counselors. *Journal of Counseling and Development, 69,* 209–217.

Erikson, E. (1968). *Identity: Youth and crisis.* New York: Norton.

Garcia-Coll, C. (1997). Building connection through diversity. In J. Jordan (Ed.), *Women's growth in diversity: More writings from the Stone Center* (pp. 176–182). New York: Guilford Press.

Gertner, D. M. (1994). Understanding and serving the needs of men. *Counseling and Human Development, 27,* 1–16.

Gilligan, C. (1982). *In a different voice.* Cambridge, MA: Harvard University Press.

Good, G. E., Dell, D. M., & Mintz, L. B. (1989). Male role and gender role conflict: Relations to help seeking in men. *Journal of Counseling Psychology, 36,* 295–300.

Good, G. E., & Mintz, L. B. (1990). Gender role conflict and depression in college men: Evidence for compounded risk. *Journal of Counseling and Development, 69*(1), 17–21.

Good, G. E., Robertson, J. M., Fitzgerald, L. F., Stevens, M., & Bartels, K. M. (1996). The relation between masculine role conflict and psychological distress in male university counseling center clients. *Journal of Counseling and Development, 75,* 1, 44–49.

Good, G. E., & Wood, P. K. (1995). Male gender role conflict, depression, and help seeking: Do college men face double jeopardy? *Journal of Counseling and Development, 74*(1), 70–75.

Haddock, S. A., Zimmerman, T. S., & Lyness, K. P. (2003). Changing gender norms: Transitional dilemmas. In F. Walsh (Ed.), *Normal family process* (pp. 301–336). New York: Guilford Press.

Haider, R. (1995). *Gender and development.* Cairo, Egypt: American University in Cairo Press.

Hays, P. A. (1996). Addressing the complexities of culture and gender in counseling. *Journal of Counseling and Development, 74,* 332–338.

Hoffman, R. M. (2001). The measurement of masculinity and femininity: Historical perspective and implications for counseling. *Journal of Counseling and Development, 79,* 472–485.

Horst, E. A. (1995). Reexamining gender issues in Erikson's stages of identity. *Journal of Counseling and Development, 73,* 271–278.

Jordan, J. (1997a). A relational perspective for understanding women's development. In J.

Jordan (Ed.), *Women's growth in diversity: More writings from the Stone Center* (pp. 9–24). New York: Guilford Press.

Jordan, J. (1997b). Clarity in connection, empathic knowing, desire, and sexuality. In J. Jordan (Ed.), *Women's growth in diversity: More writings from the Stone Center* (pp. 50–73). New York: Guilford Press.

Kaplan, A. G. (1987). Reflections on gender and psychotherapy. In M. Braude (Ed.), *Women and therapy* (Vol. 6, pp. 11–24). New York: Haworth Press.

Lemkau, J. P., & Landau, C. (1986). The "selfless syndrome": Assessment and treatment considerations. *Psychotherapy, 23,* 227–233.

McBride, M. (1990). Autonomy and the struggle for female identity: Implications for counseling women. *Journal of Counseling and Development, 69,* 22–26.

Mencher, J. (1997). Structural possibilities and constraints of mutuality in psychotherapy. In J. Jordan (Ed.), *Women's growth in diversity: More writings from the Stone Center* (pp. 110–119). New York: Guilford Press.

Mintz, L. B., & O'Neil, J. M. (1990). Gender roles, sex, and the process of psychotherapy: Many questions and few answers. *Journal of Counseling and Development, 68,* 381–387.

Moir, A., & Jessel, D. (1991). *Brain sex: The real difference between men and women.* New York: Delta.

Nelson, M. C. (1996). Separation versus connection: The gender controversy. *Implications for Counseling Women, 74,* 339–344.

Okazawa-Rey, M., Ward, J. V., & Robinson, T. (1987). Black women and the politics of skin color and hair. In M. Braude (Ed.), *Women and therapy* (pp. 89–102). New York: Haworth Press.

Ossana, S. M., Helms, J. E., & Leonard, M. M. (1992). Do "womanist" identity attitudes influence college women's self-esteem and perceptions of environmental bias? *Journal of Counseling and Development, 70,* 402–408.

Pinderhughes, E. (1989). *Understanding race, ethnicity, and power: The key to efficacy in clinical practice.* New York: Free Press.

Pleck, J. H. (1984). Men's power with women, other men, and society: A men's movement analysis. In P. P. Ricker & E. H. Carmen (Eds.), *The gender gap in psychotherapy: Social realities and psychological processes* (pp. 79–89). New York: Plenum Press.

Renzetti, C. M., & Curran, D. J. (1992). *Women, men, and society.* Boston: Allyn & Bacon.

Robinson, T. L. (2001). White mothers of non-White children. *Journal of Humanistic Counseling, Education and Development, 40,* 171–184.

Robinson, T. L., & Watt, S. K. (2001). Where no one goes begging: Gender, sexuality, and religious diversity. In D. Locke, J. Myers, & E. Herr (Eds.), *Handbook of counseling,* (pp. 589–599). Thousand Oaks, CA: Sage.

Sadker, M., Sadker, D., & Long, L. (1993). Gender and educational equity. In J. Banks & C. McGee-Banks (Eds.), *Multicultural education* (pp. 111–128). Boston: Allyn & Bacon.

Scott, D. A., & Robinson, T. L. (2001). White male identity development: The Key model. *Journal of Counseling and Development, 79,* 415–421.

Skovholt, T. M. (1993). Counseling and psychotherapy interventions with men. *Counseling and Human Development, 25,* 1–16.

Slater, S. (1997). Contributions of the lesbian experience to mutuality in therapy relationships. In J. Jordan (Ed.), *Women's growth in diversity: More writings from the Stone Center* (pp. 119-126). New York: Guilford Press.

Spence, J. T., & Helmreich, R. L. (1978). *Masculinity and femininity: Their psychological dimensions, correlates, and antecedents.* Austin: University of Texas Press.

Stevens, M. J., Pfost, K. S., & Potts, M. K. (1990). Sex role orientation and the willingness to confront existential issues. *Journal of Counseling and Development, 68,* 47–49.

Swanson, J. L. (1993). Sexism strikes men. *American Counselor Counseling and Development, 68,* 21–25.

Thompson, E. H., & Pleck, J. H. (1987). The structure of male role norms. In M. S. Kimmel (Ed.), *Changing men: New directions in research on men and masculinity* (pp. 25–36). Newbury Park, CA: Sage.

Turner, C. W. (1997). Clinical applications of the Stone Center theoretical approach to minority women. In J. Jordan (Ed.), *Women's growth in diversity: More writings from the Stone Center* (pp. 74–90). New York: Guilford Press.

Uba, L. (1994). *Asian Americans: Personality patterns, identity, and mental health.* New York: Guilford Press.

West, C., & Zimmerman, D. H. (1991). Doing gender. In J. Lorber & S. A. Farrell (Eds.), *The social construction of gender* (pp. 13–37). Newbury Park, CA: Sage.

White, E. C. (1994). *The Black women's health book: Speaking for ourselves.* Seattle, WA: Seal Press.

Wiegman, R. (1994). Feminism and its mal(e)contents. *Masculinities, 2,* 1–7.

Wilkinson, D. (1997). Reappraising the race, class, gender equation: A critical theoretical perspective. *Smith College Studies in Social Work, 67,* 261–276.

Worell, J., & Remer, P. (1992). *Feminist perspectives in therapy: An empowerment model for women.* New York: John Wiley.

Zinn, H. (2003). *A people's history of the United States: 1492–present.* New York: HarperCollins.

Chapter 10

Converging Socioeconomic Class

My grandparents and parents come from small pueblos in Zacatecas, Mexico. My grandparents lived off a few hectares, farming sugar cane. Zacatecas is one of the poorest states in Mexico. After the forests were cut down in the interest of corporate profits, the land dried up, the rivers dried out, all the kids started to leave for Mexico City, Guadalajara, or the United States. Few can live there now. My mom came here [the U.S.] legally and got a job flipping burgers at a fast food place. She's been working at Target for about ten years without a promotion. Younger White people usually pass her up for manager positions, mostly because of her accent, even though she speaks English well. Dad paid a coyote to come across illegally when he was 20. He came here "Mojado" (wet). He has worked all his life as a day laborer, laying bricks, driveways, or other masonry. My dad has worked six days a week, leaving home at 5.30 a.m. and returning around 5 or 6. He works on rich people's houses in the wealthier parts of Los Angeles.

Alberto, Facing You, Facing Me: Race, Class, and Gender Among U. C. Berkeley Student Leaders

Alberto's (2001) words illuminate the fact that talking about class means talking also about race and gender. This chapter is dedicated to an examination of the effects of class on identity. A case study is provided to facilitate the integration of the material discussed throughout the chapter. This chapter attempts also to explore both the meanings and the implications of a middle-class bias on the training of students in graduate counseling programs nationwide.

CLASS: AN IDENTITY CONSTRUCT

Class is an identity construct that has a significant impact on identity development. Like culture, people are often oblivious to it. Fortunately, since the first edition of this book, there is now more literature that addresses race, gender, and class as interconnected constructs. One activity that will help students and established counselors gain insight into the effects of class on their identity is to recall memories from childhood that were connected to class and that evoked feelings of pride, embarrassment, guilt, superiority, and shame. Remember similar stories from when you were in college and as an adult. Was there an event that you did not attend because you did not have the appropriate attire or accessories? Were there sporting events or clubs that you could not participate in because your family did not have the money? Were there friends you did not invite to your home because you were ashamed of where you lived and how your home looked? Did you consciously downplay your wealth by dressing in attire typically associated with low-income people? Did you choose mates or shun others because of their income or lack thereof? Have you ever worked hard to convince people that although you had wealth, you were still a kind person?

McLoyd and Wilson (1992) found that working- and lower-class parents placed less emphasis on happiness during the rearing of their children. This research targeted the psychological effects of class on people's lives. Although class is fluid and prone to change throughout a person's life, I was intrigued at how one's childhood experiences within a particular class group shaped identity. In the case of these parents, survival issues took precedence over happiness.

In exploring the effects of class, middle-class status should not arbitrarily be associated with feelings of power, security, and privilege, or lower class with feelings of anxiety, depression, and low self-esteem. Storck (1998), a psychologist, proposed that the definition of social class be expanded to include psychosocial class, which is "defined by a person's education and occupation, and correlated behaviors, thoughts, and feelings" (p. 102). She went on to say that a working-class person tends not to be defined as college educated and is typically employed as a factory worker, with thoughts such as, "life starts after working hours," or "psychotherapy means that they will lock you up." Storck (1998) also stated that "both 'lower' and 'higher' ranking individuals and groups may feel disadvantaged or disempowered, in different contexts" (p. 101). Yet, a person from a lower psychosocial class may have higher feelings of marginalization or feel ignored and denied access. These class-determined feelings, according to Storck, are important contributors to depressive symptoms.

What are some of the long-term effects of class on psychosocial development? One way to make sense of class and its influence on development is to query friends. I have made the following observation among persons who grew up in working-class families: Among middle-class urban-dwelling adults with access to an array of stores, there is a tendency to buy in bulk. This behavior seems to be directly related to the childhood experience of constantly running out of items used on a daily basis. Because of limited resources, their parents may have bought a small box of soap powder that cost less than the larger container but was more expensive in the long run. As adults with greater disposable income, these people do not have to tolerate this annoyance endured as children. I have also noticed the tendency of some people from working-class families to save new purchases. Uncertainty about when new items will come again and a desire to prolong their novelty explains this behavior.

THE NEGLECT OF CLASS AS A STATUS VARIABLE

Other disciplines, such as sociology and anthropology, have devoted ample attention to class issues, particularly within the context of educational equity (Fine, 1991; Lareau, 1997; Ogbu, 1997). Class as a status variable, however, has been largely neglected in the counseling literature. The effects of socioeconomic class on students' career identities and vocational choices have been explored (see McWhirter, McWhirter, McWhirter, & McWhirter, 1995; Rojewski, 1994), however socioeconomic class as a psychosocial identity construct has received scant attention in the counseling literature.

Ladany, Mellincoff, Constantine, and Love (1997) discussed at-risk urban high school students' commitment to career choices. They stated,

> In the context of at-risk urban high school settings, students are often
> forced to make vocational decisions regarding their intent to go to college
> or to identify options for employment, while simultaneously contending with
> poverty, unstable family structures, and inhospitable environments. (p. 46)

These authors also discussed the significance of considering how class issues (e.g., extreme financial hardship) may impinge on students' ability to pursue career choices or even to contemplate them seriously. Ladany et al.'s work underscored the effects of class on career commitment and vocational identity. Students who tended to be uncommitted to their career choices also experienced difficulty in other vocational areas. Robinson (1990) found in her analysis of Black student persistence that the students who were most likely to graduate from college in four years came from two-parent households and had participated in anticipatory socialization experiences such as Future Teachers of America and Future Business Leaders while in high school. These variables associated with persistence and success, as measured by graduation, are representations of class but not necessarily income, and support other findings regarding the effects of class on career commitment and vocational identity.

The major emphasis in cross-cultural counseling has been on race, ethnicity, and, more recently but to a lesser extent, gender. Career choices, vocational identity, and other occupational themes are usually regarded as job measures or class indicators. This may explain why the majority of the research on class has focused narrowly in this area. Race, gender, ability and disability, and class converge and affect the discourses about the ways people engage in self-definition. Jones (1985) articulates this point in describing Black women during slavery whose identity as women included working alongside men.

> Together with their fathers, husbands, brothers, and sons, black women
> spent up to fourteen hours a day toiling out of doors, often under a blazing
> sun. In the Cotton Belt they plowed fields; dropped seed; and hoed,
> picked, ginned, sorted, and moted cotton. On farms in Virginia, North
> Carolina, Kentucky, and Tennessee, women hoed tobacco; laid worm
> fences; and threshed, raked, and bound wheat. (p. 15)

Unlike the large numbers of white women newly entering the workforce Black women have a history as workers, slaves, servers, domestics and field and factory hands (Jones, 1985). This identity is imprinted on the American psyche, thus dictating the perception that society at large has of Black women, particularly when they newly occupy class positions not initially meant or reserved for them.

MIDDLE-CLASS BIAS AND COUNSELOR TRAINING

Alinsky (1990), a self-confessed radical, referred to three class groups that are useful for understanding class distinctions in society: (a) the haves, (b), the have-nots, and (c) the haves a little; wants more. He said that the purpose of the haves (e.g., the middle class) is to maintain the status quo, and the have-nots (the poor) is to seek to change it—by appealing often to laws that are above and beyond human-made laws (e.g., religiosity).

Counseling students receive very little information about socioeconomic class as it relates to influences on identity development and subsequent implications for counseling. Moreover, the training caters to the haves, as opposed to other social classes (e.g., working and lower classes). A client's discussions about economic exploitation and oppression can be extremely difficult for a counselor to hear who is a member of the very group about which the client is talking/bemoaning (Cardemil & Battle, 2003). The counselor's inability to hear should not be the client's problem, but it becomes the client's problem when the counselor is unavailable emotionally.

Part of this middle-class bias is related to the nature of graduate education itself, which is steeped in privilege. Graduate students are college graduates who have distinguished themselves from others in the general population as capable of meeting the rigors of an academic program. Just being in graduate school is an esteemed position in society that carries middle-class connotations, independent of students' class-linked childhood socialization experiences or their current and most likely temporary state of poverty. In other words, the graduate school environment acculturates its members to a middle-class direction given its emphasis on success, competition, control, individualism, and the expectation of future employment and class mobility. Graduate students are preparing themselves for jobs that will designate them as having middle-class social standing, prestige, and power. It is hoped that students' future salaries will reflect their elite standing; the pay is often not good, but the professional status is evident.

Despite the privileged status of graduate school, some students make considerable financial sacrifices (e.g., working and going to school, borrowing money from family, securing school loans) to attend school. The majority, then, of graduate students in the United States could be described as having embodied traditional values anchored within a middle-class framework: success, motivation, perseverance, self-reliance, Standard English, hard work, and delayed gratification.

What does it mean for a middle-class bias to pervade the training of counselors? Is it possible that the effects of socioeconomic class on psychosocial identity have been neglected in the counseling literature because the middle-class bias is so pervasive and has rendered the profession oblivous to itself? Sue and Sue (1990) identified two aspects of middle-class bias within counselor training. The first pertains to the emphasis on Standard English within society at large. The second refers to the 50-minute counseling sessions that typically characterize the counseling event.

Standard English represents a class issue because dialect, accent, and use of English are often used in drawing conclusions about a person's educational, occupational, income, intellectual, legal, and ultimately class status (see the Storytelling "The Curtains"). Standard English operates as a form of power and access within society. Alberto, at the beginning of the chapter, mentioned this very point when he discussed how his mother was passed over for managerial positions at Target because of her accent despite her strong English skills. For many, an accent is symbolic of differtness and not belonging.

STORYTELLING: The Curtains

My first job as a 16-year-old was working at Sears Catalog taking orders over the phone. One day, a woman phoned and said that she wanted to order some curtains. I took her order and she inquired about the thickness of the curtains. I read the specifications indicated in my notes. She then said, "I want thick curtains to keep those colored people from looking through my windows." This woman assumed by my Standard English that I was White and thought the same base thoughts as she did.

Delpit (1997) talked about the power embodied in language and dialect. Although she argued against obliterating the unique cultural or speaking style of a group, she advocated educating people about the sociopolitical context that has standards and rules regarding the status quo:

> To imply to children or adults that it doesn't matter how you talk or how
> you write is to ensure their ultimate failure. Tell them that their language
> and cultural style is unique and wonderful but that there is a political power
> game that is also being played, and if they want to be in on that game
> there are certain games that they too must play. (pp. 590–591)

Delpit demonstrates the dialectic: a both/and perspective, where on the one hand the cultural style is embraced and esteemed, while on the other hand students understand that others perceived as powerful (e.g., teachers, prospective employers) may denigrate it. This means having knowledge about the appropriate contexts in which one's language style can be celebrated and where it will not.

Judgments and evaluations about people are made on the basis of their proximity to normative standards of behavior, these norms being White, able-bodied, heterosexual, and using Standard English (Reynolds & Pope, 1991). **Cultural encapsulation,** or defining reality on the basis of a limited unidimensional cultural orientation (Wrenn, 1962), contributes to counselors' bias toward normative standards. Schofield's (1964) use of the acronym YAVIS (*y*oung, *a*ttractive, *v*erbal, *i*ntelligent, and *s*uccessful) may enable counselors to see their tendency to favor this type of client. Perhaps it is related to the counselor's perception that the client is more similar to the counselor's actual or imagined sense of self.

Some counselors regard clients from lower socioeconomic groups as undesirable and more difficult to be with in counseling relationships because of noticeable differences in communication and behavioral styles (e.g., the use of slang, street talk, or non-Standard English). If counselors think in this way, then one's best practice is not likely to result, particularly if the counselor is annoyed that the client is on a sliding scale and not paying the full fee for the hour of counseling time.

At the same time, some counselors from middle-class backgrounds may not be equipped to deal with the multiple challenges and life problems that characterize some of their poor clients' lives, such as homelessness, pregnancy, appalling living conditions, hunger, mistreatment by the police and schools, crime, transience and chronic violence or the threat of violence (Boyd-Franklin, 2003).

Another middle-class bias in counseling identified by Sue and Sue (1990) is the 50-minute counseling session. The American Counseling Association (ACA) Code of Ethics does not dictate 50- or 60-minute counseling sessions. Sometimes clients, depending on the type of work they do or can get, have work schedules that fluctuate from week to week. This disallows having a fixed day and time for therapy. For example, a client may work the 11:00 p.m. to 7:00 a.m. shift at a gas station one week but work 3:00 p.m. to 11:00 p.m. during the next week. One's work schedule may not be posted until a few days prior to the beginning of a new shift. For some clients, a 90-minute session every other week might be preferable and should be offered if it is consistent with the counselor's schedule. A flexible schedule applies to a variety of clients across socioeconomic groups, from highly paid physicians on call to shift workers receiving minimum wage.

Which privileges are we as professionals willing to relinquish to better accommodate a diverse clientele? Wachtel (2002) stated it this way,

> What is required of us, however, in working with a broader range of patients, is more than just explaining why we do things the way we do. At times, what is required is that we do things differently . . . It is extremely difficult to be succesful in therapeutic work with patients outside the White middle class if one maintains traditional notions about "the frame." (p. 205)

Class issues are not discussed in counselor training because the context in which class occurs is normative and reflective of an American value. An implicit expectation that clients have jobs and conventional work hours based on standard work fuels this oversight. What about clients who do not own cars, live in cities where reliable public transportation is nonexistent, can't leave 15 minutes early from their jobs without being docked, or spend an entire afternoon catching and waiting for buses—and then walking part of the way? Some clients experience obstacles trying to get some therapy as a direct result of the ways class shapes people's lives, including our own. Do we subtract the time from the client's hour, even if another client is not scheduled immediately, because of the middle-class cultural adage that "time is money"? Although we as counselors need to make a living, perhaps we need to recruit paying clients to balance the ones who are on a sliding scale. Conversely, if clients drive up for their appointments in expensive cars and wear expensive clothing, how are we impacted by these indicators of wealth or debt? Components of class include art, music, tastes, religion, food, and furniture (Bourdieu, 1984). When high-status clients appear, how self-conscious do we become of our work environments and other indicators of our proximity to middle-class status? And how might our intimidation/being impressed detract from our ability to extend our best professional practice to wealthy clients? Counselors need to look beneath the glamour of socioeconomic class and privilege to avoid being blinded by its allure. There are clients with financial means who come to counseling with great woundedness.

THE FLUIDITY OF CLASS

Acquiring middle-class status or suddenly becoming poor in one's life does not erase the effects of early conditioning. Middle-class persons can move into a lower income level because of unemployment, physical and mental illness, violence, divorce or loss of another significant relationship, disability, death of the primary provider, or traumatic event. Class is fluid, and this issue can be overlooked if it is assumed that clients and their counselors have had similar and consistent class socialization experiences from childhood to adulthood. A change in income does not translate into a loss of values to which one has become accustomed.

The U.S. economic recession began in March 2001. Between 2000 and 2001, there was a widespread decline in median income. In 2001, the median household income in the United States was $42,228. It was $43,162 just a year earlier in 2000. In 2001, the median income for non-Hispanic Whites was $46,305; it was $29,470 for Blacks, $53,635 for Asians, and $33,565 for Latinos. Between 2000 and 2001, each of these racial groups and non-Hispanic Whites showed declines in income. During this time, the income of the Hispanic population remained unchanged (U.S. Census Bureau, 2001b).

MIDDLE-CLASS BIAS AND ETHICAL STANDARDS

A middle-class bias is seen in the very basic tenets of counseling, such as confidentiality. Students learn early in their programs that counselors can even be sued for violating a client's confidentiality. Pedersen (1997) said,

> In an individualistic culture, personal space and personal time are valued as property to be privately owned, and any infringement of those boundaries is considered a form of theft. . . . In other more collectivistic cultural contexts, . . . personal privacy is less valued and may even be perceived as selfish.

Another middle-class bias exists in the expectation that clients will self-disclose. Actually, this is a hallmark of Rogerian counseling, which assumes that, after disclosure, people experience a measurable and identifiable benefit and catharsis. Clearly, the roots of positivism are at work. Isn't it possible for some clients actually to feel violated, given the unidirectional nature of the counseling exchange that could be perceived of as inconsistent with community, kinship, and reciprocity? Another assumption embedded in disclosure is that an individual will be articulate (in Standard English) and should, after rapport has been developed, feel comfortable enough to discuss private and personal issues with a professional stranger independent of family or community involvement and support. Many poor people, because of limited education and/or migrant status, do not speak Standard English. Inability to speak Standard English is not synonymous with lack of intelligence or the ability to learn.

The roots of a middle-class cultural bias are also reflected in the official documents used to standardize the profession and provide its membership with rules and guidelines for their professional practice. For example, the ACA Code of Ethics (Section A.10c) discourages bartering for services. It reads as follows:

> Counselors ordinarily refrain from accepting goods or services from clients
> in return for counseling services because such arrangements create inher-
> ent potential for conflicts, exploitation, and distortion of the professional
> relationship. Counselors may participate in bartering only if the relationship
> is not exploitative, if the client requests it, if a clear written contract is
> established, and if such arrangements are an accepted practice among
> professionals in the community. (ACA, 1995)

Pedersen (1997) critiqued this narrow position. He argued that a cultural slant presumes money is associated with fairness across cultures. Yet, depending on the cultural context and whether the focus is on the very rich or very poor, money can take on different meanings. Instead, greater emphasis should be placed on that which is fair and equitable rather than on money as the particular medium of exchange.

In some contexts, money may not be as readily available or even esteemed in the same ways as other forms of currency. A woman may not be able to afford $100 an hour for therapy (or even a greatly reduced amount based on a sliding scale), but she may value doing housework, gardening, or providing child care as an expression of gratitude and as a means of giving back to the one who helped her in a time of need. This sounds like bartering and understandably can be and is problematic.

Interestingly, but not surprising, the ACA Code of Ethics does not encourage dual relationships. Again, in certain contexts, such as the size of the community and the availability of resources, dual relationships may not be easily avoided. It is a middle-class bias that presumes such avoidance is preferred. Often times, collectivistic communities are dependent on overlapping relationships where role diffusion can not be avoided. Counselors, themselves, may be involved in conflicting roles (Pedersen, 1997). If there are few counselors of color in a community (urban and rural), it is likely that clients of color and the select counselors will frequent the same churches, community and recreational activities and may even have the same employer. Thus, the clear division of roles assumes an abundance of resources that are diverse enough so as not to intersect. The assumption is that clients and their counselors function and live out their lives in different social and political circles. This simply is not the case in some rural communities, communities of color, and ethnic communities—where, for instance, the family rabbi might be the marriage counselor and the child's Hebrew tutor.

An examination of core and dominant cultural values allows one to see why a middle-class bias prevails in the training of counselors. Competition, the Protestant work ethic, and self-reliance all stem from an individualistic and Western culture (Sue & Sue, 1990). Yet, some communities are more collective, wherein greater dependence on others is the norm. Perceptions of dependence also seem to be fostered by class status. Perhaps it is easier to live without cultivating a relationship with neighbors if one is not financially interdependent on others. The California community in which I was reared was collective and collaborative in orientation. In my community, neighbors depended on one another for community. We borrowed household flour and sugar from one another, helped raise each other's children, shared resources, and even watched television in one another's homes when someone's "tube" was in the shop for repair. Class may dictate one's ability to provide for personal material needs independent of others. Having middle-class status, particularly within an individualistic context, may make it easier not to be in relationship with persons in close proximity to oneself. This is most likely different from poor or collectivistic communities (independent of class differences), where value is placed on kinship networks. Within collectivistic contexts seen among many Arab, African, Asian, Native American and Latino families, an extension of the personal self is part of the culture or tribe.

CULTURAL LINKS AND CLASS EFFECTS

Just as middle-class status has value in society, the opposite is also true. Being poor in American society and staying poor is not valued. Being poor and then becoming rich is often admired; the values of hard work, pulling oneself up by one's bootstraps, change, and perseverance are showcased. Being poor and staying that way is looked upon with disdain. Such a position does not mirror the American values of competition, success, change, progress, rising above one's situation, and controlling one's life. The inability to significantly alter one's station in life is inconsistent with core American values.

Socioeconomic class as discussed earlier is fluid and the lines between class groups are very soft. For example, many working-class families are governed by middle-class values, such as education as a means of self-help, hard work, money management, perseverance, and delayed gratification. Ogbu (1997) discussed the transient nature of class membership:

> Because the basis for membership in class groups can be acquired by an individual during a lifetime, social classes are open entities. Although they are more or less permanent, the entities have no clear boundaries; furthermore, their membership is not permanent because people are continually moving in and out of them. (p. 768)

Ogbu's words, as well as the most recent recession, help us to acknowledge that the white-collar worker can quickly become the blue-collar laborer. Newman (1999), an anthropologist and researcher on poverty said, "the working poor are perpetually at risk for becoming the poor of the other kind; they are one paycheck away from what is left of welfare, one sick child away from getting fired, one missed rent payment short of eviction" (p. xiv).

Within the home there are cultural experiences that assist children in their adjustment to school, such as being read to, seeing people read books, waiting in line, and organizing one's work or play. (Bourdieu referred to such experiences as cultural capital that have middle-class connections.) The home environment, along with a host of other agents (e.g., school, church, neighborhood, extracurricular activities), socializes children toward a middle-class perspective. Linguistic structures, styles of interacting, and authority patterns characterize cultural resources that can be turned into highly beneficial and socially lucrative cultural capital.

Lareau (1997) conducted research on two very different school populations. At the first school, 60% of parents were professionals, compared with 1% at the other. The majority of the professional parents had college degrees, and many fathers had advanced degrees. Parents in the unskilled jobs had either a high school education or had dropped out of high school. Only 1% of parents at the first school were unskilled workers, compared with 23% at the second one. Lareau found that interactions between professional parents and teachers were more frequent and comfortable. Professional parents were also more involved in the academic preparation of their children. Parents at the school where the majority of parents were semiskilled or unskilled tended to have uncomfortable and infrequent interactions with teachers. Also, many unskilled parents left the training and education of their children to teachers, although both sets of parents truly valued educational success and achievement. Lareau wrote, "In the middle-class community, parents saw education as a shared enterprise and scrutinized, monitored and supplemented the school experience of their children" (p. 712). This difference could be a reflection of the parents' lack of confidence in their own ability to be of academic assistance to their children. Children from middle-class families had greater cultural capital than children from lower income families. This is not to say that the family-school relationship among the middle class was better for children in comparison with children from the working class. Lareau stated, however, that "the social profitability of middle-class arrangements is tied to the school's definition of the proper family-school relationship" (p. 713).

School counselors need to be mindful of the ways culture can work against parents' perception of schools as accessible, particularly for working-class parents and their children. What may appear to be apathy from parents may actually be feelings of fear and uncertainty. For many of these parents, the quality of interactions with school personnel is linked to the discourses predominant from their own educational contexts that were perhaps alienating and fraught with shame and difficulty. Brantlinger (1993) said,

> In my own interviews with low-income parents, I discovered strong
> feelings and well-formulated opinions about a number of school-related
> issues. Although asked to discuss their children's school experiences,
> these parents inevitably launched into lengthy and emotional accounts
> of their own school careers, detailing a profusion of humiliating and

painful experiences. Even elderly parents recalled conversations and events that had happened many years earlier. It was clear that school had been a setting of great significance and that the parents carried the mental baggage of their own problematic school careers into parenting. (p. 11)

Kenway (1988) conducted research on privileged girls in private schools in Australia, also a Western nation. She was interested in looking at self-esteem within an educational context. In talking with the girls about their experiences, Kenway found that the girls used words such as *proper, right, perfect, education, manners,* and *success* to describe their status as upper class. Kenway said,

There is a tendency to equate high self-esteem with the confidence which many private school girls exude, but such confidence may be illusory, as the girls have learned that "what we appear to be is what people think we are." . . . Self-esteem may be bought via the right "casual-chic" designer label. In the culture of consumption within which private schools are immersed, success also can be bought alongside approval, acceptance, and social honour. (p. 155)

Kenway encouraged her readers to see the costs to these young girls in their efforts to maintain an image based on elite class distinctions as measured by an exclusive school environment.

RACE, GENDER, AND CLASS

Social class is complicated—this may also explain its relative absence in the counseling literature. In the social sciences, there has been a tendency to minimize race issues and esteem class particularly in light of increases among middle-class families of color. Class, however, particularly for people of color, does not operate as a primary status trait because race and gender tend to be more conspicuous than class and can override it. "In the race-class-gender-nexus, race constitutes more than a social construction. It is a permanent and salient identity marker, self-indicator, and status locator that defines one's being, along with gender, sexuality, and class" (Wilkinson, 1997, p. 270).

Within a materialistic and consumeristic society, the structural inequities that can work against a person's best efforts to be successful can be overlooked. It is perhaps easy to blame people for failing to transcend their situations despite structural and institutional forces. For instance, women systematically earn less money than men. Often, men in nontraditional jobs (e.g., nursing) earn more money than their female counterparts (Chusmir, 1990).

Defining **racial stratification** as "the hierarchical organization of socially defined 'races' or groups on the basis of assumed inborn differences in status, honor, or material worth, symbolized in the United States by skin color" (Ogbu, 1997, p. 768), Ogbu argued that "the inequality between Blacks and Whites is one not of class stratification but of racial stratification" (p. 766).

The intersections of class with gender and race are clear. In 2001, the poverty rate for non-Hispanic Whites was 7.8%; 22.7% for Blacks; and 10.2% for Asians and Pacific Islanders. For Latinos, who can be of any race, it was 21.4%. Among women in general, the poverty rate in 2001 was 22.3% and 17.3% among men (U.S. Census Bureau, 2001a). According to the United States Census Bureau (2001a), the poverty rate among single mothers of color is much higher than it is for White mothers. For White women, the poverty rate was 22.4%, 35.2% for Black women, 14.6% for Asians, and 37% for Latinas.

Women of color, as a consequence of poverty, are more likely to suffer from inadequate access to medical and mental health services. In comparison to White women, Black women have lower mean earnings due to their overrepresentation in low-status occupations and by a disproportionately low level of education (Napholz, 1994).

Children suffer because of the economic situation of their single mothers. As such, the poverty rate for children was 16.3% in 2001. This was higher than any other age group (U.S. Census Bureau, 2001a). The higher unemployment, underemployment, and incarceration rates of men of color have an adverse affect on women of color, who are most likely to be in relationships with these men. Failure to look at the situation from this perspective can lead to locating pathology within women of color who are more likely to be raising their children on their own than with a partner.

Membership in groups that are more valued is a mediating variable in conjunction with membership in groups that are less valued (Robinson, 1999). As an African American woman, I share some of the experiences of poor African American women; however, my educational status and university faculty position afford me certain earned benefits in a variety of sectors that I can and do cash in. I live in a neighborhood where there is no gun violence although one can be killed going through a drive-thru to pick up dinner. I am able to purchase cancer-fighting fruits and vegetables (the healthier food is more expensive). I have access to reliable vehicles; my home is safe (as far as I know there is an absence of toxic chemicals that kill poor, unsuspecting people). I have good medical benefits. Yet it is not my goal to minimize the place that class occupies in my life. Class does not negate the effects of racism although class may minimize these effects. The quality of our lived experiences is greatly influenced by perceptions of safety and access to that which will keep us safe. People who are poor experience more chronic health problems, live in crowded places, contend with noise, injury on the job, and are more likely to engage in the behaviors that are associated with chronic disease. Over time, these experiences contribute to lower life expectancy (Newman, 1999).

Race affects the ways gender and class linked messages are communicated. Renzetti and Curran (1992) cited research that stated Black boys and girls tend to be more independent than White boys and girls. Parents' strong emphasis on hard work and ambition and the less frequent gender stereotyping and exposure to strong mothers that characterizes the lives of many Black children may explain this finding (Cole & Guy-Sheftall, 2003).

In American society success is often defined and measured by material acquisition. Homes, cars, boats, jewelry, and other "things" are indicators of income and occupation, which are often suggestive of even moral attributes such as being honest, hard working, smart, happy, and morally good. Not surprising are the socialization practices that most men are exposed to that promotes the idea that manhood is tied to being a provider and having success in one's chosen career (Swanson, 1993). The inability to be successful in this fashion has and continues to have far-reaching implications for men who, for a variety of personal and systemic reasons, are unable to attain success in this manner. Washington (1987) talked about this issue as it relates to Black men: "Economic stressors such as unemployment, underemployment, job losses, health catastrophes, loss of personal property, and gross indebtedness also exert an unacceptable level of chronic stress" (p. 194). The stress is tied into not being able to achieve society's clear standards about manhood, which are synonymous with career and material success.

IMPLICATIONS FOR COUNSELORS

Unraveling the effects of class on one's life is not easy and can be painful. Dominant discourses within society and particularly within the nation's training programs connect class and self-worth. More often than not, the poor are seen as lazy, unmotivated, and intellectually inferior. The middle-class represent the referents for society. Counselors need to hear the prevalence of class conditioning when listening to their clients' stories and, where necessary, help their clients make important connections between their identity and the effects of class on their lives. For example, an adult client from a working-class family might be reluctant to take certain occupational risks because of socialization experiences that emphasize security, saving for a rainy day, and being practical about the future. The counselor could ask the client, "What is the effect of growing up poor on your willingness now to change jobs?" or "What kinds of messages did you receive about being poor or taking risks?" Anxiety about change and taking risk might be higher among clients who, as children and now as adults, have difficulty meeting basic needs. This is not to say that middle-class clients would not be reluctant about the uncertainty of change, but having access to an inheritance and other financial nets that augment one's exisiting resources may make it more psychologically comfortable and financially possible to engage in risk-taking behavior. Such resources include, but are not limited to, a trust fund, a family loan, the family home, the beach house, an inheritance, and furniture (see the Storytelling "The Furniture").

STORYTELLING: The Furniture

I was visiting one of my oldest friends. We successfully balanced catching up with each other's lives while she managed her children. The furniture throughout her home was beautiful—sturdy, solid, lovingly carved pieces. I commented on how beautiful it was. She thanked me and stated that except for maybe three pieces, all of this furniture came from either her or her husband's parents and grandparents. I found myself thinking about the multigenerational effects of class—that wealth and goods are handed down. In order to hand something down one has to have something to give. Middle-class status for many people, particularly people of color, is a first-generational phenomenon. New middle-class status is very different in terms of overall wealth from established middle class.

CASE STUDY
Class Divide

Amber Collins is a 23-year-old European American counseling student. She will graduate at the end of her practicum with her M.S. in counseling. She grew up with her mother after her father left the family when she was 3 years of age. Her mother often worked two jobs (waitressing and cafeteria server) to support Amber and her sister. To finance her education, Amber has a part-time job and she is also an RA in the residence halls. Amber is facilitating a group for women in their 30s and 40s who have had difficulty conceiving and are considering international adoptions. Many of the women in her group appear wealthy and have paid $20,000 if not more for expensive reproductive technology treatments such as in-vitro fertilization. Some have already spent that much and more on trying to adopt a child. This boggles Amber's mind. She has never been around people with so much money and she is sometimes intimidated by their wealth. Some of the women are her mother's age.

QUESTIONS

1. How might Amber's class experiences impact her therapeutic interactions with wealthy clients?
2. What, if anything, can Amber do about her feelings of intimidation?
3. How might age contribute to Amber's feelings of intimidation?

DISCUSSION AND INTEGRATION
The Counselor, Amber

In Amber's situation, her modest class upbringing contributes to her feelings of intimidation and inadequacy when interacting with wealthy clients who are perceived to be powerful. The fact that Amber is much younger than these clients is also a variable that may tilt the power balance (Robinson, 1993). Poor people are more vulnerable within institutional structures including the school, courts, and the police (Robinson, 1999). For instance, the interest rate on Amber's credit card is over 18%. Just making the minimum monthly payment is difficult, and she finds the debt nearly impossible to pay off. It would be helpful to Amber to answer the questions posed at the beginning of this chapter related to memories of class and associated feelings. What is it about her interactions with these women in her group that she finds intimidating? What are the indicators of their privileged financial position that are imbalancing for Amber? Amber wants to nurture an egalitarian relationship with her clients, but at the same time, there is an unequal power dynamic. Amber is the professional. Feelings of intimidation can contribute to a counselor's acquiesence of her power. This is defeating to both the counselor and the counseling event.

Amber's recognition of her tenacity, and her ability to "make a dollar holler" (e.g., excellent budgeting skills), delay gratification, save, plan, and survive are invaluable skills that should promote feelings of security, confidence, and power both inside and outside of the counseling event. Her empathy for her clients is also needed. Their wealth does not erase their anxiety, vulnerability, and depression in their attempts to become mothers.

SUMMARY

This chapter on class explored the neglect of class within the literature as a psychosocial variable. The middle-class bias in graduate counseling training programs was discussed at length. Work conducted by sociologists on school inequity was an important link in this discussion. A case study about a counselor from a low-income background working with upper middle-class women in a therapy group who are the age of her mother allowed for further integration of the material. Implications for counselors were explored.

REFERENCES

Alberto, (2001). Class. In D. Stark & J. D. Griffin (Eds.), *Facing you, facing me: Race, class, and gender among U.C. Berkeley student leaders* (pp. 129–132). Berkeley, CA: Stiles Hall.

Alinsky, S. D. (1990). *Rules for radicals: A primer for realistic radicals.* New York: Random House.

American Counseling Association (ACA). (1995). *Code of Ethics.* Alexandria, VA: American Counseling Association.

Bourdieu, P. (1984). *Distinction: A social critique of the judgment of taste.* Cambridge, MA: Harvard University Press.

Boyd-Franklin, N. (2003). Race, class, and poverty. In F. Walsh (Ed.), *Normal family process* (pp. 260–279). New York: Guilford Press.

Brantlinger, E. A. (1993). *Politics of social class in secondary schools: Views of affluent and impoverished youth.* New York: Teachers College Press.

Cardemil, E. V., & Battle, C. L. (2003). Guess who's coming to therapy? Getting comfortable with conversations about race and ethnicity in psychotherapy. *Professional Psychology: Research and Practice, 34,* 278–286.

Chusmir, L. H. (1990). Men who make nontraditional choices. *Journal of Counseling and Development, 69*(1), 11–16.

Cole, J. B., & Guy-Sheftall, B (2003). *Gender talk: The struggle for women's equality in African-American Communities.* New York: Random House.

Cottone, R. R., & Tarvydas, V. M. (1998). *Ethical and professional issues in counseling.* Upper Saddle River, NJ: Merrill/Prentice Hall.

Delpit, L. (1997). The silenced dialogue: Power and pedagogy in educating other people's children. In A. Halsey, H. Lauder, P. Brown, & A. Wells (Eds.), *Education: Culture, economy, society* (pp. 582–594). Oxford, UK: Oxford University Press.

Fine, M. (1991). Invisible flood: Notes on the politics of "dropping out" of an urban public high school. *Equity and Choice, 8,* 30–37.

Jones, J. (1985). *Labor of love, labor of sorrow.* New York: Vintage Books.

Kenway, J. (1988). *High-status private schooling in Australia and the production of an educational hegemony.* Unpublished doctoral dissertation, Murdoch University, Western Australia.

Ladany, N., Mellincoff, D. S., Constantine, M. G., & Love, R. (1997). At-risk urban high school students' commitment to career choices. *Journal of Counseling and Development, 76,* 45–52.

Lareau, A. (1997). Social-class differences in family-school relationships: The importance of cultural capital. In A. Halsey, H. Lauder, P. Brown, & A. Wells (Eds.), *Education: Culture, economy, society* (pp. 703–717). Oxford, UK: Oxford University Press.

McCandless, J. N., Lueptow, A., & McClendon, D. (1989). Family socioeconomic status and adolescent sex-typing. *Journal of Marriage and the Family, 51,* 625–635.

McLoyd, V. C., & Wilson, L. (1992). Telling them like it is: The role of economic and environmental factors in single mothers' discussions with their children. *American Journal of Community Psychology, 20,* 419–444.

McWhirter, J. J., McWhirter, B. T., McWhirter, A. M., & McWhirter, E. H. (1995). Youth at risk: Another point of view. *Journal of Counseling and Development, 73,* 567–569.

Naphloz, L. (1994). Sex role orientation and psychological well-being among working Black women. *Journal of Black Psychology, 20,* 469–482.

Newman, K. S. (1999). *No shame in my game: The working poor in the inner city.* New York: Vintage Books and Russell Sage Foundation.

Ogbu, J. U. (1997). Racial stratification and education in the United States: Why inequality persists. In A. Halsey, H. Lauder, P. Brown, & A. Wells (Eds.), *Education: Culture, economy, society* (pp. 765–778). Oxford, UK: Oxford University Press.

Pedersen, P. B. (1997). The cultural context of the American Counseling Association code of ethics. *Journal of Counseling and Development, 76,* 23–28.

Renzetti, C. M., & Curran, D. J. (1992). *Women, men, and society.* Boston: Allyn & Bacon.

Reynolds, A. L., & Pope, R. L. (1991). The complexities of diversity: Exploring multiple oppressions. *Journal of Counseling and Development, 70,* 174–180.

Robinson, T. L. (1990). Understanding the gap between entry and exit: A cohort analysis of Black student persistence. *Journal of Negro Education, 59,* 207–218.

Robinson, T. L. (1993). The intersections of race, gender, and culture: On seeing clients whole. *Journal of Multicultural Counseling & Development, 21,* 50–58.

Robinson, T. L. (1999). The intersections of dominant discourses across race, gender, and other identities. *Journal of Counseling and Development, 77,* 73–79.

Rojewski, J. W. (1994). Career indecision types for rural adolescents from disadvantaged and nondisadvantaged backgrounds. *Journal of Counseling Psychology, 41,* 356–363.

Schofield, W. (1964). *Psychotherapy: The purchase of friendship.* Upper Saddle River, NJ: Prentice Hall.

Storck, L. E. (1998). Social class divisions in the consulting room: A theory of psychosocial class and depression. *Group Analysis, 31,* 101–115.

Sue, D. W., & Sue, D. (1990). *Counseling the culturally different: Theory and practice.* New York: John Wiley.

Swanson, J. L. (1993). Sexism strikes men. *American Counselor, 1,* 10–13, 39.

U.S. Census Bureau (2001a). Poverty in the United States. Washington, DC: Annual Demographic Supplement. U.S. Department of Commerce.

U.S. Census Bureau (2001b). Money income in the United States. Current population survey. Washington, DC: Annual Demographic Supplement.

Wachtel P. L. (2002). Psychoanalysis and the disenfranchised: From therapy to justice. *Psychoanalytic Psychology, 19,* 199–215.

Washington, C. S. (1987). Counseling Black men. In M. Scher, M. Stevens, G. Good, & G. Eichenfield (Eds.), *Handbook of counseling and psychotherapy* (pp. 192–202). Newbury Park, CA: Sage.

Wilkinson, D. (1997). Reappraising the race, class, gender equation: A critical theoretical perspective. *Smith College Studies in Social Work, 67,* 261–276.

Wrenn, C. G. (1962). The culturally encapsulated counselor. *Harvard Educational Review, 32,* 444–449.

Chapter 11

Converging
Sexual Orientation

We are lesbians and gay men who, as the most obvious target of the New Right, are threatened with castration, imprisonment, and death in the streets. And we know that our erasure only paves the way for erasure of other people of color, of the old, of the poor, of all of those who do not fit that mythic dehumanizing norm.

Audre Lorde, Sister Outsider

It has been my experience that some students have greater hostility, animosity, and fear about discussing sexuality than they do about race. I have taught students who believe that heterosexuality is normal and that being anything other than heterosexual is disordered. My hope is that they will never counsel a gay, lesbian, bisexual, or transgendered (GLBT) client with such a disdainful attitude.

This chapter focuses on sexual orientation. Sexuality exists on a continuum representing variations within and between homosexuality, bisexuality, and heterosexuality. This chapter also recognizes the fluidity of sexuality over the developmental cycle. One goal is to expose readers to the heterosexual bias that exists in this culture and how an assumption of heterosexuality can be very damaging to lesbian and gay clients. If counselors are not aware of their own biases, service delivery can be seriously hampered; yet, far too often counselors do not receive adequate training in this area. Feeling inadequately trained and lacking knowledge about gay, lesbian, and bisexual clients does not make most therapists unwilling to treat GLBT clients. Yet working outside of areas of expertise is a violation of the ethical standards of the American Counseling Association (ACA) and the American Psychological Association (APA).

Definitions are provided, and, as customary, a case study concludes the chapter.

DEFINITIONS AND TERMINOLOGY

To eliminate confusion, appropriate language and terminology particular to therapy with gay and lesbian clients is provided (Dworkin & Gutierrez, 1992). "As with any group, language has a strong impact on gay and lesbian culture. As times change and as words develop new connotations, some words fall out of favor" (Hunt, 1993, p. 2). The following terms are considered nonbiased and accepted terminology among gay men, lesbians, and bisexuals. These terms are used as the standard terminology in this chapter.

Heterosexism is the belief that everyone is heterosexual and that heterosexual relationships are preferred and necessary for the preservation of the family, particularly the nuclear family. Heterosexism is institutionalized through religion, education, and the media and leads to homophobia (Robinson & Watt, 2001). It describes the institutionalization of antigay, antilesbian, and antibisexual beliefs, attitudes, and behaviors. Heterosexism is the deeply ingrained notion that heterosexuality is the superior sexual orientation (Wall & Evans, 1992). Pharr (1988) stated that heterosexism has been defined as a worldview, a value system that prizes heterosexuality, that assumes it is the only appropriate manifestation of love and sexuality, and that devalues homosexuality and all that is not heterosexual.

Although similar to heterosexism, **homophobia** is the irrational fear of anyone gay or lesbian or of anyone perceived to be gay or lesbian. Homophobia is a weapon of sexism because it works to keep men and women in rigidly defined gender roles (Pharr, 1988). *Homophobia* comes from the Latin *homo,* meaning "same" (in this case, referring to same-gender attraction), and *phobia,* meaning "fear of"; thus, the term's original application to individuals was an extreme and persistent fear and loathing of homosexuals (Pharr, 1988).

Homosexual defines attraction to the same sex for physical and emotional nurturance and is one orientation on the continuum from homosexual to bisexual and heterosexual. This term has become associated with the historical belief that homosexuality is unnatural, a sin, and a sickness. For this reason, females who are homosexual/gay often prefer the term **lesbian** to describe their sexual orientation. The difference in terminology, which arose during the feminist movement, reflects the difference between gay men and lesbians. The term *lesbian* gets its origins from the Greek poet Sappho (c. 600 B.C.), who lived on the Greek island of Lesbos in the Aegean Sea. Sappho's poems are exclusively about women.

Someone who acknowledges his homoerotic orientation and incorporates this knowledge into his identity and carries this identity into interpersonal relationships is defined as **gay.** The term *gay* signifies more self-awareness, self-acceptance, and openness than the term *homosexual*. Often, in developmental literature, the process of coming to terms with one's sexuality involves moving from being homosexual to becoming gay.

Transgender refers to persons who may be biologically one sex but identify within their bodies, souls, and minds as the other sex. People may refer to themselves as transgender and still consider themselves gay, lesbian, bisexual, or heterosexual. A male-to-female transsexual might put it this way, "I see myself being with a man, but I did not see myself as a man with a man. I saw myself as a woman with a man" (see the Storytelling "Paula").

One consequence of homophobia is **internalized homophobia.** It is produced by the negative messages about homosexuality that lesbians and gay men hear throughout their lives. Because gay men and lesbians are stereotyped, uninformed, or fed inaccurate, distorted information about homosexuality, the messages are

STORYTELLING: Paula

When I was in college, I met a person who had been born male. Paul knew that he was in the wrong body. The *DSM–IV TR* refers to this as gender identity disorder. As an adult, Paul married and fathered two children. Paul then decided to have gender reassignment surgery. As a woman, Paula was very tall and her voice was heavy. She agreed to come and speak to my Abnormal Psychology class. I was doing a project on transsexuals and had contacted a church in the Los Angeles area to get additional information. I was fortunate to be put into contact with Paula. I was attending a small, liberal arts Christian college in southern California. Needless to say, the word had gotten out that a transsexual was coming to campus. The class was packed. The theology majors were ready to do battle. Paula was honest and talked of her early identity struggles before her decision to have the surgery, the surgery itself, the hormones, the changes in her body, and her continued attraction to women, which did not change from when she was Paul. Paula was judged that night by many of my classmates. What many failed to realize is that gender is multifaceted, certainly not dichotomous, and intersects with sexuality.

internalized and result in low self-esteem. Internalized homophobia can lead to self-hatred and other psychological problems (Dworkin & Gutierrez, 1989).

When gay men and lesbians come to accept being gay or lesbian as a salient component of their identities, it is descriptive of the process of **coming out.** Numerous developmental models describe the stages of the coming-out process, such as those of Cass (1979) and Coleman (1982). Gay and lesbian people have struggled throughout history with the notion that their sexual identity was a choice—and the wrong choice. Because of socialization, some gay men and lesbians have behaved heterosexually even though their identity was gay or lesbian. Many remember feeling different at an early age and see this as stemming from their gay and lesbian orientation. For this reason, the term **sexual orientation,** rather than *sexual preference,* is preferred. By owning this orientation, gay men and lesbians make a conscious choice to let their behavior conform to their orientation, just as a heterosexually oriented person makes a choice not to behave in a homosexual manner.

Heterosexism affects everyone, covertly and overtly, in this society. It is not only harmful to the victims but to the perpetrators as well. According to Smith (1982), heterosexism is intimately associated with other discriminatory practices (e.g., classism, sexism, racism, ageism) in our society. She stated that verbal and behavioral expressions of heterosexism are acceptable and go uncontested in contexts where other discriminatory comments or gesticulations (e.g., racist, sexist, or anti-Semitic remarks) would be challenged or prohibited.

Sexual politics ensures the dominance of males over females and the dominance of heterosexuals over persons who are gay and lesbian (Pleck, 1984). Within a system of **hegemony** (a historical situation where power is won and held) and androcentrism, in which the complementarity of women and men implies women's subordinate social position to men, homosexuality becomes a threat for heterosexual men. Heterosexual men are socialized into believing that to reject anything that remotely resembles homosexuality, they must oppress women. For this reason, "any kind of powerlessness, or refusal to compete among men becomes involved with the imagery of homosexuality" (Pleck, 1984, p. 84). Within heterosexuality, a central dimension of the power that men exercise over women is found. Clearly, sexism and homophobia are interlocking paradigms.

Sexual inequality and heterosexuality cannot be discussed without addressing sociopolitical power dynamics within society, such as the suppression of women's sexuality, forced sexuality through incest and rape, the idealization of heterosexual marriage, and the contradicting and confusing roles of motherhood.

Traditionally, a healthy or ideal personality has included a concept of *sexual identity* with three basic components: (a) a sexual preference for members of the opposite sex, (b) a sex role identity as either masculine or feminine, depending on one's gender, and (c) a gender identity that is a secure sense of one's maleness or femaleness. Bem (1993) set out to refute these components by stating that sexual preference ought to be considered orthogonal to notions of mental health. She also indicated that the terms *heterosexual* and *homosexual* should be used to describe acts rather than persons.

NARRATIVE QUESTIONS

It is often through exposure to other people's personal narratives that students gain insight into the lived experiences of others. Gaining insight into one's own personal stories and histories is essential to self-knowledge. Consider your responses to the following questions (Falco, 1991, p. 174):

1. What was the first reference to gays or lesbians you ever remember hearing?
2. What do you remember about the first person you ever saw or met who you identified as gay or lesbian?
3. What did your parents teach you about people who are gay and lesbian?
4. What type of treatment did gay and lesbian clients receive in your therapy or counseling course?
5. How were gay or lesbian student therapists treated in your training program? Gay or lesbian supervisors or instructors?
6. Do you currently have friends or acquaintances whom you know to be gay or lesbian? If not, why do you think this is so?
7. Who do you think might be gay or lesbian? What are they like? Do you think they are typical of gays or lesbians?
8. What is the most memorable same-sex experience of your life? The most traumatic? The most meaningful and/or eye-opening?

THE IMPORTANCE OF A FOCUS ON GAY, LESBIAN, BISEXUAL, AND TRANSGENDER ISSUES IN COUNSELING

To be effective, counselors need to receive adequate training in counseling persons who are gay, lesbian, and bisexual. Rudolph (1990) projected that approximately 25% to 65% of the gay, lesbian, and bisexual population seek psychotherapy, a percentage 2 to 4 times higher than in the heterosexual population. Moreover, a significantly larger percentage of gay men and lesbians report dissatisfaction with their treatment, compared with heterosexuals. Although there is a need to provide psychotherapy in the gay/lesbian community, many mental health professionals have not been provided the appropriate training to assist gay men, lesbians, and bisexuals effectively through their coming out or identity development process. Survey and anecdotal literature reveals that the source of dissatisfaction often is the counselor's ignorance or prejudice toward people who are gay (Bell & Weinberg, 1978). Just as counselors must be aware of their racial biases regarding cultural and racial groups, they must also assess their biases as they relate to gay, lesbian, and bisexual clients (Pope, 1995). Counselors, too, have been influenced by living in a society that socializes people toward racist and homophobic attitudes.

Caroline Pace (1991) conducted an in-depth study on the attitudes of mental health professionals and graduate students in training programs toward gay men and lesbians. She found that "counselors, like other individuals socialized by hetero-sexist institutions in the United States, hold negative attitudes toward lesbians and gays" (p. 73). The mental health professionals and counselors-in-training scored in the "low grade homophobic" range of the Index of Attitudes Toward Homosexuals Scale, which was developed by Hudson and Ricketts (1980). This scale has been used in studies designed to measure attitudes toward gay men and lesbians in several populations.

Gays, lesbians, bisexual and transgender people experience homophobia not only in the counselor's office, which should be a safe place to explore identity issues, but from the general public as well. In a study of 1,669 students, staff, faculty, and administrators at 14 private and public colleges and universities, 29% of respondents reported that they had been harassed because of their sexual orientation or gender identity. Harrassment was defined as "conduct that has interfered unreasonably with your ability to work or learn on this campus or has created an offensive, hostile, intimidating working or learning environment" (Rankin, 2002, p. 26). The harrassment was most likely, at 57%, to occur in public space on campus or while people were walking or working on campus. The harrassment most frequently occurred through derogatory remarks, at 89%; verbal harassment or threats, 48%; graffiti, 39%; and pressure to be silent about sexual orientation/gender, 38%. This study also found that the majority of respondents, 71%, perceived transgender people to be the most likely to be harrassed on campus. The actual percentage of harassment that occurred against transgendered people was 41%. In an environment that should support the universe of expression, ideas, and exploration, colleges and universities have been bastions of heterosexist and homophobic activity.

Other crucial issues that face the gay population are substance abuse, depression, runaways, HIV and AIDS, partner abuse, and attempted suicide. Researchers maintain that substance abuse among lesbians and gay men is high. The gay bar may be the most accessible and visible place to persons who are "out" to interact with others who are also "out" (Rothblum, 1994). Gay men and lesbians attempt suicide 2 to 7 times more often than heterosexual comparison groups (Durby, 1994; Hammelman, 1993). Gay youths have a plethora of problems during adolescence, such as intensified feelings of isolation, depression, and lack of healthy role models (Browning, Reynolds, & Dworkin, 1994). School counselors should be aware of, and be prepared to work with, a diversity of youths because an estimated 3 million adolescents across the country are gay, lesbian, or bisexual. Unfortunately, because of the lack of role models and sympathetic support systems, another 20% to 35% of these young individuals attempt suicide (O'Connor, 1992). Gay youth are vulnerable and need caring adults.

DEVELOPMENTAL PROCESSES

Everyone has sexual orientation. The need to develop a clear sense of one's sexual identity is not limited to GLBT people only. Robinson and Watt (2001) argued that "the socially endorsed experience of heterosexuality and the unconscious and unearned privilege afforded heterosexuals often deems them unaware of the importance to transition through sexual identity formation" (p. 594). Thus, not thinking about oneself as a heterosexual (similar to not thinking about oneself as White) may reflect an individual who is less developed in his sexual identity. Below, two models of gay identity development are presented for gay, lesbian, and bisexual populations. Cass and Troiden are the authors. Sullivan's model for heterosexuals and gay people is also presented.

CASS'S MODEL OF GAY, LESBIAN, AND BISEXUAL SEXUAL IDENTITY FORMATION

Vivian Cass (1979) developed a model to assess the growth, development, and awareness of gay, lesbian, and bisexual individuals. Most counselors will work with a gay, lesbian, or bisexual client at some juncture during their professional careers. The Cass model is provided as a guideline for assessing a client's level of development. It is important to note, however, that the client may remain "stuck" in a given stage, skip certain developmental levels, or regress from a higher stage to a lower stage, depending on the events that occur in his life.

Coping strategies vary for the GLBT client. Often, a therapist can assess the gay client's level of identity development in the coming-out process. According to the Cass model (1984), the gay identity formation process occurs in six stages, beginning with the individual having a sexual self-portrait that is heterosexual. For example, if the client were talking about a female, the female would see herself and her behavior as heterosexual as well as perceive others to view her as heterosexual. For the most part, the person's sexual self-portrait is consistent or congruent with heterosexuality. At some point in life, however, a change occurs. It might happen in childhood, in adolescence, in early adulthood, in middle age, or even very late in life.

STAGE 1: IDENTITY CONFUSION Identity confusion is characterized by a growing awareness of thoughts, feelings, or behaviors that may be homosexual in nature. These self-perceptions are incongruent with earlier assumptions of personal heterosexuality and constitute the first developmental conflict of this model. Entrance into this stage begins with the conscious awareness that information regarding homosexuality is somehow personally relevant. When the continuing personalization of this information can no longer be ignored, the individual's sexual self-portrait feels inconsistent, or incongruent. The process of gay identity formation has begun.

Examples of questions a person in Stage 1 may be asking are "Who am I?," "Am I homosexual?," and "Am I really a heterosexual?" The individual sometimes feels, thinks, or acts in a homosexual way but would rarely, if ever, tell anyone about this. The individual is fairly sure that homosexuality has something to do with him personally.

With continuing personalization of information regarding homosexuality, the person begins privately to label his own behavior (or thoughts or feelings) as possibly gay. Publicly, the person maintains a self-image as heterosexual and perceives others as maintaining the same image. To deal with this incongruity, the person adopts one or more of the following three strategies (Berzon, 1988). The first is the *inhibition strategy* and describes the person who regards the definition of his behavior (thoughts, feelings) as correctly gay, but finds this definition undesirable and unacceptable. Several actions are taken: The person restricts information regarding homosexuality (e.g., I don't want to hear, read, or know about it) or inhibits behavior (e.g., It may be true, but I'm not going to do anything about it). Denying the personal relevance of information regarding homosexuality is also an action taken (e.g., It has nothing to do with me). Other possible behaviors include becoming hypersexual (e.g., within the context of heterosexual interactions) or becoming asexual wherein the person seeks a "cure." Another action is to become an antigay moral or religious crusader. If the inhibition strategies employed are successful in enabling the person to inhibit, redefine, or disown responsibility for gay behavior, a foreclosure of gay/lesbian identity will occur at Stage 1.

Personal innocence strategy is a second strategy. Here, the person rejects either the meaning or the context of the homosexual behavior so as not to have to own it. He then redefines the meaning or context of the behavior. For example, in U.S. society, genital contact between males is acceptable in a variety of situations without the participating individuals being defined as gay. Little boys have "circle jerks." Men confined for long periods of time without access to women, such as in prison or other confined situations, have genital contact with one another, and they are not necessarily defined as gay. The shift occurs in the contextual meaning when males develop emotional attachments to the other males with whom they are having sex or when they have repeated contacts with the same male, increasing the possibility of emotional involvement.

For females in U.S. society, just the opposite is true. Girls can be inseparable, experience deep emotional involvement with one another, and spend more time with each other, even into adulthood, than they do with the men in their lives, and this behavior is not regarded as gay or unusual. For this reason, it may be easier for girls and women to hide their lesbian behavior or identities longer. The shift occurs when they have genital contact in addition to their emotional involvement, which is more likely to be considered lesbianism but may not be. Quite a bit of same-sex sexual experimentation occurs in adulthood among persons who had been or currently are in heterosexual marriages. Qualitative research is needed in this area to understand this phenomena.

Another personal innocence strategy is categorized as redefining context. The individual disowns responsibility for his homosexual behavior by redefining the context in which it occurred. Examples of these rationalizations are "I was just experimenting," "I was drunk," "I just did it for the money," "I did it as a favor for a friend," "It was an accident," and "I was taken advantage of."

Success in the use of the inhibition and personal innocence strategies depends on the individual's ability to avoid provocative situations and to employ the psychological defense of denial. It is impossible to avoid erotic dreams and physiological responses to persons of the same sex to whom the individual is attracted. In this instance, these strategies will be only partially successful, and the individual may very well experience the beginning of a negative or self-rejecting sexual identity.

The person in the information-seeking strategy is likely to adopt this third strategy if the meaning attributed to his homosexual behavior is perceived as correct, or at least partially acceptable. Now the individual seeks more information in books, in therapy, or in talking with anyone who might have expertise or experience related to this topic. The question being addressed is "Am I homosexual?" How individuals perceive these characteristics or behaviors will influence the way they seek to resolve the incongruence, either through repression (identity foreclosure) or by moving into Stage 2. This strategy of seeking more information moves the person along to Stage 2.

STAGE 2: IDENTITY COMPARISON   Individuals begin to investigate those qualities first experienced in Stage 1. As they begin to gather information and seek out contacts with gay others, there is increased congruence between self-perceptions and behaviors but increased conflict with others. Stage 2 statements of *Identity Comparison* would include "I feel like I probably am gay, although I am not definitely sure. I feel different. I think I may want to talk with someone, maybe someone gay about feeling different, but I'm not sure if I really want to or not" are statements that a person would make at this stage.

As the person accepts the possibility that he may be gay the individual begins to examine the wider implications of being gay. Whereas in Stage 1 the task was to handle the self-alienation that occurs with the first glimmerings of homosexuality, the main task of Stage 2 is to handle the social alienation that is produced by feeling different from peers, family members, and society at large. A particularly troubling aspect of relinquishing one's heterosexual identity is the giving up of behavioral guidelines and the expectations for one's future that accompany them. If marriage and family are not in one's future, then what is? What will give form, structure, and a sense of normalcy to one's life? With the letting go of a perception of a self that is clearly heterosexual, one can experience a profound feeling of loss.

Certain conditions heighten the feeling of alienation from others, such as (a) living in geographic isolation with no other gay people or resources available and (b) being from a family that is deeply religious and with strong convictions about homosexuality as a sin.

Here are four strategies the individual may employ to reject homosexual self-definition while continuing homosexual behavior:

1. *Special Case.* The person characterizes what is happening as the product of the liaison with one person and this one person only.
2. *Ambisexuality.* The person says he can be sexual with anybody; it doesn't matter what gender the other person is.

3. *Temporary Identity.* The person regards his homosexuality as only temporary: "I could be heterosexual again any minute."
4. *Personal Innocence.* The person blames his homosexuality on anyone or everyone else.

As conflict heightens, individuals may move to Stage 3.

STAGE 3: IDENTITY TOLERANCE *Identity tolerance* is marked by increased contact with the gay community, leading to greater empowerment. At this point, individuals hold an increasingly strong gay self-image but continue to present themselves (outside the community) as heterosexual. "I feel sure that I'm homosexual, and I tolerate it. I see myself as homosexual for now, but I'm not sure about the future" are statements that a person would make at this stage. It occurs when the person has come to accept the probability that he is gay and recognizes the sexual, social, and emotional needs that come with being homosexual.

With more of a commitment to a gay identity, the person is now free to pursue social, emotional, and sexual needs. Doing this accentuates the difference between the person and heterosexuals even more. To deal with the increased social alienation from heterosexuals, the person seeks out gay people and the gay subculture. Involvement in the gay/lesbian community has distinct advantages in terms of movement toward a more positive gay/lesbian identity. According to Berzon (1988), it (a) contributes to a ready-made support group that understands and shares the individual's concerns, (b) provides opportunities to meet a partner, (c) gives access to positive gay and lesbian role models, and (d) provides opportunities to practice feeling more at ease as a lesbian or a gay man. However, if the person has poor social skills, is very shy, has low self-esteem, has strong fear of exposure (of sexual identity), or has a fear of the unknown, positive contacts are made more difficult.

A negative experience may occur if the person encounters gay men and lesbians who are still employing the inhibition and denial strategies of Stages 1 and 2. These lesbians and gay men will be perceived as unhappy, self-rejecting individuals with whom one would not want to be affiliated. However, individuals at this stage will be empowered by people who are accepting of their own gay and lesbian identities. A shift occurs when the individual's significant others are gay rather than heterosexuals.

If the contacts made are experienced as negative, a reduction of involvement with gay subculture is probable, resulting in a foreclosure at Stage 3. If contacts are perceived as positive, it is likely that the strategies employed have broken down and that the individual will want to explore further. This breakdown of strategies will result in movement into Stage 4. In any case, the commitment to gay identity is now sufficient for the person to say, "I am a homosexual."

STAGE 4: IDENTITY ACCEPTANCE At this point, the conflict between the self and nongay others' perceptions is at an intense level. This conflict may be resolved through passing as "straight," having limited contact with heterosexuals, or selectively disclosing to significant (heterosexual) others. A person at this stage may say,

"I am quite sure that I am gay/lesbian, and I accept this fairly happily. I am prepared to tell a few people about being gay/lesbian (e.g., friends, family members), but I carefully select whom I tell." Identity acceptance occurs when the person accepts, rather than tolerates, a gay self-image and contact with the gay/lesbian subculture continues and increases.

The individual now has a positive identification with other gay people. The questions of earlier stages (What am I? Where do I belong?) have been answered. Attitudes toward sexual orientation of the gay men and lesbians with whom the person becomes associated are crucial at this point. If these individuals regard being gay as partially legitimate (being gay is okay in private, but being public about it is not okay), then the person is likely to adopt this attitude as his own philosophy and to live a compartmentalized, "passing" gay life.

To reduce the stress involved in interfacing with a homophobic society, the person has less and less to do with heterosexuals. Some selective disclosure of gayness to nongay family, friends, and coworkers occurs, but as much control as possible is exercised over the potentially discrediting information. The emphasis is on fitting into society and not making waves. If, on the one hand, this strategy is successful, the person forecloses at this identity acceptance stage. If, on the other hand, the person comes to associate with people who regard being gay as fully legitimate (in private and public), this attitude is likely to be adopted. Greater acceptance of one's gay orientation tends to increase the distance the person now feels from a society that is still homophobic. Homophobic attitudes are now particularly offensive to the person characterized by this stage.

To deal with the anger toward a rejecting society, in combination with the increasing self-acceptance that is occurring, the person moves into Stage 5. Those who find that the strategies described effectively manage the conflict may stay at this level comfortably; otherwise, the continuing conflict pushes them onward.

STAGE 5: IDENTITY PRIDE   Identity pride is marked not only by strong pride in the gay community and in identity, but also by intense anger directed toward, and isolation from, the heterosexual society. The conflict is managed through fostering a dichotomized homosexual (valued) and heterosexual (devalued) worldview. How others, particularly those who are not gay, respond to the expression of these feelings influences whether individuals move to the final stage. Persons who have arrived at this stage may say, "I feel proud to be a gay/lesbian and enjoy living as one. I am prepared to tell many people about being gay/lesbian and make no attempt to hide this fact. I prefer to mix socially with other gay men/lesbians because heterosexuals are typically antigay." This stage occurs when, accepting the philosophy of full legitimation, the person becomes immersed in the gay/lesbian subculture and has less and less to do with heterosexual others.

As identification with the gay/lesbian community deepens, pride in accomplishments of the community increases. Daily living still requires continuing encounters with the heterosexual world and its homophobic attitudes. These encounters produce feelings of frustration and alienation. The combination of anger and pride energizes the person into action against the heterosexual establishment and creates "the activist."

Confrontation with the heterosexual establishment brings the person more into public view, and earlier strategies to conceal sexual orientation must be abandoned. Doing so precipitates disclosure crises with significant heterosexuals, such as family and coworkers. It is better to tell the folks yourself than to let them hear that you are gay as you are interviewed on a news program.

What becomes crucial at this point is whether those significant heterosexuals in the gay person's life react negatively to the disclosure as expected or react positively. If the reaction is negative, confirming the person's expectations that it would be so, the view of the world as being divided into gays (who are okay) and nongays (who are not okay) gets reinforced. In this instance, the person forecloses at the identity pride stage. If the reactions of the heterosexuals to whom the person discloses are positive and inconsistent with her or his negative expectations, the person tends to change those expectations, which moves him into Stage 6.

STAGE 6: IDENTITY SYNTHESIS Movement to identity synthesis most likely occurs when individuals experience positive reactions from heterosexual others. The need to dichotomize the world into gays who are okay and nongays who are not is gone. The gay/lesbian aspect of one's identity can now be integrated with all other aspects of self.

Sexuality is regarded as one part of the individual's total identity. There is some conflict but it is at the lowest and most manageable point. The person at this stage says, "I am prepared to tell anyone that I am gay/lesbian. I am happy about the way I am but think that being gay/lesbian is not the most important part of me. I mix socially with fairly equal numbers of gay men/lesbians and heterosexuals and anyone who is accepting of gay men and lesbians." The individual now acknowledges that some nongay people are as supportive of his gay identity as other gay people are. Because heterosexuals as a class are no longer seen as hostile, it is no longer necessary to sustain the high level of anger seen at Stage 5. Increasing contact with supportive nongays produces more trust.

TROIDEN'S HOMOSEXUAL IDENTITY DEVELOPMENTAL MODEL

Troiden (1989) also developed a nonsequential model of homosexual identity. *Sensitization* is the first stage and occurs before puberty. Here the child is more concerned with gender identification than with sexuality. *Identity confusion* is the next stage. Movement occurs during adolescence, around the age of 18 for females and 17 for males. There is a shift to sexuality and conflict exists between the identity developed during childhood and the identity demanded during adolescence. Often adolescents struggle tremendously in this stage because they are ill-prepared from their heterosexual socialization to deal with these feelings and perceptions. *Identity assumption* is the third stage and occurs around ages 19–21 for males and 21–23 for females. One of the key tasks here is learning to make sense out of and negotiate social stigma. *Commitment* is the final stage and occurs around ages 21–24 for males and 22–23 for females. It includes commitment to a same-sex love marked by identifying oneself as gay, lesbian, or bisexual. There is less dependence on passing strategies here.

SULLIVAN'S MODEL OF SEXUAL IDENTITY DEVELOPMENT

Sullivan's model has five stages that include active and passive phases. It is relevant for both gay and heterosexual people. The first stage is _naivete_ and reflects little awareness of sexual orientation. The _acceptance_ stage is characterized by a predominance of heterosexist thinking. _Resistance_, the third stage, as is consistent with many identity development models, reflects a state of dissonance. Oppression is now seen. _Redefinition_ is the fourth stage. Here the person is reformulating his notions of heterosexuality not dictated by the discourses of heterosexism. The final stage is _internalization_ and reflects the person's efforts to integrate newfound values into all aspects of his life.

IMPLICATIONS FOR COUNSELORS

There are several helping strategies that counselors can employ: (a) be aware of personal feelings toward gay men and lesbians; (b) validate confusion, (c) provide a safe, supportive environment conducive to the exploration of this struggle and confusion; (d) explore what it means to be gay (e) dispute myths about homosexuality; (f) suggest readings; (g) help the client move beyond the grief by acknowledging and expressing the loss of a heterosexual blueprint for life; (h) become familiar with local resources for gay men, lesbians, bisexuals and trangendered people and suggest supportive organizations to assist the client in building a support structure within the gay community; (i) assist the client in overcoming barriers to positive socialization; (j) be sensitive to the impact a gay/lesbian identity may have on the context surrounding the problems and issues faced by the individual; (k) encourage the client to create a support system within the gay/lesbian community before coming out to heterosexual significant others; (l) have some type of gay, lesbian, or bisexual literature on the bookshelf; (m) display something as small as a pin (one pin available for heterosexuals says "Straight but not narrow"), a poster, or a quote that depicts a multicultural and nonbiased view of the world; (n) attend workshops on counseling gay men, lesbians, bisexuals, and transgendered people; (o) stay informed of local gay events that can serve as a resource to clients; (p) personally and honestly assess one's level of sexual identity development; and (q) be aware of sexual identity models for heterosexuals as well as models for GLBT clients.

COUNSELING GAYS, LESBIANS, AND BISEXUALS OF COLOR

Even in generally supportive gay and lesbian social communities, people of color who are gay, lesbian, bisexual, and transgender are often oppressed and do not receive the affirmation that White GLBT people receive (Loiacano, 1989).

Battle, Cohen, Warren, Fergerson, and Audam (2002) conducted a study in conjunction with the National Gay and Lesbian Task Force with 2,465 Black GLBT people—58% men, 43% women, and 3% transgendered. They found that two thirds indicated that homophobia was a problem within the Black community. Half of the respondents agreed that racism is a problem for Black GLBT people in their relations with White GLBT people. Gender differences were found regarding the most important issues facing Black GLBT people. Approximately 72% of the men stated that HIV/AIDS was the most important issue facing Black GLBT people, while 55% of the women responded the same way. Women were more likely, at 50%, to say that hate crime violence was the most pressing issue; less than 40% of the men responded in this way. In addition to contending with hate crime, there is the pressing issue of domestic violence in same sex relationships which the National Coalition Against Domestic Violence estimates at 25% to 33% (Peterman & Dixon, 2003).

The racism and oppression faced by gay men and lesbians of color often urge them to turn to their same-race communities for the development of coping techniques, help with maintaining a positive identity and potential support (Icard, 1986). Because of the level of homophobia, few gay men and lesbians of color actually find needed support psychologically and socially. The African American community often reflects the attitude that homosexuality is inconsistent with being Black (Riggs, 1994).

Black gay males are faced with a problem of complying with male role expectations that include propagating the race and holding allegiance to the African American community, which generally maintains an antihomosexual attitude (Icard, 1986). Similarities are found within the Native American Indian and Asian American cultures. Greene (1994) said that "bearing some similarity to Asian cultures, gender roles are clearly delineated among Indian families, and obedience to parents is expected" (p. 247).

In working with Native American Indian gay clients, the devastation of colonialism and Western influences need to be considered in interpreting sexuality. It is crucial that Spirit, and not the material world, be held as sacred in traditional Native American Indian cultures. Gunn Allen (1992) talked about the gynecentric societies, which value the centrality of women, honor the young, and revere all of life that is part of the whole. In traditional society, there were sacred places for men and women who were embodied by Spirit and did not want to marry persons of the other gender, and there were men who dressed and lived like women. Among Native Americans, the term *berdache* has been misapplied to both gay men and lesbians. It is an Arabic word meaning "sex-slave boy" and has no relevance to American men or women (Gunn Allen, 1992). Concerning contemporary Native American Indians who are gay, Greene (1994) stated that acceptance may be less on reservations than in large urban centers. Gunn Allen (1992) pointed to acculturation and fundamental Christianity as major influences on homophobic attitudes among some Native people.

The Policy Institute of the National Gay and Lesbian Task Force interviewed 912 Latino gay men drawn from New York, Miami, and Los Angeles as part of a project called Nuestras Voces (Our Voices). The men reported widespread experiences with oppression (homophobia, racism, and poverty). Sixty-four percent were verbally insulted as children for being gay or effeminate, 31% reported experiences of racism in the form of verbal harrassment as children, 35% reported having been treated rudely as adults on account of their race or ethnicity, and 61% experienced a shortage of money for basic necessities, with 54% borrowing money to get by during the last 12 months before the interview (Diaz & Ayala, 2002). The report found that men who were high risk (less likely to use protection when engaging in anal intercourse with a nonmonogamous partner) had higher rates of oppression when compared to low-risk men. To survive or cope with the pain of societal oppression and accompanying feelings of powerlessness, many men turn to drugs or alcohol as aids and comforters. Diaz and Ayala (2002) stated, "Substances are used to cope not only with homophobic messages but also with the anger and frustration caused by poverty, racism and many other forms of social discrimination and abuse" (p. 16). The authors proposed that HIV prevention programs must also help men learn to cope with (*and resist*—emphasis mine) the toxic forces of racism, poverty, sexism, and homophobia because these social forces weigh heavily on Latino gay men's lives.

CASE STUDY
Staying Closeted or Coming Out

David is a 26-year-old Jewish male. His great grandparents emigrated from Israel to New York where David was born, raised, and currently resides. David is completing medical school and will begin his residency in the fall. His partner is Darren, also 26. Darren is a chemist and works for a pharmaceutical company. They have lived together for 2 years and are very committed to one another. Although David is out with his family, Darren is not. Darren is Chinese, his father is a minister, and Darren feels that being out will cause shame and disgrace to his family. David has "had it up to here" with the hiding and secrecy. According to David, he struggled to finally come out to his Jewish parents. He does not see how Darren's problem is any worse than his own. Darren tells David that he really does not care about what heterosexuals think about his being gay and that's why he does not bother telling them. David and Darren are looking for a good therapist to deal with their relationship problems.

QUESTIONS

1. Would a heterosexual counselor be appropriate for David and Darren?
2. How do culture and ethnicity intersect with sexuality?
3. What types of therapeutic techniques could be used to help David and Darren?

4. What kinds of questions should David and Darren ask a potential therapist to assess his or her suitability for providing professional therapeutic services?

DISCUSSION AND INTEGRATION
The Clients, David and Darren

Bradford, Barrett, and Honnold (2002) report that as of the 2000 Census, there were nearly 600,000 same-sex couples or nearly 1.2 million people. The largest proportional increases in the number of same-sex couples self-reporting in 2000 compared to 1990 were in rural and sparsely populated areas. For instance, Wyoming reported 30,000 same-sex couples in 1990 and 807,000 in 2000. The five cities with largest number of same-sex couples were New York, Los Angeles, San Francisco, Washington, DC, and Chicago.

David and Darren are similar to other couples. They are required to negotiate relationships with one another, in-laws, and other family and friends, balance work and family life, mediate conflicts, and establish boundaries (Laird, 2003). Despite these similarities, Darren's "closetedness" is indicative of a difference—being gay is not an acceptable type of relationship in the eyes of many and the ante is raised when a person of color is also gay. In one study the GLBT respondents of color surveyed were more likely to conceal their sexual orientation or gender identity to avoid harrassment. They were also more likely in comparison to White people to fear for physical safety. One woman said, "As a chicana, I felt ostracized even more. Forget about feeling a sense of community when you're a member of two minority groups" (Rankin, 2002 p. 25).

The notion of coming out, both to the self and to others, has been regarded as fundamental to a coherent sense of self and to self-esteem. Yet, some gay people in disclosing their sexuality have been disowned by their families and friends. Many people keep their sexualities closeted (Laird, 2003). The silence can interfere with intimacy because energy is expended hiding and not being one's authentic and true self. Such is the case with David and Darren.

David and Darren's monogomy is also reflective of a trend. AIDS may have fostered a move toward monogomous and committed relationships. A recent study reported by Laird (2003) indicated that 70% of gay male partners reported being in monogomous relationships.

As a person of color, Darren's experience as a gay man differs from David's, who is white and Jewish. Darren will face discrimination as a gay Asian man (Chan, 1992). As a visible man of color, Darren's sexual orientation and race need to be considered, particularly within the context of societal racism, sexism, and homophobia (Greene, 1994). A tremendous amount of oppression and isolation exists within communities of color around homosexuality. The impact of having multiple identities that are devalued in society represents a lack of support from communities of color and the White-dominated gay and lesbian populace. As is the case with Darren, Asian American gay people find themselves "caught between two conflicting cultural values, between Asian and Western influences" (Chan, 1992, p. 116). Asian American and Native American Indian gay men and lesbians also contend with strong traditional family roles, subsequent expectations, and community values that are often collectivistic, as opposed to individualistic, in orientation (Greene, 1994). This is not to say that David does not contend with strong

family roles because he does. According to Rosen and Weltman (1996), "The family's centrality cannot be underestimated in looking at Jewish cultural dynamics. Jewish 'familism' stems primarily from the idea that it is a violation of God's law not to marry. The first commandment of the Torah is, 'You shall be fruitful and multiply'" (p. 613). Not only has David not married a woman, he is gay. David does not belong to a synagogue or temple, but he is very attached to his Jewish identity. At the same time, David is committed to his sexuality and to Darren. His ability to juggle conflicting interests and priorities adds to his confusion and disappointment at Darren's silence. David's parents were deeply distraught at hearing he was gay and distanced themselves from him for awhile. David's desire to be a parent to either biological or adoptive children was good news to his parents and allowed them to deal more effectively with their son's homosexuality.

Darren maintains that he minimizes the judgments that heterosexuals have regarding his being gay and this explains his silence, but this appears to be a defense mechanism. Cass (1984) discussed approaches that gay people take in coping with alienation. A person may react positively to being different and devalue the importance of heterosexuals in his life. Darren has always felt different because of feelings for the same sex, and it was a relief for him to know that others have had the same experience. However, devaluing the importance of heterosexuals in Darren's life only works if he is able to avoid negative confrontation from heterosexuals about being gay. In other words, he needs to be able to pass or pretend heterosexuality and that is what he is doing, at least with his family. This passing strategy is coming under attack. Darren even took a female friend to a company holiday party; David was livid. Darren states that he is very committed to David but he is also very controlling of his personal information and his manner of dressing and behavior to ensure against being typed as homosexual. He is concerned that coming out could cost him his employment or a promotion. Rothblum (1994) cited a model of sexual orientation formation in which the various levels of identity are regarded as multidimensional, congruent, and/or incongruent. For example, Darren may say that he is gay, but is not yet out to his parents. This may differ for David.

The Counselor

All persons should have an opportunity to receive the services of a well-trained, qualified, and empathic mental health professional. These services should not be offered by a few sympathetic counselors in the field, but rather be available from therapists who seek to empower and enhance their gay clients' identity development.

A heterosexual counselor could be effective with David but not unless the counselor had worked through his own homophobic attitudes, which counselors, along with the general population, are socialized into (Holahan & Gibson, 1994). Chojnacki and Gelberg (1995) connected Cass's model to developmental stages of heterosexual counselors. A counselor who is at Stage 1 (confusion) may not clearly comprehend the oppressive contexts in which gay, lesbian, and bisexual persons live. Therefore, such a counselor may not understand the need for clients to be in a support group. Counselors in the latter stages, such as Stage 5 (identity pride) begin to feel pride about the quality of the services they provide to their clients and recognize the importance of understanding "the history, culture, ethics, jargon, and sense of community that define the gay and lesbian culture" (Pope, 1995, p. 302). Counselors at this stage also begin to experience greater alienation from colleagues perceived to be homophobic. Many gay and lesbian clients are cautious about entering therapy because they are aware of the homoprejudice among society at large and even among members of the helping profession (Rothblum, 1994). Gay, lesbian, or bisexual persons are disadvantaged when the helping professional is ignorant of sexual orientation, developmental processes, identity development, counseling techniques, and overall challenges with which this population contends on a daily basis. Referring a client to a different counselor who can be more effective is the standard course of action. This is particularly the case when the first counselor is unable or not adequately trained to provide the necessary support the client needs. Yet, counselors may want to ascertain whether their unwillingness to work with persons who are gay and lesbian is indicative of an intolerance for other sources of diversity, such as race, class, and, ability.

It may be helpful for the counselor to disclose his sexuality and talk about his qualifications to provide therapy as well as his openness to do so. Counselors need to be prepared to help clients create a support system within the gay/lesbian community before the clients come out to heterosexual significant others.

It is important for therapists who work with gay immigrant, ethnic, and other clients of color to ask themselves the following questions:

Is the client an immigrant or American born?
To what ethnic group does the client belong?
What are the specific cultural values of this
    group? Of the client's family? Of the client?
How strongly does the client follow traditional
    customs?
What is the client's socioeconomic status?
What is the client's level of bilingualism?

SUMMARY

This chapter examined sexual orientation and acknowledged that it exists on a continuum. Definitions were provided, and developmental processes, identity models, and implications for counselors, particularly in working with gay, lesbian, and bisexual clients, were discussed. A case study allowed readers to apply the material contained throughout. The importance of studying this topic was provided. Clients of color who are gay, lesbian, or bisexual were also discussed in an effort to help the reader in understanding the convergence of multiple identities.

REFERENCES

Battle, J., Cohen, C. J., Warren, D., Fergerson, G., & Audam, S. (2002). Say it loud I'm Black and I'm Proud. *Black Pride Survey 2000.* New York: The Policy Institute of the National Gay and Lesbian Task Force. Retrieved from http://www.ngltf.org/pi/blackpride.htm

Bell, A., & Weinberg, M. (1978). *Homosexuality: A study of human diversity among men and women.* New York: Simon & Schuster.

Bem, S. L. (1993). *The lenses of gender: Transforming the debate on sexuality inequality.* New Haven, CT: Yale University Press.

Berzon, B. (1988). *Permanent partners: Building gay and lesbian relationships that last.* New York: E. P. Dutton.

Bradford, J., Barrett, K., & Honnold, J. A. (2002). *The 2000 Census and same-sex households: A user's guide.* New York: The Policy Institute of the National Gay and Lesbian Task Force. http://www.ngltf.org/downloads/Census/CensusFront.pdf

Browning, C., Reynolds, A. L., & Dworkin, S. H. (1994). Affirmative psychotherapy for lesbian women. *Counseling Psychologist, 19,* 177–196.

Cass, V. C. (1979). Homosexual identity formation: A theoretical model. *Journal of Homosexuality, 4,* 219–235.

Cass, V. C. (1984). Homosexual identity: A concept in need of definition. *Journal of Homosexuality, 9,* 105–126.

Chan, C. S. (1992). Cultural considerations in counseling Asian American lesbians and gay men. In S. H. Dworkin & F. J. Gutierrez (Eds.), *Counseling gay men and lesbians: Journey to the end of the rainbow* (pp. 115–124). Alexandria, VA: American Association for Counseling and Development.

Chojnacki, J. T., & Gelberg, S. (1995). The facilitation of a gay/lesbian/bisexual support-therapy group by heterosexual counselors. *Journal of Counseling and Development, 73,* 352–354.

Coleman, E. (1982). Developmental stages of the coming out process. *American Behavioral Scientist, 25,* 469–482.

Diaz, R. M., & Ayala, G. (2002). *Social discrimination and health: The case of Latino gay men and HIV risk.* New York: The Policy Institute of the National Gay and Lesbian Task Force. http://www.ngltf.org/downloads/DiazEng.pdf

Durby, D. D. (1994). Gay, lesbian, and bisexual youth. *Journal of Gay and Lesbian Social Services, 1*(3/4), 1–37.

Dworkin, S. H., & Gutierrez, F. J. (1992). *Counseling gay men and lesbians: Journey to the end of the rainbow.* Alexandria, VA: American Association for Counseling and Development.

Falco, K. L. (1991). *Psychotherapy with lesbian clients: Theory into practice.* New York: Brunner/Mazel.

Greene, B. (1994). Ethnic-minority lesbians and gay men: Mental health and treatment issues. *Journal of Consulting and Clinical Psychology, 62,* 243–251.

Greene, B., & Herek, G. M. (1994). *Lesbian and gay psychology: Theory, research, and clinical applications.* Thousand Oaks, CA: Sage.

Gunn Allen, P. (1992). *The sacred hoop: Recovering the feminine in American Indian traditions.* Boston: Beacon Press.

Hammelman, T. L. (1993). Gay and lesbian youth: Contributing factors to serious attempts or considerations of suicide. *Journal of Gay and Lesbian Psychotherapy, 2*(1), 77–89.

Holahan, W., & Gibson, A. A. (1994). Heterosexual therapists leading lesbian and gay therapy groups: Therapeutic and political realities. *Journal of Counseling and Development, 72,* 591–594.

Hudson, W. W., & Ricketts, W. A. (1980). A strategy for the measurement of homophobia. *Journal of Homosexuality, 5,* 357–372.

Hunt, B. (1993). What counselors need to know about counseling gay men and lesbians. *Counseling and Human Development, 26*(1), 1–12.

Icard, L. (1986). Black gay men and conflicting social identities: Sexual orientation versus racial identity. In J. Gripton & M. Valentich (Eds.), Social work practice in sexual problems [Special issue]. *Journal of Social Work and Human Sexuality, 4*(1–2), 83–93.

Laird, J. (2003). Lesbian and gay families. In F. Walsh (Ed.), *Normal family processes* (pp. 176–209). New York: Guilford Press.

Loiacano, D. K. (1989). Gay identity issues among Black Americans: Racism, homophobia, and the need for validation. *Journal of Counseling and Development, 68,* 21–25.

Lorde, A. (1984), *Sister Outsider : Essays and speeches.* Freedom, CA: The Crossing Press Feminist Series.

O'Connor, M. F. (1992). Psychotherapy with gay and lesbian adolescents. In S. H. Dworkin & F. J. Gutierrez (Eds.), *Counseling gay men and lesbians: Journey to the end of the rainbow* (pp. 3–22). Alexandria, VA: American Association for Counseling and Development.

Pace, C. (1991). *A description of factors affecting attitudes held by mental health professionals and students toward lesbians and gays.* Unpublished master's thesis, University of Florida, Gainesville.

Peterman, L. M., & Dixon, C. G. (2003). Domestic violence between same sex partners: Implication for counseling. *Journal of Counseling and Development, 81,* 40–47.

Pharr, S. (1988). *Homophobia: A weapon of sexism.* Little Rock, AR: Chardon.

Pleck, J. H. (1984). Men's power with women, other men, and society. In P. P. Ricker & E. H. Carmen (Eds.), *The gender gap in psychotherapy: Social realities and psychological processes* (pp. 79–89). New York: Plenum Press.

Pope, M. (1995). The "salad bowl" is big enough for us all: An argument for the inclusion of lesbians and gay men in any definition of multiculturalism. *Journal of Counseling and Development, 73,* 301–304.

Rankin, S. (2002). *Campus climate for gay, lesbian, bisexual, and transgender people: A national perspective.* New York: The Policy Institute of the National Gay and Lesbian Task Force. http://www.ngltf.org/downloads/CampusClimate.pdf

Riggs, M. (Producer/Director). (1994). *Black is . . . Black ain't* [Video]. San Francisco: California Newsreel.

Robinson, T. L., & Watt, S. K. (2001). Where no one goes begging: Gender, sexuality, and religious diversity. In D. Locke, J. Myers, & E. Herr (Eds.), *Handbook of counseling,* (pp. 589–599). Thousand Oaks, CA: Sage.

Rosen, E. J., & Weltman, S. F. (1996). Jewish families: An overview. In M. McGoldrick, J. Giordano, & J. K. Pearce (Eds.), *Ethnicity and family therapy* (pp. 611–630). New York: Guilford Press.

Rothblum, E. D. (1994). "I only read about myself on bathroom walls": The need for research on the mental health of lesbians and gay men. *Journal of Consulting and Clinical Psychology, 62,* 213–220.

Rudolph, J. (1990). Counselors' attitudes toward homosexuality: Selective review of the literature. *Journal of Counseling and Development, 65,* 165–168.

Smith, B. (1982). Toward a Black feminist criticism. In G. Hull, P. Scott, & B. Smith (Eds.), *All the women are White, all the Blacks are men, but some of us are brave* (pp. 157–175). Old Westbury, NY: Feminist Press.

Sullivan, P. (1998). Sexual identity development: The importance of target or dominant group membership. In R. C. Sanlo (Ed.), *Working with lesbian, gay, bisexual, and transgender college students: A handbook for faculty and administrators* (pp. 3–12). Westport, CT: Greenwood Press.

Troiden, R. R. (1989). The formation of homosexual identities, *Journal of Homosexuality, 17,* 43–73.

Wall, V. A., & Evans, N. J. (1992). Using psychosocial development theories to understand and work with gay and lesbian persons. In N. J. Evans & V. A. Hall (Eds.), *Beyond tolerance: Gays, lesbians, and bisexuals on campus* (pp. 25–28). Alexandria, VA: American College Personnel Association.

Chapter 12

Converging Physical Attractiveness, Ability, and Disability

I am confident that Oprah's beauty and inner radiance at 50 are a result of loving intensely, forgiving extensively, and embracing her power, spirit, and wisdom in ways not possible as a younger woman.

Tracy Robinson

Cultural values of independence, thinness, physical strength, and athleticism pervade U.S. society. Both print and audiovisual advertisements are a primary medium for the transmission of images. Chronic dieting among women; preoccupation with body sculpting among men, even to the point of damaging the body with steroids; and eating disorders, such as anorexia and bulimia, are common and even epidemic within the culture. These behaviors seem to have their genesis in cultural images and values that far too often place a greater premium on physical attractiveness than on developed inner character strength. In this chapter, implications for the development of self-esteem based on possession of valued physical characteristics are examined. Race, gender, and body size are integrated into this discussion of physical attractiveness. The need for counselors to be aware of the salience of physical attractiveness as a status variable in everyday life is crucial to understanding clients as whole beings. That narrow definitions of physical attractiveness have implications for mental health attitudes, body validation, and the development of coping strategies to cope meaningfully with both unanticipated and normal maturational changes in physical appearance and body ability is articulated. Integrated into this discussion is an examination of the culture's clear preference for the able-bodied and intolerance for persons with disabilities. Implications for the development of a healthy relationship with the body, regardless of being able-bodied or having a disability, are presented. Multiple components of physical attractiveness exist and encompass facial beauty, skin color, physical ability and strength, visible signs of aging, height, weight, and hair length and texture. The discussion of physical attractiveness is broadened to include personal empowerment.

PHYSICAL ATTRACTIVENESS AS A STATUS VARIABLE

It has been said that literature reveals life. If this is so, the literature clearly supports a reality that societal distinctions are made between those persons who are regarded as physically attractive and those who are not (Cash & Duncan, 1984; Downs, 1990; Unger, Hilderbrand, & Madar, 1982). Numerous research findings have consistently shown a pattern across all age groups in which people react more favorably to attractive infants, children, and adults than they do to individuals perceived as unattractive (Ponzo, 1985). Physical attractiveness has even been linked to assumptions of moral character, intelligence, marital satisfaction, dating frequency, and quality of life (Dion, Berschid, & Walster, 1972; Webster & Driskell, 1983).

As highly valued traits in this society, beauty and physical attractiveness influence the assumptions held about individuals and the choices made about with whom to associate. Ponzo (1985) stated, "We desire to be with those who are physically beautiful because we have bought the 'beauty is good' hypothesis. We also believe that we will be viewed more positively by association" (p. 483).

Because of the hierarchical relationship that emerges between those who are perceived to have the commodity of attractiveness and those who are not, physical attractiveness is a **status variable.** More specifically, the attractive have more social power, meaning that, as with other forms of privilege, they are able to exercise this power on a daily basis to negotiate their lives more effectively.

Hahn (1988a) discussed beauty power and its close association with mate selection and sexual intimacy. She said, "As long as physical beauty determines sexual choices, human relations will be guided by fortuitous pleasing compositions of bone, muscle, and skin" (p. 27). Hahn observed that inner beauty and character will take a back seat in the competition for partners. Perceived as a prized commodity, beauty operates to "snare a mate who can give her the opportunity to live out her biological and social destiny" (Hutchinson, 1982, p. 60).

Definite privileges and benefits are associated with physical attractiveness. At the same time, physical attractiveness can be a hindrance to healthy interpersonal relationships. Attractive people may be perceived to be more vain and egotistical, to feel less sympathetic toward the oppressed, and to be more bourgeois in their attitudes than persons who are not as attractive (Okazawa-Rey, Robinson, & Ward, 1987). These and other perceptions and, arguably, prejudices toward attractive persons may adversely affect approachability and the cultivation of trusting alliances with persons perceived as attractive.

THE CONVERGENCE OF PHYSICAL ATTRACTIVENESS WITH GENDER AND RACE

Undoubtedly, race and skin color are variables in the beauty business. From a cultural perspective, American standards of beauty are often based on blond-haired, blue-eyed European ideals. The physical features of many White women, as well as those of women of color, more often than not differ from societally based rigid beauty standards.

Pursuit of the thin beauty ideal has meant different things for women. One percent of the 10- to 20-year-old American female population has anorexia nervosa. Four percent of college-age women have bulimia nervosa. Ten percent of anorexics and bulimics are men. About 72% of alcoholic women under the age of 30 also have eating disorders (ANRED, 2003). Disordered eating is far too often associated with becoming or remaining thin. Large numbers of young women in high school report that they use maladaptive weight control techniques such as fasting (39.4%), appetite suppressants (8.1%) and skipping meals (33.5%) to lose weight (Tylka & Subich, 2002).

Emmons (1992) found that African American teenage girls were more likely than any other race and gender group examined to use laxatives as a dieting ploy. In contrast, European Americans were more likely to vomit to lose weight. Cultural factors, values, and institutional variables such as racism and religious discourses all converge to influence the presence and diagnosis of eating disorders in women. Mastria (2002) maintains that cultural components of Latina culture predispose girls to defer and sacrifice themselves. She said, "From childhood, females are taught to repress sexual desires, and conditioned to be extremely modest and 'virginal' in terms of their bodies, which may cause conflict and shameful feelings about their bodies" (p. 71).

Among Black women, stress associated with the struggle to deal with acculturation, success, racism, and family responsibilities may trigger bingeing and purging behavior in some who did not evidence disordered eating during adolescence. Research conducted by Lester and Petrie (1998) on 139 female Mexican American college students found evidence of bulimia nervosa among 1.4% to 4.3% of the sample. Emmons's (1992) research points to an erroneous assumption about eating disorders—that they are rare among people of color. The stereotypes about which groups are affected by eating disorders and the dearth of people of color doing research on eating disorders contribute to this mistaken belief. Despite strongly entrenched beliefs about the protective aspects of race, a relationship may exist between increasing opportunities for social mobility for women of color and increasing vulnerability to disordered eating (Root, 1990).

The desire to bring honor and not disgrace to the family, coupled with the "model minority myth" may contribute to disordered eating among Asian American girls (Mastria, 2002). The changing roles of women within the family and workforce have to be considered when understanding the etiology of eating disorders and its relationship with power and control. According to Chernin (1985), eating disorders "must be understood as a profound developmental crisis in a generation of women still deeply confused after two decades of struggle for female liberation, about what it means to be a woman in the modern world" (p. 17).

Family of origin plays a pivotal role in the life of the girl who has an eating disorder. Brouwers (1990) reported that negative attitudes toward the body begin in the family and that, after self-body evaluation, the daughter's belief that the mother was critical of the daughter's body was the second biggest predictor of bulimia in female college students.

Research by Rogers and Petrie (2001) found that among 97 college women (27 non-White), dependency and assertion of autonomy were important in explaining the variance on the Eating Attitudes Test. It appears that symptoms of anorexia are characterized by dependency on and need for approval from a significant relationship, as well as the need to deny this reliance. Restricting food intake may be a way to assert one's sense of individualism within the gender role. Women's power comes from their beauty and physical allure as approved and esteemed by others.

College campus factors or values may influence a girl's vulnerability to eating disorders. Kashubeck, Walsh, and Crowl (1994) discovered that the literature on one college Web site emphasized physical appearance, attention to fashion, and participation in the sorority-fraternity system. Another college, a liberal arts institution, emphasized political activism and intellectual talent. The rate of eating disorders did not differ between the two schools, but the study found that at the first school, the factors associated with eating disorders were the perceived pressure to dress a certain way, to be smart, and having a marginal grade point average. At the second school, being a girl and having low masculine gender role identity were the strongest predictors to disordered eating behaviors.

Despite African American youths' positive self-esteem (Gibbs, 1985; Gibbs, Huang, & Associates, 1989; Ward, 1989), feeling enormous pressure to look according to European ideals may adversely affect self-concept among this group as well as other women of color. They may feel compelled to change hairstyles, dress, body size, and makeup to be accepted and thus keep the doors of opportunity wide open. Robinson and Ward (1991) indicated that obesity among many African American women may be a quick-fix resistance strategy to negotiate the pressures and frustrations of daily racism and sexism.

Oppressive stereotypes about women of color are pervasive throughout the media. For instance, Root (1990) identified that

> Women of color are either fat and powerless (African American and Latina women); fat, bossy, and asexual; corrupt and/or evil (Asian/Pacific Island Americans and African Americans); obedient, quiet, and powerless (Latinas and Asian/Pacific Americans); exotic (Asian Americans, mixed race); or hysterical and stupid. (p. 530)

In an effort to conform to accepted standards of beauty, many women of color will seek to fulfill Eurocentric beauty standards equated with status, acceptance, and legitimacy. Some Asian women have undergone plastic surgery to make their eyes appear more round or double-folded, as opposed to single-folded, for a more Western look. This drastic physical change may be fueled by Uba's (1994) statement, "There is evidence that Asian Americans have lower self-concepts than Euro-Americans do when it comes to physical appearance" (p. 83) (see the Storytelling "Is She Pretty?"). Rhinoplasty to obtain a nose that is smaller, narrower, and finer is a surgical procedure many Jewish women have undergone. African American women have been known to bleach their skin, and there is the monumental issue of hair, on which Black women spend an inordinate amount of time, psychic energy, and money. Many of them, along with their Jewish sisters, have for decades been "relaxing" their hair by applying chemicals to make it straight and less naturally coiled or curly. The author Alice Walker refers to this relaxing process as "oppressing" the hair.

Among Black Americans, appearance is not solely linked to skin color but to a variety of phenotypical traits, such as body shape, facial features, and hair texture (Rockquemore, 2002). Skin color has social power and status within the African American community (Okazawa-Rey et al., 1987). Mullins and Sites (1984) found that the inheritance of light skin color, which generally came from the mother, who tended to be lighter than the father, along with the mother's education, occupational

STORYTELLING: Is She Pretty?

I was sitting at Starbucks one afternoon, grading papers. I overheard three Asian women speaking. They were talking about another Asian woman who was not there. One of the women asked, "Is she pretty?" Another woman said as she laughed, "Oh no, she has the big Korean face."

attainment, and income, served to bolster a family's social position over time. Within a society preoccupied with skin color as a barometer for assignment to a racial category, the desirability of lighter skinned women stems from their closer proximity to European beauty standards, which research has found affects income, educational attainment, and perceptions of success (Rockquemore, 2002). Intraracial conflict around **colorism,** or stereotyped attributions and prejudgments based on skin color, has been documented in the literature (Okazawa-Rey et al., 1987; Robinson & Ward, 1995). Colorism is often manifested as a preference for lighter skin tones over darker ones, because color-consciousness is rooted in the social, political, and economic conditions that existed during and after slavery; however, discrimination against persons with lighter skin tones occurs as well. Colorism in the Black community may be a double-edged sword, affecting those who are seen perhaps as "too black" and those who may be seen as "not black enough." Robinson and Ward (1995) found that African American adolescents reported high levels self-esteem, yet students who were at the extremes of skin color, lighter or darker than most African Americans, were less satisfied with skin color than students who were somewhere in the middle. Clearly, skin color attitudes are connected to several variables, including the particular ethnic group, group cohesiveness, the group's status in society and factors such as family, school and peers (Phinney & Rosenthal, 1993).

In qualitative research conducted by Rockquemore (2002) with 16 men and women who had one Black biological parent and one White biological parent, three main themes were reported: (a) racialized negotiations with Black women (the primary theme), (b) internalized negativity toward Blackness, (c) racial socialization by parents. In comparison to men from the larger survey sample conducted as part of the same study, women had a higher frequency of negative encounters with Black women. The status and commodity of lighter skin color within the Black community was noted as were strong anti-Black sentiments. According to Rockquemore (2002), "at different times during the interviews, Black people were broadly characterized as being drug addicted, ignorant, unemployed, uneducated, impulsive, and ill-mannered" (p. 495). Fifty percent of the interview sample had parents who were not married due to divorce or separation or never had been married. Most of the respondents from single parent homes were raised by White women. Two difficulties expressed by these women were dealing with their parents' explicit racism or negotiating the racialized negativity that White mothers had for Black fathers. Consistent with national data on Interracial unions, the majority of Black/White unions in this study were between White women and Black men.

It should be remembered that skin color issues are connected to broader themes of identity and an awareness of the sociopolitical context of race in America. As people of African descent celebrate various hues, skin color as a status variable may hopefully take on less prominence.

Appearance is important to people, yet personal beauty is frequently considered the most important virtue a woman can possess. According to Lakoff and Sherr (1984), "beauty is power," and many women have gained social success banking on the social marketability of their perceived physical attractiveness. The socialization process in this culture equates self-worth with mobility, thinness, beauty, and, far too often, dress size. From a very early age, little girls are conditioned, in both subtle and overt ways, that fulfillment in life is hugely dependent on being physically beautiful. As children, many African American women remember being cautioned by their mothers that unless their newly washed hair was done (which usually meant being pressed and curled but sometimes braided), they could not go outside. The implicit and sometimes explicit message in this statement was that one's natural state was synonymous with being unpresentable and unkept.

In addition to learning that beauty is a valuable commodity, young girls learn passivity from the pressure imposed on them to stay clean and neat, correlates of femininity, purity, and acceptability. Adult women continue the legacy by restricting their movement, in an effort to be socially desirable, by oppressing themselves in fashions that are uncomfortable, tight, or even painful. Most American women have worn uncomfortable shoes just because they accompany an outfit, add height, slenderize the entire body, and elongate the legs. The bunions, corns, and other foot problems that millions of women suffer are often a result of this socialization standard. Men, too, seek to beautify themselves, but their bodies, although this is changing, appear to be less dependent on external beauty standards as necessary to self-definition and validation.

It is not surprising that many women behave in a manner that suggests beauty is something to be acquired and at any cost (Okazawa-Rey et al., 1987). Billions of dollars are spent annually on products and services in Herculean effort to beautify, freshen, and defy the aging process. Looking one's best is not being assailed. What is problematic is the excessive emphasis placed on physical attractiveness, which is dangerously linked to self-worth, dignity, desirability, and quality of life. As Rockquemore (2002) stated, "For women, appearances are power in the mating market therefore differences and distinction serve as the primary level at which negative interactions occur" (p. 492).

Attractiveness and sexual desirability are themes that even concern women confronting life and death issues. A survivor of breast cancer spoke movingly about the impact of the disease, but noted the silence around attractiveness and desirability:

> I was worried about my appearance; perhaps that was easier than worrying
> about the threat to my life. I worried about how the mastectomy would affect
> our married life. I could never get anyone to talk about that! It turned out
> that my husband was more worried about losing me than my losing a breast.
> I now know (a year later) how unaware other people are of it. (Elder, 2000)

Standards of beauty have been different over time, across cultures, and among racial groups. Age is most likely the one identity construct that has the greatest bearing on beauty. **Ageism,** or discrimination against middle-aged and elderly people, differs between men and women. According to Nuessel (1982), "Ageism is distinct from other forms of discrimination because it cuts across all of society's traditional classifications: gender, race, religion, and national origin" (p. 273). Ageism affects women in that in the normal and inevitable maturational process, men mature and become refined, whereas women wilt and wither. Consider the naturally occurring conditions of menstruation and menopause. Much of the research and studies done in these areas express deep hatred and fear of women and their bodies. Menstruation has been perceived as an impediment and an illness, and menopause has been labeled a disease and a social problem. Because women's bodies are different from men's, they have been regarded as abnormal. More than 600,000 hysterectomies are performed in the United States each year, yet very few of these operations are performed because of life-threatening situations. Some are even suspected of being unnecessary. Per capita, "half as many hysterectomies are performed in Great Britain as in the United States" (Balch & Balch, 1997, p. 337).

Could the historical devaluation of women and their bodies among the male-dominated medical community contribute to this extremely high rate of costly hysterectomies? Menopause is big business, so is weight loss, the eating disorders anorexia and bulimia, Botox, liposuction, and other forms of plastic surgery. The medical community has used estrogen against women to support a belief that this hormone is essential for femininity and youth. Conversely, this same chemical has been viewed as responsible for erratic and strange behavior. Now there is rampant confusion about whether women should be using hormone replacement therapy. Although there are benefits, there are also definite disadvantages. The social contexts of women's lives must be addressed during the menopausal years.

As women mature and develop a sense of personal power and an internal locus of control, how is their beauty perceived? Power in this context is associated with the knowledge that selflessness is a less desirable trait than responsible self care and respect for others. Powerful women have come to critique and challenge externally defined constructions of beauty and femininity.

SEX ROLE TYPOLOGY, BODY IMAGE, AND SATISFACTION

Attitudes about body image and subsequent levels of satisfaction are socially constructed and can be deconstructed or challenged and changed so that new discourses about their meanings are created (Monk, Winslade, Crocket, & Epston, 1997). For instance, research (Jackson, Sullivan, & Rostker, 1988; Unger et al., 1982) strongly suggests that a masculine sex role type, as opposed to a feminine one, may be related to a more favorable body image. This could be a function of the psychological nature of masculinity. A person's high dependence on external validation of the self may contribute to external locus of control (McBride, 1990).

In other research conducted on the attractiveness of the androgynous male, researchers found that masculinity, too, is a double-edged sword. Masculine subjects were rated less favorably than androgynous males; however, androgynous men who were seen as too feminine were rated as less likable (Cramer, Cupp, & Kuhn, 1993).

Other research related to sex role type has found that, among children, both boys and girls rated as more attractive were more likely to play with feminine-typed toys and less likely to play with masculine-typed toys, in comparison with children rated as unattractive (Downs, 1990). Attractive adolescents were more likely to hold on to traditional sex-typed values for themselves and others (Downs & Abshier, 1982). Being regarded as attractive may affect one's ability to develop an androgynous sex role type. Females judged as attractive may be challenged in their development of a masculine sex role and attractive men may have difficulty developing a feminine sex role. This concern is important, given the effect of androgyny on self-esteem, attitudes about success, and ability to cope with existential issues (Cano, 1984; Cook, 1987; Stevens, Pfost, & Potts, 1990).

Despite the noble efforts of the women's movement, negative body image continues to be with us into the 21st century. According to Hutchinson (1982), "Body image is not the same as the body, but is rather what the mind does to the body in translating the experience of embodiment into its mental representation" (p. 59). Birtchnell, Lacey, and Harte (1985) indicated three aspects of body image: (a) *physiological,* which involves the brain's ability to detect weight, shape, size, and form; (b) *conceptual,* which is the mental picture of one's own body; (c) and *emotional,* which refers to the feelings about one's body weight, shape, and size. Brouwers (1990) argued that the emotional aspect of body image is the crux of the eating disorder known as **bulimia,** characterized by recurrent episodes of binge eating and feelings of lack of control over eating behavior during binges. This makes sense—intense dissatisfaction with body image and strong hatred of one's body is correlated with bulimia. Such strong negative emotion regarding the body often elicits severe feelings of depression and powerlessness.

Where does such intense dislike for the body originate? For young girls, they are socialized that their primary role in life is to please and to be pleasing to others, tending to be much more anxious and worried than boys about being socially desirable. If the body deviates from acceptable cultural standards, and it often does, dissatisfaction may ensue when the girl child is not empowered to celebrate her body and the joys of it. Adult women are incapable of assisting young women in this celebration process if they themselves cannot honor their own desires within their bodies.

A closer relationship exists among beauty, thinness, success, power, acceptance, and self-worth for girls and women than it does for boys and men. In fact, one study found that overall body dissatisfaction was higher among girls than among boys (Paxton et al., 1991). This finding may explain why 87% of persons undergoing plastic surgery are women (Steinem, 1992).

In the United States, over 90% of persons suffering from **anorexia nervosa,** or self-starvation of the body, are young females (Andersen, 1986; ANRED, 2003). Adolescents are particularly vulnerable to eating disorders because anorexia nervosa has its highest incidence at the beginning of adolescence and bulimia nervosa has its highest incidence at the end (Emmons, 1992). From a psychodynamic perspective, the earlier scripts that are set in motion will have a powerful impact on behavior and cognition unless early information is replaced with new information. Arrival to adulthood does not ensure clarity about the existence or elimination of dysfunctional tapes.

One task of adulthood is to unlearn many of the negative tapes received during childhood and adolescence and to replace them with tapes that affirm the self and are more reflective of who the individual has sculpted the self to be. The media, church, educational institutions, other women, family members, and men create an environment wherein men "construct the symbolic order" within which gender inequity and male supremacy are reproduced. Clearly, not all men feel powerful and exert power over all women within a system of male supremacy. There are women by virtue of their race and class privileges who exert power over some men. Nonetheless, an androcentric culture exists and dictates for both women and men images and standards of acceptability which influence one's body image and self-esteem.

In this system, women (and, arguably, men because the privilege to define reality often comes with a price) become detached from their bodies in a warring fashion. This is particularly true when a gap exists between perception of body image and approximation to the socially constructed standard. In short, intense body dissatisfaction and a sense of disembodiment can ensue when one's body does not conform to the standard. Hutchinson (1982) stated, "The body is experienced as alien and lost to awareness. . . . The body has broken away or has been severed from the mind and is experienced as a foreign object, an albatross, or a hated antagonist" (pp. 59–60).

Alienation from the body interferes with the important work of appreciating and ultimately accepting the multiple identities of the self regardless of how it is configured. Perceptions of the body amid parts that cause pain, create difficulty, or are defined by society as unattractive and therefore deemed unacceptable can be transformed and embraced through deliberate paradigm shifts. New discourses or ways of bringing meaning to bear on the value of the body can emerge and take root interpersonally (Monk et al., 1997).

MEN AND BODY IMAGE

American society places an inordinate amount of emphasis on thinness as a criterion for physical attractiveness in women more than in men (Downs, 1990). Whereas the majority of American women seek to lose weight, American men seem to be equally split between those who desire to lose weight and those who wish to gain some (Davis, Stuart, Dionne, & Mitchell, 1991). **Patriarchy,** women's dependence on men for economic gain, and the objectification of women's bodies are partly responsible for this dynamic. But men, too, are affected by societal notions of attractiveness. Athletic leanness (Emmons, 1992) and a sculpted, muscular body (Gillett & White, 1992) are often the criteria for men's attractiveness and social acceptability. Thus, men are now more concerned with their body image and physical appearance than they were a few decades ago (Davis et al., 1991). This standard is evidenced in advertising that often depicts men in erotic poses with emphasis on their bulging and sculpted muscles as well as the phallic symbol (Kervin, 1989).

Adult men are affected by societal dictates but adolescents are more vulnerable, in part, because of the dramatic physical changes that take place during puberty. To achieve an ideal body image, teenagers have been known to resort to a variety of methods that include fasting, dieting, using laxatives, and purging. Although females represent the majority of eating disorder cases, boys and men are not immune to these disorders. Andersen (1986) stated that similarities are found between males and females with eating disorders, yet some differences are found with respect to preillness weight, psychotherapeutic needs, and modality themes. Overall, males are less conscious of the desire to achieve a certain weight or clothing size. Instead, they place greater emphasis on muscle definition and avoiding fat and flab on the body. Boys are socialized to believe that masculinity is synonymous with being a protector, provider, and worker. Athleticism and body strength create the basis for virility. Men with physical disabilities often struggle with oppressive and internalized notions of masculinity that tend to be inconsistent with the presence of disability. Emmons (1992) found that boys, too, were engaging in dieting behaviors, meaning that adolescent males, as a group, are under considerable pressure to shape and sculpt their bodies to fit societal standards. Perhaps greater emphasis on fashion advertisements and product lines wherein the young, muscular male body is revered (Mishkind, Rodin, Silbersein, & Striegel-Moore, 1987) has contributed to this pressure.

The male body and its muscles are associated with strength and power. It is argued that in times of psychocultural stress, through bodybuilding and maintenance of a health regime, a male can gain discipline over the body, which is a form of salvation in itself (Gillett & White, 1992). Moreover, masculinity is reclaimed by attaining a hypermasculine body image through bodybuilding. Pumped muscles demonstrate strength, power, and authority. Psychologically for men, bodybuilding may be a way to resist perceived oppression or as a counteraction to the accomplishments of women.

To achieve the ideal body, steroids are often employed, not only among professional athletes but also among high school seniors (Ham, 1993). Anabolic-androgenic steroid hormones can enhance body size toward achieving the "chiseled" body look, increase speed, and boost performance. Steroids also have been known to have adverse effects on the liver, cardiovascular and reproductive systems, and even psychological health. Both men and women are subject to increased risks of cancer, liver dysfunction, kidney disorders, and heart disease (Ham, 1993). Despite the risks and the potential lethal effects of steroids, they are often used to achieve an ideal body image. The culture's obsession with beauty comes with a heavy price tag.

DISABILITY AND EXPERIENCES IN AND OF THE BODY

Having an able body is so highly valued in U.S. society that persons with disabilities are discriminated against, stereotyped, ignored, and in many instances, presumed to be biologically inferior, particularly if the disability is congenital as opposed to acquired (Marini, 2001). Hahn (1988a) said, "The most salient features of many disabled

STORYTELLING: The Stairs

I had arrived in Scotland for a conference. I decided to take public transportation from the airport to get an initial feel for the city. As I disembarked from the subway with my luggage, I noticed a very long flight of stairs. I looked for the escalator and upon not seeing one, I asked a man where it was. He looked at me with amusement, grabbed my bags, and said as he glided up the stairs taking every other one, "There isn't one." I asked, "What do people with disabilities do?" He said, "They are out of luck unless they can get someone to help them."

persons are bodily traits similar to skin color, gender, and other attributes that have been used as a basis for differentiating people for centuries and without which discrimination would not occur" (p. 26). Hahn (1988b) observed that men and women with disabilities, unlike groups of color, have been unable to refute discrimination-based notions of biological inferiority. Persons of color with disabilities represent persons who have the highest poverty and unemployment rates (Marini, 2001).

Zola (1991) stated that preference for specific body types over others represents another societal "ism." In this work, this form of discrimination has been termed "able-body-ism" (see Chapter 3). Just as being male is a biological fact, so is having a disability. Being handicapped, however, is a psychosocial outgrowth of this biological reality (Weeber, 1992). Considerable silence surrounds the experiences of those who have disabilities (see the Storytelling "The Stairs"). This is particularly relevant among able-bodied persons who assume that lack of membership in the disability community entitles them to ignorance or apathy.

Societal attitudes toward disability are numerous and degrading. Many persons perceive the disability to be the only salient element in a person's life. Fowler, O'Rourke, Wadsworth, and Harper (1992) said, "When one's physical and/or mental abilities are considered as the primary status for characterizing individuals, the resulting polarity implicitly divides all persons into two groups: the able and the unable" (p. 14). Much like race, physical disability can be elevated to a primary status trait, where it overrides other characteristics, even achieved ones, and can produce feelings of invisibility. Often, people with disabilities are seen as helpless, childlike, dependent, unattractive asexual, and economically subordinate. In addition to such dangerous myths, able-bodied people are too often embarrassed when it comes to talking about or associating with those who have disabilities (Weeber, 1992).

As with other identity constructs, disability intersects with gender. In a society in which masculinity is often equated with virility, strength, sexuality, and self-reliance, it is understandable how men with physical disabilities can be perceived as a contradiction to hegemonic masculinity. Gerschick and Miller (1994) stated that "men with physical disabilities are marginalized and stigmatized because they undermine the typical role of the body in United States culture. . . . Men's bodies allow them to demonstrate the socially valuable characteristics of toughness, competitiveness, and ability" (p. 35). To arrive at the place of acceptance of one's self in one's body, there has to be, as Collins (1989) indicated, (a) a confrontation of the societal standard that maintains that masculinity is not only narrowly defined but also in contradiction to the disabled man's body, (b) repudiation of this socially constructed norm, and (c) affirmation of the self through a recognition that the norms and discourses, and not the person, are problematic. From this perspective, the man is able to reconstruct, for himself, alternative gender roles and practices (Gerschick & Miller, 1994).

Real-life stories in which people experience dramatic and sudden changes in their bodies are numerous (see the Case Study "Redefining Manhood" at the end of this chapter). Wendell (1989), for example, wrote powerfully about the sudden overnight process of going from being able-bodied to being disabled as a result of a disabling chronic disease:

> In 1985, I fell ill overnight with what turned out to be a disabling chronic disease. In the long struggle to come to terms with it, I had to learn to live with a body that felt entirely different to me—weak, tired, painful, nauseated, dizzy, unpredictable . . . I began slowly to identify with my new, disabled body and to learn to work with it. (p. 63)

Waiting to return to her original state was indeed dangerous because the likelihood of this occurrence was remote. So, in time, she was required to learn how to identify and coexist with her new disabled body but not without struggle. Within a culture where normalcy and disability are regarded as antonyms, Wendell (1989) wrote, "Disabled women struggle with both the oppressions of being women in male-dominated societies and the oppressions of being disabled in societies dominated by the abler-bodied" (p. 64).

Both Wendell (1989) and Zola (1991) maintained that a theory on disability and the body is needed. Because of the strong cultural assumptions of able-bodiedness and physical attractiveness, such a theory is beneficial to all, regardless of current or, better yet, temporary physical status.

One way that many people with disabilities experience their bodies is through pain. Wendell (1989) stated that persons who live with chronic pain can teach the general public what it means to share space with that which hurts. Crucial questions emerge, such as how a person welcomes pain into his or her life, especially if it is feared. In turn, are people with chronic pain feared and loathed by those who are reminded of their own vulnerability? Feeling the pain, as opposed to endeavoring to medicate it away (Wendell, 1989), meditating on the pain, and engaging in visual imagery and thereby making peace with it are examples of being in, listening to, and embracing one's body for what it is. Indeed, this increased consciousness is a gift of pain. Such a gift can move a person to a place of unconditional acceptance of his or her body despite the circumstances. Writer Audre Lorde (1994) said, "There is a terrible clarity that comes from living with cancer that can be empowering if we don't turn aside from it" (p. 36). It is in the not turning away, the bold and yet humble confrontation of the source of pain, that strength is found for the journey. Note how all of us can benefit from this lovely truth because pain, in its various forms, is a feature of living and is independent of physical ability status.

The wisdom among some people with disabilities may benefit many able-bodied persons. The psychological tendency to regard persons who differ from a societal referent point as "other" can interfere with receiving life lessons. Yet, how would this culture be enhanced by listening to dismissed or silenced voices? Wendell (1989) stated that "if disabled people were truly heard, an explosion of knowledge of the human body and psyche would take place" (p. 77). Many persons with disabilities have much to teach the able-bodied about this process of acceptance, dignity, and empowerment.

IMPLICATIONS FOR COUNSELORS

Helping professionals are not exempt from attitudes that favor children and adults regarded as attractive over those regarded as unattractive (Ponzo, 1985). Guidance counselors need to be particularly mindful of the power of words in shaping children's constructions of themselves. Lerner and Lerner (1977) wrote, "Evidence suggests that when compared to the physically attractive child, the unattractive child experiences rejecting peer relations, the perception of maladjustment by teachers and peers, and the belief by teachers of less educational ability" (p. 586). Professionals are encouraged to ascertain their own beliefs about body image and physical attractiveness. Some professionals may be more inclined to gravitate toward able-bodied and attractive clients. This is biased behavior and discredits the profession that should be oriented toward empowerment and respect. The counselor should be aware that some ethnic clients may not value and thus not strive for independence or mastery over their environment. Refusing to do so is not a form of pathology but such attitudes have to be examined in the context of culture (Marini, 2001).

Counselors need to assess for themselves the impact of the culture's messages about weight, beauty, size, and disability on their self-esteem and on their perceptions, favorable and otherwise, of others.

CASE STUDY
Redefining Manhood

Ryan is a 22-year-old athletic White male from a working-class family. He works at a lumber yard. He was crushed by logs that fell off a trailer that he had hitched to a crane. His injury damaged his spine and he is now a paraplegic. He will never walk again. Ryan barely survived and is grateful to be alive although he is mourning the loss of his mobility and able body.

QUESTIONS
1. How can a counselor help Ryan to heal?
2. How does Ryan's status as a paraplegic affect his masculinity and, more specifically, his sexuality?
3. Can a woman effectively counsel Ryan?

DISCUSSION AND INTEGRATION
The Client, Ryan

Any client who experiences a loss needs time and space to mourn. Only the client gets to decide how long this process will take. Ryan's life after the accident can continue to be meaningful, but first he has to redefine success, attractiveness, masculinity, desirability, and sexuality. Fowler et al. (1992) indicated that "a disability is a characteristic which carries sufficient conceptual power to stereotype an individual, regardless of whether the disability was present at birth or acquired later in life" (p. 102). Ryan's conceptualization of self must shift. Part of this shifting self-conceptualization encompasses notions of what it means to be a man.

In a patriarchal society that is designed by men for men, U.S. cultural values of the Protestant work ethic, individualism, capitalism, and self-reliance, become inextricably bound to notions of physical attractiveness, power, mobility, strength, and dominance over one's body. Vulnerability and uncertainty simply do not coexist well in a society that values domination and conquest. The belief is that the body can be controlled—that somehow illness and perhaps subsequent disability are a result of the individual's doing. Wendell stated, "The demand for control fuels an incessant search for the deep layered explanations for causes of accidents, illness, and disability" (p. 72). "The body beautiful" is central to self-expression (Gillett & White, 1992). An insatiable hunger to be alluring, lovely, and desired permeates the culture and emanates from a conceptual framework.

Myers et al. (1991) stated that, in society today, with all of its isms, "the very nature of the conceptual system is itself inherently oppressive and that all who adhere to it will have a difficult time developing and maintaining a positive identity" (p. 55). Essentially, a suboptimal system operates within a paradigm where self-worth is attached to external factors separate from the self. Optimally, self-worth is intrinsic to the self. Accidents and illness can suddenly change the ability of one's body and one's control over it.

A multiculturally competent counselor understands the essential process of rage, anger, and depression associated with Ryan's major life crisis. At the appropriate time, the counselor can serve as an educator helping Ryan to critique traditional notions of masculinity. For instance, physical strength is associated with manhood. Men with disabilities are often not perceived by society as strong because a large part of this strength and manhood equation is having an able body. There are different types of strength, physical as well as character, that are not typically identified by society.

Asking for psychological help is a form of self-reliance and control (Roberts, Kisselica, and Frederickson, 2002). Spiritual and human resources that radiate love and acceptance are vital to healing. Research has shown that supportive social networks are associated with psychological well-being and adjustment to one's disability (Belgrave, 1991; Swanson, Cronin-Stubbs, & Sheldon, 1989). Prior to the accident, Ryan had a very active life involving the full use of his legs. As the healing progresses, it is hoped that Ryan could continue to be physically, socially, and sexually active. Although he is unable to walk, he can develop his upper body strength. He can also be mobile via the use of a wheelchair, which is another form of mobility. Zola (1989) indicated that a shift in society's perceptions of a wheelchair would have far-reaching implications for society.

Through journaling, within small groups, or both, Ryan can collectively begin to unravel the strongholds of socially constructed notions of desirability and attractiveness and how these have had an enormous impact on his self-concept. Ryan's counselor needs to reframe meanings of strength, realizing that Ryan's abilities can exhibit strength through his lived experiences of dignity, interdependence, competitiveness, and peace.

Ryan's counselor needs to supplement his knowledge about Ryan's disability and accompanying functional limitations (Marini, 2001). Many of the issues Ryan is grappling with are sensitive and related to his sexual impotence. Thus, a woman would most likely be an inappropriate counselor. At the same time, homophobia interferes with the ability of many men to share intimately with other men. Ryan has major concerns about his sexuality and the expression of it given his impotence. How will he experience sexual gratification? He may also wonder about the ability to provide sexual pleasure without an erect penis. How will he satisfy his sexual partner or any other person? Fortunately, a series of technological devices are available that assist couples with achieving satisfying sex lives in the event of spinal cord injuries, medication-induced impotence, and other barriers to erection. Penile implants made of silicone or polyurethane can be surgically installed. One type consists of two semirigid but bendable rods; the other type consists of a pump, fluid-filled reservoir, and two cylinders into which the fluid is pumped to create an erection. Vacuum devices can also be used to increase blood flow to the penis (Balch & Balch, 1997, p. 340).

Ryan has the full use of his body above his waist. His body, mind, spirit, and heart are sources of giving and receiving intense pleasure. Notions of what constitutes a normal sex life have to be altered if

Ryan is going to seek and eventually find meaning in his life. Genital sex is certainly one way to give and receive pleasure but it is not the only way.

Finally it is also crucial to remember that what is perceived as attractive is a cultural dictate mediated by the values of society. For example, many Native Americans do not regard disability as punishment for having sinned and tend not to judge or stigmatize people (Marini, 2001). Gunn Allen (1992) observed that American society would be different if various traditions from Native American culture were followed, saying

> If American society judiciously modeled the traditions of the various Native Nations, the ideals of physical beauty would be considerably enlarged to include "fat" strong-featured women, gray-haired, and wrinkled individuals, and others who in contemporary American cultured are viewed as "ugly." (p. 211)

SUMMARY

This chapter examined the culture's fascination and preoccupation with physical attractiveness. A case study examined able-body-ism in a male client who had become disabled as a result of a work-related accident. Implications for counselors were discussed with respect to the convergence of physical attractiveness, race, age, ability, disability, and gender. Statistics were presented on eating disorders and their potentially deadly impact on young women and men.

REFERENCES

Andersen, A. E. (1986). Males with eating disorders. In F. E. F. Larocca (Ed.), *Eating disorders* (pp. 39–46). San Francisco: Jossey-Bass.

ANRED (2003). Anorexia and Related Eating Disorders. Retrieved January 23, 2004 from http://www.anred.com/ stats.html

Balch, J. F., & Balch, P. A. (1997). *Prescription for nutritional healing.* Garden City Park, NY: Avery.

Belgrave, F. Z. (1991, January–March). Psychosocial predictors of adjustment to disability in African Americans. *Journal of Rehabilitation*, 37–40.

Birtchnell, S. A., Lacey, J. H., & Harte, S. (1985). Body image distortion in bulimia nervosa. *British Journal of Psychiatry, 47*, 408–412.

Brouwers, M. (1990). Treatment of body image dissatisfaction among women with bulimia nervosa. *Journal of Counseling and Development, 69*, 144–147.

Cano, L. (1984). Fear of success: The influence of sex, sex role identity, and components of masculinity. *Sex Roles, 10*, 341–346.

Cash, T. S., & Duncan, N. C. (1984). Physical attractiveness stereotyping among Black American college students. *Journal of Social Psychology, 1*, 71–77.

Chernin, K. (1985). *The hungry self: Women, eating, and identity.* New York: Harper & Row.

Collins, P. H. (1989). The social construction of Black feminist thought. *Signs, 14*, 745–773.

Cook, E. P. (1987). Psychological androgyny: A review of the research. *Counseling Psychologist, 14*, 471–513.

Cramer, R. E., Cupp, R. G., & Kuhn, J. A. (1993). Male attractiveness: Masculinity with a feminine touch. *Current Psychology, 12*, 142–150.

Davis, C., Stuart, E., Dionne, M., & Mitchell, I. (1991). The relationship of personality factors and physical activity to body satisfaction in men. *Personality and Individual Differences, 12*, 689–694.

Dion, K., Berschid, E., & Walster, E. (1972). What is beautiful is good. *Journal of Personality and Social Psychology, 14*, 94–108.

Downs, A. C. (1990). Physical attractiveness, sex-typed characteristics, and gender: Are beauty and masculinity linked? *Perceptual and Motor Skills, 71*, 451–458.

Downs, A. C., & Abshier, G. R. (1982). Conceptions of physical attractiveness among young adolescents: The interrelationships among self-judged appearance, attractiveness stereotyping, and sex-typed characteristics. *Journal of Early Adolescence, 2*, 57–64.

Elder, P. (2000). An entirely routine test. In M. Clark (Ed.), *Beating our breasts: Twenty New Zealand women tell their breast cancer stories* (pp. 29–35). New Zealand: Cape Catley Limited.

Emmons, L. (1992). Dieting and purging behavior in Black and White high school students. *Journal of the American Dietetic Association, 92*, 306–312.

Fowler, C., O'Rourke, B. O., Wadsworth, J., & Harper, D. (1992). Disability and feminism: Models for counselor exploration of personal values and beliefs. *Journal of Applied Rehabilitation, 23*, 14–19.

Gerschick, T. J., & Miller, A. S. (1994). Gender identities at the crossroads of masculinity and physical disability. *Masculinities, 2*, 34–55.

Gibbs, J. T. (1985). City girls: Psychosocial adjustment of urban Black adolescent females. *Sage: A Scholarly Journal on Black Women, 2*, 28–36.

Gibbs, J. T., Huang, L. N., & Associates. (1989). *Children of color: Psychological interventions with minority youth.* San Francisco: Jossey-Bass.

Gillett, J., & White, P. G. (1992). Male bodybuilding and the reassertion of hegemonic masculinity: A critical feminist perspective. *Play and Culture, 5*, 358–369.

Gunn Allen, P. (1992). The sacred hoop: Recovering the feminine in American Indian traditions. Boston: Beacon Press.

Hahn, H. (1988a, Winter). Can disability be beautiful? *Social Policy*, pp. 26–32.

Hahn, H. (1988b). The politics of physical differences: Disability and discrimination. *Journal of Social Issues, 44*(1), 39–47.

Ham, E. L. (1993, August). Steroids: Wrestling with the issues. *Trial*, pp. 36–42.

Hutchinson, M. G. (1982). Transforming body image: Your body—friend or foe? In *Current feminist issues in psychotherapy* (pp. 59–67). New York: Haworth Press.

Jackson, L. A., Sullivan, L. A., & Rostker, R. (1988). Gender, gender role, and body image. *Sex Roles, 19*, 429–443.

Kashubeck, S., Walsh, B., & Crowl, A. (1994). College atmosphere and eating disorders. *Journal of Counseling and Development, 72*, 640–645.

Kervin, D. (1989, Winter). Advertising masculinity: The representation of males in *Esquire* advertisements. *Journal of Communication Enquiry, 14*(1), 51–70.

Lakoff, R. T., & Scherr, R. L. (1984). *Face value: Politics of beauty.* Boston: Routledge, Kegan, & Paul.

Lerner, R. M., & Lerner, J. L. (1977). Effects of age, sex, and physical attractiveness on child-peer relations, academic performance, and elementary school adjustment. *Developmental Psychology, 13*, 585–590.

Lester, R., & Petrie, T. A. (1998). Prevalence of disordered eating behaviors and bulimia nervosa in a sample of Mexican American female college students. *Journal of Multicultural Counseling and Development, 26*, 157–165.

Lorde, A. (1994). Living with cancer. In E. C. White (Ed.), *The Black women's health book: Speaking for ourselves* (pp. 27–37). Seattle, WA: Seal.

Marini, I. (2001). Cross-cultural counseling issues of males who sustain a disability. *Journal of Applied Rehabilitation Counseling, 32*, 36–44.

Mastria, M. R. (2002). Ethnicity and eating disorders. Psychoanalysis and Psychotherapy, *19*(1), 59–77.

McBride, M. (1990). Autonomy and the struggle for female identity: Implications for counseling women. *Journal of Counseling and Development, 69*, 22–26.

Mishkind, M. E., Rodin, J., Silbersein, L. R., & Striegel-Moore, R. H. (1987). The embodiment of masculinity: Cultural, psychological, and behavioral dimensions. In M. S. Kimmel (Ed.), *Changing men: New directions in research on men and masculinity* (pp. 37–52). Newbury Park, CA: Sage.

Monk, G. D., Winslade, J. S., Crocket, C., & Epston, D. (1997). *Narrative therapy in practice: The archeology of hope.* San Francisco: Jossey-Bass.

Mullins, E., & Sites, P. (1984). Famous Black Americans: A three-generational analysis of social origins. *American Sociological Review, 49*, 672.

Myers, L. J., Speight, S. L., Highlen, P. S., Cox, C. I., Reynolds, A. L., Adams, E. M., & Hanley, P. (1991). Identity development and worldview: Toward an optimal conceptualization. *Journal of Counseling and Development, 70*, 54–63.

Neal, A. M., & Wilson, M. I. (1989). The role of skin color and features in the Black community: Implications for Black women and therapy. *Clinical Psychology Review, 9*, 323–333.

Nuessel, F. H. (1982). The language of ageism. *Gerontologist, 22*, 273–276.

Okazawa-Rey, M., Robinson, T. L., & Ward, J. V. (1987). Black women and the politics of skin color and hair. *Women and Therapy, 6*, 89–102.

Paxton, S. J., Wertheim, E. H., Gibbons, K., Szmukler, G. I., Hillier, L., & Petrovich, J. L. (1991).

Body image satisfaction, dieting beliefs, and weight-loss behaviors in adolescent girls and boys. *Journal of Youth and Adolescents, 20*, 361–379.

Phinney, J., & Rosenthal, P. A. (1993). Ethnic identity in adolescence: Process, context, and outcome. In F. Adams, R. Montemayor, & T. Oulotta (Eds.), *Advances in adolescent development* (Vol. 4, pp. 145–172). Newbury Park, CA: Sage.

Ponzo, Z. (1985). The counselor and physical attractiveness. *Journal of Counseling and Development, 63*, 482–485.

Porter, C. (1991). Social reasons for skin tone preferences of Black school-age children. *Journal of the American Orthopsychiatric Association, 61*, 149–154.

Roberts, S. A., Kisselica, M. S., & Fredrickson, S. A. (2002). Quality of life of persons with medical illnessess: Counseling & holistic contribution. *Journal of Counseling and Development, 80*, 422–432.

Robinson, T. L., & Ward, J. V. (1991). A belief in self far greater than anyone's disbelief: Cultivating resistance among African American adolescents. *Women and Therapy, 11*, 87–103.

Robinson, T. L., & Ward, J. V. (1995). African American adolescents and skin color. *Journal of Black Psychology, 21*, 256–274.

Rockquemore, K. A. (2002). Negotiating the color line: The gendered process of racial identity construction among Black/White biracial women. *Gender and Society, 16*, 485–503.

Rogers, R. L., & Petrie, T. A. (2001). Psychological correlates of anorexic and bulimic symptomatology. *Journal of Counseling and Development, 79*, 178–187.

Root, M. P. P. (1990). Disordered eating in women of color. *Sex Roles, 22*, 525–536.

Steinem, G. (1992). *Revolution from within: A book of self-esteem.* Boston: Little, Brown.

Stevens, M. J., Pfost, K. S., & Potts, M. K. (1990). Sex role orientation and the willingness to confront existential issues. *Journal of Counseling and Development, 68*, 47–49.

Swanson, B., Cronin-Stubbs, D., & Sheldon, J. A. (1989). The impact of psychosocial factors on adapting to physical disability: A review of the research literature. *Rehabilitation Nursing, 14*, 64–68.

Tylka, T. L., Subich, L. M. (2002). Exploring young women's perceptions of the effectiveness and safety of maladaptive weight control techniques. *Journal of Counseling & Development, 80,* 101–110

Uba, L. (1994). *Asian Americans: Personality patterns, identity, and mental health.* New York: Guilford Press.

Unger, R. K., Hilderbrand, A., & Madar, T. (1982). Physical attractiveness and assumptions about social deviance: Some sex-by-sex comparisons. *Personality and Social Psychology Bulletin, 8.*

Ward, J. V. (1989). Racial identity formation and transformation. In C. Gilligan, N. P. Lyons, & T. J. Hanmer (Eds.), *Making connections: The relational worlds of adolescent girls at Emma Willard School* (pp. 215–232). New York: Troy Press.

Webster, M., Jr., & Driskell, J. E., Jr. (1983). Beauty as status. *American Journal of Sociology, 89,* 140–164.

Weeber, J. (1992). *The importance of a disability identity theory: Implications for gender.* Unpublished manuscript.

Wendell, S. (1989). Toward a feminist theory of disability. *Hypatia, 4,* 63–81.

Zola, I. K. (1989, October–December). Aging and disability: Toward a unified agenda. *Journal of Rehabilitation,* 6–8.

Zola, I. K. (1991). Bringing our bodies and ourselves back in: Reflections on a past, present, and future "medical sociology." *Journal of Health and Social Behavior, 32,* 1–16.

Part Four: Reimaging Counseling

Chapter 13

Diversity in Relationships

She said, "bad cow" as she sat down. This adult woman had come to realize that her mother was incapable of filling her cup with the nurturance and love that she both wanted and deserved to have. It is liberating, albeit painful, to learn that one's biological or family of origin—husbands, wives, partners, mothers, fathers, sisters, brothers—may be ill-equipped to respond appropriately to any one of our many legitimate needs. There are people who can and desire to fill our cups with mutuality, reciprocity, love and understanding. They may not however, be related by blood.

Tracy Robinson

This chapter looks at the changing face of relationships in the 21st century. A focus is on demographic trends from census data and the way in which the counseling profession can honor the challenges that people face in their efforts to be in relationships that are authentic and yet configured differently than in decades past. A case study and related questions begin this chapter. Students are asked to form working groups and answer the questions while creating additional ones.

CASE STUDY
Two White Mothers, One Black Male Child

The following case is presented for students to discuss in working groups.

Thirteen years ago, a White lesbian couple adopted a Black male child, Rodrick, age 12. The couple has now split up. Together they share custody of the child. The child is your client. Each of his moms has a new partner. Everybody is White and female. Rodrick is required to repeat the sixth grade because of failing grades and truancy. For 6 months, he has been fighting with other children, stealing repeatedly from the neighborhood store, and throwing rocks at new cars to dent them. He is defiant and disobedient to his mothers and teachers.

1. How do you assess the situation and what additional information do you need?
2. What would be a provisional DSM-IV TR diagnosis?
3. What resources do you organize to assist the child?
4. How do you feel about working with this family?
5. What are your concerns, judgments, and biases?
6. How do you work therapeutically with the mothers?

DEMOGRAPHIC OVERVIEW OF LIVING AND FAMILY ARRANGEMENTS

According to the 2000 Census, nonfamily households were more common and family households less common in comparison to 1970. The most noticeable trend was the decline in the number of married households with their own children present. In 2000, 24% of homes were married couples with their own children. This percentage was 40.3% in 1970. Other-family households were 16% of the population in 2000 compared to under 11% in 1970. This category includes families whose householder has no spouse present and is living with other relatives with children present. In 2000, women living alone represented 58% of single-person households. In 1970, this figure was 67%, so the number of men living alone has increased.

Households have become smaller, and households with their own children comprised only one third of all households in 2000 (U.S. Census Bureau, 2000).

Divorce, fertility changes, and mortality all contribute to declines in the size of households. According to census data, there are now more single-parent families. Single-mother families increased from 3 million in 1970 to 10 million in 2000, and single-father households also saw an increase, from 393,000 to 2 million during the same period. The reasons for single parenting differ across race and ethnicity. Among White women, it is most likely a function of divorce. Most Black women who are single mothers have never been married. Independent of race, one-parent families maintained by women are more likely than those maintained by men to have family incomes below the poverty line. The rise in the divorce rate over the last several decades is no surprise. What is surprising is the influence of gender and race on getting married in the first place. Among African American women in particular, there have been substantial decreases in marriage rates. The percentage of married Black women declined from 62% in 1950 to 36.1% in 2000. There are a number of factors that have already been identified throughout this text that contributed to this decrease, including high rates of unemployment among Black men (people are less likely to marry during times of economic instability), high incarceration rates among Black men, high homicide rates among Black men ages 15–44, and increases in the number of Black men, particularly those with some college or a college degree, who marry outside of their racial group.

People are also delaying marriage. The median age for marriage among men is 26.8. It was 23.2 in 1970. The median age for marriage among women is now 25.1. In 1970 it was 20.8. The proportion of women ages 20 to 24 who had never married doubled between 1970 and 2000, from 36% to 74%. Increasingly high numbers of children under the age of 18 reside in stepfamilies. In 1996, 5.2 million children lived with one biological parent and either a stepparent or adoptive parent. This figure is up from 4.5 million just 5 years earlier in 1991 (U.S. Census Bureau, 2001a). There were 2.1 million adopted children as estimated from the Census 2000 (Kreider, 2003). Disproportionately, African American children are represented among those who have been separated from families of origin, placed in foster care, and are in need of adoption (Bradley & Hawkins-Leon, 2002).

Another trend in marriage is the increase in the number of interracial married couples in the United States. As of the 2000 Census, there were 1.46 million interracial couples. Black-White couples have increased seven-fold between 1960 and 2000, from 51,000 to 363,000, respectively. The majority of Black-White unions are between Black men and White women. Despite the large increase in Black-White marriages, they represent only 24.7% of all interracial marriages, which is lower than the 34% proportion in 1960. Approximately 70% of Latinos marry outside of their ethnic group. When Blacks and Latinos marry interracially, their spouses are more likely to be White. Non-Latino Whites who marry outside of their race are more likely to marry Native Americans and Asians. The majority of Asian-White unions are between Asian women and White men. Among Native Americans and Whites, there are equal numbers of White men and Native women to Native men and White women.

THE ECONOMY AND RELATIONSHIPS

The United States and other Western cultures have experienced significant social, cultural, and economic changes. Marked economic growth increased the number of available jobs. Rising inflation rates increased the cost of living. The women's movement, the civil rights movement, and associated legal actions improved the access of women, individuals with disabilities, and people of color to the workplace. Politically and economically based transitions in the past 2 decades have considerably reshaped the family landscape in this country. Family form and structure have been influenced by a host of factors, including the feminist movement, economic insecurity, the increase in dual-earner households, the recession, more mothers in the workforce, the rising rates of divorce, single-parent households, remarriage, and cohabitation (Fenell & Weinhold, 1996).

During the 1990s, the breadwinner-homemaker model of the two-parent family was replaced by dual-earner families, in which both partners participate in the job market for pay. The predominance of dual-earner families has occurred both by choice and by necessity. Some women have wanted to work and others responded to economic necessity because of declining family incomes hit hard by the recession that began in March 2001. In 1975, 47% of all American mothers with children under age 18 worked for pay. By 2000, the rate had risen to 73%. High percentages of women with very young children are going to work. In 1975, 34% of mothers with children age 3 and under were doing paid work, and in 2000, this figure had risen to 61% (Hochschild, 2003). Many of these parents with young children are also caring for their aging parents. For the first time in history, more American children live in families with mothers who are working outside the home than with mothers who are full-time homemakers. These trends in maternal workforce participation are dramatic. Their impact, both real and feared, on family functioning, marital relationships, and child development has received national attention. Despite this trend, the labor participation rates of mothers with infant children actually fell from 59% in 1998 to 55% in 2000 (U.S. Census Bureau, 2001b). It should be noted that these "declines occurred primarily among mothers in the workforce who were 30 years old and over, White women, married women living with their husbands and women who had completed one or more years of college" (p. 1).

GENDER AND RELATIONSHIPS

Statistics and trends are important because they describe the families that counselors interact with on a daily basis, professionally and personally. The very definition of family has a bearing on the way family policy is constructed and on those whom counselors will serve. Current family policy rewards and punishes certain kinds of family forms, as it defines and privileges particular relationships within certain groups. Heterosexual marriage is priviliged and protected; single persons with no children or property pay the federal government mightily in taxes for not having legitimate tax write-offs.

Clearly, the form and structure of the American family is changing. Much discussion and speculation surrounds the loss of the traditional father/breadwinner and mother/homemaker pattern to the dual-earner or single-parent family pattern and its impact on child development and family well being. It often is assumed that the traditional family pattern is best and that nontraditional family patterns, which often include nonfamily-related child care arrangements, are less desirable. But the general trend of research findings does not readily identify one family pattern or child care pattern as clearly superior or inferior to the others in terms of children's adjustment, child-rearing practices, or family functioning.

The traditional family pattern with distinct sex role separations between homemaking and wage earning always has been and remains the societal norm. In a compelling historical review of the origins of the traditional family, Lamb (1982) noted that although women universally have had primary responsibility for the care of young children, these responsibilities rarely prevented them from relying to a substantial extent on supplemental child care arrangements or from contributing to the economic survival of the family. When U.S. society was more agrarian and local-community-based, both parents typically worked in the fields or in a location close to home. Most women entered the paid workforce and remained employed except for brief childbearing and child-rearing interruptions. With the Industrial Revolution, work locations moved farther away from the family home, but most women continued their employment.

The materialistic culture impresses a value of "more is better," and the debt burdens most people carry are staggering. It is no wonder family members are stressed, confused, and dysfunctional because of frequently conflicting work, school, and personal schedules; regimented and chaotic socialized routines; and little or no intimate space with each other to communicate what has been occurring in each other's lives. These situations often create a struggle for the semblance of a shared life; thus, family discord and confusion occur.

Families have been affected by society's infusion of gender role socialization for centuries. The socialization process requires that heads of the household and siblings conform to rigid gender role expectations created by a patriarchal system (Goldenberg & Goldenberg, 1996; Nelson, 1997). Although the patriarchal structures of intimacy that serve as the hegemonic ideal of family are perhaps the structures among all others that have silenced and exploited women, they are also the structures—or something like structures—of many feminists' families (Nelson, 1997). The vast majority of families in this society are affected by the covert and overt models of socialization that ultimately form the framework and functioning in most households (Hanna & Brown, 1995; Lott, 1994).

The literature on gender role socialization discusses the power base of men as providers gaining recognition from sources outside the home, whereas females' power base and recognition come from their work as caregivers and relationship-maintenance providers inside the home (Burck & Speed, 1995; Lott, 1994; Nicholson,

1997). Even when women work, traditional roles such as child care, household chores, as well as sustaining contact and communication with family and friends, continue to be part of their daily routine (Hochschild, 2003). These roles are socially sanctioned and imposed on individuals on the basis of gender. The assumption is that these roles are symmetrical and equivalent in power. However, the inherent inequality of power is based on what is valued most highly in this society—economic stability. "The contribution of women's family work continues to be minimized, perhaps because it does not directly produce income" (Hare-Mustin, 1988, p. 40).

Society imposes certain behavioral expectations on women and men within families. Women in families often experience a responsibility to uphold the traditions and rituals in those families. Men are expected to be the financial providers and to play less of an emotional role in their caring networks. The socially sanctioned roles within families have left behind generations of women and men who have, at different stages in their lives, felt inadequate and isolated from others because of their narrow gender experience.

Women are expected to assume responsibility for maintaining family relationships and connections. If they do not take on this role and no one else fills in the gap, the connections in the family unit start to deteriorate. The breakdown of family ties or inability to provide nurturance in relationships leads to women experiencing an overwhelming sense of shame and inadequacy (Efthim, Kenny, & Mahalik, 2001). The socialization of women to assume this caretaking role is handed down from generation to generation within families by the demands of an androcentric society. These positions of gender role rigidity can serve to restrict the experiences of family members. Men can begin to feel like strangers to the family and defined primarily within the context of money. Women feel responsible for the survival of the family ties while at the same time their position outside the family is limited.

Families in this new millennium are composed of female-headed households, gay or lesbian couples, biracial partnerships, blended (divorced or widowed) families, and grandparents or extended family members raising the family's children. These new families need to be comfortable with the therapist and the therapist with them. Inquiring about gender and family roles allows the therapist to assess the family dynamics operating between members and perhaps across generational lines. Questions that could be asked might include:

1. What family traditions or rituals stressed specific roles or activities for boys and for girls?
2. Does your family discuss how gender roles affect girls and boys in our society?
3. In what ways, if any, do you think these ideas and traditions might be related to the presenting problem?

These are a few questions the counselor can ask during the assessment process. Care should be taken to eliminate any question that does not seem to resonate with the client. The therapist should always keep the factors of race, gender, disability, religion, sexual orientation, age, and socioeconomic status in mind when talking with the client because the personal is political.

The family system plays a key part in helping the counselor gather background information on the client and determine whether the client has the ability to process his innermost thoughts and connect them with the impact of gender role socialization or race. This structural approach to family therapy is a theoretical framework that provides a conceptual map to understanding families.

COUNSELING THEORIES FOR FAMILY PRACTICE

The theoretical framework and theorist most commonly used for family issues is the **structural family approach,** developed by Salvador Minuchin who began his work with families in the 1960s. The structural family approach gives the practitioner a concrete, conceptual map of what should be happening in a family if it is to be functional; it also provides maps of what is awry in the family if it is dysfunctional (Becvar & Becvar, 1993). The structural family approach gives students and practitioners definite ideas about the therapeutic processes that should be carried out. These processes inevitably vary in practice; however, they should reflect the personality of the therapist and the particular structure of the family. Structural family therapy is one of the most heavily researched models, and its efficacy has been demonstrated with a variety of what are generally termed "difficult families." Thus, families with juvenile delinquents, families with anorexic members, families with chemically addicted members, families of low socioeconomic status, and alcoholic families (Fenell & Weinhold, 1996) have all been successfully counseled with the structural family approach. The influence of this approach may also be seen in other models of family therapy, particularly the strategic approach.

Structural family therapy sees the family as an integrated whole—as a system. Accordingly, it is also a subsystem in that its members belong to other agencies and organizations in the community of which it is a part and that affect its basic structure and pattern of organization. In the language of the theory, there are three key concepts or constructs: structure, subsystems, and boundaries.

STRUCTURAL FAMILY THERAPY

Structural family therapy focuses on the patterns of interaction within the family that give clues to the basic structure and organization of the system. **Structure** refers to the invisible set of functional demands that organizes the way family members interact, or the consistent, repetitive, organized, and predictable modes of family behavior that allow the counselor to consider that the family has structure in a functional sense. The concepts of *patterns* and *structure* therefore imply a set of covert rules that family members may not be consciously aware of but that consistently characterize and define their interactions.

The structure of a family is governed by two general systems of constraints. The first constraint system is referred to as *generic,* an observation that all families everywhere have some sort of hierarchical structure according to which parents have greater authority than children. An important aspect of this generic structure is the notion of reciprocal and complementary functions, which can be discerned by the labels applied to family members that indicate their roles and the functions they serve. Members of a family evolve roles (without a conscious awareness of their roles) to maintain the family equilibrium and to keep it functioning.

A second constraint system is that which is *idiosyncratic* to the particular family. Rules and patterns may evolve in a family although the reason for such characteristic processes may be lost in the history of the family. The rules and patterns become a part of the family's structure. Family structure governs a family in that it defines the roles, rules, and patterns allowable within the family.

SUBSYSTEMS

Structural family theory defines three subsystems: the spouse subsystem, the parental subsystem, and the sibling subsystem. The rule among these subsystems for the functional family is that of hierarchy. The theory insists on appropriate boundaries between the generations.

The *spouse subsystem* is formed when two people marry and thus create a new family. The notion of a spouse assumes heterosexual marriage. The processes involved in forming the spouse subsystem are known as *accommodation,* which implies adjustment, and *negotiation* of roles between spouses. The early part of the marriage formation of the spouse subsystem necessitates evolving such complementary roles. Although some of these roles may be transitory and others may be more permanent, the keys to the successful navigation of life as a family are negotiation and accommodation, especially as they concern rules and roles. The adjustment for couples may be difficult and slow because each has certain expectations about the performance of various functions and roles. Negotiation and accommodation are enhanced to the degree that each spouse is his own person and is not overly tied to the family of origin or its rules, patterns, and roles. Finally, an important requirement of the spouse subsystem is that each spouse be mutually supportive of the other in the development of his unique or latent talents and interests. Accordingly, neither spouse is so totally accommodating of the other as to lose his own individuality. Both sides give and take, each remains an individual, and as each accommodates the individuality, resources, and uniqueness of the other, they are respectfully bound together.

In the *parental,* or executive, *subsystem,* each spouse has the challenge of mutually supporting and accommodating the other to provide an appropriate balance of firmness and nurturance for the children. The parents are in charge, and an important challenge is knowing how and when to be in charge about specific issues. Parents need to negotiate and accommodate changes in the developmental needs of their children. A family is not a democracy, and the children are not equals or peers of the parents. From this base of authority, the children learn to deal with authority and to interact in situations in which authority is unequal.

By establishing the spouse and parental subsystems, structural family theory also defines the sibling subsystem. The *sibling subsystem* allows children to be children and to experiment with peer relationships. Ideally, the parents respect the ability of the siblings to negotiate, to compete, to work out differences, and to support one another. It is a social laboratory in which children can experiment without the responsibility that accrues to the adult. Children also learn to coalesce to take on the parental subsystem in the process of negotiating necessary developmental changes.

BOUNDARIES

Boundaries are invisible, but they nevertheless delineate individuals and subsystems and define the amount and kind of contact allowable between members of the family. Structural family theory describes interpersonal boundaries among subsystems as falling into one of three categories: clear, rigid, and diffuse.

Clear boundaries are firm and yet flexible. Clear boundaries also imply access across subsystems to negotiate and accommodate situational and developmental challenges that confront the family. Indeed, situations that occur each day are a test in how to live that necessitates negotiation, accommodation, and experimentation with a new structure over and over again until the family gets it "right," only to find its circumstances have changed once more. Clear boundaries in a family increase the frequency of communication between subsystems, and thus negotiation and accommodation can successfully occur to facilitate change, thereby maintaining the stability of the family.

Rigid boundaries refer to the arrangement both among subsystems and with systems outside the family. Rigid boundaries imply disengagement within and between systems. Family members in that instance are isolated from one another and from systems in the community of which the family is a part. Members in such families thus rely on systems outside the family for the support and nurturance they need and desire.

The family defined by *diffuse boundaries* is characterized by enmeshed relationships. In this case, everybody is into everybody else's business, and the hovering and the providing of support even when not needed is extreme. The parents are too accessible, and the necessary distinctions between subsystems are missing. There is too much negotiation and accommodation; the cost to both the developing children and the parents is a loss of independence, autonomy, and experimentation. The spouse subsystem devotes itself almost totally to parenting functions, and the parents spend too much time with the children and do too much for them. Such children may be afraid to experiment, perhaps to succeed, perhaps to fail. They may feel disloyal to a parent if they do not want to accept what the parent offers. They probably have difficulty knowing which feelings are theirs and which belong to others. The clear boundary is preferred and represents an appropriate combination of rigid and diffuse characteristics.

For Minuchin, the ideal family builds on a spouse subsystem in which each accommodates, nurtures, and supports the uniqueness of the other. The spouses have attained a measure of autonomy from their families of origin. Ideally, in the family of origin, each spouse felt supported and nurtured and yet experienced a degree of autonomy, independence, and responsibility. Similarly, spouses need to be able to maintain a delicate balance between proximity and distance. On this base, the couple negotiates complementary roles that are stable but flexible and through a process of negotiation and accommodation evolves different structures and role complements to deal with changing circumstances. The spouse subsystem maintains itself even when children are born and the parental/executive and sibling subsystems come into existence.

The ideal family will face expected and unexpected crises appropriately by recognizing and facilitating necessary changes in structure. Such behavior requires a great deal of patience and wisdom. So, with the challenge of each new crisis, a new culture (structure) must be evolved—in many cases, a structure and transition process for which the participants have no direct experience to guide them. That is, families are organisms in a continuous process of changing while trying to remain the same.

GOALS

Problem solving is not the goal of structural family therapy. Symptomatic behavior is viewed as a function of the structure of the family; that is, it is a logical response in the family, given its structure. Problem solving will naturally occur when appropriate structural adaptations have been made. Thus, problem solving is the business of the family; structural change so that problem solving can occur is the business of the structural therapist. Symptom removal without the appropriate change in structure would not be successful therapy from the structural perspective.

The structural therapist must join the family and respect its members and its way of organizing itself. Thus, the therapist gets into the family and accommodates to its usual style. Such joining is a necessary prerequisite of attempts to restructure. The structural therapist also respects the hierarchy of the family by asking for the parents' observations first. Problems thus get redefined relative to the family structure. Structural family therapy is action oriented and aimed at influencing what happens in the therapy session.

Becvar and Becvar (1993, pp. 207–208) noted specific techniques and activities the structural therapist might conduct while in therapy:

1. Meet with family members separately to discuss therapeutic boundaries
2. Assist family members who are not communicating effectively toward increasing their dialogue with one another
3. Help specific dyads find ways to end conflictual relationships without intrusion from other family members
4. Help family members find ways to cognitively view themselves differently by embracing a positive frame of reference

Structural family therapy primary processes include being clear about family structure and having respect for the family's efforts to achieve higher levels of functioning. Additionally, the therapist should respect the family's traditional modes of operation, yet provide a healthier model of behavior. This can be achieved by "supporting members, challenging them to try new methods in session and praising them generously when they are successful. There must be an intensity sufficient enough to gain the attention of the family members" (Becvar & Becvar, 1993, p. 208).

MULTICULTURAL THEORETICAL PERSPECTIVES IN FAMILY THERAPY

The structural family approach and multicultural theoretical paradigms should be viewed and implemented as complementary approaches to treatment. Gushue and Sciarra (1995) stated that two models currently in the counseling literature provide a framework for the impact of culture on family therapy and family systems: (1) the intercultural dimension and (2) the intracultural dimension, which delineates the issues of (a) acculturation (b) racial and cultural identity, and (c) bilingual theory.

When looking at the *intercultural dimension,* the counselors working with White, middle-class, heterosexual males used this paradigm to guide all work with their clients. But they began to realize that, for families, diversity was normative. Different cultures had differing ways of understanding "appropriate" family organization, values, communication, and behavior. Although the family perspective had revolutionized the individual view of the client by taking family context into account, it now needed to understand its own unit of analysis (the family) in the light of a cultural culture.

In the *intracultural dimension,* the counselor must turn to three crucial questions of within-group difference: (a) To what extent does this particular family conform to or differ from the "typical" patterns of family functioning for its culture? (b) What cultural differences may exist within the family itself (among the various subsystems)? and (c) If cultural differences exist within the family, what consequences do these differences have for interactions both among the subsystems and between the various subsystems and the counselor? (See the Storytelling "All in the Family.") Answering these questions leads the therapist to the issues of (a) acculturation, (b) racial and cultural identity, and (c) bilingual theory.

Acculturation initially referred to the potentially mutual influence that two cultures have on each other when they come into contact (Ivey, Ivey, & Simek-Morgan, 1997; Mindel, Habenstein, & Wright, 1988). Over the years, however, it has more commonly come to refer to the interaction between a dominant and a nondominant culture in which one is affected much more profoundly than the other.

The models of *racial* and *cultural identity* presented in Chapter 8 are important to integrate into family systems therapy because they provide the therapist with

STORYTELLING: All in the Family

I was talking to a woman in Cairo, Egypt. She looked liked she was in her early 30s. She told me that she was divorced and living at home with her family. I asked her if she ever had concerns about her privacy (a very Western and individualistic question). She looked at me with some confusion and replied no. I asked her if any women lived alone in Cairo. She said not many did and that those who did came from not-so-good families. Her cultural expectations informed this woman of appropriate behavior at various developmental junctures. She honored these cultural expectations and perceived them to be normal.

information regarding within-group differences and an individual's psychological orientation to membership in both the dominant and nondominant cultures in the United States.

Bilingual theory questions whether intracultural differences in a given family can be attained by observing and understanding the function of linguistic difference within the family system. As emigration from non-English-speaking countries continues to rise, bilingual persons in therapy will become an increasing phenomenon. Some issues that need to be addressed for the bilingual client are related to the immigration experience, language barriers within the family, and language barriers between therapist and client. "Family therapists must take great care before using norms that stem from the majority cultural matrix in assessing the attitudes, beliefs, and transactional patterns of those whose cultural patterns differ from theirs" (Goldenberg & Goldenberg, 1996, p. 36). The behaviors described in the next section provide important information that the therapist must be keenly aware of to empathize with the issues affecting people of color in this country.

NATIVE AMERICAN INDIANS

Native American Indian children have extended self-concepts by self-descriptions that indicate an emphasis on family ties, traditional customs and beliefs, and moral worth (John, 1988). The extended family network includes several households (Goldenberg & Goldenberg, 1996; John, 1988). Cousins may be referred to as brother and sister. The primary relationship is with the Grandparents which can include a great aunt or godparents. Relationship, not blood, determines family, thus families are blended, not joined, through marriage (Sutton & Broken Nose, 1996). "A non-kin family member through being a namesake of a child, consequently assumes family obligations and responsibilities for child rearing and role modeling" (Goldenberg & Goldenberg, 1996, p. 37). The presence and impact of these strong family ties once made possible the social controls that existed throughout life and that shaped concepts of the self. In some tribes, during earlier periods, control by the family over social behavior and sexuality during all phases of life was absolute (John, 1988).

In the extended Indian family responsibility is shared. This shared responsibility includes food, shelter, cars, and all available services, including child care (John, 1988). The Native American Indian community expects decisions by tribal consensus, institutional sharing as a source of social esteem, and a characteristic indirection in attempts to control the behavior of others. As a result of an extended concept of self, the community is enabled to enforce values and to serve as a source of standards by using a loose structure or flexible nexus of support. An example of extended self-concept is *tiospaye*. In Lakota Sioux, it refers broadly to harmonious and reciprocal family ties.

Examples of an extended self-concept include obligations to other human beings and to the native community. An extended self-concept serves to provide a continued group identity (John, 1988). This group identity increases the likelihood of prolonged individual survival in an alien and hostile mainstream culture in which the natural and social environments are increasingly less responsive to native persons.

In addition to tribal beliefs the composition of the self-concept of any individual Native American Indian is affected by the level of assimilation into the larger culture. Despite education, occupation in nontraditional jobs, and bicultural status, many Native American Indians have shown a significant retention of cultural values (John, 1988). Despite the tremendous diversity across tribes, the homogeneity of beliefs among Native American Indians may be greater than is characteristic of other cultural groups in this country. The cultural loss and devastation that many Native American clients feel deeply should be acknowledged and attended to by the counselor (Sutton & Broken Nose, 1996).

LATINOS

Personal identity for Latino Americans is sociocentric in nature, with the self and self-interest often subordinated to the welfare of *la casa* and *la familia* (Becerra, 1988). The balance of group and individual prerogatives, however, depends on the individual manner of dealing with the culture in traditional, bicultural, nontraditional, or marginal terms. For traditional and bicultural persons, the balance will often be in favor of needs in the extended family. For nontraditional and marginal persons, the balance may favor more egocentric decisions and actions.

Traditional sex roles are clearly defined by *machismo* for men and *marianismo* and *hembrismo* for women (Becerra, 1988). *Machismo* is more than male physical dominance and sexual availability. It includes the role of a provider responsible for the welfare, protection, honor, and dignity of his family. *Marianismo* refers to the spiritual superiority of women and their capacity to endure all suffering, with reference to the Virgin Mary. After marriage, the *Madonna* concept includes sacrifice and femaleness, or *hembrismo,* in the form of strength, perseverance, and flexibility. These *hembrista* behaviors ensure survival and power through the children.

Personal identity is also associated with being strong. *Strong* refers to inner strength, or *fuerza de espiritu,* characterized by toughness, determination, and willpower (Dana, 1993). A strong person can confront a problem directly and be active in resolving it, thereby delaying the admission that help may be needed. *Controlarse,* or controlling oneself, is the key to being a strong person and includes *aguantarse,* or being able to withstand stress during bad times; *resignarse,* or resigning oneself and accepting fate; and *sobreponerse,* or imposing one's will or overcoming circumstance. A weak person will have little or no self-control and be less able to exercise responsibility or to display *orgullo,* or pride, and *verguenzza,* or shame. As a result, he is more easily influenced by people or events and is relatively unable to become strong.

The family name is very important to Latinos, with a man, along with his given name, adopting both his father's and mother's names. It is often expected, as well as encouraged, that family members will sacrifice their own needs for the welfare of the family (Goldenberg & Goldenberg, 1996). Thus, the family constellation is loyal, committed, and responsible to each other and has a strong sense of honor.

BLACKS AND AFRICAN AMERICANS

There is great diversity among Black families yet there are similarities independent of place within the Diaspora. According to Black (1996), people of African descent are set apart from other ethnic groups by the following: (a) the African legacy rich in custom and culture, (b) the history of slavery and its insidious attempts to destroy people's souls while keeping their physical bodies in servitude, (c) historical and contemporary racism and sexism, (d) and the victim system in which people are denied access and then blamed for their marginalized positions.

African American families have demonstrated a stability and cohesive functioning that is often culture specific. Competence among intact inner-city African American families includes shared power, strong parental coalitions, closeness without sacrificing individual ego boundaries, and negotiation in problem solving. Many of these competent families are at risk because of economic conditions, appalling neighborhood conditions, violence, and uncertainty in employment status (Ingrassia, 1993).

As a result of economic conditions, families often do not include only blood relations but may have uncles and aunts, cousins, "big mamas," "play sisters," and "home boys and girls." In many Black American families there is a three-generation system.

The extended families encourage an elastic kinship-based exchange network that may last a lifetime. These families exhibit spiritual strength, role flexibility, and interchangeability in which male-female relationships are often egalitarian because of the presence of working wives, mothers, and grandmothers (Hines & Boyd-Franklin, 1996; Staples, 1988). Members of the extended family may also exhibit "child keeping," using an informal adoption network.

Despite a feminist perspective that characterized large numbers of Black homes prior to women's liberation, African American men have identity as the nominal heads of households, tied in to their ability to provide for their families. Women often socialize their daughters for strength, economic independence, family responsibility, and daily accountability (Boyd-Franklin, 1989).

Women are identified as possessing fortitude, perseverance, and strength during adversity. As such, women are also generally more religious than men and function to tie the family into a complete church-centered support system of persons in particular roles, activities, and social life (Boyd-Franklin, 1989; Hines & Boyd-Franklin, 1996). This is especially notable in Black Christian (e.g., Baptist) churches. Other major religious groups with similar functions include the African Methodist Episcopal, Jehovah's Witnesses, Church of God in Christ, Seventh-Day Adventist, and Pentecostal, and the Nation of Islam sects to which more Black people are converting (Black, 1996).

This culture-specific description of the African American family is not intended to suggest that all families are extended and nonconsanguineous in composition. Increasing numbers of Blacks are single and many marriages have an increasing fragility as reflected in the higher rates of divorce and separation when compared to the general population (Boyd-Franklin, 1989; Ingrassia, 1993). Many African Americans are acculturated, have opted for identification with the dominant European American culture, and are more egocentric in lifestyle and less communal in orientation.

ASIAN AMERICANS

Asian Americans typically have patriarchal families with authority and communication exercised from top to bottom, interdependent roles, strict adherence to traditional norms, and minimization of conflict by suppression of overt emotion (Kitano, 1988; Min, 1988; Tran, 1988; Wong, 1988). Guilt and shame are used to control family members, and obligations to the family take precedence over individual prerogatives (Kitano, 1988; Sue & Sue, 1990; Wong, 1988). Under the aegis of the family, discipline and self-control are sufficient to provide an impetus for outstanding achievement to honor the family. Negative behaviors such as delinquency, school failure, unemployment, or mental illness are considered family failures that disrupt the desired harmony of family life. In addition is the belief in external control, a fatalism that allows an equanimity and acceptance without question of life as it unfolds.

In China and the United States, absolute control by the family as a major ingredient in the formation of a traditional self-concept has not only diminished but is being openly questioned (Wong, 1988). Despite questioning of traditional filial identity, strong evidence suggests, at least among Hong Kong Chinese students, the continued presence of an extended self or collective orientation.

Similarly, in Japan the emphasis on the importance of collectivity has been increasing, particularly in the form of corporate family effectiveness instead of intrafamily lineal authority or filial piety (Goldenberg & Goldenberg, 1996; Kitano, 1988). However, this collectivity may also be expressed in humanistic or socialist terms.

The primary tradition is **filial piety**, which is the dedication and deference of children to their parents (Goldenberg & Goldenberg, 1996). In the United States, problems faced by first- and second-generation Chinese may differ as a result of inability to express this tradition properly (Sue & Sue, 1990; Wong, 1988). Although first-generation men in particular are required to achieve and to be good providers for their families, sufficient achievement to fulfill family expectations has not always been possible for them. Second-generation individuals also may fail to be unquestioningly faithful to the traditional values of their parents. Their self-worth is increasingly defined either by dominant culture values or by pan-Asian values, in which a common response to racism and personal pride may take precedence over filial piety. As a result, individuals in both generations may experience considerable guilt and anxiety. It may be argued that the locus of loyalty within the Chinese community is in the process of shifting from the family, including ancestors, to other collectivities, including the pan-Asian community in the United States. Overall, the traditional Asian American family believes in loyalty and devotion to its values (Goldenberg & Goldenberg, 1996).

IMPLICATIONS FOR COUNSELORS

Therapists attempting to develop a process that will take into account the impact of culture could follow Hanna and Brown's (1995, p. 101) assessment questions of racial and cultural factors:

1. How does your racial/cultural/religious heritage make your family different from other families you know?
2. Compared to other families in your cultural group, how is your family similar?
3. What are the values that your family identified as being important parts of your heritage?
4. At this particular time in your (family's) development, are there issues related to your cultural heritage that are being questioned by anyone?
5. What is the hardest part about being a person of color in this culture?
6. When you think of living in America versus the country of your heritage, what are the main differences?
7. What lesson did you learn about your people? About other peoples?
8. What did you learn about disloyalty?
9. What were people in your family down on?
10. What might an outsider not understand about your racial/cultural/religious background?

SUMMARY

This chapter identified some complex and intricate issues affecting diverse families. The role gender plays in the maintenance of relationships was discussed. The approach presented here emphasized the need to attend to both intergroup and intragroup cultural differences when working within relationships. Gender socialization issues, societal trends, and biases the counselor has internalized need to be identified and challenged. It is important to have a factual perspective of the worldview and specific values of a given family's culture. Therapists must also take into account their own worldviews and family values and assess how their personal perspectives may influence, or spill over into the therapeutic process. To be effective in cross-cultural contexts, the therapist must be linguistically cognizant and culturally aware. Ethnocentrism, gender bias, and stereotypical beliefs will confuse the counseling process. Multiple identities must be taken into account. The unfortunate result may be early termination, protracted family strife and dysfunction, and a continuation of such behaviors by the therapist, who then endangers many more families. The case study provided an opportunity for students to think about how they would approach a family characterized by separation, same-gender relationships, and cross-racial adoption. Interactions between and among diverse family members as well as the therapist can be very rewarding for those in therapy and to society.

REFERENCES

Becerra, R. M. (1988). The Mexican American family. In C. H. Mindel, R. W. Habenstein, & R. Wright (Eds.), *Ethnic families in America: Patterns and variations* (3rd ed., pp. 141–159). New York: Elsevier.

Becvar, S. B., & Becvar, R. (1993). *Family therapy: A systematic integration* (2nd ed.). Boston: Allyn & Bacon.

Black, L. (1996). Families of African origin. In M. McGoldrick, J. Giordano, & J. K. Pearce (Eds.), *Ethnicity and Family Therapy* (pp. 57–65). New York: Guilford Press.

Boyd-Franklin, N. (1989). *Black families in therapy: A multisystems approach.* New York: Guilford Press.

Bradley, C., & Hawkins-Leon, C, G. (2002). The transracial adoption debate: Counseling and legal implications. *Journal of Counseling & Development, 80,* 433–440.

Burck, C., & Speed, B. (1995). *Gender, power, and relationships.* New York: Routledge.

Dana, R. H. (1993). *Multicultural assessment perspectives for professional psychology.* Boston: Allyn & Bacon.

Efthim, P. W., Kenny, M. E., & Mahalik, J. R. (2001). Gender role stress in relation to shame, guilt, and externalization. *Journal of Counseling and Development, 79,* 430–438.

Fenell, D. L., & Weinhold, B. K. (1996). Treating families with special needs. *Counseling and Human Development, 28*(7), 1–10.

Goldenberg, I., & Goldenberg, H. (1996). *Family therapy: An overview* (4th ed.). Pacific Grove, CA: Brooks/Cole.

Gushue, G. V., & Sciarra, D. P. (1995). Culture and families: A multidimensional approach. In J. G.

Ponterotto, J. M. Casas, L. A. Suzuki, & C. M. Alexander (Eds.), *Handbook of multicultural counseling* (pp. 586–606). Thousand Oaks, CA: Sage.

Hanna, S. M., & Brown, J. H. (1995). *The practice of family therapy: Key elements across models.* Pacific Grove, CA: Brooks/Cole.

Hare-Mustin, R. T. (1988). Family change and gender differences: Implications for theory and practice. *Family Relations, 37,* 36–41.

Hines, P. M., & Boyd-Franklin, N. (1996). African American families. In M. McGoldrick, J. Giordano, & J. K. Pearce (Eds.), *Ethnicity and Family Therapy* (pp. 66–84). New York: Guilford Press.

Hochschild, A. R. (2003). *The Second Shift.* New York: Penguin Books.

Ingrassia, M. (1993, August 30). Endangered family. *Newsweek,* pp. 17–29.

Ivey, A. E., Ivey, M. B., & Simek-Morgan, L. (1997). *Counseling and psychotherapy: A multicultural perspective* (4th ed.). Boston: Allyn & Bacon.

John, R. (1988). The Native American family. In C. H. Mindel, R. W. Habenstein, & R. Wright (Eds.), *Ethnic families in America: Patterns and variations* (3rd ed., pp. 325–366). New York: Elsevier.

Kitano, H. H. L. (1988). The Japanese American family. In C. H. Mindel, R. W. Habenstein, & R. Wright (Eds.), *Ethnic families in America: Patterns and variations* (3rd ed., pp. 258–275). New York: Elsevier.

Kreider, R. (2003). Adopted children and stepchildren 2000. Census 2000. Special Reports. Economics and Statistics Administration. Washington, D. C.: U. S. Department of Commerce. www.census.gov/prod/2003pubs/censr-6.pdf

Lamb, M. E. (1982). Parental behavior and child development in nontraditional families. In M. E.

Lamb (Ed.), *Nontraditional families: Parenting and child development*. Hillsdale, NJ: Erlbaum.

Lott, B. (1994). *Women's lives: Themes and variations in gender learning* (2nd ed.). Pacific Grove, CA: Brooks/Cole.

Min, P. G. (1988). The Korean American family. In C. H. Mindel, R. W. Habenstein, & R. Wright (Eds.), *Ethnic families in America: Patterns and variations* (3rd ed., pp. 199–229). New York: Elsevier.

Mindel, C. H., Habenstein, R. W., & Wright, R. (1988). *Ethnic families in America: Patterns and variations*. New York: Elsevier.

Minuchin, S. (1974). *Families and family therapy*. Cambridge, MA: Harvard University Press.

Minuchin, S. (1984). *Family kaleidoscope*. Cambridge, MA: Harvard University Press.

Minuchin, S. (1991). The seductions of constructivism. *The Family Networker 15*(5), 47–50.

Mishkind, M. E., Rodin, J., Silberstein, L. R., & Striegel-Moore, R. H. (1987). The embodiment of masculinity: Cultural, psychological, and behavioral dimensions. In M. S. Kimmel (Ed.), *Changing men: New directions in research on men and masculinity* (pp. 37–52). Newbury Park, CA: Sage.

Nelson, H. L. (1997). *Feminism and families*. New York: Routledge.

Nicholson, L. (1997). The myth of the traditional family. In H. L. Nelson (Ed.), *Feminism and families* (pp. 27–42). New York: Routledge.

Staples, R. (1988). The Black American family. In C. H. Mindel, R. W. Habenstein, & R. Wright (Eds.), *Ethnic families in America: Patterns and variations* (3rd ed., pp. 303–324). New York: Elsevier.

Sue, D. W., & Sue, D. (1990). *Counseling the culturally different: Theory and practice* (2nd ed.). New York: John Wiley.

Sutton, C. T., & Broken Nose, M. A. (1996). American Indian families: An overview. In M. McGoldrick, J. Giordano, J. K. Pearce (Eds.), *Ethnicity & Family Therapy* (pp. 31–44). New York: The Guilford Press.

Tran, T. V. (1988). The Vietnamese American family. In C. H. Mindel, R. W. Habenstein, & R. Wright (Eds.), *Ethnic families in America: Patterns and variations* (3rd ed., pp. 276–302). New York: Elsevier.

U.S. Census Bureau (2000). America's families and living arrangements. Washington, DC: U.S. Department of Commerce.

U.S. Census Bureau (2001a). The nuclear family rebounds. Census Bureau reports. U.S. Department of Commerce News. Retrieved on March 12, 2004, from http://www.census.gov/Press-Release/www/releases/archives/children/000326.html

U.S. Census Bureau (2001b). Labor force participation for mothers with infants declines for first time, Census Bureau reports. U.S. Department of Commerce News. Retrieved on March 12, 2004, from http://www.census.gov/Press-Release/www/releases/archives/fertility/000329.html

Wong, M. G. (1988). The Chinese American family. In C. H. Mindel, R. W. Habenstein, & R. Wright *(Eds.), Ethnic families in America: Patterns and variations* (3rd ed., pp. 230–257). New York: Elsevier.

Chapter 14

Mutuality, Empathy, and Empowerment in Therapy

Strong clinical skills are essential for good therapy, but they alone are insufficient. The holding environments that we create, the sincere regard for our clients' well-being that we convey through our eyes and smiles, and our respect for their courage to embrace struggle as they put one foot in front of the other toward healing, is nothing short of love. It is this love that our clients need to feel from us in order for therapy to be truly good. It is our mutual need for connectedness, clinician and client alike, that marks the counseling event as inherently spiritual.

Tracy Robinson

A primary goal of the therapeutic process is to foster self-empowerment for the client and to encourage greater psychological functioning. To facilitate client empowerment, counselors first need to understand their own multiple identities and to confront unresolved issues that could eventually rob them of their personal power and overall efficacy during the therapeutic event.

Empowerment is viewed as one goal of psychotherapy. Many definitions exist. Pinderhughes (1995) said that "empowerment is defined as achieving reasonable control over one's destiny, learning to cope constructively with debilitating forces in society, and acquiring the competence to initiate change at the individual and systems level" (p. 136). According to McWhirter (1991), empowerment is a process wherein people or groups of people who lack power become cognizant of the power dynamics that operate in their lives (e.g., prejudice, discrimination) and as a result are able to acquire reasonable control in their lives without encroaching on others' rights. An example of empowerment is recognizing how internalized homophobia, manifested through restricting behaviors, such as avoiding friendships with gay people if one is heterosexual, and self-denigrating cognitions, such as "I must be sick if I am gay" impedes the formation of a healthy self-image. Subsequent to expanded awareness, an observable change in thoughts and behavior takes place that leads to more control without infringing on others' rights and that involves the support of others. Finally, Dulany (1990) stated that empowerment "is another term for finding one's own voice. In order to speak, we must know what we want to say; in order to be heard, we must dare to speak" (p. 133).

In this chapter, power, individually and interpersonally, is presented as a salient theme in the discussion of empowerment. Factors that render people voiceless and leave them feeling incapacitated are also a point of focus. The conflict between the traditional male role, empowerment, and seeking therapeutic assistance is also a focal point of discussion throughout this chapter.

POWER AND POWERLESSNESS

Powerlessness is operationalized as the "inability to direct the course of one's life due to societal conditions and power dynamics, lack of skills, or lack of faith that one can change one's life" (McWhirter, 1991, p. 224). It results in persons feeling unable to have any meaningful impact on their lives. Feelings associated with this disempowered state were identified by Pinderhughes (1989) as less comfort and pleasure, less gratification, more pain, feelings of inferiority and insecurity, and a strong tendency for depression.

Several conditions contribute to a sense of powerlessness. Loss of a meaningful relationship, dream, or hope or a change in status (including poor physical health, financial strain, or career immobilization) can leave an individual feeling insecure, depressed, and emotionally troubled. Likewise, gains in these areas can be vehicles for transporting power. Often, when students are asked what makes them feel powerful, many will respond with being listened to, being in a loving relationship, having money in the bank, getting a good education, and having physical health.

Myers et al. (1991) believed that oppression, which is an outgrowth of feelings of powerlessness, occurs when one's power, an internal construct, is externalized or dictated by a force or entity outside the self. Persons who are oppressed adopt a suboptimal conceptual system characterized by the validation of the self as a basis of external legitimation, as opposed to an intrinsic orientation that contributes to a solid sense of self. Racism, sexism, ageism, and poverty wreak havoc on people's mental, social, and physical health and are forms of oppression. A disproportionate share of persons in poverty are people of color. Most jobs are stratified by race, ethnicity, and gender, with women of color at the bottom of the occupational hierarchy and White males at the top: The rates of morbidity, mortality, incarceration, and criminal victimization for Black men are higher than those of both White men and women and Black women. These data, however, do not automatically translate into internalized feelings of less power for low-income women, disabled people, and people of color, yet this is a dominant theme in society and in the minds of many counseling graduate students. Middle-class students often fail to understand that poor people and people of color, unemployed people, immigrants, and disabled people have relied on kinship networks, a relationship with the land, and infinite strength from cultural and spiritual power to live their lives with dignity and power (Robinson, 1999). This is not to say that people are not vulnerable; indeed they are, but empowerment is learning not to chronically inhabit the same mental and spiritual space of oppression.

More power is characterized by less tendency to depression, more pleasure, less pain, and feelings of superiority (Pinderhughes, 1989). White people, the able-bodied, heterosexuals, middle-class, Christians, and males are perceived as the referent point for normalcy, and power is attributed to these identities. These identities do not ensure psychological empowerment nor are they inherently moral (Robinson, 1999), yet many students believe that these identities are automatically associated with goodness. Counselors need to assess for themselves to what extent they have internalized this societal standard. Client empowerment cannot happen when the counselor is oriented in this way.

POWER AND THE THERAPEUTIC PROCESS

Power and powerlessness are by no means mutually exclusive categories in people's lives. Swanson (1993) maintained that each gender and race has unique feelings of power and powerlessness. Yet, the faulty notion remains that one group's power engenders the other's powerlessness. Consider masculinity, which is construed with hegemonic power and men's dominance over women. Men are dependent on women and perceive women as having expressive power over them or the power to express emotion (Pleck, 1985). Another form of power that women are perceived to have over men is *masculinity validating power,* or men's dependence on women to affirm their masculinity and validate their manhood. A system of this nature reinforces homo-phobia and heterosexism because it is dependent on rigid adherence to gender and sex-role-appropriate behaviors that operate exclusively in the context of heterosexuality or the semblance of heterosexuality.

Helping professionals who operate from clients' strengths and believe in clients' abilities to positively affect the quality of their own lives are in a better position to facilitate client empowerment (McWhirter, 1991; Pinderhughes, 1989). Mental health professionals who maintain that clients are victims because of the oppressiveness of the social context and that clients have little opportunity to change power dynamics directly are not instrumental in creating hope and healing.

Counselors need to be careful about mystifying the counseling event, particularly if it accentuates the power differential between client and counselor. Counselors and therapists possess knowledge of human development and an understanding of how to facilitate client empowerment, yet the counseling process is by no means a magical one in which the therapist is free of any personal conflicts and the client is solely dependent on the counselor (McWhirter, 1991).

Power can be abused by fostering client dependence; it can also be used constructively to facilitate growth and insight. *Productive and constructive power* is at the center of a counseling relationship when a counselor creates a holding environment for a client to make passage through a difficult period. *Destructive power* occurs when one has access to resources and dominates another and imposes one's will through threats or the withholding of certain desired rewards despite implicit or explicit opposition from the less powerful.

Pinderhughes (1989) stated that accepting the reality of one's powerless position can bring a sense of power, an admittedly ironic statement. Reframing the situation to one's advantage (through the help of a skilled counselor) and choosing not to internalize negative behaviors and attitudes are in themselves acts of empowerment. To balance the power differential between client and counselor, empathy is a necessary tool because it represents one of the most important themes in therapy or counseling (Pinderhughes, 1989).

Kaplan (1987) described **empathy** as a function of both advanced cognitive and affective dimensions. She said empathy is "the capacity to take in the experience and the affect of the other without being overwhelmed by it on the one hand or defensively blocking it out on the other hand" (p. 13). She went on to say that the therapist must be able to yield (yielding is a traditionally female quality) to the affect of another person while being able to interpret the meaning of this affect within the cognitive domains. Incidentally, the act of yielding denotes enormous power. In short, the therapist needs to be comfortable with a range of emotions—hers and those of another.

Empathy allows the therapist to be touched, moved, and affected by stories of change and resistance shared by another (see the Group Case "Firm Ground" at the end of this chapter.). Harry Stack Sullivan once described the therapeutic relationship as "two people, both with problems in living, who agree to work together to study those problems, with the hope that the therapist has fewer problems than the patient" (Stiver, 1997, p. 306).

The client is in a position of authority regarding her life. In collaboration with the therapist, the client seeks to improve on a situation or to cope more effectively. When

STORYTELLING: I Cry for You

A therapist shared the story of erupting into tears as one of her clients mechanically explained being raped by her father when she was just a child. The client was moved by the therapist's tears which conveyed to the client that she was worthy of crying over, that her story was sad, and that the therapist was deeply sorry for her struggle and pain. The therapist also realized that she was unconsciously connecting to her client's repressed pain. Counselors are not emotion-free nor are they free from their own pain, trigger points, and troubles.

future challenges arise, insight is available and can be accessed for better negotiating the situation. Counselors are not superior (see the Storytelling "I Cry for You"), yet clients sometimes experience shame from a therapist's haughty attitude that seems to suggest that the therapist knows better than the client does. A therapist's interpretation of dreams and other unconscious material or the use of DSM-IV TR terms can feel condescending and shaming to the client (Jordan, 1997).

Empathy allows a respect for differences that exist between counselor and client, as well as an acknowledgment of the similarities. Where appropriate, the counselor advocates on behalf of the client by, for example, making out-of-office interventions. Empowerment and advocacy differ substantially from rescuing. McWhirter (1991) reminded us that taking responsibility for doing what another person is capable of doing for the self is disempowering. There are some acts that require the abiding presence of another and although this is not rescuing, it is being with another. This process of "being with" describes mutuality in counseling and represents an intimate space inhabited by two people that is governed by a professional context.

Counselors bring themselves into the counseling room. They bring their pain, disappointment, success, arrogance, insensitivity, and empathy. They bring their attitudes about race, gender, class, sexual orientation, culture, abortion, politics, gender roles, and interracial marriages. Some counselors will find it difficult to bear witness to certain stories or emotions from their clients. The stories themselves are not the problem nor is the difficulty that a therapist encounters in hearing them. It is the inability or unwillingness to make sense out of the way in which our clients' lives contribute to and affect our feelings, thoughts, and sensitivities that is problematic. Counselor unwillingness does not encourage client empowerment.

GENDER, EMPOWERMENT, AND THERAPY

As discussed in Chapter 9, the socialization differences for men and women have been documented widely. Essentially, men tend to be socialized to be assertive, powerful and independent and to restrict emotion. Women are often socialized to be nurturant and emotional and to direct achievement through affiliation with others, particularly men (Mintz & O'Neil, 1990). Such socialization patterns in early childhood have implications for adult intrapersonal and interpersonal relationships. For example researchers maintain there are gender differences in intellectual development. Again, the male pattern is often presumed to be superior, with men often being regarded as objective or "separate knowers," and women termed subjective or "connected knowers" (Crose, Nicholas, Gobble, & Frank, 1992). Brown and Gilligan (1992) criticized this perspective:

> To call women connected and men separate seems to us profoundly mis-
> leading; to say that men wanted domination and power while women
> wanted love and relationship seemed to us to ignore the depths of men's
> desires for relationship and the anger women feel about not having power
> in the world. (p. 11)

Historically, the role of women in multicultural counseling has not been explored in great depth in the literature. Therapists have traditionally taken a unidimensional approach to counseling that negates the female experience by failing to see how gender interacts with other identities and oppressive forces such as racism, sexism, class elitism, and homophobia. Yet, gender similarities do not negate racial differences, nor do racial similarities negate gender differences. Chow (1991) discussed gender, cultural, and ethnicity messages among Asian American women. She stated, "These women have been socialized to accept their devaluation, restricted roles for women, psychological reinforcement of gender stereotypes, and a subordinate position within Asian communities as in the society at large" (p. 256). Chow's observation need not be true for Asian men, although certain Asian men occupy subordinate positions because of their membership in groups that are devalued. When race and gender emerge as primary status-determining variables, gender and racial oppression within similar gender and racial groups is dismissed or minimized.

In an effort to honor the client's cultural, gender, religious, and political backgrounds and the cumulative impact on the therapeutic process, each client must be viewed from her worldview (Arredondo, Psalti, & Cella, 1993). Although it is true that the majority of people in therapy are girls and women, the prevalence of females in therapy need not be related to a higher degree of mental disturbances among this population. Socialization processes and the stigma of counseling may be associated with the greater tendency among women in comparison with men to seek help.

FEMINIST THERAPY FOR WOMEN AND MEN

Feminist therapy differs philosophically from traditional psychotherapy in that it seeks to understand the experiences of women within their social contexts while challenging systematic gender inequality. Devoe (1990) stated that "feminist therapy emphasizes the need for social change by improving the lives of women rather than by helping them adjust to traditional roles in society" (p. 33). In feminist therapy, a critique of how a male-dominated and patriarchal society often deems women as other, inferior, and invisible is ongoing. Because psychotherapy is largely influenced by dominant cultural values, the mental health system has participated in the oppression of women by assessing women from a male model. One strength of feminist therapy is that it acknowledges the sexist and unjust society in which women and men live and thus seeks to educate women and men about this while respecting women's anger and men's sadness (Devoe, 1990). Counselors need to consider how men have been impacted under the system of patriarchy and sexism as well (Robinson, 1999).

Western psychotherapy is largely influenced by a psychoanalytical framework, European philosophers, and a hierarchical structure based on hegemonic power. More specifically, the therapist, most likely a male, is seen as the expert, and the client, traditionally a woman, is recognized as dependent. Within the context of therapy and psychiatry, women have been more likely to receive a diagnosis of mental disorder, are more often prescribed psychotropic medication, and take more prescription and over-the-counter drugs than men (Crose, et al. 1992). Ethnic minority clients are also more likely to receive inaccurate diagnoses; be assigned to junior professionals; receive low-cost, less preferred treatment consisting of minimal contact, medication, or custodial care rather than individual psychotherapy (Ridley, 1989, p. 55). Feminist therapy questions this construction of power and proposes a more collaborative, egalitarian relationship between client and counselor if therapy is to be therapeutic and ultimately empowering. Devoe (1990) spoke about an egalitarian relationship and the importance of an emotional link between the client and her counselor prior to effective therapeutic work occurring. "The counselor must view the client as an equal both in and out of the counseling relationship . . . [T]he personal power between the client and counselor should be equal whenever possible" (p. 35).

More contemporary forms of psychotherapy have challenged the premises of Freudian psychology, such as Adler and Rogers (see Corey, 1991). These theorists, however, have often been silent about the social-political contexts in which women exist—contexts constructed by gender and race relations, which for many women are perceived as oppressive and marginalizing.

Personal power should be egalitarian, whenever possible, between client and therapist (Devoe, 1990). If the therapist's underlying premise is that the woman intuitively knows what is in her best interest, then the therapist accepts a different power position. Professional training and years of relevant experience provide insight into mental health issues, but this learned and external knowledge does not supplant the woman's subjective and constructed knowledge even if she has yet to tap into it. Finally, a feminist perspective allows the counseling process to unfold at the pace that is most comfortable for the client.

A substantial number of women may not understand the value of psychotherapy in general and feminist or womanist therapy in particular. Although participation in movements for social justice can increase gender consciousness, some women of color perceive that uniting with men of color toward racial equality is a higher priority than increasing gender consciousness with White women (Chow, 1991). From a dialectical perspective, increasing both racial and gender consciousness is crucial because women of color are always, at all times, both female and racial and ethnic beings. Tatum (1997) says these multiple identities cannot be separated like "pop beads" (p. 91). Comas-Diaz and Greene (1994) also spoke about the intersections of these identities: "Due to the pervasive effects of racism and the concomitant need for people of color to bond together, women of color experience conflicting loyalties in which racial solidarity often transcends gender and sexual orientation solidarity" (pp. 4–5). Consequently, becoming aware of gender issues may be difficult for women of color who contend with both racial and gender discrimination. It is common for women to feel overwhelmed at the dynamics of multiple layers of oppression, but layers of oppression should not be confused with race and gender. Racism is different from being Black and sexism is different from being a woman.

IMPLICATIONS FOR COUNSELORS

It is true that the therapist exercises certain kinds of authority and the client moves into a place of vulnerability; however, the attitude is one of empowerment rather than "power over" (Jordan 1997, p. 143).

There are unique structural elements to the therapeutic relationship (Mencher, 1997). These include (a) the formal beginning and ending, (b) the client or insurance company pays and the therapist is paid, (c), the client asks for help with some clinical distress and the therapist provides help based on her training and expertise, (d) the client shares more information about his life than the counselor shares about her life, (e) the therapist agrees to keep the information confidential whereas the client can share this information with whomever he pleases, (f) the relationship is dedicated to the growth of the client, and (g) counselors operate within these structures and, in an effort to empower clients, need to respect their clients and the values that clients bring to counseling. Counselors also need to acknowledge their clients' cultural practices and their own ability to coexist comfortably with these. The ability to change beliefs and to think differently and flexibly are empowerment skills that counselors need (Pinderhughes, 1995). Traditional counseling and psychotherapy are located within a Western cultural paradigm. Yet, cultural competence is critical to empowerment as noted by Pinderhughes (1995) who said, "Empowerment of diverse populations requires culturally competent practitioners. To intervene effectively, they must be able to avoid using such automatic responses to difference as stereotyping, projection, or distancing" (pp. 132–133).

Within the therapeutic context, the constellation of the client's and counselor's cultural identities has to be considered, particularly given that both culturally diverse clients and White people have been treated poorly by the mental health establishment, which has been insensitive to sociopolitical realities that affect mental and social functioning.

In some circumstances, having a one-on-one client-counselor relationship is not possible or even desirable. For instance, some women may prefer seeing a female counselor, but the agency or practice or group may not have an appropriate match although female counselors are available. Yet many counselors are inadequately prepared to work with diverse clients who present with particular concerns, such as worrying about safety levels, confronting sociopolitical barriers to racism (Washington, 1987) or dealing, for example, with a Black female child's self-esteem around her hair, weight, and skin color. Being a counselor of color or a woman or both does not ensure that one is able to work effectively with diverse clients. Wilkinson (1997) pointed out that Black educators and mental health professionals internalize racism and the negative scripts around race just as White people do. This in turn can result in Black professionals' exaggeration of "middle-classness to an art form" (p. 271) and make Black people unable to relate to other Blacks who are of a lower income bracket or who were born on the Continent. Despite this reality among some clinicians of color, a same-race counselor is often a result of identification of "similar emotional and physical experiences with racism, and more of a willingness to confront this external barrier" (Washington, 1987, p. 198). Men who are more traditional may, within the context of help seeking, react favorably to bibliotherapy, telling stories, and relating to metaphors (McCarthy & Holliday, 2004).

Finances are yet another factor that may hinder a client-counselor interaction. Costs may be a factor for people who lack insurance or whose insurance does not give them access to a preferred counselor of their choice. Sliding scale fees can make counseling more accessible to many clients, and although it is not encouraged by the American Counseling Association bylaws, in some communities across race and class, bartering for counseling services is done and may be effective.

There are times when the most valiant inquiries into the far reaches of the soul do not yield satisfying answers. The ability to yield to the hurt that by all appearances is grossly unfair is indicative of power. Help is needed for people to recover. To heal properly, ample energy and time are required for transition through the normal depression associated with grief and loss. When clients drink or engage in drugging behavior, or promiscuity, fighting, or excessive shopping or sleeping, the motivations for these behaviors should become a source of clinical inquiry. Alcohol can serve as a temporary anesthetic in that it can reduce the intensity of one's feeling. Antidepressants, by their very nature, have a similar effect. The gift of counseling is that good therapy can assist people in their efforts to bring meaning, wisdom, and sanity into their lives while being in the abiding presence of a competent and spiritually loving therapist.

GROUP CASE STUDY
Firm Ground

Several years ago I facilitated support groups for Black Christian women who were survivors of childhood incest. The following are examples of sources of empowerment for them and myself.

1. the freedom to say what they wanted without concerns of being nice, polite, appropriate "good Black girls"

2. the choice to not speak when they did not want to

3. the solace that came from knowing they were not alone

4. the power of saying and believing, "it was not my fault, it was not my fault"

5. the anger they felt at God for not intervening to stop the assault(s)

6. the anger they felt at their mothers for not intervening to stop the assault(s)
7. the right to be angry
8. the realization that, in relationships, others also brought baggage to the table
9. the ability to identify and name their feelings
10. the skills learned to cope on the bad days
11. the freedom to name and claim sexual desire as distinct from sexual abuse
12. the belief that I cared about them and was sorry for their suffering
13. the hope that I held for them that a better day was coming
14. the peace they felt from God
15. my ability to wait with them when it appeared that the better day was not coming
16. my ability to hold their anger, shame, rage, vulnerability, secrets, and disgust

SUMMARY

In this chapter, the therapeutic process as a means of fostering self-empowerment for the client toward greater self-reliance and functioning was discussed. The importance of counselors understanding their own identities and confronting unresolved issues that could rob them of their own personal power and inevitably hinder the counseling process was also examined. A case study was presented to illustrate sources of empowerment observed from a support group.

REFERENCES

Arredondo, P., Psalti, A., & Cella, K. (1993). The woman factor in multicultural counseling. *Counseling and Human Development, 25*(8), 1–8.

Brown, L. M., & Gilligan, C. (1992). *Meeting at the crossroads: The landmark book about the turning points in girls' and women's lives.* New York: Ballantine Books.

Chow, E. N.-L. (1991). The development of feminist consciousness among Asian American women. In J. Lorber & S. A. Farrell (Eds.), *The social construction of gender* (pp. 255–268). Newbury Park, CA: Sage.

Comas-Diaz, L., & Greene, B. (1994). Overview: An ethnocultural mosaic. In L. Comas-Diaz & B. Greene (Eds.), *Women of color* (pp. 3–9). New York: Guilford Press.

Corey, G. (1991). *Theory and practice of counseling and psychotherapy.* Pacific Grove, CA: Brooks/Cole.

Crose, R., Nicholas, D. R., Gobble, D. C., & Frank, B. (1992). Gender and wellness: A multidimensional systems model for counseling. *Journal of Counseling and Development, 71,* 149–156.

Devoe, D. (1990). Feminist and nonsexist counseling: Implications for the male counselor. *Journal of Counseling and Development, 69,* 33–36.

Dulany, P. (1990). On becoming empowered. In J. Spurlock & C. Robinowitz (Eds.), *Women's progress: Promises and problems* (pp. 133–142). New York: Plenum Press.

Jordan, J. (1997). Relational development: Therapeutic implications of empathy and shame. In J. Jordan (Ed.), *Women's growth in diversity:*

More writings from the Stone Center (pp. 136–161). New York: Guilford Press.

Kaplan, A. G. (1987). Reflections on gender and psychotherapy. In M. Braud (Ed.), *Women and therapy* (pp. 11–23). New York: Haworth Press.

McCarthy, J., & Holliday, E. L. (2004). Help-seeking and counseling within a traditional male gender role: An examination from a multicultural perspective. *Journal of Counseling and Development, 82,* 25–30.

McWhirter, E. H. (1991). Empowerment in counseling. *Journal of Counseling and Development, 69,* 222–227.

Mencher, J. (1997). Structural possibilities and constraints of mutuality in psychotherapy. In J. Jordan (Ed.), *Women's growth in diversity:* More writings from the Stone Center (pp. 110–119). New York: Guilford Press.

Mintz, L. B., & O'Neil, J. M. (1990). Gender roles, sex, and the process of psychotherapy: Many questions and few answers. *Journal of Counseling and Development, 68,* 381–387.

Myers, L. J., Speight, S. L., Highlen, P. S., Cox, C. I., Reynolds, A. L., Adams, E. M., & Hanley, P. (1991). Identity development and worldview: Toward an optimal conceptualization. *Journal of Counseling and Development, 70,* 54–63.

Pinderhughes, E. (1989). *Understanding race, ethnicity, and power: The key to efficacy in clinical practice.* New York: Free Press.

Pinderhughes, E. (1995). Empowering diverse populations: Family practice in the 21st century. *Families in Society: The Journal of Contemporary Human Services,* CEU Article No. 50, 131–140.

Pleck, J. H. (1985). Men's power with women, other men, and society: A men's movement analysis. In P. Ricker & E. H. Carmen (Eds.), *The gender gap in psychotherapy: Social realities and psychological processes* (pp. 79–89). New York: Plenum Press.

Ridley, C. R. (1989). Racism in counseling as an aversive behavioral process. In P. B. Pedersen, J. G. Draguns, W. J. Lonner, & J. E. Trimble (Eds.), *Counseling across cultures* (pp. 55–78). Honolulu: University of Hawaii Press.

Robinson, T. L. (1999). The intersections of dominant discourses across race, gender, and other identities. *Journal of Counseling and Development, 77,* 73–79.

Stiver, I. P. (1997). A relational approach to therapeutic impasses. In J. Jordan (Ed.), *Women's growth in diversity* (pp. 288–310). New York: Guilford Press.

Swanson, J. L. (1993). Sexism strikes men. *American Counselor: Counseling and Development, 68,* 21–25.

Tatum, B. D. (1997). Racial identity development and relational theory: The case of Black women in White communities. In J. Jordan (Ed.), *Women's growth in diversity* (pp. 91–106). New York: Guilford Press.

Washington, C. S. (1987). Counseling Black men. In M. Scher, M. Stevens, G. Good, & G. Eichenfield (Eds.), *Handbook of counseling and psychotherapy* (pp. 192–202). Newbury Park, CA: Sage.

Wilkinson, D. (1997). Reappraising the race, class, gender equation: A critical theoretical perspective. *Smith College Studies in Social Work, 67,* 261–276.

Chapter 15

Diverse Counseling and Healing Strategies

The highest compliment that I ever received as a teacher was when a student told me that I "shake everything from the tree." Counseling is enormously similar in that the therapist must have the ability to be silent, to wait, and to ask the same questions, patiently, with a spirit of anticipation that unseen change is occurring.

Tracy Robinson

The rich diversity of this nation has been echoed throughout this book and thoroughly discussed in the preceeding chapter. This final chapter explores different approaches to counseling in a diverse and multicultural world. Transcultural and universal approaches that acknowledge and appreciate the multiple identities embodied within each person are emphasized.

New and effective ways of envisioning the world are paramount for counseling practitioners in a new century. Counselors who can behold a new vision are needed, as are models that critique modalities that encourage imbalance disharmony and, are inherently silencing. Instead, egalitarianism between client and counselor, in a climate of respect where connection with others is regarded as central to healing is desperately needed. This ultimately means crossing borders that so easily divide, such as race, gender, culture, and sexual orientation, and gaining insight into the cultural socialization processes that shape personal attitudes, beliefs, behaviors, and perceptions. Once a person moves beyond an intellectual understanding of another and begins to experience the reality of diverse people as a personal and spiritual encounter, a border crossing has commenced.

Within the past 2 decades, cross-cultural and multicultural perspectives have emerged both in the literature and in research methodologies. They have helped bridge the gap between traditional psychological theories and current mental health issues related to gender, race, culture, ethnicity, and sexual orientation. Because of embeddedness in dominant Western cultural contexts, many theories and their frameworks may not be suitable or optimal for clients of color, clients with disabilities, or GLBT clients. A model of resistance is featured, with several case studies that offer a way of integrating this construct into counseling (see Table 15.1, The ABC's of Resistance).

HEALTHY RESISTANCE

Ample literature espouses the need for healthy psychological resistance as a strategy for countering oppression and cultivating empowerment. *Oppression* represents an act that prevents a person from being fully human or alive (Freire, 1988). It is a dehumanizing process that involves acts of "violence" that range from psychological to physical injury being inflicted on a person. A person who is psychologically dependent on others to define who he is is likely to perceive himself as an object or is a person who lacks power to determine his destiny. Once a person's thinking is externally determined by others, past or present, his behavior is more susceptible to external manipulation. Such a person is vulnerable to accepting an inferior societal status.

There are sociopolitical forces such as racism, sexism, ethnocentrism, homophobia, able-body-ism, and classism that oppress people. These are the forces that require optimal resistance from people. People also engage in healthy and or unhealthy resistance strategies or modalities as they contend with these infrastructure inequities.

TABLE 15.1   The ABC's of Resistance

Optimal Resistance Affect	Suboptimal Resistance Affect
• Strength • Confidence • Inner peace • Entitlement • Hope • Normal sadness and depression	• Inferiority • Insecurity • Chronic pain, sadness, anger, rage, and depression • Hopelessness • Cynicism and bitterness • Listlessness
Optimal Resistance Behaviors	**Suboptimal Resistance Behaviors**
• Asking for help; giving help to others • Knowing when you are in and out of trouble • Recognizing harmful practices and saying no • Recognizing opportunity and saying yes • Setting goals and pursuing them • Being able to feel sad feelings • Being able to delay gratification • Knowing how to wait	• Addictive behaviors (drugs, alcohol) • Disordered eating • School failure • Violence (girl fighting, gang behavior) • High-risk sexual behavior • Externalizing power • Selflessness • Victimization of self and others
Optimal Resistance Cognitions	**Suboptimal Resistance Cognitions**
• A belief in self-agency and self-worth • A belief in one's dreams and goals • A belief in the goodness of others • A spiritual belief that "it's all good," despite appearances • An understanding that failure and crises are necessary aspects of life	• The belief that you are unworthy, unattractive, unloved • The belief that you are unable to change the course of your life • The belief that life would be better if you were someone else • The belief that things are as they seem • A belief in self that is not greater than others' disbelief

The development of empowering resistance paradigms are needed. Energy is expended to live optimally within a society that is discriminatory, demeaning, and depleting (Brookins & Robinson, 1996; Robinson & Howard-Hamilton, 1994; Robinson & Ward, 1991). The model of resistance was originally developed for Black teen girls with the purpose of helping Black girls optimally resist their socially constructed and marginalized racial, gender, and class statuses through conscious use of a culturally oriented and empowering framework. Resistance as universal and transcending sources of difference among women was proposed via case vignettes in Robinson and Kennington (2001).

The resistance modality adapted from Robinson and Ward (1991) distinguishes between resistance that is survival oriented and oppressive and resistance that is optimal, empowering, and liberating. *Optimal resistance* is oriented toward empowerment and is characterized by a person's ability to avoid internalizing negative societal messages that can foster unhealthy self-images and self-depreciatory behaviors. An understanding and recognition of the sociopolitical context of oppression allows the person to engage in optimal resistance which is different from mere coping.

Healthy forms of resistance are directly tied to an accurate knowledge of one's historical, racial, and cultural connections (Robinson & Ward, 1991). Reflected in this mode of resistance are the seven principles of the *Nguzo Saba*. According to Karenga (1980), the Nguzo Saba represents a basic value system that is African in origin and that enables people to establish "direction" and "meaning" in their lives. The seven basic values that constitute the Nguzo Saba system are *Umoja* (unity), *Kujichagalia* (self-determination), *Ujima* (collective work and responsibility), *Ujaama* (cooperative economics), *Nia* (purpose), *Kuumba* (creativity), and *Imani* (faith). These seven primary values, combined with elements of the resistance modality model (Robinson & Ward, 1991), may serve as a paradigm for enhancing personal growth across race, culture, and gender. The case studies depicted in this chapter seek to demonstrate the versatility and adaptability of this model.

Unhealthy or suboptimal resistance represents dysfunctional and short-term adaptations to an oppressive environment, an environment that facilitates chronic feelings of powerlessness within the person and the community. Self-determination is not a primary operating factor because the person's self-image is largely shaped and defined by external and economic forces that have oppressive roots.

UMOJA

The first principle, *Umoja*, refers to unity, solidarity, and harmony that transcends many societal differences that are far too often divisive, such as race, religion, age, and gender. Suboptimal resistance is characterized by disconnectedness from self-knowledge, as well as alienation from communities of support. During the process of learning to adopt a healthy resistance framework, a period of inner dissonance is likely while survival orientations are gradually abandoned and replaced by liberation-oriented thinking. Communicating this natural developmental process to the client may help ease some of the irregular rhythm associated with this growing process (see the Case Study "*Umoja*").

CASE STUDY
Umoja

An example of optimal resistance is 26-year-old Sara, a Puerto Rican graduate student majoring in statistics at a large private university. Sara is one of a few women of color in her department and college.

On a regular basis, she contends with statements from colleagues and faculty that suggest to her their view of her as an outsider. One of Sara's colleagues recently asked whether she was self-conscious about having received a minority research grant. She responded politely but firmly that she was very proud of having received her grant, that it funded her studies more than adequately, and that it was a confirmation to her that she was an excellent researcher and an apt grant writer. Sara also belongs to a meditation group, is a mentor to a teen girl from Guatemala, and attends a book club that meets monthly. Her support systems outside the university, as well as her open communication with her adviser and other committee members, provide her with a sense of connection and access to internal and external opportunities. Sara definitely feels the stress of graduate school, but she is self-knowing, spiritually centered, and committed to her primary goal: getting her PhD.

Although there are some people Sara would do well not to spend time with, there are those who can be tremendous sources of support. Fortunately, Sara knows this. Because resistance oriented toward survival involves disconnection from others (Robinson and Kennington, 2001), a suboptimal portrait of Sara would depict a young woman who was isolated from supportive personal and professional academic communities. If Sara's life were primarily characterized by suboptimal resistance, then the enormous psychological and physical stress from academic timelines, competition with other graduate students, fear of not completing her studies successfully, and the stress of constantly being scrutinized and evaluated would monopolize Sara's life.

KUJICHAGALIA

The second principle is *Kujichagalia,* which means self-determination. In terms of resistance oriented toward survival, the self is largely defined by external influences, including the media (see the Case Study "*Kujichagalia*"). The media have a long history of depicting men as unidimensional, selfish, and sex dominated. Such depictions contribute to inaccurate depictions and lead to stereotypes.

Persons who are self-determined define themselves through a subjective knowledge base. Possessing knowledge of the oppressive dynamics that exist within society, persons are empowered to confront and resist oppressive messages through defining *self* in alternative ways.

CASE STUDY
Kujichagalia

A healthy resistor is 14-year-old Damon, an African American male whose school experiences are alienating. The history of his people is not accurately reflected in the curriculum, and his teachers often assume that he lacks ambition because of his quiet, unassuming manner. Damon does not like being at school. What sustains him are his connections to his family, community, and church. Damon recognizes that he needs to remain in school despite the difficulty he has with being there. He has access to his own constructed knowledge and has found it

necessary to keep two sets of notes while in class—the teacher's notes that talk about Europeans contributions to the new world and his notes about the contributions of Africans to world civilization. Suboptimal resistance for Damon would resemble school failure, violence, and other unhealthy ways of negotiating the discrimination all around him. Young people must have the support of positive and involved adults to resist optimally. It is important not to label Damon as pathological but to understand racist environments for what they are—toxic.

UJIMA

The third principle is *Ujima*, which represents collective work and responsibility. Suboptimally, the person is excessively individualistic and overly self-reliant (see the Case Study "*Ujima*"). This profile describes the U.S. culture regarding the commonly held values of individualism and independence. Many people, including counseling students and their faculty members, have difficulty with the idea of seeking therapy even when it may be sorely needed. Therapy is needed even if for the opportunity to focus on the self and grow emotionally, which everyone has space for. Needing help is stigmatized because it is likened to being weak and inadequate.

CASE STUDY
Ujima

Arthur is a 26-year-old Mexican American teacher. He recently has been diagnosed with prostate cancer. Although he is in a lot of pain and suffers from depression, he refuses to share his diagnosis with his family or community, who are eager to help. Arthur has become rather distant and irritable. He wants to deal with his problem on his own and in his own way. Arthur is engaging in suboptimal resistance strategies as he copes with his cancer diagnosis.

If Arthur were resisting optimally, he would still feel scared and depressed and angry that at such a young age he has this awful disease, but in time, he would also understand the importance of community and come to respect, as Stephanie Mills sang, "the power of love" from his communities of support.

UJAAMA

Ujaama, the fourth principle, refers to cooperative economics. Emphasis is on the sharing of resources through the convergence of the "I" and the "we." Suboptimal resistance reflects an attitude of "I got mine, you get yours." This paradigm involves extreme selfishness and individualistic behavior (see the Case Study "*Ujaama*").

CASE STUDY
Ujaama

An example of suboptimal resistance behaviors is Lani, a 46-year-old single Jewish American office manager. Lani's family of origin lived in near poverty. Through hard work and perseverance, she earned bachelor's and MBA degrees and received several job promotions over the years. She believes in the American dream, in meritocracy and a just world ideology, and that if you work hard, then you will be rewarded with material things. She feels that people who do not have are those who simply do not work hard enough. After 26 years with her employer, Lani has been released because of downsizing. She comes to counseling for help with a series of losses: her job loss and the loss of a 23-year relationship with her husband, Ted. Ted left the marriage shortly after their oldest child left for college. He was tired of coming in fourth after work, the kids, and Lani's parents.

Within an optimal resistance framework, Lani would understand the benefit of sharing resources (financial and human) with others, knowing that without meaningful human connections, she is experiencing a lesser life. Within the counseling event, Lani would be encouraged to explore the fear of poverty that surrounds her work ethic and the notion that bad things happen only to lazy people. To be effective with Lani, it is important to understand her childhood experiences with poverty and some of the tenets of Jewish culture, such as the role of family and children, attitudes about divorce, and the expectations that parents have for their children.

NIA

Nia is the fifth principle and represents purpose that benefits not just the self but the collective body as well. Resistance oriented toward empowerment emphasizes meaningful work and purposeful relationships for life to be as fulfilling as it can be (See the Case Study "*Nia*").

CASE STUDY
Nia

Taki, a 67-year-old Japanese American retiree, widow, and breast cancer patient is an optimal resistor. She enjoys her extended family composed of friends, children, and grandchildren. She is involved in community and volunteer work, dates, and is engaged in lifelong learning. Although she is receiving chemotherapy, she feels optimistic about her healing, meditates, takes herbs, exercises, and is a member of a support group.

Survival-oriented resistance seeks to meet immediate needs and is characterized by a pervading sense of meaninglessness. In desiring escape from drudgery, poor choices or "quick fixes" such as alcohol addiction, obesity, and unplanned pregnancy can and do result. Unhealthy resistance for Taki would be to view life without purpose and meaning. Alone, ill, and with no place to go during the day, Taki's emotional and physical health could easily decline. Being out of contact with other healthy resistors from whom she can learn and teach, she would be depressed and merely surviving.

KUUMBA

Kuumba is the sixth principle and represents creativity. Suboptimal resistance is maintaining the status quo and replicating existing models, although they may be irrelevant (see the Case Study "*Kuumba*").

CASE STUDY
Kuumba

Thirty-nine-year-old Cantina is the mother of a murdered child. In a random act of violence her son was shot while waiting for a train. Cantina has survived debilitating depression and is now an activist, working to empower other women and families whose children have been killed by violence in primarily poor communities of color. Although an optimal resistor, Cantina has put on a large amount of weight—she finds that food is a source of comfort especially at night when her other chilldren are asleep and she is all alone with the lights off. Cantina illustrates that resistance is not a dichotomy, or an "either/or," but that both optimal and suboptimal modalities can be active in each person's life. A person may be more of an optimal resistor in his professional life but suboptimal in intimate relationships or with respect to addictions such as food.

IMANI

The last principle is *Imani,* or faith. Optimal resistance involves an ability to wait and to believe that good is happening independent of external appearances (see the Case Study "*Imani*").

CASE STUDY
Imani

Foster has been diagnosed with HIV and his health is declining. He is depressed and has suicidal ideation—he questions why he should go on anyway with his partner dead and his family not speaking to him. As an optimal resistor, Foster would know that this is a dark night of the soul and would trust that it will not remain as such, believing that the creator is doing a mightier work in his life despite the appearance of things.

Suboptimal resistance is being fixated on the present circumstances. It is characterized by loss of memory, of not seeing the connections with others, the unborn and the deceased, and the entire universe as a whole. It is believing that things are not working or improving because they do not look as if they are. This form of resistance is limited to the present and to what can be discerned through the physical senses.

NARRATIVE THERAPY

Narrative therapy that emanates from a postmodern paradigm has emerged primarily from the work of Michael White and David Epston. Primary sources of inspiration for them were Gregory Bateson and Michael Foucault. With narrative therapy, counselors seek to deconstruct a problem. In other words, the counselor is interested in knowing how the problem originated and its impact on people's self perceptions. Facets of narrative therapy include discourses, mapping influences, and externalizing conversations. In narrative therapy, discourses operate within the context of power in relationships and are the problem; people are not the problem. Take, for example, Susan, whose pathological gambling has contributed to job loss, lying to obtain funds for gambling, failure to honor her household and child care responsibilities, and chronic absence away from the home to gamble. An externalizing conversation would not see gambling and the woman as one and the same. Yes, she is a gambler and she gambles, but her spirit is above and beyond this addiction from which she can recover. Mapping the influences of the problem refers to the counselor and the client better understanding what effect the gambling has had on Susan and her family (Monk, Winslade, Crocket, & Epston, 1997). Often, with seemingly intractable problems, clients feel that nothing is changing; however, narrative therapy looks at change no matter how microscopic. In doing so, the client is more able to trust development in relation to the story that is problem focused.

Discourses are a set of ideas and structuring statements that underlie and give meaning to social practices (Monk et al., 1997). Racist discourses promote the importance and legitmacy of one group's racial experience over another group. Discourses serve to objectify people and deprive people from agency or voice (J. Winslade, personal communication, April 1998).

ALTERNATIVE HEALING STRATEGIES

The number of helping professionals is insufficient to adequately address the psychological and emotional needs of the general population. Church and community groups, in consultation with mental health professionals, can and do offer paraprofessional sensitivity training to leaders. Individuals, couples, or groups who are experiencing transition and need support can benefit greatly from these low-cost, highly effective services. Training can also review when to refer people if and when problems exceed the paraprofessional's scope of training. As people recover from various emotional and psychological wounds, supportive community support is needed.

hooks (1993) said that if places of healing do not exist to help people process their grief, that they must be created because "bottled-in-grief can erupt into illness" (p. 104). In healing, balance and harmony are restored (Shore, 1995).

"Home psychoanalysis" (hooks, 1993), or informal spaces where people feel free to share their stories and receive nonjudgmental support, is not inconsistent with professional help when necessary. Loving and authentic spaces need to be created so that people may heal and move forward, catch their breath, regain and create new rhythms, and reclaim their voices. Granted, therapists and counselors provide valuable service to people in need, but other havens can and do promote healing.

EFFECTIVE LAY-LED HEALING

The following incomplete list may be helpful:

- *Book and film circles* describe the gathering of people, not just to talk about the books and films they are reading and seeing, but to think reflectively about the connections between the written texts and the motion pictures on their lives and the lives of others.
- *Storytelling* allows people to think of their own personal stories or those told by another person and reflect on their meaning and importance. Alice Walker talks about her mother's blue bowls. Although it seemed like there was nothing to eat in the house, her mother, with creativity and care, would prepare the most delicious and nutritious food. As a child, I, too, remember marveling at my mother's ability to perform this same feat and vividly recall thinking that this had to be the mark of a real woman—to take what looks like nothing and make it into something special. It is empowering for clients to realize that they can author their own lives and live the stories they choose.
- *Affirmations* written on a daily basis provide ritual and rhythm to life while promoting positive thinking. Shinn (1989) offers wonderful examples: (a) My supply is endless, inexhaustible, and immediate and comes to me under grace in perfect ways; (b) Rhythm, harmony, and balance are now established in my mind, body, and affairs; and (c) Infinite Spirit, give me wisdom to make the most of my opportunities. Never let me miss a trick.
- *Poetry*—others and one's own. Iyanla Vanzant's (1998) poem, "Yesterday I Cried," is really a story about a woman who cried over losses and disappointment. She ends the poem on a triumphant note, embracing her own wisdom and place of power and vulnerability.
- *Kitchen table talk* is an informal gathering of friends around the kitchen table to eat and to talk about whatever is in people's hearts and on their minds. An adaptation of this activity can take place in therapy (see the Storytelling "Being and Becoming").

STORYTELLING: Being and Becoming

I have encouraged my clients in therapy to compile a list of any and all adjectives that in their view best describes them. I then ask them to compile another list that speaks to who they would like to become. A woman might, on the first list, indicate that she is accommodating and selfless. On the list of who she would like to be, she may say that she would like to have clear boundaries and be less concerned about others' approval of her. One of the goals of therapy could be to move in the desired direction while unpacking the scripts, socialization experiences, others' commentary, and rewards that influenced and perpetuated her tendency to be overly concerned about pleasing other people while denying herself.

- *Burning Bowls.* I used to do this on New Year's Eve at my church. The minister would direct each of us to write down on a piece of paper that which we did not want to take with us into the new year. Finances, relationships, physical health, and spirituality were topic areas for us to consider and organize our thoughts around. People do not have to wait for the end of the year to participate in this activity of literally incinerating the pieces of paper that reflect what is no longer desired. They could be encouraged to think about what they do not want to take with them into the next day, or the next hour. Vanzant (1998) identified several "lessons" one could burn: (a) making decisions in fear, (b) being afraid to say no (or yes), (c) believing that I should not get angry, (d) being afraid to trust myself, (e) not asking for help when I need it, (f), not telling the truth, (g) being afraid to make a mistake, and (h) feeling afraid that I want too much.

- *Letters to oneself.* I have asked my students to write a letter to themselves at an earlier point in their lives. In this letter, they need to offer support, forgiveness, understanding, and wisdom to the younger person they are. A graduate student once wrote to herself as a high school student. She had made a decision to attend a college closer to her home to accommodate her boyfriend who had moved to another state to attend college. He expected her, however, to be able to receive him during holidays and breaks, thus not wanting her to attend the college of her choice several states away. As a graduate student, she came to realize that she forfeited her desires for his and had been encouraged to do so by both women and men alike.

- *Who would you choose to be you?* is an activity that can foster understanding of self through identification with another. A person is asked to identify an actor that he would want to portray him in his biography and why. I would choose Alfre Woodard. She is expressive, smart, so talented, self-respecting, and a proud Black woman.

- *Massage* is a loving way to affirm oneself, relax, and experience soothing human touch.

- *Latin and swing dancing* are high touch, and the music is soulful and stirring.

- *"Howling at the moon"* sessions (J. Weeber, personal communication, March 1996) occur when men and women gather each month during the time of the full moon to celebrate the faithfulness and continuity of nature and the universe, commune with each other, and restore ritual to life.

- *Methaphor* can be very therapeutic with clients who may have a difficult time naming and articulating intense feelings. A client who has a conflicted relationship with her mother could be asked, "What color is the relationship you have with your mother?" "What shape is it?" "Is it an ocean, river, pond, stream, or gutter?" "How does it sound?" and "Who are its friends?" Such questions enable the client to externalize the pain and conflict in order to talk about it.

- *Tell me when to stop* is an activity that I have done with clients who have a difficult time clarifying their feelings around conflicting issues. I have asked them to tell me to stop when the width of my hands arrives at a point that represents the depth of their feelings. I had one client who told me that my arms were not wide enough to describe how angry she was at her husband. It was not until that moment that she became aware of the extent of her rage at his infidelity during her pregnancy.

OTHER APPROACHES

Other approaches that are instrumental in healing include physical exercise, prayer, meditation, yoga, journaling, aromatherapy, and hydrotherapy. There are times when drug therapy or antidepressants under the careful supervision of a medical doctor are warranted and can assist people as they journey to a time when life does not hurt so much.

CREATIVE ARTS

Creative arts can be very helpful to the therapeutic event. According to Gladding (1997), "Creative arts refers to any art form, including visual representations (paintings, drawings, sculpture), poetry, drama, and music, that helps individuals become more aware of themselves or others" (p. 354). The National Coalition of Art Therapies Association (NCATA) is an interdisciplinary organization that supports all art therapies. Drawings, photography, cartooning, drama, cinema, games, poetry/metaphor, bibliotherapy, working with sand, writing, and music and movement all fall under the umbrella of creative therapies. It helps for counselors to understand the importance of the creative process as a part of the healing taking place. Shore (1995) said that "when clients become artists they have tools for activating their own compost and fertilizing their inner lives" (p. 93).

WELLNESS

To encourage healing, whether using creative therapies or more traditional ones, a holistic and multidimensional approach is essential in which mind and body are seen as one. Myers, Sweeney, and Witmer (2001) proposed a Wheel of Wellness. Five life tasks for healthy functioning are depicted and include (a) spirituality, (b), self-direction, (c) work and leisure, (d) friendship, and (e) love. There are additional components for self-direction such as sense of humor, physical fitness, sense of worth, and cultural identity. This ecological model interacts dynamically with other life forces including religion, education, family, and community.

IMPLICATIONS FOR COUNSELORS

Is it truly possible to conceptualize counseling from a different lens? Speight, Myers, Cox, and Highlen (1991) offered a new definition of multicultural counseling that emanates from optimal theory. In this new definition, individual uniqueness, human universality, and cultural specificity are all recognized and seen as interrelated.

> With this redefinition, multicultural counseling courses would be organized around themes that seem to cut across various racial, ethnic, and cultural

groups. Rather than having each identified group as a class topic, theoretical issues relevant to all groups would be addressed, including identity development, oppression, worldview, ethics, and spirituality. (Speight et al., pp. 32, 33)

RELABELING AND REFRAMING

Essential counseling tools are part of a new paradigm for understanding diversity. One such tool is **relabeling** (Pinderhughes, 1989). Via relabeling, the counselor has an opportunity to focus on the client's strengths and to work toward helping the client see coping strategies as legitimate in a climate where these may have previously been mislabeled. For example, from the resistance paradigm presented previously, 15-year-old Than, a Vietnamese high school student, would be regarded as assertive and tenacious with strong leadership potential, instead of as aggressive and disruptive when he respectfully challenges his teachers in class or politely asks for explanations regarding policies and procedures. As a means of rechanneling energy, a guidance counselor could encourage Than to occupy leadership roles at his school. In this way, Than's assertiveness would be better understood.

Reframing is also an important counseling tool. Here, the counselor helps the client see her situation with more hope. Hatha, 45, is now a widow. She commented sadly when looking at a family photograph taken with her husband that then there were two of them. Now, she is all alone and has nothing. A counselor reframe would be to encourage Hatha to look at those two people in the photograph. While they were able, they loved, laughed, shared, and cared for one another deeply. Her decision and commitment to love was a source of life and strength then and can be at another time as well.

SUMMARY

Prior to assisting others, counselors are encouraged to spend time and effort gaining the necessary awareness of their multiple and intersecting identities. It is true that training multiculturally competent counselors is the responsibility of all training programs, but it is essential that counselors graduate from those programs with more than a cursory understanding of how to work with clients across diverse identities. A comprehensive theoretical scheme or model from which to operate is desired. The primary aim of this chapter was to explore various alternative and less well-known approaches that could be used in conjunction with traditional therapeutic approaches to empower counselors to work more effectively with all their clients.

REFERENCES

Brookins, C. B., & Robinson, T. L. (1996). Rites of passage as resistance to oppression. *Western Journal of Black Studies*.

Freire, P. (1992). *Pedagogy of the oppressed.* New York: Continuum.

Gladding, S. T., (1997). *Community and agency counseling.* Upper Saddle River, NJ: Merrill Prentice Hall.

hooks, b. (1993). *Sisters of the yam: Black women and self-recovery.* Boston: South End Press.

Karenga, M. (1980). *Kawaida theory.* Los Angeles: Kawaida.

Monk, G. D., Winslade, J., Crocket, K., & Epston, D. (1997). *Narrative therapy in practice: The archaeology of hope.* San Francisco: Jossey-Bass.

Myers, J. E., Sweeney, T. J., & Witmer, J. M. (2001). Optimization of behavior: Promotion of wellness. In D. Locke, J. Myers, & E. Herr (Eds.), *The handbook of counseling* (pp. 641–652). Thousand Oaks, CA: Sage Publications.

Pinderhughes, E. (1989). *Understanding race, ethnicity, and power: The key to efficacy in clinical practice.* New York: Free Press.

Robinson, T. L., & Howard-Hamilton, M. (1994). An Afrocentric paradigm: Foundation for a healthy self-image and healthy interpersonal relationships. *Journal of Mental Health Counseling, 16,* 327–339.

Robinson, T. L., & Kennington, P. A. D. (2001). Holding up half the sky: Women and psychological resistance. *Journal of Humanistic Education, Counseling, and Development, 41,* 164–177.

Robinson, T. L., & Ward, J. V. (1991). A belief in self far greater than anyone's disbelief: Cultivating resistance among African American adolescents. *Women and Therapy, 11,* 87–103.

Shinn, F. S. (1989). *The wisdom of Florence Scovel Shinn.* New York: A Fireside Book.

Shore, L. I. (1995). *Tending inner gardens: The healing art of feminist therapy.* New York: Harrington Park Press.

Speight, S. L., Myers, L. J., Cox, C. I., & Highlen, P. S. (1991). A redefinition of multicultural counseling. *Journal of Counseling and Development, 70,* 29–36.

Vanzant, I. (1998). *Yesterday I cried.* New York: A Fireside Book.

Epilogue

How would our lives be different if we were not afraid?

Tracy Robinson

I dream of a world where people can talk freely and honestly about hard issues. And when people get mad, or sad, or confused, they don't stop talking—they may leave the room, get something to drink or eat, go away for a while, but the commitment to dialogue and truth does not end. I dream of a world where people can take their whole selves out somewhere and not feel that their transgendered self or White self, or locked hair self, or their self in a scooter will be unwelcomed. I dream of a world where everyone knows the gift of good community during times of celebration and plenty as well as during times of struggle, limited understanding, and unmet need. And I dream of a world where people are not afraid to love people who are perceived to be different—a world where human differences are not better or worse than other human differences.

I have attempted to present a way for the counseling event to honor the multiple and simultaneous identities in people's lives. My hope is that people will talk about the cases—about the models, and the research, and the census data, and the stories. I would like people to talk about their feelings and listen to other people talk about theirs. And that when it is all said and done, we will each know that we have been changed at depth.

NAME INDEX

SUBJECT INDEX